Yacht

PRINCIPLES OF
ADOLESCENT PSYCHOLOGY

BY

EDMUND S. CONKLIN

INDIANA UNIVERSITY

NEW YORK
HENRY HOLT AND COMPANY

To the students and faculty of the University of Oregon, who were my loyal friends and colleagues for more than twenty years, this volume is affectionately dedicated

PREFACE

This volume is another consequence of my persistent effort to understand human nature. To me there is nothing in life more fascinating than a bewildering bit of human behavior, and nothing more satisfying than a good approximation toward its explanation. The next most fascinating thing is to lead others into an understanding of the explanations I have found.

For many years I have taught classes of older college students who were consciously preparing for the responsibilities of social leadership and parenthood. For our use I have searched the literature of the psychology of adolescence, and have directed researches, that we might have at our command the best that was available. In more recent years I have been repeatedly called upon to conduct courses in the same subject matter for the information and guidance of ministers and social workers seeking a better understanding of the young people among their charges. Deans of men and deans of women, teachers, physicians, and parents have constantly come to me for counsel concerning their more difficult problems in adolescent behavior. And in addition to these, many hundreds of students have sought me in my home and in my office for aid toward a better understanding of their immediate difficulties. All this has brought me the values of a rich personal experience in the problems of adolescent behavior.

These demands have influenced my point of view. While I have sought generalizations wherever the literature of the subject made them safe, I find myself constantly thinking in terms of the point of view of the student leader, the parent, the dean, the teacher, the physician, the pastor, and the social worker who must use this knowledge for the interpretation of particular behavior problems. As I have sought to lead these people to think of adolescent problems as but phases in the growth of personality, or distortions of such growth, so in this book I have sought to present adolescence as a progressive change in the personality pattern and as normally a progressive integration of the many behavior patterns contributing to the personality as a whole.

The literature is vast. My bibliographies include far more than two thousand titles, and most of these bear dates of publication later than that of G. Stanley Hall's encyclopedic survey of the literature published in 1904. I have not therefore tried to include bibliographies in this book; but I have given with each topic discussed references which will give to the reader who desires a ready introduction to the literature on that subject. In the selection of these footnote references I have given preference to those which included good bibliographies. In so far as possible I have chosen references published in English; but where publications in other languages were of exceptional merit or without English equivalents I have not hesitated to include them. I believe that in these footnote references any reader will find a useful guide to the literature on every subject here treated.

I trust that the trained psychologists who read this volume will note how often it has been necessary for me to point out gaps and uncertainties in our knowledge. Vast as is the literature I am nevertheless convinced that adolescence is a neglected field of research. With the better orientation which we now have and the contributions of recent years to research methods, many of these gaps and uncertainties would quickly yield to research attack. While I have thought of this volume as primarily a teaching aid, I shall be disappointed if it does not at the same time stimulate some much-needed research.

For permission to reproduce copyrighted material I am indebted to the following persons and publishers: the *American Journal of Psychology*, A. S. Barnes and Co., the University of Chicago Press, Professors Floyd H. Allport and Daniel Katz.

E. S. C.

Bloomington, Indiana.
November 1, 1934.

CONTENTS

vii

PRINCIPLES OF
ADOLESCENT PSYCHOLOGY

CHAPTER I

INTRODUCTION

DEFINITION OF ADOLESCENCE, ADULT AS NORM, NATURE OF
PERSONALITY, INTEGRATION OR SYNTHESIS, INSTABILITY, IN-
CONSISTENT BEHAVIOR, BIOLOGICAL THEORIES OF DEVELOP-
MENT

There is a period of several years in the life of every human
being when he is no longer a child nor is he yet a mature adult.
The length of that period varies greatly. Some individuals and
some peoples mature early. Others enjoy, or suffer, a considerable period of growth after childhood has passed and before the
full development of powers and abilities has been achieved, before life settles down into the routine of an adjusted efficient
adult. It is this period which has come to be termed adolescence.

Definition. The definition of the term adolescence is not easy.
It is sometimes defined as meaning the "teen age." Others say
it designates the period between the development of sexual maturity (pubescence) and the achievement of adulthood. But both
of these dividing lines are still harder to define with any degree
of exactitude. Arbitrary points of physical growth may be selected to represent the dividing lines. But such physical marks
tend to distract attention from those changes of behavior and
experience which gave rise to the psychological studies of this
period. For legal purposes, chronological boundaries have been
set out; but most students of psychology, especially those who
have looked at all into the problems of genetic psychology, know
full well that a chronological dividing line touches people of
many different stages of mental development. It seems better
then to concentrate upon the nature of adolescent behavior and
not to be too anxious for the sharp delimitation of its range in
the life cycle.

Since the dawn of the twentieth century there has been a vast

1

amount of material published on what has been termed the "boy problem" and the "girl problem." Some of this has been devoted to the problems of childhood, but much of it has been concerned with young people who are approaching maturity. Parents and moralists have been concerned about the delinquencies of young people who either ought to know better or who do know better, and yet for some reason do not act according to their knowledge. The clergy and other religious leaders have been concerned about the inconsistencies of youth as well as their delinquencies, and have sought to understand and through religion to stabilize and to moralize each rising generation. Welfare workers have been concerned about the problems of vocational placement because they have seen so many mistakes, and consequent unhappiness, resulting from the unguided efforts of youth to find vocational placement in life. It is the period of leaving school, of breaking away from parental domination, of vocational selection and adjustment, of establishing self-reliance and self-responsibility in conduct; it is the period of sexual restraint in the years between sexual maturation and the age when marriage is approved; it is the period in which the body as a whole reaches its mature proportions and is normally a time of vigorous health; it is a period in which religion plays a large and often changing function in life; and it is above all a period of social adjustment, one in which the social situation has perhaps a larger influence upon the personality pattern than at any other time in life. It is a period so freighted with problems and possibilities as to make it a most critical period of growth.

Adult as Norm. It is customary to evaluate adolescent behavior in terms of adult behavior. By this comparison the adolescent appears to be inconsistent, erratic, romantic, childish, impulsive, idealistic, selfish, altruistic, excitable, and so on through a long list of differentiating traits. Obviously if we had no adult norm and only adolescent behavior before us we should use very different terms in the description of these and other forms of behavior. We should then be thinking only in terms of individual differences, of central tendencies and deviations from them. But we do have adult behavior about which we are fairly well informed, and we know that adolescents are in process of becoming adults. So it is probably wise to follow the custom of evaluating adolescent behavior in terms of adult norms.

But in so evaluating adolescent behavior there is grave danger of setting up false standards of what is adult. It requires but little reflection to realize that adults differ greatly. Some are sociable while others are not; some are well poised and self-controlled, while others are impulsive and erratic; some have wide ranges of interest, while others are limited in their interest range; some are extroverted, and some are introverted; some are well adjusted to their social situation, while others are poorly adjusted; some have high ideals and some have low; some are optimistic and some are pessimistic; some have achieved a working philosophy of life while others have not. It would thus be wide of the mark to think of that adulthood toward which all adolescents are in course of approximation as highly uniform. Rather is it quite the opposite. Adolescents are thus not converging in their growth toward adulthood as a focal point. They are in the course of a progressive divergence. As they grow they are approximating to some one or other of the vast number of different personality patterns which make up the adult population. Adolescence may thus be thought of as primarily a period in which the personality is differentiated and molded into that which is to be characteristic of the individual in the years of adult life.[1]

Definition of Personality. The term personality as here used connotes nothing metaphysical nor anything metapsychological. It is used as the most inclusive term available to the psychologist for the designation of an individual. Personality means the sum total of what an individual human being is. It includes all that is native and all that has been acquired.[2] It means that the personality is the combined product of a vast number of traits, abilities, characters, trends, drives, tendencies, and the like, much of which is still beyond scientific knowledge. It means that the

[1] Clearly as this seems to be indicated by all the many studies of interests and attitudes and social adjustment and the like, it is also true that studies of physical features and certain mental functions do not indicate an increase of variability in adolescence. See Henmon, V. A. C., and Livingston, W. F., "Comparative Variability at Different Ages," *J. Educ. Psychol.*, 1922, 13, 17-29; Hollingworth, H. L., *Mental Growth and Decline*, pp. 268-270.

[2] Prince, Morton, *Clinical and Experimental Studies in Personality*, chap. 6. Warren, H. C., and Carmichael, L., *Elements of Human Psychology*, p. 333.
Woodworth, R. S., *Psychology* (Third ed.), chaps. 5 and 6.

anatomical size and shape, the peculiarities of individual physiology, the health of the body, the degree of intelligence, the
range and nature of knowledge acquired, all the native abilities
and the degrees of their development and utilization, the ideals
past and present, the pattern of emotional development, the
whole social experience, especially the parental experience, the
habits, the complexes (however they be defined), the adjustments
and the maladjustments—that all of these and any other features
or traits which may have been omitted from the above list enter
into the grand synthesis or sum total termed the individual personality. As these traits and factors and functions differ from
individual to individual so personalities differ. And, still more
important for our present purposes, as any of these differ with
growth changes so will adolescent personalities differ from each
other and also from adult personalities.

Differences of Personality Integration. Personality differences
are, however, to be thought of not only in terms of differences of
pattern but also in terms of differences in what is called synthesis
or degree of integration. This latter is a most useful concept,
and especially important in the understanding of adolescent behavior, although the nature of what is designated by it is not yet
known in full.[1]

These differences in synthesis or degree of integration are a
matter of everyday experience for those who are accustomed to
observation of human behavior. Here is a person who is well
educated, cultured, trained in a variety of physical activities, enjoying an excellent range of knowledge, and known to possess
the most acceptable of ideals; but the day-to-day conduct of this
person is such as to acquire the reputation of being unstable, un-
predictable, jumpy, unreliable, impulsive, of one who "goes off
at half cock." Associates complain that there seems to be little
control or inhibition. What the person knows, the background
as it were, seems to have little influence upon the immediate response. Such a person is defective in the development of personality synthesis. Numerous behavior patterns have been estab-

[1] This concept has been taken over from psychopathology and so is ordinarily presented from a medical point of view. For an introduction to such
literature see the following: Diethelm, O., "Non-organization and Dis-organi-
zation of the Personality During Psychoses," *Arch. Neur. & Psychiat.*, 1933,
29, 1289-1304; Janet, P., *Major Symptoms of Hysteria.*

lished, but they are apparently not sufficiently connected with each other, not sufficiently organized for the exercise of an adequate and effective influence upon each other.

Fortunately, one more often meets people who are better organized, whose organization is indicated by better control or more poise. Most efficient and successful business men are of this variety. Actions are deliberate and under the full influence of habits, knowledge, the background of experience and training. They have the reputation for reliability and wisdom because their responses are controlled and because their conduct is consistent with their past and their ideals.

Between these two extremes most adults may be placed. And it is helpful at times to think in terms of such a dimension and to attempt, crudely of course, to judge people in terms of their place on such a scale, running from the most poorly to the most highly integrated. But when one comes to apply this concept to the changes of personality in the growing years, one soon discovers that growth from birth to maturity may be thought of as a progressive development of the personality synthesis.

The infant has a personality, to be sure, because it has a sum total; but there is little about its behavior, except for some vegetative functions, which can be thought of as integrated. Arms and legs and voice apparatus and the like respond to stimuli, although in a notably incoordinate fashion. But it is not long before arms and legs respond in a coordinated manner, in creeping or hitching and later on still in walking. These means of locomotion are in turn organized with perceptions and later with conceptions, and also with emotional reaction patterns. The synthesis is becoming manifest. But with growth there is much acquisition as well as development of synthesis, hence for years the progress in synthesis ordinarily does not, perhaps cannot, catch up with the establishing of new patterns. Hence the growth in synthesis continues on up to adulthood, by which time some considerable degree of it is ordinarily achieved. Perhaps individuals who become prematurely adult, who settle down early, achieve a synthesis too soon; others, for reasons not yet known, seem never to develop much of a synthesis, or at least not enough for their happiness and efficiency.

With childhood past and adulthood not yet attained, the

adolescent is but midway in the course of the development of this personality integration. Many behavior patterns have been acquired. Many more are being acquired. Some degree of integration has been established, but much more is needed before the poise and consistency of maturity appear. To this imperfection of integration or synthesis much of the erratic, impulsive, and inconsistent conduct of adolescence is attributable. Instances of this will appear again and again in the chapters which follow.

Instability of Adolescence. By contrast with maturity youth has often been characterized as a period of relative instability. On first reading, the meaning of this term appears to be obvious; but unfortunately it has meant different things to different people. The consequence is a confusion of meanings and a proper alarm on the part of some [1] that its significance may be distorted. The difficulty seems to lie in a failure to distinguish between instability and inconsistency. Instability of personality in adolescence should mean insecurity of development, liability to fail or to fall, and thus point directly toward the possibility of defect and of degeneration or disease of personality. Inconsistency of adolescent behavior might of course be related to instability, but it is far from being necessarily so. Inconsistency may be and doubtless more often is merely an indication of the immaturity of development and of integration of the personality.

When one thinks of instability as a condition in which degeneration and disease is easily brought about and asks if adolescence is a period in life characterized by such instability, one will find that contemporary specialists in psychopathology will answer with great caution. That there are nervous and mental diseases occurring in personalities of adolescent age none will deny; but there is grave doubt if adolescence as a developmental period is any more liable to such instability than other periods of life.

It is quite true that intrinsic defects may not become apparent until adolescent years; and it is possible that the greater demands and the strains of the complicated life which adolescents must live in our civilization may serve to bring out intrinsic defects not before apparent. This is no doubt true of many epilepsies,

---

[1] See for example Hollingworth, L. S., *Psychology of the Adolescent,* p. 192.

although the onset of epilepsy may occur in childhood and may be delayed until after full maturity has been achieved.[1] Not infrequently it has been assumed that every individual began life with a certain amount of capacity for development. This might be wholly adequate to carry the individual through all the stresses and strains of growth up to a full maturity, or it might be inadequate and therefore exhausted before maturity is reached. Certainly there are individuals who grow well up to somewhere in adolescent years and deteriorate into a condition of dementia. This was once termed adolescent insanity or dementia præcox. In recent years, however, the interpretation of this disease is changing rapidly. It is now known to be no longer in anywise peculiar to adolescence, and the notion of an intrinsic defect at its base is being discarded by many.

Students of all the many forms of hysteria have frequently asserted that adolescence was a stage of development peculiarly susceptible to hysterical disturbance. It is quite true that hysteria is more easily produced in those personalities which lack well-organized inhibitions, in which emotions are easily aroused and are poorly controlled; and it is also quite true that conflicts between ideals and native impulses or drives contribute to the development of hysterical behavior. Young people in the teen ages are imperfect in the development of control and frequently have conflicts to struggle with; and hysterias do appear with a fair degree of frequency in adolescent years. But it is also true that there is much hysteria in mature years. There are many adults with poorly integrated personalities and many others whose control breaks down under the strains of life. Figures on the relative frequency of hysteria at different times in life as well as of the other borderline abnormalities are notoriously unreliable. Consequently it is unsafe to conclude that adolescence is a period characterized by any special predisposition toward hysterical disturbance.

These, epilepsy and dementia præcox (schizophrenia) and hysteria, are the three diseases of personality most frequently mentioned as appearing in adolescence. If adolescence is to be thought of as a period of instability then it must be a period of

[1] For more detailed presentation of epilepsy and the other abnormalities of development mentioned here see chap. XVII.

relatively greater susceptibility to these diseases, and that cannot now be substantiated. There are individuals who are decidedly unstable in adolescence and it is the function of mental hygiene so to guide and protect them that they may pass through the tensions of adolescence without breaking down. These deserve special study, and they will receive special consideration from time to time in this volume, but one must not of course describe adolescence as a period of instability because some adolescents are unstable, requiring special attention and study.

Inconsistency of Adolescent Behavior. Of this there can be no question. It has been recognized at least since the days of Aristotle who described the inconsistent behavior of youth in a way that is almost as applicable in our day as in his.[1] In a charming and illuminating essay Dean Briggs has given expression to similar observations coming from his many years of experience with Harvard students.[2] Among the psychologists G. Stanley Hall[3] has no doubt described the inconsistencies of adolescent conduct most effectively. He summarized his observations in pairs of antithetic or contrasting modes of behavior. While the original should be read in its entirety the following abstract of his presentation in terms of paired contrasts will present the substance of his thinking:

1. Oscillations between activity and idleness.

Youth is represented as being more savage than civilized in work habits. Instead of working regularly by the clock as does the modern adult, youth is prone to spasms of prolonged and intense activity, training with severe application and self-discipline for some athletic event or studying with equal persistence; and likewise to spells of indifferent, lazy, apathetic neglect of responsibilities and opportunities.

2. Fluctuations between euphoria and disphoria.

The mood changes of childhood become in adolescence modified into periods of happiness or euphoria and periods of depression or melancholy or disphoria which are of much longer duration. There is the oft-described careless and even silly gaiety of youth; and there are likewise the blue moods which in rare cases terminate in suicide but more often in meditation and poetizing.

[1] Welldon, J. E. C., *Rhetoric of Aristotle*, 1886, pp. 164-166.
[2] Briggs, LeB. R., *School, College and Character*, chap. 3.
[3] Hall, G. Stanley, *Adolescence*, Vol. 2, pp. 75-94.

3. Self-confidence versus self-depreciation.

Youth often manifests an extraordinary consciousness of self and personal capacity. Teachers, parents, and other formerly respected adults now sink into the background. There is much of arrogance and annoying assertiveness in the behavior. Often there is much that is fine and highly idealistic. But there is also the contrasting timidity, lack of self-confidence, shame, abasement, feelings of incapacity and with reflection upon the recent past not a little humiliation.

4. Oscillations between selfishness and altruism.

Youth is often petty and disgustingly selfish. Rights of others seem to be utterly ignored. And along with such behavior there are comparable instances of unselfishness, of self-sacrifice. Societies are formed for and vows taken for life-long service to the welfare of mankind, to missionary endeavor, social reform or what not.

5. Good and bad conduct.

Benevolent, kindly, thoughtful conduct is rarely to be found more graciously and sweetly manifest than in the acts of youth. But it is also in adolescence that the curve of delinquency rises rapidly. The apex of the curve of religious conversions comes at about the same age as the greatest frequency of commitment for criminal acts.

6. Oscillations between society and solitude.

Clubs, gangs, societies, fraternities and sororities—all forms of organization and social contact at this age have a strong appeal. Youth seems to crave such social contacts and affiliations. But there is also to be observed the contrasting craving for solitude. Youth has periods of longing to be alone, to be away from people and social activities of every sort, to be alone, to meditate.

7. Nice sensitivity alternating with hard-heartedness.

Youthful murderers, child torturers, etc., are mentioned as extreme examples of the harshness of youth, and in contrast (sometimes in the same individuals who manifest these extremes) there is the exquisite tenderness shown toward pets, children, and those who suffer.

8. Enthusiasm for knowledge versus indifference.

Eagerness and zestful enthusiasm for knowledge manifested from time to time in periods of intense devotion to some form of study is contrasted with the indifference which all teachers know so well, so often manifested in a fear of appearing "highbrow" and in the attitude that it is bad form to do well in school.

9. Knowing versus doing.

Hall did not elaborate this very much. What he evidently had in mind is what we should now call an oscillation between extrovertive and introvertive interests. There is the contrast between times when the individual seems primarily to desire to know, to live with the things of the mind, and the times when he prefers the world of overt action.

10. Conservatism alternating with radicalism.

Here the familiar beliefs of youth that society is all wrong, that educational systems and governmental establishments and religious institutions and the rest must soon be thoroughly overhauled and remade, are contrasted with the equally familiar adolescent trait of adhering to the status quo, to the maintenance of school traditions, to devotion to fundamentalistic doctrines religious and social.

11. Proximity of wisdom and folly.

In the same youth we often meet instances of conduct that reveal the finest of mature judgment and also instances of absurdly foolish conduct.

Hall wrote in a day when the inherent, the racial, the instinctive, the intrinsic, was primarily and almost habitually looked to for interpretation. For him growth was largely determined from within. For him the developing human being was much like the growing plant so long thought of as unfolding from the seedling to the plant, to the bud, to the flower. So the adolescent was in a human period of blossoming. With this general point of view in mind one can better understand the quaint figure Hall used in the interpretation of these inconsistencies in adolescent behavior. He said that the self was growing, reaching out, trying now this and now that, finding slowly footholds here and there for further advance. He likened it to the rapidly growing vine which puts out new growth shoots that sway about and at last find places of fixation. In this "circumnutating" progress of the growing plant Hall saw a striking resemblance to the growing self of the human youth. The self in adolescence is new and green and inexperienced and unestablished. It is growing and trying itself out in all these many contrasting modes of conduct. As it oscillates it learns, finds points of fixation and bases for further growth.

Alluring as such a figure of speech may be we cannot today

think of the growing personality or self as growing by such an unfolding process from within. Nor can we wisely look upon the self or personality as one grand whole and neglect the details which various studies have made available to us. Adolescent conduct is certainly inconsistent and there can be no objection to the marshaling of the various forms of adolescent conduct under such pairs of contrasting titles as Hall did, but what we seek today is a glimpse within the personality pattern to determine if possible the forces which produce now this form of conduct and now that. Instead of merely saying in poetic figure that the self is growing and seeking higher levels for attachment we would prefer to be able to say why growth moves now in this direction and now that.

A full explanation of all these many forms of inconsistent behavior would require all that is presented in this volume and much more knowledge not yet discovered. But the general outline of their explanation can be grasped from a few rather condensed statements of trends and points of view. Certainly the immaturity of personality synthesis in adolescence, as has been described in an earlier part of this chapter, will frequently explain inconsistency of behavior. Because the behavior patterns are not yet fully integrated with each other and there is a lack of pervasive domination by some one or more of them, it is possible for highly inconsistent conduct to appear. The rapidly growing body means changes of internal as well as external pattern with which are associated a wealth of effects upon the physiology and the conceptions of the self. What the youth may think and feel one day may be considerably different from what he may think and feel a couple of months later. The adult, however, whose pattern and habits of thought are well established judges by himself and thinks of the impossibility of anticipating the conduct of the youth and stresses the youth's inconsistency.

With the maturation of the sex organs there is known to be a significant shift in the pattern of hormones in the body. Endocrine glands whose secretions were once dominant come to take a less prominent place in the pattern and others come into greater prominence if not dominance. The endocrines are also known to factor in emotional reactions, and so their changes must mean changes of emotional reaction which to the adult appear as inconsistent. Associated with these are of course the steadily growing changes in the perceptions of life and affairs which bring many new stimuli to emotional arousal. By processes of conditioning and de-conditioning changes of behavior take place so that what was once emotionally exciting loses its power and other thoughts and events acquire the capacity to stir emotion.

Too little is known yet about personality types, but enough is known to make many suspect that type differences of personality, or large individual differences, are either intrinsically determined or established so early in life as to be mistaken for intrinsic determination. By adolescent years these type differences are coming to prominence. Youths are by growth changes being differentiated into the types they will have in maturity. And this progressive differentiation of type may frequently be a cause of conduct which is characterized as inconsistent.

But above all must the inconsistencies of adolescent conduct be related to growth changes taking place through the effects of adjustment to the world in which the growth itself occurs. Ideals are established and changed and developed, and gradually become more and more pervasively influential. The self concept which was brought into being in infancy or early childhood is worked over and changed in far more ways than we are yet able to enumerate. Social attitudes are developed and established. Feelings of inferiority and superiority, especially the former, come to play a large place in the motivation of behavior. Sometimes complexes result as a consequence of the struggle with inferiority troubles. Interests grow and change. Love comes into the life and with it the struggle over sex impulses and thoughts and desires. Religion and morals and explanations of the problems of life, the seeking of a vocation and training for it, and a vast number of other responses to the needs of the individual and the pressures of society and social institutions contribute their share to the molding of the personality. All contribute to the alteration of behavior, and as these alterations come about the observing adult is prone to think of the changes as manifestations of inconsistency. Doubtless it were far better to think in terms of the changes of personality pattern and the causes of those changes, for by such thinking progress is made toward a genuine understanding of youth. No one can hope to understand the ways of youth who merely observes the inconsistency in youthful behavior and fails to think beyond the fact of that inconsistency.

Biological Theories of Development. The older genetic psychology was much influenced by biological ways of thinking. There was much inclination to think in terms of racial evolution and to relate developmental features in the growth of the individual to possibly corresponding features in the development of the race. The then current stress upon instincts, upon intrinsically determined traits of development and of behavior, doubtless contributed much to this pervading consciousness of racial relations and similarities.

Much emphasis was placed upon the order of trait appearance in individual development. As is well known, all modes of behavior do not appear immediately after birth. Some appear at one time and some at another. There is a period when climbing is a dominant interest, one when collecting something is above all attractive, another when interests are controlled by what the gang does, and much later on all interests seem centered in some one of the other sex. Interest in the explanation of this order of development was reinforced by the belief that there was an order which was truest to nature, the violation of which was likely to be fraught with danger to the health of the child and the following of which would be the most effective and most economical basis upon which to build a program of education.

This led to an extension of the recapitulation theory of the biologists for psychological purposes; and later, with loss of faith in the recapitulation theory, to the development of other modes of explanation. These have left a large impress upon the thinking of many genetic psychologists and appear so frequently in the literature, especially the older literature, the student of today cannot afford to ignore them.

1. The recapitulation theory. This was proposed by the distinguished biologist Ernst Haeckel [1] and adapted for psychological purposes by G. Stanley Hall,[2] who is largely responsible for its widespread influence in both psychology and education. Briefly stated in its biological form it is that ontogeny recapitu-

---

[1] Haeckel, Ernst, *The Evolution of Man,* chap. I.
[2] Hall, G. Stanley, *Adolescence.*

lates phylogeny. For psychological purposes it may be formulated as follows:—the growth of the individual both pre-natal and post-natal rehearses the growth stages of the race. Comparison of the brief course of individual development with the very long course of racial evolution reveals at once that the ontogenetic rehearsal is much more rapid in the earlier months and years than it is in the later. The whole course of evolution from the beginning to the vertebrate animal must be rehearsed in the nine months before birth; and the first twelve years of post-natal development rehearses a period many times that rehearsed from the ages of twelve to twenty-four.

Support for the theory was found in the similarities between individual growth and racial development. While the biologist pointed to anatomical similarities, the psychologist called attention to behavior similarities. The climbing propensities of small children were supposed to rehearse a tree-dwelling stage in the life of our ancestors; the tendencies to run away, to wander, were assumed to rehearse the nomadic life of later ancestors; the strange new food desires of pubescents were thought to be reflections of a time when wandering or climatic changes forced upon our ancestors new food habits. Many who have never psychologized at all are prone to characterize children at times as little savages, and thereby unwittingly contribute their support to belief in a recapitulation.[1]

One intriguing consequence of the psychological use of the recapitulation theory was the development of the catharsis doctrine.[2] If the sequence of growth changes in the individual is intrinsically determined and is rehearsing the order of racial evolution, then each stage becomes necessary to the development of the next. If the environment is such as to suppress any stage, the course of development must thereby be distorted, hindered, or perverted. Thus good hygiene would stress the importance of permitting full expression, full living out, of each stage as a stim-

[1] Fascinating presentations in support of the theory will be found in the following:

Beebe, Wm., Hartley, G. I., and Howes, P. G., *Tropical Wild Life in British Guiana* (N. Y. Zoo. Soc.), chap. XI.
Hrdlička, Ales, *Children Who Run on All Fours*, 1931.
[2] This must not be confused with the psychoanalysts' use of the same term to designate a feature of their psychotherapeutic procedure.

ulus to the appearance of the next. This was termed catharsis. Some stages cause trouble in our civilization. The way to handle them according to this catharsis doctrine was to permit them free expression as a means of outgrowing them as quickly as possible. If for example some child manifested a propensity to play with fire, then that child was passing through the period when man lived especially by the use of fire and in close daily contact with it. The way to eliminate the troublesome trait in the child would then be to give the child ample opportunity to play with fire under protecting supervision. That would aid growth and more quickly bring on the next stage of development which would replace the troublesome fire building.

In the early years of the present century this cathartis doctrine was widely discussed and believed by many to have much moral value. Educators under the influence of the recapitulation idea developed the culture epochs theory for educational practice. It was thought that the curricula of the schools should be made to conform to the racial course of development in order to achieve the greatest efficiency. Thorndike pointed out that the cathartis doctrine was contrary to all that we knew of habit formation; and the opponents of the culture epochs doctrine pointed out the disturbing speed with which some racial periods were rehearsed and the large individual differences. But these arguments to the contrary were slow in taking effect.[1]

Gradually the defects in the evidence for the recapitulation theory became evident and convincing. There are quite as marked dissimilarities between the development of the individual and the evolution of the race. The head of the human embryo develops rapidly and at birth is about one quarter of the length of the infant. There is no known stage in the evolution of the race which corresponds to this. Specialized sexual reproduction comes much too late in the development of the individual to compare favorably to racial evolution. And there are many other dissimilarities. There are in fact so many dissimilarities that some have asserted that there never would have been a recapitulation theory had as much attention been given to the dissimilarities as was given to the similarities.

[1] Thorndike, E. L., *Educational Psychology*, Vol. 1, pp. 275-282. See also the article on culture epochs theory in the *Cyclopedia of Education*.

Furthermore, the recapitulation theory makes the mistake of considering as developmental only the years from conception to maturity. The rest of the life cycle is neglected. The recapitulation theory necessitates the acceptance of the inheritance of acquired characters in some form. And according to the recapitulation theory no stage of development could ever be eliminated entirely, which appears to be contrary to fact.[1]

2. The utility theory. Recognition of the weakness in the recapitulation theory led to other means of explanation. This utility theory, advocated especially by Thorndike,[2] has been widely accepted. It is much simpler and is based on a conception of evolution in terms of variation and selection. It assumes that those factors which have brought some trait into being through variation and survival by selection for its value, also determine the time in the order of development that it shall appear. The order of development is thus thought of as an order which has come into being because it was somehow useful.

According to this utility theory new traits may arise and old traits may disappear when no longer useful. And in like manner the time of appearance of an intrinsically determined trait may vary, and, if the variation is useful, the time, or place, in the order of development may accordingly become changed. It has also the advantage of not depending upon the doubtful assumption of inheritance of acquired characters.

3. The correspondence theory. This is scarcely a theory of relationship to the race at all. It is merely a statement that the growth of living organisms is likely to correspond to the growth of other living organisms when the environmental factors are similar. Similarities when they occur, then, between the development of the individual and the evolution of the race are merely similarities and nothing more. There is a correspondence merely because the growth situations happened to be enough alike to produce similarities. According to such a conception there would be far more similarity between the growth of the individual and the development of the race in the earlier stages, which does appear to be true. And there would be far less simi-

---

[1] An excellent summary of this material will be found in the following: Davidson, P. E., *The Recapitulation Theory and Human Infancy*, 1914.
[2] Thorndike, E. L., *Educational Psychology*, Vol. 1, pp. 252-254.

larity in the later stages, which also appears to be true. For our present interests this is significant because it obviously means that similarities in the adolescent years would be fewer in number and of minor importance.

With the shift of emphasis in recent years away from thinking in terms of intrinsic determination of trait development and appearance, there has been far less use made of these biological theories by students of genetic psychology. They still appear from time to time in the literature and it is quite possible that there may be a revival of interest in them,[1] but for the present it is far more important to make a direct attack upon individual behavior development. While reference to these theories will appear occasionally in this text, the emphasis will be decidedly upon other and less speculative ways of interpretation.[2]

SUPPLEMENTARY REFERENCES ON PERSONALITY AND ADOLESCENCE

Allport, F. H., *Social Psychology,* chap. 5.
Bridges, J. W., "A Theory of Personality," *J. Ab. & Soc. Psychol.,* 1926, 20, 362-370.
Brooks, F. D., *Psychology of Adolescence,* chap. 12.
Hollingworth, H. L., *Mental Growth and Decline,* 1927.
Hollingworth, L. S., *Psychology of the Adolescent,* 1928.
Murchison, Carl (Ed.), *A Handbook of Child Psychology,* second edition, 1933.
Prince, Morton, "The Problem of Personality: How Many Selves Have We?" *Ped. Sem.* 1925, 32, 266-292.
Richmond, Winifred V., *The Adolescent Boy,* 1933.
——— *The Adolescent Girl,* 1925.
Smithies, Elsie M., *Case Studies of Adolescent Girls,* 1933.

[1] This is already true in psychoanalytic thinking. See for example Jelliffe, S. E., "Paleopsychology," *Psychoanal. Rev.,* 1923, 10, 121-139.
[2] For a more detailed presentation of these theories see Koffka, K., *The Growth of the Mind,* pp. 42-49.

CHAPTER II

PHYSICAL MATURATION AND ITS EFFECTS

HALL ON GROWTH CURVES, LATER STUDIES, SEX DIFFERENCES
IN GROWTH, EFFECTS OF PATTERN CHANGE, PUBESCENCE,
RELATION OF PUBESCENCE TO INTELLIGENCE, PUBESCENT
KNOWLEDGE OF SEX, PERSONALITY EFFECTS

For a long time it was supposed that much information of psychological value could be obtained through a careful study of all the stages and changes in the course of physical development. Much attention was given to the measurement of height and weight and diameters and girths and a variety of ratios between such measures were obtained. Averages were calculated for each age-year, and growth curves were plotted. The same thing was done for childhood years and so far as possible for the course of development prior to birth. Then total curves for the whole growth period from impregnation to maturity were available. Comparisons were made between the sexes, and the curves were carefully scrutinized for indications of nodal points, for plateaus, for periods of marked acceleration, for any peculiarities in fact which might perhaps be meaningful.

Valuable as such studies still are for anatomical and physiological and biological purposes their significance for psychology now appears to be far less and certainly far more indirect than it was assumed to be twenty-five and thirty years ago. This, like so many other changes of point of view in genetic psychology, is largely the product of a shift of emphasis from heredity to environment. When both physical and mental growth were accepted as primarily determined from within, from some sort of determining factors in the germ plasm, then a careful scrutiny of every phase of growth change was a most logical procedure for the psychologist as well as for the anatomist and the biologist. In the days of emphasis upon the intrinsic in growth determination, the recapitulation theory was in the background of the thinking of most genetic psychologists. It influenced the nature of their work and largely influenced their interpretations. One must keep this in mind if one would understand the differences of emphasis and even of point of view which are to be found in the literature of genetic psychology. Older ways of thinking still linger, older books still stand on our library shelves. Older books are still read, and properly so because in spite of the changes of emphasis and theory there is much in them of value, if the reader has learned to read with caution and criticism.

The most significant among these older students of adolescence is G. Stanley Hall. Great as have been the changes in methods of research and modes of interpretation since his time his ways of working and thinking are still so widely influential and appear so often in the literature of the subject every student needs to become familiar with them.[1]

Hall on Growth Curves. On this subject of physical development, Hall's interpretations were curiously well supported by the nature of the then available data. The curves of growth with which he worked did show a marked cessation of growth for a time prior to the onset of pubescence. Some of them gave indications of a similar retardation along about six or seven years of age; and there were vague indications of yet earlier steps in the curves. Hall was even inclined to suspect the presence of such in prenatal development. Hence the course of physical growth came to be looked upon as irregular, as characterized by periods of retardation alternating with periods of acceleration. Adolescence was thought to be initiated by a special outburst of physical development.

Hall believed that mental growth paralleled the physical development. For him therefore these periods of retardation and acceleration were just as important psychologically as they were physically. Thinking as he did in terms of intrinsic determination and the recapitulation theory he proceeded to look upon the growth curve as a sort of graphic record of the history of the race rehearsed in the development of every individual. Each period of retardation represented an ancient period of racial

[1] Here the careful student should read especially the first two chapters of Hall's *Adolescence*.

maturity; and each period of acceleration represented a time in the evolution of man when both physically and mentally the race was making rapid progress. Growth was thus looked upon as characterized by a succession of spasmodic outbursts, of which adolescent development was but the most recent. Each spasm of growth was thought of as a new unfoldment, the course and appearance of which was determined from within.

Later Studies of Growth. After the influence of this mode of thought had become widespread new studies appeared, especially on height and weight, which were made with much more accurate methods and on larger numbers of cases. These presented growth curves that are much more smooth and regular than the earlier studies. The recapitulation theory was also subjected to rigorous criticism and largely rejected. The behavioristic movement came with its emphasis upon the environment. Instinct concepts were subjected to a severely critical overhauling. There was in consequence a reaction against the older thinking in terms of spasmodic outbursts of growth and of intrinsic determination. There was a swing to the belief that the normal growth curve for physical development was continuous from impregnation to maturity; and that any outbursts of growth, any indications of spasmodic development, or any periods of retardation, were to be thought of as disturbances in the normal course of development which could be traced to circumstances in the environment (diet, disease, etc.).[1]

The drift of contemporary studies of physical growth, however, is in the direction of emphasizing two periods of acceleration. One of these is in prenatal development and the other is in the early years of adolescence. While the adolescent acceleration is not so great as that high period of growth before birth, there is still an acceleration which must be recognized as normal.[2]

---

[1] See Hollingworth, H. L., *Mental Growth and Decline*, chap. 3.
[2] The literature here is extensive. The reader can, however, get a very good introduction to it through the following:

Baldwin, B. T., *The Physical Growth of Children from Birth to Maturity,* Univ. of Iowa Stud. in Child Welfare, 1921, No. 1.
Boas, F., "Observations on the Growth of Children," *Science,* 1930, 72, 44-48.
Brooks, F. D., *Psychology of Adolescence,* chap. 2.
Davenport, C. B., "The Human Growth Curve," *J. Gen. Physiol.,* 1926, 10, 205-216.
—— "Human Metamorphosis," *Amer. J. of Physical Anthropology,* 1926, 9, 205-232.

The reason for this early adolescent acceleration is not yet clear. Apparently it is related to the maturation of the sex organs and the sex functions, and this in turn leads to the supposition that it is related to the change in the pattern of hormones within the body.

But there is no tendency today to think of the adolescent acceleration in physical development as indicative of a corresponding acceleration in mental development. While there is a general correspondence between physical and mental development, a positive correlation between the two, one cannot use the growth curve as more than a rough indication of the mental development. The correlation is positive but not perfect and as such merely indicates a general tendency. Furthermore, the studies upon which our present knowledge of the relationship between physical and mental development are based have been made very largely with measures of intelligence and on the purely cognitive processes. The older idea of a spasmodic outburst of mental development at adolescence was rather that of a sudden blooming of instincts and emotions. Concerning these features we know far less, but there is little tendency to think of a psychological development here that is intrinsically determined. Whatever emotional developmental changes there may be accompanying this adolescent acceleration of physical development are looked upon as the indirect effect through changes in the concept of the self.

Sex Differences in Growth. In these matters of physical growth one sex difference stands out clearly. That is the earlier appearance of the adolescent acceleration in girls than in boys. From about eleven to about thirteen or fourteen years of age girls are larger on the average than boys. Then the curve for the boys rises slightly above that for the girls.

This has often been attributed to a supposed earlier appearance of puberty in girls than in boys, a sex difference which now seems very doubtful.[1] Why this growth difference between the sexes exists is today unexplainable. And we do not know if there is any corresponding psychological difference. Of indirect

[1] See pp. 24-25.

effects we suspect many, and these will be presented below in other connections.[1]

Not a little attention has also been given to the development of different parts and organs of the body.[2]

The different internal organs mature at different times and have different periods of most rapid development. One must not think of the internal organs of the body as always bearing the same size ratio to each other. The pattern of relative size changes notably from time to time. Some organs mature early and some late. The brain grows very little after puberty (very little in size, but much in organization) while the heart and liver and digestive system manifest conspicuous growth changes during adolescence. But again we are much in the dark as to the psychological significances of these growth changes. One may suspect that changes in the pattern of the heart and liver and digestive tract may have some effect upon the feelings and emotions, and these may be very important, but we know little of which we may be certain.

Effects of Pattern Change. Changes in the external physical pattern are not only more observable but more observably influential upon the behavior of the adolescent. With the growth in height, the achievement of adult stature, there comes a change in the perception of the world. No longer is it necessary to look up when addressing adult associates. Sometimes this change comes very rapidly and there is the curious experience of now even looking down to adults who had hitherto always been looked up to when addressed. The boy's shoulders broaden, the jaw becomes more prominent, the Adam's apple noticeable, and the sex organs attain adult proportions. The girl's breasts develop and the nipples increase in size, the pelvis broadens, and new distributions of adipose tissue bring curves to the figure. Both boys and girls develop their sex's characteristic distribution of body hair with large individual differences in amount. For a time, features of these anatomical changes appear to be out of proportion. Hands and feet may seem too large and certainly

[1] Concerning this earlier development of the female G. Stanley Hall proposed several possible theories which are at least thought provoking. They will be found in his *Adolescence*, Vol. 1, pp. 40-44.

[2] Brooks, F. D., *Psychology of Adolescence*, chap. 2.
  Hall, G. Stanley, *Adolescence*, chap. 2.

their owners are often very awkward in their management. Mrs. Hollingworth [1] thinks that the nose often reaches its maximum of development so early as to be out of proportion to the other features. Many other disproportions and noticeable changes could doubtless be isolated. Certainly there are many individual instances of marked variation from the average in which the growth pattern seems to be even embarrassingly distorted for a time. [2]

Of the effects of these changes of size and of pattern upon the self concept, the self feelings, and the attitudes toward others every one can recall something. Unfortunately there have been all too few systematic studies, but fortunately there have been many clinical observations and personal recollections written out for our instruction. Consciousness of the achievement of adult stature contributes much to the rapidly changing concept of the self. The new physical point of view and the new reactions of others, expressed verbally or apparent only in manner of address, contribute their share to the changing attitudes toward others. Perception of personal awkwardness, consciousness of feet and hands and nose or other feature disturbs what little social poise may have been achieved and may contribute not a little to notions or complexes of inferiority. And these size changes must be articulated with adolescent interest in clothing, because the changes of stature bring many clothing improprieties and hence much clothes consciousness. Clothes that are bought too large as insurance against being too early outgrown and clothes that are so far outgrown as to make the youth look boobish contribute much to the embarrassments and trials of being youthful. [3]

Physiological Maturation (Pubescence). No one can say with certainty just when adolescence begins in any individual instance. While it is commonly asserted that adolescence begins with puberty, it requires but a moment's thinking to realize that no one can determine just when the changes of pubescence start, nor when they are complete. Age tables in plenty have been presented but these differ not a little, probably because of differences in criteria used, possibly because of differences in social

[1] Hollingworth, L. S., *Psychology of the Adolescent*, p. 8.
[2] For a good general description of pubescence from a medical point of view see Schwab, S. I., and Veeder, B. S., *The Adolescent*, chap. 2.
[3] See chap. VIII for fuller presentation of psychology of clothing.

status, and perhaps also because of racial differences in the groups studied. The general indication of these studies is toward a mode about fourteen years of age. But as with all measures of central tendency it must be ever kept in mind that there are quite normal variations above and below this mode. Boys may become pubescent three or four years earlier than this or as much later without any cause for thinking them abnormal. This also means that within these age years any group of boys of the same chronological age is almost certain to include some who are not yet pubescent, some who are undergoing the pubescent changes, and some who have passed through them. And because of these physiological differences there will of course be an accompanying range of psychological differences.[1]

The maturing sex structures and functions produce new sensory experiences. How these will be perceived, what they mean to any individual boy, will depend of course upon his background of knowledge at the time. Whatever may have been the educational preparation it is certain that the new sensory experiences will command and receive attention. A new experience has come into the life of the boy and like all new experiences, whether for good or bad, it is interesting and attention compelling. There will be much thought about it. The feelings and emotions aroused will be determined by the meanings which accrue to the new sensations. If they are perceived as something evil or dangerous or sinful or somehow abnormal, fears and inferiorities are the ordinary accompaniment. If they are perceived as a new and desirable and normal step in growth toward manhood (an interpretation which is all too rare), there may be little of fear and something of the thrill of achievement, of joy, of exaltation, of superiority. These interpretations and these emotional reactions in turn have their effect upon the content of the growing concept of the self and must accordingly mold the pattern of the self-regarding sentiment.

[1] The special studies here can be readily reached through the following references, especially by using the bibliographies which they present:

Baldwin, B. T., *The Physical Growth of Children from Birth to Maturity*, Univ. of Iowa Stud. in Child Welfare, 1921, 1, No. 1.
Brooks, F. D., *Psychology of Adolescence*, chap. 3.
Crampton, C. W., "Physiological Age," *Amer. Phys. Educ. Rev.*, 1908, 13, 144-154, 214-227, 268-283, 345-358.

The new sensations which give rise to all these new cognitive and emotional reactions are not of course limited to those aroused by the sex structures. Secondary sexual developments also factor. There is the accompanying growth of the vocal cords and the often distressing changes of the voice. The girlish voice of the little boy gradually changes to the heavier voice of the adult male. All the world knows very well the amusing breaks of voice which so often appear in the course of this change; but far too often the world forgets to perceive the distress and embarrassment which these vocal mishaps bring. The boy may be proud of his new bass voice, but he is not proud of his inability to control it.[1] Sometimes the boy does not know what is going on, and, more remarkable still, instances are reported of parents who bring their boys to behavior clinics to discover what has caused the disturbance in the voice. Development of hair on the face brings sooner or later the necessity for shaving. This again is a new experience. Sometimes it is a happy one, but not always. Older members of the family and older associates generally are much given to the practice of teasing the boy about his first shaving. The experiences of learning to shave are often thus made additionally embarrassing. But of these experiences we have practically no records that are useful. The conviction is growing that a thorough study of the process of learning to shave which shall include so far as possible all of the imaginative and emotional accompaniments will reveal much of value to the psychology of adolescence.

The onset of puberty in the female is somewhat more easily determined. It is customary to use the age of first menstruation as the line of demarcation, although it must be obvious that some pubertal growth changes have taken place before the first menstrual flow is possible. Still it is a much more definite measure than any available for the male. It has long been customary to state that girls mature sexually somewhat earlier than do boys; but the difference given, usually about a year, is too small to present with any degree of certainty where the measures are so unreliable and where the actual evidence for an age difference is

---

[1] An amusing and at the same time pathetic description of this will be found in H. A. Shute's *The Youth Plupy.*

really very slight.[1]   It is safe to recognize the modal age for girls
at approximately fourteen years of age, the same as that given
for boys.   It is possible, as some studies seem to indicate, that
this modal age may differ somewhat in warmer and colder cli-
mates and perhaps there are characteristic racial differences as
well.   Again, as with boys, it is important to keep in mind that
there is a considerable deviation above and below this mode
which must still be included within the range of normality.   In
practice the appearance of menstruation as early as the ninth
year is not looked upon as abnormal nor is it considered abnormal unless it is delayed later than seventeen or eighteen years
of age.

What has already been said concerning the sensory and perceptual and emotional effects of pubescence in the boy can be
applied in most of its detail to the experiences of the girl.   Of
course the actual sensory experiences are different but there are
the same interpretation problems.   Some are frightened; some
give to the first menstruation most absurdly morbid interpretations because of their ignorance or misinformation; some who
have been better prepared for it are exalted as by a great new
achievement in growth.[2]   These reactions must in turn have
their reflex effects upon the self concept and the self-regarding
sentiment.

The hygiene of functional periodicity brings, however, into
the life of the girl, many factors of habit and interpretation
which the boy does not experience.   Care of the person during
the period raises questions and problems, and concerning this
there is a wide range of practice and belief to be faced.   Expert
medical knowledge and advice differ greatly from much of the

[1] For the literature on the age of first menstruation the reader should see
those references given above for the age of puberty in boys and also the
following:

Dickinson, R. L., and Pierson, H. H., "The Average Sex Life of American
    Women; Relation Between Experiences and Genital Findings," I. Intro-
    duction to Studies, *J. of the Amer. Med. Assoc.*, 1925, 85, 1113-1117.
Hall, G. Stanley, *Adolescence*, Vol. 1, chap. 7.
Hollingworth, L. S., *Psychology of the Adolescent*, pp. 2-3.
Terman, L. M., *Genetic Studies of Genius*, Vol. 1, p. 208.

[2] In an unpublished study made under the writer's direction, 475 girls
reported as follows concerning their emotional reactions to their first menstruation: terrified, 7%; chagrined, 12%; indifferent, 51%; curious and interested, 24%; delighted and proud, 6%.

alleged knowledge which has been handed down by word of mouth for many generations. This must bring confusion to the thinking of many girls. Then again the periodicity is not always established at once. The usual interval of twenty-eight days may be departed from with much irregularity for a time, even for several years. Many suffer actual pain at their periods, headache, cramps, soreness, weariness, fatigue, bladder irritability and other disturbances. Emotional disturbances, so easily aroused at this age, may be the cause of irregularity or even of temporary suppression of the menses. Emotional shock, prolonged strain, change of scene as well as disease may bring this disturbance which unless wisely interpreted may cause more emotion and yet more disturbance. That many girls react to their periods with disgust and hatred is not to be wondered at, regrettable as it is.[1]

Relation of Pubescence to Intelligence. It would be very helpful if we knew exactly what the relationship is between the development of puberty and the development of intelligence. If, for instance, one is confronted by a boy of fifteen years of age, who is backward in school work, with tests indicating that he is somewhat under fifteen years of age mentally, and one learns that the boy is not yet pubescent, can one safely advise that the boy will probably catch up in intelligence and school work when he experiences the effects of pubescence? In other words, is mental development dependent upon sexual maturation? Many problems arise which could be handled much more satisfactorily if definite answers could be made to such questions.

There does seem to be a low positive correlation between mental development and pubertal development. Terman found in his extensive study of boys and girls of superior ability that their pubescence came on the average somewhat earlier than in comparable unselected groups of boys and girls.[2] And it also appears to be true that feeble-minded children develop pubescence somewhat later on the average. But one cannot as a consequence

---

[1] The psychology of menstruation is so little developed that recently a reputable medical journal printed an editorial appeal for more research on this problem. See *Medical J. and Record*, 1929, 130, 106-107.

For a very wholesome semi-popular statement of the physio-psychological problems of menstruation see Winifred Richmond's book entitled *The Adolescent Girl*, chap. 2.

[2] Hollingworth, L. S., *Gifted Children*, chap. 6.

Terman, L. M., *Genetic Studies of Genius*, Vol. I, chap. 8.

safely conclude that the earlier pubescence comes the more precocious the child will be mentally; nor can one conclude that a
child is dull minded because it is slow in reaching pubescence.
The correlation between mental and pubertal development is
positive, to be sure, but it is low. That means that there are
many exceptions and that there are many other factors operative
in the development of the two functions. A few cases have been
reported where pubescence came at an extraordinarily early age,[1]
as early as the second year in some instances; but the rate of mental development seems not to have been affected by this early
pubescence. The determiners of mental development seem to be
in large part other than those which control sexual maturation.

Pubescent Knowledge of Sex. As has already been indicated,
the major effect upon the growing personality of the development of sexual maturity must come through the interpretations
of the new experiences and then through the emotions aroused.
As these reactions to the new physical developments in any individual must depend upon the amount and nature of the information acquired before pubescence begins, some attention has
been given to the discovery of what information pre-adolescents
have and from whence that information came. Most of these
studies indicate that boys and girls on the average come up to
pubescence with very little information concerning sexual development. Much of that which they do have has come from
sources that give it an undesirable coloring and unhealthy emphases. Davenport studied over eight hundred questions asked
spontaneously by one hundred and sixty girls in later adolescent
years concerning matters of sex relation and sex hygiene. The
summary [2] indicates that even these girls of better than average
education who had been through pubescence themselves manifested a most surprising ignorance about the most commonplace
facts concerning menstruation, reproduction, marital relations,

[1] Doe-Kulmann, L., and Stone, C. P., "Notes on the Mental Development
    of Children Exhibiting the Somatic Signs of Puberty Præcox," *J. Abn.
    & Soc. Psychol.,* 1927, 22, 291-324.
    Gesell, A., "Precocious Puberty and Mental Maturation," *27th Yr. Book,*
    Nat. Soc. Stud. Educ., Part I, 1928, pp. 399-409.
[2] Davenport, F. I., *Salvaging American Girlhood,* New York, 1924. The
same material will be found also in her dissertation entitled "Adolescent Interests," *Arch. of Psychol.,* 1923, No. 66.

and associated diseases. Blanchard and Manasses [1] obtained answers to a questionnaire from over two hundred and fifty girls in their later adolescent years representing a rather wide range of social status. Seventy-two percent of these reported that they had acquired some information prior to their first menstruation; but twenty-six percent reported that their knowledge had come entirely after menstruation began.[2] In response to a question asking whence they obtained their information a number of sources was mentioned of which the following were the most frequent:

	Percent
From mother	45
From a girl friend	25
From relatives	4
From books	3

Davis found that of 1,200 women less than one-third could recall having received their first information concerning sex from parents and guardians. The others had learned from other children, servants, and so on.[3]

Peck and Wells [4] questioned a large group of college-graduate men and report the following list of frequencies with which different sources of information were mentioned:

	Percent
From companions	28
From the home	27
From books	12
From school	12

(Remainder scattering.)

Another study of more than a thousand school and employed boys revealed that seventy-eight percent believed their first knowledge of sex matters to have come from the talk of other boys.[5]

Such studies verify the daily observations of those who live and

1 Blanchard, P., and Manasses, C., *New Girls for Old*, 1930.
2 The remainder, five in all, did not answer this question.
3 Davis, K. B., *Factors in the Sex Life of Twenty-two Hundred Women*, chap. 12.
4 Peck, M. W., and Wells, F. L., "On the Psycho-Sexuality of College-Graduate Men," *Ment. Hygiene*, 1923, 7, 697-714.
5 Hughes, W. L., "Sex Experiences of Boyhood," *J. Soc. Hygiene*, 1926, 12, 262-273.

work with young people. Boys and girls in large numbers come up to the physical changes of sex maturation with little informational preparation; and even after they have passed through it, and have come into the later years of adolescence, their knowledge of such vital matters is extraordinarily inadequate and frequently erroneous. They have acquired what they know at haphazard. That they are often frightened and worried and depressed and go about seeking information in a furtive manner is not to be wondered at. Nor should one be surprised to learn that many of the nervous and mental troubles of adolescence are rooted in sexual maladjustments.

Personality Effects. Of the many effects of physical maturation upon personality the first and most obvious is that of the *definitization of sex* in the pattern. Prior to the Freudian (psychoanalytic) movement in genetic psychology it was customary to think of childhood as psychologically asexual, and of pubescence as being an entirely new development. The point of view is quite different today. While many of the extremes of the psychoanalysts are still rejected, there is a widespread acceptation of their conclusion that there is a sexuality in childhood but of a diffused or generalized nature. With the maturation of the sex organs in pubescence, sexuality becomes definitized and focalized in the personality pattern. It is not something new, but a development into detail of that which had all along been present in a rather vague fashion. Prior to puberty sex is relatively inconspicuous in the conscious life of the child. In adolescent years sex occupies a prominent if not a dominant place in conscious experience, and is perhaps more widely influential in the general behavior of the adolescent than most adults have been inclined to think.

Pubescence and all of the growth changes of adolescent years must bring about significant *changes in* both the core and meaning *patterns of the self concept*. The background or core of the self concept has, ever since the days of William James, been recognized as lying in the pattern of organic or kinesthetic sensations. Perhaps the number and anatomical location of the intero- and propioceptors may remain as before, but their relative locations change and certainly the patterns of stimulus values are altered. Changes in size and relative position, changes in functional habits, as well as the changes in and new stimulations coming from the sex organs themselves, must bring about a very large change in this essential matter of the self concept. No wonder adolescents feel themselves as queer and new and different. The simultaneous shift in the endocrine pattern no doubt has its effects upon the emotional patterns. The thymus subsides, the thyroid becomes prominently active, and there is the addition of those hormones which come from the interstitial cells of the reproductive organs. While of many of these changes the youth is not directly (perceptively) aware, there are many others of which he is. He can see for himself the changes in stature and anatomical pattern, the changes in attitudes of others, the awkwardness and disproportion into which he has grown, the new manliness (or womanliness) of physical appearance, and there are of course direct perceptions of many of the developments in the reproductive organs. These are all perceptions of his own person which add to and alter greatly what he himself means to himself, alter the meaning pattern of the self concept.

If these perceptions are in terms of his being abnormal or defective or backward or precocious, then there will be corresponding effects upon his concept of himself. Not infrequently peculiarities of social behavior can be traced back to distorted meanings in the self concept, self feelings or self-regarding attitudes and sentiments, due to some peculiarity in the course of physical development.

Growth anxieties appear easily in adolescence and should be listed as another of the possible personality effects of physical maturation. The girl who has learned the importance of physical beauty may watch her own physical development with some fear that she may not herself be as charming in personal appearance as her dreams had led her to hope. Disproportions which a few months more of growth will wipe out entirely may be the cause of much temporary anxiety. Ignorance and misinformation easily lead to misperceptions of growth changes, especially those which have to do with the sex organs and their functions, and these in turn to disturbing fears and anxieties. The general ignorance and lack of educational preparation for these changes and the surreptitious seeking of information contribute largely to these misperceptions and attendant emotional distresses. Allied to these are the not infrequent instances of disturbing self-consciousness which may also be traced to the misinterpretations of physical development. All instances of self-consciousness are not of course traceable to these misunderstandings of physical development, but many of them are; and frequently they are among the more serious because their very nature leads the sufferer to seek concealment rather than reliable information and counsel.

New dream experiences must be listed also as an effect of physical development in adolescence. Sex dreams appear where such had not existed before. This is true of both nocturnal and daydreams. This may be in some instances a relatively minor feature of development. On the other hand there are instances wherein the dreams aid in the development of complexes. Sex dreams may easily be misinterpreted as having some morbid significance, especially when the information about sex is limited or inaccurate.

The beginning of *autoerotic practices* (masturbation) is largely associated with pubescence. While the initiation of such habits may occur in childhood, or be delayed until adult years, or never occur at all, there is nevertheless ample evidence for the statement that autoerotism is frequently a feature of adolescent behavior.[1] Its effect upon the developing personality, except in the comparatively rare instances of gross excess, appears now to be entirely indirect. What the youth thinks about himself and his autoerotic acts is ordinarily of far greater importance than any direct physiological effect of the act itself. But what he thinks is certainly very important.

There is current a vast amount of misinformation concerning autoerotism coming from the earlier days of hygienic and reli-

---

[1] For literature on this consult the following, noting especially the additional references in the summary by Davis:

Achilles, P. S., *The Effectiveness of Certain Social Hygiene Literature,* Amer. Soc. Hygiene Asso., 1923.

Davis, K. B., *Factors in the Sex Life of Twenty-Two Hundred Women,* chap. 6.

Exner, Max J., *Problems and Principles of Sex Education;* a Study of 948 College Men, Association Press, 1915.

Harvey, O. L., "Some Statistics Derived from Recent Questionnaire Studies Relative to Human Sexual Behavior," *J. Soc. Psychol.,* 1932, 3, 97-100.

Peck, M. W., and Wells, F. L., "On the Psycho-Sexuality of College-Graduate Men," *Ment. Hygiene,* 1923, 7, 697-714.

gious teaching and also in no small part from the surreptitiously circulated propaganda of unethical physicians. By word of mouth most young people pick up these notions to the effect that as a consequence they will develop insanity, feeblemindedness, that the habit is actually that designated in the Bible as the unpardonable sin, that it is not only unforgivable but incurable, that they will never again be normal, never be able to become a parent as all healthy youth hope some time to be. Curious notions are also current about so-called "tell-tales" by which it is believed that any observer may know who is autoerotic in his habits. Most of these are peculiarities of the eyes or other features of the face, which actually have no sexual significance. Traditional notions and unfounded beliefs are readily available, and reliable sources of information still fail to touch a large percentage of young people in any thorough and effective manner. The result is a vast amount of distorted perception and beliefs that are emotionally disturbing.

Fear in its chronic subacute forms of anxiety and worry is the most common and direct *effect* of such *misinterpretations*. Often there is a disinclination to believe these popular notions, with enough shame to prevent the seeking of information from reliable sources. Attention may be badly disturbed. Boys and girls alike with such beliefs and emotional reactions find themselves unable to keep their minds on their studies, or whatever their tasks may be. The chronic fear or anxiety disturbs digestion and may bring on feelings of weakness and incapacity. Sleep may be broken and this also may contribute to the weakness and feelings of helplessness. The concept of the self may change into that of one who is hopelessly enslaved, hopelessly diseased, worthless, inferior, sinful and the like. Efforts at repression and concealment may easily eventuate in the production of inferiority or other complexes with all of their disturbing consequences.

As a matter of fact, such information as we have indicates that autoerotic practices begun in early adolescent years do not as a rule endure for long. From one source or another better information is obtained. Adjustments of a sort take place and eventually marriage comes with the newer problems of adjustment which that relation involves. There are large individual differences in the intensity of the sex urge.[1] Consequently it must not be assumed that all adolescents suffer the distresses just mentioned. Some do and are for a time much troubled by them. Others have a prolonged struggle which leaves a permanent effect upon the personality pattern.

Generalizations are thus dangerous but of this much we may be certain that when complaints are made by young people of inattention and self-consciousness and embarrassment, of feelings of weakness, of worry, and the rest, one should consider the possibility of emotional disturbances from autoerotism. And it should also be kept in mind that those very same complaints may have quite other causes.

Speech disturbances can be in many instances traced to adjustment difficulties related to pubescence. The self-consciousness aroused by growth in size and weight, anatomical disproportion and awkwardness, consciousness of the new sexuality and efforts at concealment of normal functions, and the rest can easily become so aggravated as to disturb speech. The misinterpretations and struggles over autoerotism just described can also be the cause of speech disturbance. In the whole wide range of pubescent changes there is plenty which may under appropriate circumstances causes self-consciousness and speech inhibitions. Hesitations from self-consciousness may be of no more importance than any emotional disturbance of verbal utterance, but it must always be kept in mind that the adolescent personality is not yet well integrated. Disruptions are thus easier than in later years. From these disturbances of speech, which may be and often are but temporary, habits sometimes come into being which remain as permanent features of the personality.

Sex in Conversation. Pubescence also stimulates much curiosity concerning all matters pertaining to sex, and consequently not only much thought but also much talk and not a little reading. Careful investigation has revealed that even as late as college years sex remains one of the most frequent topics of conversation among adolescents of both sexes. Smutty jokes and

[1] This long-accepted statement is now being doubted by some very competent people. What has been attributed to differences in degree of sexuality they are attributing to differences in training, ideas, habits, attitudes, etc. But the burden of proof still seems to be upon those who contest the belief in large individual differences in the sex drive itself.

sexy literature of many kinds have a wide circulation.[1] Some
have thought that there was a cathartic value in this much talk
about matters of sex, that through it there was some release of
tension. Others believe that such talk, even also the carefully
designed lectures of specialists in personal hygiene, is primarily
exciting in its effects. Probably both points of view are right,
the actual effect depending upon the immediate circumstances.
Judgments here are not easy to make because the best of lectures
and books may be listened to or read with attitudes which utterly
pervert material presented with a high purpose. On the other
hand dirty conversations not infrequently are motivated by a desire for information rather than excitement. What the permanent effect of all this may be we little know. Habits and attitudes, desirable and undesirable, may be established, of course.
Morals may be raised or lowered. Correct information may be
disseminated or utterly false beliefs may be established. But for
good or bad it constitutes an inevitable part of the experience of
adolescence.

Many have believed that the changes of puberty stirred in each
sex a *tendency to withdraw* from association with the other sex.
The older genetic psychologists were inclined to stress the significance of this and Hall [2] even went so far as to develop a plan for
the education of adolescent girls on the assumption of the factual nature of this belief. While it may be quite true that individual boys and girls do for a time in early adolescent years find
the other sex unattractive if not abhorrent and prefer to let them
alone, it is doubtful if this can be laid down as a general characteristic of adolescence. Later studies have revealed, it is true,
indications of a "negative phase" in development when the individual is especially disinclined to associate and cooperate with
others at all, but these same studies claim that the negative phase
is prepubescent and that it disappears with the establishment of

[1] One study made on a large number of conversations in a university of
over two thousand students, showed 22% of male conversations were about
sex and 25.5% of the female conversations.

See Stoke, S. M., and West, E. D., "The Conversational Interests of College
Students," *Sch. and Soc.*, 1930, 32, 567-570. And by the same authors, "Sex
Differences in Conversational Interests," *J. Soc. Psychol.*, 1931, 2, 120-126.

[2] Hall, G. Stanley, *Adolescence*, Vol. II, p. 108, and also chap. 17.

pubescence.[1] The writer asked over three hundred college students about this period of distaste for the other sex. Fifty-four percent of them could immediately recall such a period in their development. But when asked for the age location of the period they placed it with high consistency in the years just prior to puberty.

There is also a possibility that the physical changes of early adolescence bring about directly, through actual physical needs of the body, *a change in the food appetites*. There have been many reports of changes in food desires, at this age, of the waning of old likes and dislikes, of the development of new aversions and new food preferences. Hall made much of this alleged effect of pubescence and interpreted it partly in terms of new chemical needs of the body and partly in terms of a rehearsal of some period in the history of the race when climate or change of abiding place brought some vast change in the dietary.[2] In support of this as a possible effect of pubescence there are the well known peculiarities of appetite which occasionally appear during pregnancy, when there is likewise a shift of endocrine pattern and a considerable demand being made upon the organism. But even granting a rather general shift of appetites with the dawn of adolescence, which has never been well established, the whole matter may be purely functional rather than organic. It may be that the new adjustments of life, the new emotional experiences, the new contacts, and the new interests combine to produce changes in food desires and habits as well as in other modes of behavior. And it may also be possible to explain the food fads of pregnancy in a like manner, which would rule out the strongest support for a direct physical effect of pubescence upon appetite.

Finally, pubescence brings out and *emphasizes* to each boy and girl the fact of a *sex difference*. From the anatomical and physiological differences there must arise different effects upon percep-

[1] Bühler, Charlotte, "The Social Behavior of Children." (Chap. 9 of *Handbook of Child Psychology*, 2nd ed., edited by Carl Murchison.)
Hetzer, Hildegard, "Der Einfluss der negativen Phase auf sociales Verhalten und literarische Production pubertierender Mädchen," *Quellen und Studien zur Jugenkunde*, 1926, 4, 1-43.
Vecerka, Lucia, "Das soziale Verhalten von Mädchen während der Reifezeit," *Quellen und Studien zur Jugenkunde*, 1926, 4, 49-121.
[2] Hall, G. Stanley, *Adolescence*, Vol. I, pp. 250-254.

tions and thoughts and feelings. Some of this may be direct through the structures and possibly through inherent determination of growth changes, primary and secondary sex traits and perhaps others still more remotely related; but very much comes inevitably through the changes in social attitudes and expectations and customs to which the boy and girl through pubescence will inevitably find introduction. As these matters of sex difference are so important and have been subjected to so much study and discussion they must be elaborated in a special section which follows.

CHAPTER III

SEX DIFFERENCES

INTELLIGENCE, VARIABILITY, EXTROVERSION—INTROVERSION,
PERSONALITY SYNTHESIS, GREATER EMOTIONALITY OF FE-
MALE, PSYCHOANALYTIC DIFFERENCES, INFERIORITY FEEL-
INGS, INTERESTS, SOCIAL ATTITUDES, FUNCTIONAL PERIODIC-
ITY, SELF CONCEPT

It has long been a matter of common observation that the personality patterns of boys and girls in childhood years are far more
alike than they are in adolescence. With the changes which pubescence effects and the accumulating experiences of adolescent
years, sex differences of personality become pronounced. Some
of these differences may perhaps be intrinsically determined,
inherently related to the sex-determining factors of the organism.
Of this there is much doubt and a wealth of experimental evidence in support of the doubt on such items as intelligence and
variability. But there is a very general belief among psychologists that social customs and institutions, along with secondary
or indirect influences of sex, do produce large sex differences in
personality, especially in adolescent years. For this, however, in
spite of the general confidence in its existence there is very little
experimental evidence. Probably this is because we have not yet
developed the proper means for their measurement.[1]

Intelligence. By far the largest amount of research work on

[1] The literature on sex differences is unusually large. Access to it must be
found through reviews and bibliographies. Of these the following will be
found highly serviceable:

Loutit, C. M., "A Bibliography of Sex Differences in Mental Traits," *Training School Bulletin,* 1925, 22, 129-138.
Thorndike, E. L., *Educational Psychology,* Vol. III, chap. 9.
Wellman, Beth L., "Sex Differences." (Chap. 15 of *Handbook of Child Psychology,* 2nd ed., edited by C. Murchison.)

For evidence of sex differences indicated by personality tests see the following:

the matter of sex differences has been done in the field of intelligence. As a consequence the belief supported by many investigations is widely held that if there is any sex difference in intelligence it is small and of far less significance than is the range of
differences of intelligence within either sex group. There are a
few indications that boys in the later high school years are superior on the average to the girls. This, however, still needs
careful testing to determine if uncontrolled factors of selection
may not be responsible, and the difference be apparent rather
than real. Where comparisons are made in terms of one item or
another in the test batteries used, it has not infrequently been
revealed that in certain functions the boys tested surpassed the
girls to a significant degree and that in other functions the girls
showed averages sufficiently higher to be statistically reliable.
But these differences are not yet established in a manner such
that they are of any great practical significance. For research
purposes they must be considered but for practical purposes in
working with adolescents one must know in each specific case
what the individual's relative ability may be and not trust to inferences from the sex of the individual. In molding sex differences of personality pattern other factors are of far greater
importance.

Variability. The contention has been actively asserted and as
actively denied that there is a sex difference in variability, and
that males are more variable than females. If this is true it
should be familiar to all who seek to understand the behavior
of adolescents. The notion is that when properly measured, with
sufficiency of numbers and the rest, female scores will be found
to cluster more closely around the measure of central tendency,
that there will be found comparatively few scores in the extreme
categories either side of the central tendency. Males on the
other hand are said to present as their characteristic distribution
of scores a surface of frequency which is much broader and flat-
ter. That means that scores for males would not cluster so
closely about the central tendency and would have many more
instances in the extreme categories.

Flemming, E. G., "Sex Differences in Emotional Responses," *J. Gen. Psychol.*,
    1933, 8, 430-445.
Stagner, R., "Differential Factors in the Testing of Personality. I. Sex Dif-
    ferences. II. Differences in Maturity," *J. Soc. Psychol.*, 1932, 3, 477-487.

Putting this in more concrete fashion it means that we should expect to find more male geniuses and more males among the feebleminded, that freaks of every kind physical and functional would be more frequently male, that extremes in any measure of anatomical structure or of mental function should be more frequently male. It seems on first reading as though this were a matter which could be readily determined by systematic measurement. But it has turned out to be a very difficult problem to solve. There have been many studies published with many conflicting results, and the controversies over them have not infrequently been rather warm.

One of the most active protagonists of those who accept the variability difference has been Havelock Ellis.[1] He has been almost as actively opposed by Mrs. Leta S. Hollingworth of Columbia University.[2] She has contended that the available figures on sex frequencies among the feebleminded were misleading because feebleminded females were far less often obliged to depend upon institutions for support and protection, and that present statistics were based upon institutionally protected cases. While she has admitted that historical records do reveal more famous men than women she claims that such is an unreliable criterion, that society has never given woman the opportunity for the manifestation of genius. Ellis has marshalled a vast array of data on a great variety of human abnormalities to show the greater frequency of them in the male sex and says that if feeblemindedness does not conform to that rule then it is a rare exception. On the matter of genius he quotes the studies of Cattell[3] and Castle[4] indicating the much greater frequency of genius among men and in reply to Mrs. Hollingworth he insisted that society has ordinarily opposed genius whenever it has appeared and that therefore the opportunity argument in explanation of its greater frequency among males is fallacious.

[1] See his *Man and Woman* (especially the 6th edition) and also his essay, "The Mind of Woman," *Atlantic Monthly*, 1916, 118, 366-374.
[2] See her papers as follows:
Hollingworth, L. S., "Variability as Related to Sex Differences in Achievement," *Amer. J. Sociol.*, 1914, 19, 510-530; H. L. Hollingworth's *Vocational Psychology*, chap. 10.
[3] Cattell, J. McK., "A Statistical Study of Eminent Men," *Pop. Sci. Mo.*, 1902-3, 62, 359-377.
[4] Castle, Cora, *A Statistical Study of Eminent Women*, New York, 1913. Pp. 90.

A recent survey of feeblemindedness in Great Britain reports a much greater frequency of males (30%), and this study included an effort to obtain information outside of institutions as well.[1] Terman's survey in California[2] to obtain a thousand cases of children with I.Q.'s above 140 revealed a considerably greater frequency of boys, although Terman is very cautious about making generalizations from that fact. The general tendency, however, is to look upon this as an unsolved problem, and a very intricate one. Perhaps few so-called sex differences can be attributed entirely to sex;[3] and it is quite possible that our methods of measurement are too crude to isolate that which is purely sexual in their determination. And what is termed sexual may be partly from intrinsic determination and partly from sex-regarding traditions and customs. It may be that the measurements of specific traits are not the right approach to the problem. There is some indication that a sex difference apparent in one trait may not be apparent in another or be in the reverse direction. Lincoln[4] in an admirable survey of this literature comes to the conclusion that the alleged sex difference in variability may be rather a function of the degree of maturity, and as girls are often for a time more mature than boys some have found this difference cropping out in their results. The great differences in degree of maturity in any adolescent group would make this a very difficult matter for determination, and we do not yet know if adult males are more variable than adult females. If they are, many think that such a difference should be thought of as a socially acquired difference rather than one of intrinsic determination.[5]

Extroversion—Introversion. Many believe that females are by

1 Pintner, R., "Feeblemindedness." (Chap. 20 of *The Handbook of Child Study*, 2nd ed., edited by Carl Murchison.
2 Terman, L. M., *Genetic Studies in Genius*, Vol. 1, pp. 49-54.
3 Allen, C. N., "Studies in Sex Differences," *Psychol. Bull.*, 1927, 24, 294-304.
4 Lincoln, E. A., *Sex Differences in the Growth of American School Children*, Baltimore, 1927.
5 In this connection the reader would do well to see also the following references:

Lehman, H. C., and Witty, P. A., "Sex-Differences: Some Sources of Confusion and Error," *Amer. J. Psychol.*, 1930, 42, 140-147.
Winsor, A. L., "The Relative Variability of Boys and Girls," *J. Educ. Psychol.*, 1927, 18, 327-336.

nature more introverted and that males are by nature more extroverted. And if this is true then adolescence must be the period during which that difference becomes prominent and influential. With physical maturation and the attainment of adult stature and abilities this difference, perhaps foreshadowed in childhood, would become definitely established in the personality.

A number of attempts have been made during the last few years to measure introversion and extroversion. It has been thought possible to think of each personality as classifiable somewhere along a line between an extreme of introversion and an extreme of extroversion and to express this position in terms of a score. Of course the sexes have been segregated and compared. Unfortunately these studies have not given consistent indications. Some have revealed a sex difference which corresponded well with the popular supposition. But others have found no certain indication of a sex difference and have even suggested the possibility that the male groups studied were more introverted than the females.[1]

The difficulty seems to lie in a failure to agree first upon a definition of introversion and extroversion. The terms came from psychiatry and for some workers they still carry abnormal or near-abnormal meanings. Some think of introversion as a deviation toward dementia præcox (schizophrenia), and of extroversion as a deviation toward hysteria or maniacal excitement. Some degree of introversion or extroversion under such concepts

---

[1] The reader may obtain a satisfactory introduction to this literature through the following:

Caldwell, O. W., and Wellman, B., "Characteristics of School Leaders," *J. of Educ. Res.*, 1926, 14, 1-20.

Conklin, Edmund S., "The Definition of Introversion, Extroversion, and Allied Concepts," *J. of Abn. & Soc. Psychol.*, 1923, 17, 367-382.

—— "The Determination of Normal Extrovert-Introvert Interest Differences," *Ped. Sem. and J. of Genet. Psychol.*, 1927, 34, 28-37.

Heidbreder, Edna, "Introversion and Extroversion in Men and Women," *J. of Abn. & Soc. Psychol.*, 1927, 22, 52-61.

—— "Measuring Introversion and Extroversion," *J. of Abn. & Soc.' Psychol.*, 1926, 21, 120-134.

Laird, D. A., "How Personalities are Found in Industry," *Indus. Psychol.*, 1926, 1, 654-662.

Marston, L. R., "The Emotions of Young Children," Univ. of Iowa Studies in Child Welfare, 1925, 3. Pp. 99.

Symonds, P. M., *Diagnosing Personality and Conduct*, pp. 195-205, 212-214.

might be well enough, but too much of either would approximate the abnormal if not actually be psychopathic. Then there are those who think of introversion as pathological and of extroversion as the normal or healthy condition. And there are those also who use both terms with both morbid and healthy connotations. In this last way of thinking a person may be extroverted and also quite healthy, or he may be extroverted and at the same time suffering some form of mental disease. When so used it is necessary always for the reader to discover from the context if the author be thinking of morbid extroversion or of that normal personality difference also, unfortunately, designated by the same term. A like confusion has arisen in the use of the related term introversion. There may be an introversion which is a form of mental disease and at the same time the term introversion may be used in another connection to designate a certain kind of normal personality difference. The tests of introversion and extroversion which we now have were made by different persons holding different definitions, and the tests reflect those differences.

Personality Synthesis. There is current a conviction in the minds of many students of personality development, especially those who have had much to do with abnormalities of development, that the female cannot because of some intrinsic peculiarity of her nature ever develop a degree of personality synthesis or integration comparable to that achieved by the average male. No doubt these students would admit the existence of individual variations within each sex group and that there might be some overlapping, that some women might be better integrated than some poorly integrated men; but the thought is that the averages are in this feature distinctly different.[1] Some would not insist upon an intrinsic peculiarity directly preventing the nervous system from developing a high degree of integration, but believe rather that the sex life of the female and all of the traditional ways of living into which the average girl is introduced are such as to eventuate in her failing to develop the same amount of integration that is characteristic of the average male. The responsibilities of life are said to rest more heavily upon the male. He

[1] A good example of this point of view may be found in C. D. Fox's *Psychopathology of Hysteria,* pp. 34-37. A summary of the general setting and relationships of this concept will be found in the author's *Principles of Abnormal Psychology,* chap. 7.

must be more consistent and regular and closely attentive and the consequence is his higher degree of personality synthesis.

If this be true it is obviously of much importance to the understanding of adolescence. Presumably the course of growth in the integration within the personalities of the two sexes might proceed in much the same manner up to puberty. From then on the difference would appear. It would have to be then that in adolescent years the progress toward integration would be delayed and disturbed for the girl and be far less interfered with for the boy. Of course if the whole thing is determined from the germ plasm, then no amount of educational guidance could ever help girls into a better development of personality synthesis; but if it be due to adolescent experience, by wise guidance, a proper program of education, and a certain control of the conventions of life the development of synthesis in the female personality might be relieved of many at least of the handicaps which it now suffers. On the other hand the whole matter may be no sex difference at all. The concept may be merely the consequence of hasty generalization from the kind of cases psychiatrists most often see.

Greater Emotionality of Female. One hears the assertion in both popular and scientific circles that the female is more emotional than the male. For scientific verification of this one may look long without finding much. It is again one of these convictions, firmly held by many thoughtful people, which has not yet been subjected to much systematic study. Perhaps it will not stand critical consideration and study but a conviction so widespread, and so frequently held by adolescent boys concerning the girls with whom they associate, merits inclusion until systematic study proves it utterly false.

In order to work with this concept one must clear one's thinking about the distinction intended by the phrase, greater emotionality of the female. Does it mean a greater frequency of emotional arousal? If so, then there must be something about the pattern of nerve, muscle, and gland reactions in one sex which differs characteristically from the nerve, muscle, and gland reaction patterns in the other sex. Such differences are conceivable. The male might for one reason or another tend to the development of reaction patterns which involved the skeletal muscles far more and the glandular and autonomic functions far less. If that were true any student of general psychology would recognize at once that the male would have emotional reactions far less frequently, assuming of course much the same general pattern of daily stimulation. For such a notion there is indeed some experimental evidence.[1]

Or does the concept mean a difference in the intensity with which emotional reactions occur? If so, given the same stimulating situations the strength of the emotional reaction in the female would be greater than in the male. The girl would feel more intensely about things than would the boy. But this has never been worked out. The very concept itself is vague because of the uncertainty of the meaning of the term intensity or strength of the emotional response.

Does it mean the degree of control or of inhibition? If so, then the female would have less control of her emotional reactions than would the male. It would mean more disturbance from emotions aroused. If emotions are thought of as being largely second or thalamic level functions in the brain, with control or inhibition coming from cortical patterns, then this notion would be to the effect that the cortical patterns and their organization in the female are such as to exercise a less rigid and effective control of the lower level reactions. Gradation of emotional response is interpreted in this way. The reason ordinarily accepted for the greater control and gradation of emotional response in the adult as compared with the child is the difference in the degree of development and organization of the cortex. Adolescence in this respect is midway in the course of development. And to explain emotional differences in this manner would be saying in substance that females never develop the same degree of cortical organization and cortical control. Then this difference would refer back at once to the third of the sex differences here listed, that one about the alleged difference in the degree of integration or synthesis in the female. All that was doubtful there would be doubtful here.

Does it mean a difference in the amount of superficial or overt manifestation of emotion? If so, then it would be that females

[1] Marston, W. M., "Sex Characteristics of Systolic Blood Pressure Behavior," *J. Exper. Psychol.*, 1923, 6, 387-419.

are more demonstrative than are males. And to this one can easily find people willing to subscribe. It would mean that the striated (voluntary) muscular factors in the emotional reactions of the male constitute a far less significant part of those reaction patterns or else that the striated muscle activities are far more subject to inhibition from the cortex than in the female. Perhaps this is a genuine difference. Perhaps the circumstances of life from earliest childhood are such that boys are forced into a more elaborate development of those patterns which control the superficial appearance of emotions. Girls are expected perhaps to be more expressive and therefore are so; or, in other words, they have never experienced a comparable social pressure forcing the development of control. To be sure this would not then be an intrinsic sex difference, but it would nevertheless become an important behavior difference by adolescent years.

Does it mean that judgments are influenced more by emotions in the female than in the male? To this many a casual observer would respond in the affirmative. Many believe that women permit their feelings to influence their opinions of people and policies far more than does the average man, that they are less easily swayed by facts and rational presentations than they are by an emotion-arousing appeal. For this one may find support in some of the experimental studies of testimony which indicate that women are more willing to swear to the truth of their testimonies than are men. If they believe that they recall some event, their belief is easily reinforced by feeling, which makes them less critical. This difference may be more true of adults than of children; and, if so, then adolescence must be the period during which the difference comes to the fore.

Does it mean that there is a difference in the number and nature of the situations which arouse emotion? If so, it would not then necessarily be a matter of greater emotionality in the female but a difference in that which arouses emotion. Possibly, however, there may be for the average female more situations which are adequate stimuli to emotional response. Obviously this need not be thought of in terms of intrinsic difference. It may easily be the product of training, or the accident of experience.

Some years ago the writer [1] made a study of the frequency of superstitions in the beliefs and practices of college students and found in a group of over five hundred that 90 percent of the women and 73 percent of the men could immediately recall belief or practice of superstitions. Furthermore the women mentioned more superstitions on the average than did the men; and the things which they were superstitious about were different. The women mentioned more often superstitions about the home, social relations, wishes, love, marriage and death. The men more frequently mentioned superstitions concerning sports and business activities. Similar differences concerning fear were found in a study by G. W. A. Luckey.[2] When he averaged up his reports he found that women mentioned more per individual than did the men. Both of these studies were made a number of years ago and if repeated today could have the advantage of the better methods now available. Possibly those findings would be set aside. They are mentioned here merely because they illustrate what many believe to be the essential emotional differences between men and women, that their emotional reactions have become conditioned by their experience to largely different stimuli than have the emotions of men.

Does the alleged greater emotionality of the female mean that given the same situation one emotion would be characteristically aroused in the male and another emotion would be characteristically aroused in the female? That also is within the range of possibility. And if it should prove to be true that men and women in the large habitually have different emotional reactions to the same situation, then much of the misunderstanding between the sexes should be cleared up by its general recognition. In a very clever essay on the flapper variety of adolescent girl, Hall described emotional reactions to situations which would certainly be very different, if true, from the reactions which the writer believes would be aroused in the average boy of the same age.[3] Marston has come to somewhat this conclusion from his

---

[1] Conklin, Edmund S., "Superstitious Beliefs and Practice Among College Students," *Amer. J. Psychol.*, 1919, 30, 83-102.

[2] Luckey, G. W. A., *Essentials of Child Study*, p. 92.

[3] Hall, G. Stanley, "Flapper Americana Novissima," *Atlantic Monthly*, 1922, 129, 771-780. See also chapter 9 on the Budding Girl in his *Educational Problems*, Vol. 2.

study of the blood pressure accompaniments of different emotions in the two sexes.[1] If the adolescent girl habitually reacts with awe or wonder to that which stirs disgust or fear in the adolescent boy, for instance, that would be worth knowing. It is at least worth thinking about and, for those who have the opportunity, it is deserving of experimental investigation.

Finally it is possible that all this discussion of alleged emotional differences between the sexes may eventually be resolved into the existence of emotional qualities which exist in one sex and not in the other. If the quality of an emotion depends upon the pattern of organic and muscular functioning to the extent we are now inclined to believe, then there must be instances of emotional reactions in the female which are qualitatively different from the corresponding emotional reactions in the male because of the difference in the anatomical structures involved. To this one should of course add the effects of differences in many of the physiological processes. It is thus possible that girls may have emotions and qualities of feeling which boys never have and never can have, and that boys may have qualities of feeling and emotion that girls never have and never can have. They may be designated by the same words, but they may be qualitatively quite different. Their effects upon behavior may be correspondingly different, and the efforts of one sex to completely understand the other thus be inevitably hopeless.

Psychoanalytic Differences. The psychoanalysts seem never to have produced an adequate formulation of the many sex differences which must according to their system of thinking be well established by middle adolescent years and to which the experiences of pubescence must make a not inconsiderable contribution.[2] The pattern or content of the ego and the superego must

---

[1] Marston, W. M., "Sex Characteristics of Systolic Blood Pressure Behavior," *J. Exper. Psychol.*, 1923, 6, 387-419.

[2] Through the following one may obtain a working introduction to these points of view:

Brierley, S. S., "A Note on Sex Differences from the Psychoanalytic Point of View," *Brit. J. of Psychol.*, Med. Sec., 1923, 3, 288-308.
Deutsch, Helene, "The Psychology of Women in Relation to the Functions of Reproduction," *Internat. J. Psychoanal.*, 1925, 6, 405-418.
Ellis, Havelock, "The Conception of Narcissism," *Psychoanal. Rev.*, 1927, 14, 129-153.
Harnik, J., "The Various Developments Undergone by Narcissism in Men and Women," *Internat. Jour. of Psychoanal.*, 1924, 5, 66-83.
White, W. A., *Essentials of Character Formation*, New York, 1916.

differ notably in a female from that which has developed in a male even in a very similar environment. Each sex is looked upon as predestined from earliest infancy to a different development of motivations and inhibitions because of an inherent difference in sexuality. Before puberty this sexuality difference is generalized but nevertheless is influential especially in the emotional reactions. All of the familiar psychoanalytic psychology of the Œdipus and the Electra complexes is applicable here. The love life of the girl developing within the family situation suffers peculiar influences from the relations with the father and the mother. The boy's development is the counterpart. In adolescent years substitutes for the father stir the affection of the girl, and substitutes for the mother stir the boy. The girl is supposed to rebel against the mother and to seek her place in the father's affections; the boy is supposed to rebel against the father and to seek his place in the mother's affections. The influences of all these experiences go into the content or pattern of the superego and so are in the background in adolescent years.

Narcissism, the love of the self, is thought by the psychoanalysts to undergo rather different courses of development in the two sexes. Each has its childhood stage of narcissism from which with growth the libido is normally in large part sublimated, but never so entirely. Some think that narcissism in the adolescent male is focalized on the genital organs, but that the narcissism of the female is attached to the body as a whole. On this basis they explain the female's greater concern with her own physical beauty.

The psychoanalysts make much also of an alleged lasting effect of the discovery of the difference between the sexes in the nature of the external genitals. They claim that this brings a shock and much feeling of inferiority to the female (the so-called castration complex) with all the adjustments which follow in its train. Defensive efforts and compensatory trends and the like are supposed to be apparent in the adolescent personality which are traceable to this complex. Some think that all this is accentuated by misinterpretations óf the first menstrual flow.

Inferiority Feelings. There is a persistent notion that one effect of sexuality upon the female is the development of inferiority feelings, concepts and complexes to a much greater extent than in the male. The psychoanalysts are largely responsible for this idea and have made much of it in one form or another.[1] Certainly one does meet girls who complain of the limitations placed upon them by their sex. Clinical case records abound with instances of girls who resent the alleged greater opportunities and capacities of the male, who wish that they themselves were boys, and who in some instances make themselves as boyish as possible. And there are the instances of girls who because of an unhealthy initation into the facts of menstruation are ashamed of their sex, reacting to their periods with disgust and hatred. However significant and distressing such individual instances may be systematic studies have failed to justify the belief that girls on the average are much more troubled by inferiority feelings than are boys.[2] A slight difference has been indicated but on numbers too small for safe generalization. It is also possible with proper education to produce attitudes of pride toward one's sex and the evidence of casual observation leads many to think that not a few women early develop feelings of superiority and pride in their sex which are genuine and in no sense defense mechanisms.

Physical beauty is probably more important to the female than to the male. The extent of social and commercial emphasis upon it must make it a matter of much concern to the average adolescent girl. While adolescent boys may be sensitive about their awkwardness, homeliness is probably far less troublesome to them. Their awkwardness disappears with the progress of adolescent development, but the importance of beauty to a girl increases with adolescent years. The belief, whether well founded or not, that her development is in a direction which will make her unattractive may be seriously disturbing. Perhaps in this respect a more influential sex difference in personality development may be found.

Interests. Of interest differences between the sexes there must be not a few. While these will be discussed more in detail in

[1] See discussion of psychoanalytic differences above and also the more complete discussion of inferiority troubles in chap. IX.

[2] Aikins, H. A., "Woman and the Masculine Protest," *J. Abn. & Soc. Psychol.*, 1927, 22, 259-272.

Gardner, G. E., and Pierce, H. D., "The Inferiority Feelings of College Students," *J. Abn. & Soc. Psychol.*, 1929, 24, 8-13.

other chapters (Chaps. IV and V) their existence must be noted here. Many of the studies of extroversion—introversion mentioned above involve preferences for different forms of activity and reveal sex differences in a number of instances. The play preferences of adolescent years show a sex difference. The social pressures to which a girl and a boy are subjected force a trend into activity differences and inevitably into interest differences. Clothing and other domestic activities appeal to girls rather differently from the appeal they make to boys. Studies and reading and social contacts and sports and vocational ambitions are all subject to the influences of the many factors which are producing the differentiation between the female and the male personality.[1]

Social Attitudes. Although our knowledge of social attitudes has scarcely yet passed beyond the stage of technique development,[2] there is a common and probably sound belief that the developing personalities of boys and girls diverge in the nature of their social attitudes to a no inconsiderable extent. Certainly the attitudes developed toward members of the other sex are different from those toward members of the same sex, and this would make some of the attitudes in girls quite different from some of those in boys. As courtship years approach and the incipient stages of romantic love appear, more and more each person of the other sex appears as a possible husband or wife. The petty jealousies and rivalries of such relationships enter in.[3] Gang loyalty subsides and friendships become more prominent. There is a shift to friendship attitudes. If in this there appears any sex difference we do not know; but there are many who suspect that the attitudes of a girl toward her chum are not in all respects like the attitudes of a boy toward his pal. It would be surprising also if there is not some day demonstrated a very considerable difference in the attitudes toward their individual parents.

Literary presentations often assume that a girl is typically more personal in her attitudes and that a boy is more impersonal. Novelists not infrequently bring this out in the conversations they

---

[1] Washburne, J. N., "The Impulsions of Adolescents as Revealed by Written Wishes," *J. Juv. Res.*, 1932, 16, 193-212. For sex differences in play interests see chap. IV.

[2] See chap. VII.

[3] Hollingworth, H. L., *Mental Growth and Decline*, pp. 238-241.

ascribe to their characters. The girl is presented as unable to think impersonally of the problem in hand but as always turning the conversation off into the personal relationship. The hero is not infrequently irritated by this perpetual dragging in of that which to him appears to be a minor if not insignificant feature of the problem. His inclination is to decide the problem on what appeals to him to be its merits, quite apart from his personal setting in it.[1] Systematic studies of the content of actual conversations support this view. They indicate a much greater concern on the part of females with persons and of males with objects and activities.[2]

In an extensive study of later adolescent attitudes made by Katz and Allport[3] girls checked their college studies as being of the greatest personal importance far less frequently than did boys (F. 36 percent; M. 52 percent). This the authors think points to a female tendency to value "personal experiences above reactions to things." They also observed that differences of attitude between the sexes increased with maturity, with the development of freedom from parent and teacher domination.

And there is the age-old conviction that the female is more altruistic than the male. Gina Lombroso[4] has built her whole psychology of woman upon this assumption, that the female is instinctively more altercentric and the male more egocentric. She admits, to be sure, her belief in the presence of the opposite trait also in each sex; but, by comparison, it is weak and largely insignificant. That adolescents are often highly altruistic has been well established, but it is also well known that adolescents of both sexes are often highly selfish. Even Lombroso has much to say about the feminine desire "to be first"; and in her own presentation the manifestations of this desire to be first are far from

---

[1] Charlotte Bühler says that her collection of adolescent diaries reveals a feminine tendency to stress the feelings and emotions while the boys note external or more impersonal items. *Das Seelenleben des Jugendlichen*, Jena, Fischer, 1927, pp. 30-39.

[2] Landis, C., "National Differences in Conversation," *J. Abn. & Soc. Psychol.*, 1927, 21, 354-357.

Landis, M. H., and Burtt, H. E., "A Study of Conversation," *J. Comp. Psychol.*, 1924, 4, 81-90.

Moore, H. T., "Further Data Concerning Sex Differences," *J. Abn. & Soc. Psychol.*, 1922, 17, 210-214.

[3] Katz, Daniel, and Allport, F. H., *Students' Attitudes*, Syracuse, 1931. (See especially pp. 28, 245-246, 267.)

[4] Lombroso, Gina, *The Soul of Woman*, New York, 1923.

always highly altruistic. A reader of her book is often inclined to the opinion that she makes the female appear after all to be highly selfish. But she has no systematically collected evidence for her assertions. Perhaps they are all correct to some extent. Adolescence is a period of rather more than ordinary contradiction in traits manifested, and it may be that Lombroso is right in both her apparent contradictions and in her claims for sex differences.

Functional Periodicity. No one has ever been able to demonstrate anything in the male comparable to the functional periodicity, menstruation, of the female. This constitutes an unquestioned sex difference and would continue to be such even though some one should some day discover a rudimentary periodicity of physiological functioning in the human male. Menstruation is typically female and any psychological effects which it may have will constitute a definite and incontestable sex difference. As menstruation is new in adolescent years, often slow to become settled in its periodic cycle, we should expect to observe the mental effects of it as prominently there as in any other growth period if not more so.

The physiology of functional periodicity is not well known. There is certainly a circulatory congestion relieved by the flow. Studies of blood pressure [1] during the cycle indicate a rise during three or four days preceding the period, a high pressure during the first two days, a rapid change to a pressure at the end considerably below the normal for intermenstrual days. After the period it does not return to normal immediately but does so within a week.

Of the psychological effects of the period direct and indirect we know a little. Hauptmann [2] has reported a general heightening of the activity of all mental processes during the period which accords well with the increase of blood pressure. Apparently, however, this may be considerably offset by pain disturbance. He also reports marked changes in the self feeling (Ichgefühl) in the direction of a heightening of the consciousness of

[1] Eagleson, H. E., "Periodic Changes in Blood Pressure, Muscular Coordination and Mental Efficiency in Women," *Comp. Psychol. Monog.*, 1927, 4, No. 20. (Includes an excellent review of the literature.)
[2] Hauptmann, A., "Menstruation und Psyche." (Versuch einer "verständlichen" Inbeziehungsetzung somatischer und psychischer Erscheinungsreihen.) *Archiv für Psychiatrie*, 1924, 71, 1-54.

sex difference, of the sex proprieties and the like. L. S. Holling-worth has reported the most extensive study of psychological functions subject to test methods.[1] She used tests of tapping, steadiness, motor fatigability, color naming, opposites and type-writing on six women with two men as a control group. They were tested daily for three months and while she found variations in test scores from time to time she could find nothing that was peculiar to the female subjects or that could be definitely related to effects of the functional periodicity. But it should be observed that she worked on purely cognitive or sensory-motor processes. If there were emotional effects or changes of attitude they could not have been discovered by the methods used. More recently an English study of motor control during the period has pro-duced very conflicting results and the authors [2] suggest that there may be marked differences of menstrual effect according to the social training of the individual, the general physique, and the degree of nervous instability.

The writer with the assistance of two of his students [3] made an exploratory attempt to discover what might be some of the sen-sory, emotional and attitudinal reactions to the experience of the period as well as some of its sensory phenomena. They found that in any considerable group of women between puberty and the menopause it could be assumed that approximately 18 per-cent would be in period at any given time. The amount of pain or physical discomfort experienced manifested much individual difference. The following table taken from these returns from over fifteen hundred women and girls is useful:

	Percent
No discomfort	20
Slight discomfort	45
Moderate pain	24
Intense pain	11

[1] Hollingworth, L. S., *Functional Periodicity*, New York, 1914. (Includes valuable abstract of a somewhat similar study by Voitsechovsky.)

[2] Sowton, S. C. M., and Myers, C. S. (I) Bedale, E. M. (II). Two con-tributions to the experimental study of menstrual cycle. I. Its influence on mental and muscular efficiency. II. Its relation to general functional effi-ciency. Rep. Indus. Fatigue Res. Board No. 45. London, H. M. Sta. Office, 1928.

[3] Conklin, Edmund S., Byrom, M. E., and Knips, A., *Some Mental Effects of Menstruation*, Ped. Sem., 1927, 34, 357-367.

Obviously discomfort to a greater or less degree characterizes the experience of the majority.[1] Of the reactions to the period it may be said with certainty that the general tendency is decidedly introvertive, to withdraw from the ordinary activities of life, and that this was the most pronounced where the discomfort was greatest. Curiously enough approximately one-half of one percent of the women who responded indicated reactions to the period which were most emphatically extrovertive.[2] Now and then one will meet a girl who feels impelled during the period to rush into an unusual amount of social and physical activity. Why this should be so no one yet knows.

It must be evident then that the constantly recurrent experience of the menstrual period registers effects upon the personality of the female which never appear in the male. If the female is on the average more introvertive than the male, it may be due to the effects of the functional period. That most women have more pain to suffer than men is equally obvious. Just what the effects of this may be are not yet known. Perhaps it makes them more sympathetic; perhaps less so. Possibly it makes them more sensitive to pain; possibly it hardens them and makes them more indifferent to pain. The necessity for self-protective care and for concealment every twenty-eight days must also establish habits that are peculiar to the female. How pervasive these are and to what extent they affect other activities of life remains to be discovered. Probably, as Hauptmann's study has slightly indicated, there is an effect upon the self concept and upon the pattern of self feelings. While a certain amount of adaptation to all this might come in time, some effects of the period would have been made before the adaptation was achieved.[3]

Self Concept. Nearly all of the foregoing items must have their effect upon the pattern of the self concept. The inevitable result must be that the self concept of the average girl must be quite different from that of the average boy. And as perceptions

1 A more recent investigation indicates that the proportion of college girls who report pain and discomfort is declining, although the evidence for such a change is not yet definitive.

2 This has subsequently been verified by another study which has never been published.

3 For an excellent review of the older literature the reader should see Novak, Emil, *Menstruation and Its Disorders*, New York, 1923.

and sentiments and attitudes are influenced by the content of this concept we have ample reason for thinking of much difference between the personality of the female and that of the male, a difference which is very largely a matter of adolescent establishment. Differences in variability, if they exist, may be of little significance to the self concept because they may not be perceived. If the greater introversion is perceived or believed in by a girl, that will have its reflex upon her self concept and all self-regarding functions. If the boy believes that he has better control than the girl, that will affect his attitudes as much as hers. If any or all of the possible emotional differences between the sexes are brought to the attention and perception of boys and girls, then their self concepts will be affected thereby. Likewise, if individual adolescents become conscious of any of those differences claimed by the psychoanalysts, there will be some sort of differentiating effect upon the self concepts. Differences of interest must add their share to the pattern. Altruistic impulses and acts will leave their impress and if there is any sex difference in their nature and frequency then sex differences in the self will follow. Perceptions of the physical self as male or female and all of the possible meanings which may accrue to those perceptions must cause a very large twist toward difference in the self concepts of the two sexes.

Vague as this whole subject is the preponderance of reason and of experimental fact is in the direction of believing that during adolescent years we are watching the differentiation of personalities into male and female.

CHAPTER IV

INTERESTS OF ADOLESCENCE

DEFINITIONS OF INTEREST, NATURE OF PLAY (SURPLUS EN-
ERGY THEORY, PRACTICE, RECAPITULATION, RECREATION-
RELAXATION, MISCELLANEOUS CONTRIBUTIONS, PLAY RE-
DEFINED), EFFECTS OF ADOLESCENCE UPON PLAY INTERESTS,
ATHLETICS AND ORGANIZED GAMES, DANCING, SPORT-TRAVEL-
ADVENTURE, GAMBLING, GENERAL EFFECTS OF PLAY

The interests, recreations, ambitions, and amusements of youth
have received no little attention and are deserving of much.
Their content reveals both native traits and the influence of the
social pressures to which youth in its progress is subjected. As
interests change with age one may see the effects of new ideals,
of better self-control, of changing social pressures, and possibly
also the influence of maturation in the pattern of intrinsically
determined urges or drives. Sex differences appear which were
not indicated in the interests of childhood. Participation in interest activities establishes habits, sometimes very large and influential habit patterns. It is necessary then to consider not only
the motivations of interests, amusements, ambitions, and recreations, but to seek also the relation of these to capacities and to
observe the contributions which they make to the general pattern
of the personality.

Definitions of Interest. It is wise to recall that the term interest is frequently, and in fact ordinarily, used with two very
different meanings. It is used to designate a background of
knowledge which makes attention easily aroused and held by
thoughts or sensory presentations corresponding to that background of knowledge; and it is also used to designate the state
of mind or mode of behavior when the attention of a human being is more or less continuously held with an accompanying
pleasantness. An example of the former would be one's interest

in medicine or law or the drama or in old books or in postage stamps. An example of the latter would be the experience of reading a story in some popular magazine about an adventure in Uganda, the nature of which held the attention and aroused no little pleasantness although the reader had no background of knowledge, neither of the technique of the short story nor of life in Uganda. To both the term interest is applicable, according to contemporary usage. One may speak of one's interests, and also of the experience of being interested. And the one may be without relation to the other.

A person may be temporarily interested by a situation which bears no relationship whatever to his interests, thought of as backgrounds of organized knowledge. More often, however, the experience of being interested in something (pleasantly held attention) is brought about and largely maintained by the existence of an interest (background of knowledge). One who has an interest in baseball is most likely to be attracted and held by the baseball stories on the sporting page of the daily paper. One who is interested in money and investments will be attracted and held by the news of the financial page whether he has any actual investments or not. It is just this sort of behavior with which we are most concerned in this chapter: the behavior which may be designated as interested and which is governed by an interest. Ordinarily the term interest will be used without special designation, although the emphasis of the meaning denoted may at times be more upon one phase than upon the other.

Interests have long been a subject of much importance to students of life in the adolescent years because of their possible significance in vocational counselling. In more recent years, however, they have taken on a new significance because of their possible influence in the preparation of youth for a profitable or wise use of leisure time in maturity. No longer are the recreations and amusements of youth looked upon as something to be condemned or at best to be tolerated; rather are they looked upon as an important feature of the preparation for living. Life is not merely a matter of earning a living, a matter of work; life is more than that and involves the proper use of much leisure time. It is as important that youth be prepared for leisure as for work. Toward this end it is believed that the recreations and amusements and relaxations of youth contribute much, or that they may contribute much, if they are wisely chosen and properly developed.

Among these recreations and amusements and relaxations, one thinks immediately of athletics and group games, of dancing, of the movies, and possibly also of hunting and fishing and the like, of intellectual games such as bridge and chess and checkers, and perhaps of wandering or travel and actual adventure. Gambling should doubtless also be considered, although it may be looked upon as to some extent a perversion. And there is the playful use of the fine arts, of painting and sculpture and so on, which must eventually be included.

Nature of Play. Before these individual topics can be wisely approached, however, it is necessary that the reader be fairly clear upon the interpretation of play in general. For many years there was much confusion here because of the controversy over several theories of the nature of play. Now, happily, the thinking of psychologists on these matters seems to be clarifying, as a consequence both of the discussion and also of the newer studies of play itself. The most famous of the play theories should be in mind because each has contributed more or less to contemporary thinking about the nature of play. They may be itemized as follows:

1. *The surplus energy theory.* This title is unfortunate because it is somewhat misleading. There is to be sure a long-popular notion that much play at least is due to the physical necessity of working off a surplusage of energy. The exuberant and persistent activity of children often makes adults wonder, and think in terms of this notion of consumption of surplus energy, as though nature somehow had produced more energy than was needed for the business of living. Others condemn the idea as physiologically dubious and quite inadequate for the explanation of some common instances of play activity. Animals will continue to play even when apparently nearing the point of exhaustion. Children play when tired and when ill, when it is hard to think of their having a surplusage of energy.

The theory is ordinarily associated with the names of Friedrich Schiller and Herbert Spencer as the Schiller-Spencer theory.

But if one turns to the original presentations [1] of these men one finds that they had far more in mind than has been presented in the preceding paragraph. They were not seeking primarily for an explanation of play. They were attempting to formulate an explanation for the origin of art in the evolution of man. Both present basically the same idea, that there came a time in the course of animal and human development when it was no longer necessary for all the energy and skill of the creature to be devoted to the struggle for existence. Then, in the language of Schiller, there could be some freedom and some unemployed energy. Then was it possible to "extend enjoyment beyond necessity" (Schiller). Activity not devoted to the struggle for existence is termed play when it involves only lower functions; but when it is largely a matter of the higher human functions it produces that which is called art.[2] Spencer goes on to point out that esthetic and playful behavior does not differ in its essential nature from those activities which are devoted to the satisfaction of the material requirements of living. What we should today call the same processes or functions are operative in all these forms of activity. The differences lie in the "attitude of consciousness" toward the "resulting states." In all non-esthetic activity the attitude is toward something ulterior, concerning which the activities are merely a means of achievement. But in esthetic activity the attitude is toward the processes themselves, and they are maintained as long as possible because of the pleasure which their presence produces. Play lies between these extremes. In some plays, as in games, there is still the attitude toward a distant end or purpose (the winning of the game, vanquishing of a rival), but that end is still quite close to the activity itself. From such there is a shading over into that which is purely esthetic, where the pleasure is in the activity itself. From the point of view of the place of play in the life of man it is further of interest

[1] Schiller, Friedrich, *Letters on the Esthetical Education of Man*, Letter No. xxvii.

Spencer, Herbert, *Principles of Psychology*, Vol. II, chap. 9, on the Aesthetic Sentiments.

[2] The contention has been made that Spencer's theory should not be classed with Schiller's and is not a surplus energy theory at all (Bowen, W. P., and Mitchell, E. D., *The Theory of Organized Play*, New York, 1923, pp. 182, 187-189), but in the judgment of the present author this is not justified by the original texts of Schiller and of Spencer.

to observe that Spencer believed that esthetic activities would have an increasingly important place in human life as the course of evolution progressed.

It must then be obvious that Spencer did far more than to interpret play in terms of a physiological notion of surplus energy. While utilizing the surplusage idea in his theory he also observed this psychological difference of attitude, and in the attitude difference found the differentiation of play from other forms of surplus activity.

2. *Practice or preparation theory.* This theory was contributed by Karl Groos whose two scholarly volumes on the subject have received much attention.[1] Like Spencer's, the theory is thoroughly evolutional; but unlike that of Spencer it involves a full consideration of the function of play in the development of the individual.[2] And unlike many evolutionally minded psychologists Groos in his thinking looks to the future quite as much if not more than to the past.

For Groos every infant comes into the world with a considerable number of instinctive tendencies. Some of these are well established in the race and will soon function effectively in any individual, but others are racially newer and will not through mere inherent determination mature into effective patterns. They all appear as tendencies to modes of activity; and if they are exercised they will become more or less well-defined patterns. The older and better established instincts become definitized readily. The newer ones require more exercise. The long period of infancy, childhood and adolescence provides ample opportunity for the practice and exercise of these instinctive tendencies, to the end that they shall be well established by the time maturity is reached.

Such a scheme of thinking as this does not require the assump-

---

[1] *Die Spiele der Thiere,* 1895, and *Die Spiele der Menschen,* 1899. Both of these were translated into English by Elizabeth L. Baldwin and published under the titles, *The Play of Animals* and *The Play of Man.*

[2] Spencer's presentation is not without indications of an awareness that superfluous activity would through the exercise of functions develop those functions, but his emphasis is rather upon the interpretation of play and esthetic activity in terms of superfluous activity than it is upon the function of the superfluous activity. Patrick, McDougall, and others have contended that Spencer failed to explain the form of play; but it is difficult to reconcile this criticism with Spencer's explanation of the forms of play in terms of instincts and imitation (dramatization).

tion of a specific play instinct, a notion that Groos very definitely discards.[1] He does, however, include an instinctive tendency to imitate, which helps greatly in the explanation of some forms of play. And in the light of later developments it is also of interest to observe that Groos admits an instinctive striving for supremacy which is thought of as present in all intelligent animals.[2]

But this exercise of instinctive tendencies was looked upon as yet more than a mere preparation for maturity of the individual. There is also its possible racial contribution to be considered. Perhaps this practice of new instinctive tendencies in childhood and youth contributes to their establishment as instincts in the race. Groos recognized the confusion of biological theory on this subject and was not dogmatic. This inheritance might be direct or it might be through assisting in the process of selection and survival; but, whatever be the means by which well-established instincts come into being, Groos thought that this practice of functions would tend to contribute to their establishment. And by this means did he in part explain the play of maturity. He also recognized that adults might recall the pleasure they found in the plays of their youth and desire to repeat the experiences.[3]

Many years later Groos presented another statement [4] in which he sought to relate his scheme of thinking to the doctrine of catharsis which Hall (see below) and the psychoanalysts had made popular. It also brings his thinking into closer articulation with that of Spencer. He suggests that much play is like the letting-off of steam by a safety valve, and hastens to point out that by so doing the safety valve is in no wise changed or reduced in efficiency. There is merely the removal of a burdensome or injurious excess behind it. This adds another value to many play activities and removes from them some possibly dangerous implications of the practice theory. By wrestling with a playmate emotion is worked off. Teasing is a means of releasing the energy through a sort of expression of the fighting instinct; pet-

---

[1] *The Play of Man*, p. 377.

[2] *The Play of Animals*, p. 290. In this connection it is well to observe Spencer's statement that play produces a "satisfaction of certain egoistic feelings." *Principles of Psychology*, Vol. II, p. 631.

[3] For Groos's discussion of play in adult years see *The Play of Animals*, pp. 81 and 287; and *The Play of Man*, pp. 378-9.

[4] Groos, K., "Das Spiel als Katharsis," *Zeit. f. päd. Psychol.*, 1911, 12, 353-367.

ting and flirting are presented as means of harmlessly working off energy which otherwise might result in undesirable activation of the sex instinct. Through both phantasy thinking and reading also much energy is released harmlessly. Such modes of expression do not damage the instinct pattern. The catharsis doctrine had suggested that patterns might be weakened by playful expression and subsequently deteriorate as racially old and no longer useful or desirable; but this Groos rejects.

3. *Play as recapitulation.* For the elaboration and popularization of this means of interpretation, G. Stanley Hall [1] was responsible. Fond as he was of evolutional ways of thinking he strangely rebelled against the suggestion of Groos, almost with violence. In fact he called it "partial, superficial and perverse." For Hall the whole course of development from impregnation to maturity was a recapitulation of the evolution of the race. Spontaneous activities at any stage of development were, with few exceptions, interpreted as rehearsals of the activities of the race at the corresponding stage. When children are climbing trees, they are living through the stage of racial arboreal existence; and when they are fond of wandering and camping, they are re-living the nomadic stage of race history. It was Hall's firm contention that we never practice in play that which is racially new.

He also believed, much as he regretted it, that maturity ordinarily meant the loss of play. It was consonant with his theory for him to think so. With the achievement of full maturity the recapitulation was complete and habits dominant. And yet he firmly believed that every one should fight against this domination by the ways of maturity, that by every possible means the spontaneity and creativeness of youth be retained, because he believed that impulses to new modes or stages of individual and racial progress could appear only in adolescence. They did not appear, as Groos thought, as weak tendencies which might be practiced at any time; but as impulses when the recapitulatory process neared completion and the habits of maturity were not yet fully dominant.

But if one should accept this theory, the plays of childhood and early adolescence would have more significance than as mere

[1] Hall, G. Stanley, *Adolescence*, Vol. 1, p. 202 et seq.

records of what the race had done in corresponding stages of culture. Their functioning would be necessary as stimuli to subsequent stages of development; and, having made that contribution, might subside (catharsis doctrine) and degenerate into merely rudimentary patterns. Thus the practice of these old racial traits in play would after all have a sort of preparatory value. Each would prepare for the next succeeding stage. And every play interest well cultivated in adolescence would help to postpone the day when playfulness would succumb to the habit-dominated life of maturity.

The recapitulation theory is no longer acceptable [1] and with its rejection must go much of this interesting doctrine of Hall's. But this does not mean that the plays of childhood and adolescence cannot be thought of as involving remnants or rehearsals of old racial activities. Climbing and running and hitting and throwing and the like may be intrinsically determined functional patterns, and in the use of them both boys and girls may be rehearsing the racially old. Other plays, such as the almost universal participation in string games, may be likewise rehearsals of ancient racial activities; but they may be a social rather than an organic inheritance. It does, however, mean that one must look elsewhere for explanations of the motivation of the widespread participation in the plays of childhood and youth and also for the satisfactions obtained by such participation.

4. *Recreation and relaxation.* That play is agreeable because it involves a change from activity that has become tiresome or irksome and provides opportunity for or facilitates recuperation is a very old idea indeed. It was given academic recognition and formulation as far back as (or as recently as) 1883 by Lazarus.[2] More recently it was popularized and articulated with the thinking of G. Stanley Hall by Professor G. T. W. Patrick.[3] The latter says in substance that we call the activities of childhood play because they are what adults do when they are tired and relax into activities that bring relief and pleasure.

The essential patterns of activity in the plays which children

---

[1] See chap. I.
[2] Lazarus, M., *Ueber die Reize des Spiels*, Berlin, 1883.
[3] Patrick, G. T. W., *The Psychology of Relaxation*, Boston, 1916. See especially chap. 2.

enjoy are for Patrick instinctive; and he likes to think of many
instincts, remnants of the forms of activity once useful in the
long line of our animal and human forebears.[1] To be sure, there
are not a few additions from social heredity, and there are some
instinctive tendencies which are disagreeable; but it is not to
these that he gives the bulk of his attention. Evolution has
brought into the life of the adult, and to a lesser degree of the
adolescent, demands for self-control and direction, for the strains
and efforts of inhibition. These rapidly become disagreeable
and fatiguing. Relief is necessary and is found through a slip-
ping back into those older functional patterns that were intrinsically determined, that function easily, and that require little if
any of the strains of attention and new adjustment. The lure
of baseball and of fishing and the like lies in the relief which
they bring from the tensions of business and professional affairs;
and there is also the assumption that these old activities are natively pleasurable in themselves, to all normal human beings,
quite apart from the pleasure of the relaxation or relief.

In addition to these more famous attempts at an interpretation of play, *other observations and suggestions* have been made
which merit thoughtful attention. Shand[2] thinks that the
amount of joy in any form of play or sport depends upon the
amount of effort or striving therein. Joy becomes complete only
when effort and striving disappear. So long, for example, as
there is effort to achieve a certain stroke in tennis, joy is not
complete; but when the stroke is mastered and striving to
achieve disappears then pleasure comes in full. Work would
thus differ from play in the relatively larger proportion of striving involved; and so would work become joyful as full mastery
in it is achieved. Shand also recognizes the large place which instincts have in the motivation of play; but he observes that the
joy comes not in achieving the normal end of each particular instinct. The object of play is the continuation of the joyful activity. Achieving the normal end of the instinct patterns would
put a stop to the whole thing.

McDougall[3] has made the curious suggestion that alongside

---

[1] Although he does not assume a recapitulatory order of their appearance.
[2] Shand, A. F., *The Foundations of Character*, 1914, pp. 284, 287-300.
[3] McDougall, Wm., *An Introduction to Social Psychology* (14th ed., 1921),
pp. 110-119.

each of the instincts there is a second instinct pattern derived from it and differing somewhat from it, but retaining enough of the nature of the original to be easily confused with it unless carefully observed. Rivalry is thus a sort of secondary form of instinct derived from pugnacity. In play it is not the original instincts that are exercised but these derived forms. This Mc-Dougall articulates with the preparatory theory by pointing out that the exercise of these derived instinct patterns actually increases the efficiency of these basic instincts, because there are so many features in common. For the motivation of play he rules out the notion of a special play instinct and stresses the importance of the desire for skill, of the pleasure found in make-believe, and of the pleasure in being a cause.

Woodworth has stressed the importance of the fear and escape motive in play.[1] Imagination is often important especially in the plays of children; but even in many of the plays of childhood, and especially in the sports and games of adolescence and maturity, the thrill of escape from danger gives zest to the game. The danger may or may not be actually very great. It may be nothing more than the possibility of a tumble in a snow bank, or it may be the possibility of a fatal plunge down some precipitous mountain slope. The pleasure of the sport lies in the escape through personal effort and skill. This obviously involves the enhancement of self-feeling, as Woodworth properly observes. There is a thrill of self-satisfaction in the skillful management of the skis, in the successful mountain climb, and in overcoming the opponent or opponents in some organized games.

Bradley [2] has pointed out that while that which is purely playful is without restraint, is completely free and unhampered, at the same time the vast amount of play has doubtless a fringe of consciousness of restraint. In much of the play of childhood there are limits which cannot be crossed without spoiling the play, and in the games of youth rules place still more restraint upon activity. Bradley thinks that this restraint is largely, although marginally, conscious. For this he presents no systematic investigation in support, and probably none has ever been made.

[1] Woodworth, R. S., *Psychology* (3rd ed., 1934), pp. 492-3.
[2] Bradley, F. H., "On Floating Ideas and the Imaginary," *Mind*, 1906, N. S. 15, 445-472, especially 462-472.

In a valuable monograph Reaney [1] has stressed the importance of recognizing that in play there is a significant harmony of end and means. In other than playful activities the end may be something quite different and apart from the activity itself. The factory employee repetitiously doing some process without ever seeing or knowing the nature of the completed article is working for the satisfactions to be obtained from the use of the money received in compensation. Here the end and the means are not in harmony. But where the end is the winning of the game, there the end and the means are quite harmonious. In addition, Reaney stresses the freedom for instinctive functioning in play. The activity is pleasurable because the instincts are neither hampered nor restrained, although the form of the instinctive activity may be sublimated in such a way that there is no danger of the primitive or original ends of the instincts being achieved. If there were danger of fighting plays ending in real destructive fight, there would be restraint and no joyous freedom. It is only in a sublimated form that the fighting instinct can be permitted free expression, and that we see in many group games. When in some player there is a regression to the old primitive form of the activity of the fighting instinct, then are the rules violated and the course of the game spoiled. At the opposite extreme from play is not work, which may be as free an expression of instincts as play, but drudgery; because, in what she terms drudgery, the instinctive dispositions are definitely baulked.

Lehman and Witty introduce their valuable inductive studies of play [2] by assuming that play is any activity in which an individual participates "just because he wants to"; and Robinson has wisely pointed out that much play is compensatory, that it satisfies in some substitute fashion the desires of the individual for power and achievement. [3]

In reading this brief review of the efforts to interpret play, any psychologically trained reader will have observed that some of

[1] Reaney, M. J., "The Psychology of the Organized Group Game," *Brit. J. Psych.*, Monog. Supp., 1916, No. 4.
[2] Lehman, H. C., and Witty, P. A., *The Psychology of Play Activities*, New York, 1927. (See for discussion of play definitions, chap. 2.)
[3] Robinson, E. S., "The Compensatory Function of Make-Believe Play," *Psychol. Rev.*, 1920, 27, 429-439.

the items stressed are really not psychological items. Play may, for example, be a consumption of surplus energy or a superfluous activity but that is a purely economic consideration and offers nothing which differentiates play activity from other forms of human behavior. All the discussion which has been aroused by the suggestion that play exercises and develops instinctive tendencies has some psychological significance, although it concerns rather the effects of play upon the growing individual and the evolution of the race. If it should be concluded that play is preparatory exercise, we should still be seeking for those characteristics of play which differentiate it from other forms of activity. And the same may be said of the recreational theory. Play may indeed be recreative; but this is an effect of play and not a differentiating description. Much the same is true of the recapitulation theory. To say that play is a rehearsal of the racially old is at once intriguing to all thoughtful persons, but even though the notion be accepted in some modified form it does not provide a psychological description of play.

Racially old patterns are utilized whenever a man digs a ditch, hammers a nail, walks to work or climbs a telegraph pole, but no one would think of calling these play. And then, too, racially old activities are frequently unpleasant. For many people a fight between two men is disgusting even though the Marquis of Queensberry rules be strictly adhered to. Climbing, for many, stirs too much fear for any possibility of pleasure. Such cannot be called play. And again, play is far from being always that which is racially old. Organized plays frequently involve the skilful use of the very highest of mental functions.

But through all this discussion a number of items have been mentioned which are psychologically important. Every one seems to agree that play is activity, and that in itself is important. To play, the individual must be purposefully active in some way. Play is not mere passive submission to stimulation. Many have pointed out in one way or another that in playful activity there is satisfaction of desire; there is freedom; there is an absence of the hampering influence of notions of duty, and obligation and prudence. Play is apparently an activity in which there is no conscious influence of social pressures. Every one also appears to agree that play is a pleasant activity; and this is important because it rules out many old racial patterns, and makes it necessary to observe that play is not merely freedom from the hampering effects of social pressures but it is also activity in which the inhibiting influences of fear and disgust and protective impulses for the welfare of others are not aroused. Activities which physically injure another person can be play only when tenderness and disgust are not aroused.

To this there is a partial exception in the case of organized play. But the rules of a game, while to some extent inhibitory, serve primarily to set the conditions for the manifestation of skill. The ethics of playing function, however, as actual disturbers of the play state of mind. By arousing disgust, repugnance, or anger at the self or at others for their violation the play state is dissipated.

The doctrine of play as a form of relaxation is of importance for its emphasis upon the above-mentioned freedom of action. Finally it must be recalled, also, that many students of play have stressed the thrill which comes through the consciousness of superiority. Some call it enhancement of egoistic feelings, others may speak of it as the satisfaction of the will to power drive, others may say that it is the thrill of escape from danger through one's own skill or cleverness; but, whatever it be called, it has been sufficiently recognized from Spencer down to justify its inclusion here as a differentiating characteristic of playful activity.

These items of psychological importance may now be brought together in the form of a *definition of play*. On the basis of the efforts of many students it may be said with safety that play is any form of pleasant purposeful activity which is not consciously influenced by notions of duty, prudence, or propriety (social pressure); which is unhampered by conflicting impulses (protective, repugnant, etc.) and which is desired because it often produces an agreeable feeling of superiority (mastery, personal achievement). Obviously this may be intellectual or motor or both; it may be in professional or vocational activities (playing the game of life); it may be in the gymnasium, on the tennis court, or on the golf links, in field or in forest.

As a correlative of this definition of play, it should be pointed out that *amusement* is passive responsiveness to situations which agreeably arouse any of the cognitive functions (sensation, perception, associative thinking). There is in amusement no purposeful activity; or if there is any purposeful activity it is centered merely upon the maintenance of that situation which is producing the agreeable feelings. Listening to jazz music, watching a ballet, hearing some one recount a series of ludicrous experiences—these are examples of amusement. They are agreeable and they lack purposeful activity, other than what is necessary to keep the situation in the focal point of attention. It should perhaps be unnecessary to add that the sensations aroused in amusement may be organic quite as well as peripheral. Eating may thus be a form of amusement.

Of gradations between amusement and play many will be found. Classification of specific instances will often be difficult because of the questions which are certain to arise over the presence or absence or nature of the purposeful activity. A detective story might be read for example purely for the experience of amusement; but it might also be read with much purposeful effort to solve the mystery in advance, and for thrill of egoistic feeling if the reader hits upon the correct solution. In such a case, the reading would be more of the nature of play than of mere amusement. So, too, the persons present at a football game may be experiencing mere amusement; but through much inner imitation that may be purposively participating and thus be playing rather than being passively amused.

Effects of Adolescence upon Play Interests. The old notion that the dawn of adolescence brings a great outburst of change has been rapidly dissipated in recent years by systematic studies which reveal that growth changes are normally gradual. This is true also of play interests.[1] But there are well-established differences between the play interests of adolescence and those of childhood. Childish preferences are disappearing, and with the accumulation of years the youth is becoming more and more like an adult in his play likes and dislikes. Furfey has in the following table admirably demonstrated how the play interests of childhood disappear with the progress of adolescence:

[1] Lehman, H. C., and Witty, P. A., *The Psychology of Play Activities,* chap. 5.
    See also the following articles by the same authors: "Growth Stages in Play Behavior," *Ped. Sem.,* 1926, 33, 273-288; "Periodicity and Play Behavior," *J. Educ. Psychol.,* 1927, 18, 115-118.

PUBESCENCE AND THE DECLINE OF CHILDHOOD PLAY INTERESTS [1]

(The frequency of liking at 12 yrs. of age is treated as a base.
All other age likes are expressed as percentages of
the frequency at 12 yrs.)

Kind of play	Percent 12 yrs.	Percent 13 yrs.	Percent 14 yrs.	Percent 15 yrs.	Percent 16 yrs.
Cops and thieves.......	100	108	61	22	15
Run, sheep, run	100	113	74	38	6
Follow the leader	100	91	54	44	15
Tag	100	87	57	52	18
With marbles	100	91	59	36	19
With electric trains	100	77	53	23	6
Spinning tops	100	72	37	23	14
Flying kites	100	83	43	27	14
With Meccanos	100	100	63	43	19
Walking on stilts	100	80	62	47	17
With bows and arrows .	100	84	49	31	13
Average		89.6	55.6	34.8	14.1

This means that at sixteen years of age only fifteen percent as many children say that they like to play cops and thieves as expressed a liking for such play at twelve years of age; and so on through the table.

Other evidence of changing play interests is to be found in the greater willingness to participate in team play. Before puberty, as practically all workers with boys attest, it is exceedingly difficult to get satisfactory team play because each youngster wishes to show off, to be himself the star. With the coming of the years when gang activity develops, team play appears. Hence the rise of interest in organized team games.[2] Actual participation in team plays reaches the peak of its frequency in the early years of adolescence, and then slowly declines; but interest in these team games remains high throughout adolescent years. This retention of a high place in preference rating with a decline of participation probably indicates a shift to participation by "inner imitation," a conclusion which is supported by Lehman and Witty's finding that watching athletic sports rose from 11th place

[1] Furfey, P. H., "Pubescence and Play Behavior," *Amer. J. Psychol.*, 1929, 41, 109-111. (Table reproduced by permission of the *Amer. J. Psychol.*) In this connection see also Lehman, H. C., and Witty, P. A., "A Study of Play in Relation to Pubescence," *J. Soc. Psychol.*, 1930, 1, 510-523.

[2] See psychology of the gang in chap. VIII.

in frequency rank order at 12 years of age to 5th place at 16 years, where it remained to maturity with only a slight falling off in the later years of adolescence (this for boys).

The number of different kinds of plays and amusements in which there is participation changes but little through adolescence, although the number of such plays and amusements is very much smaller than it was in childhood. The curve representing this change, admirably presented by Lehman and Witty [1] shows a high start at eight years, falling off rapidly to fifteen, and declining very slowly thereafter. Playing with dolls appears to be almost completely a preadolescent pleasure. Studies made many years apart show its disappearance during puberty.[2]

It is necessary to recognize also that the circumstances of life, possibly even the heredity, may very largely affect the play interests of any individual or group of individuals. What may be said of one group of adolescents in one time and in one place may not be so true of other groups at other times and in other places. We read often of the great age of some of our familiar games, but the meaning of that age must not be misconceived. It may mean that the games mentioned are related to instinctive tendencies. McDougall says that he tried to introduce Anglo-Saxon games to the people of the Torres Straits and failed utterly; [3] and he thinks that this was due to instinct differences. But it may also be that long-established social attitudes can account as well for the differences between races and for the persistence of games in certain races. An interesting example of a change of play interest recently brought to light concerns the practice of making collections (birds' eggs, postage stamps, etc.). In 1900 a study was published which indicated that 90 percent of

---

[1] Lehman, H. C., and Witty, P. A., *The Psychology of Play Activities,* 1927, chap. 5, especially pp. 58-9.
[2] Hall, G. Stanley, and Ellis, A. C., "A Study of Dolls," *Ped. Sem.,* 1896, 4, 129-175.
Lehman, H. C., "A Study of Doll Play in Relation to the Onset of Pubescence," *J. of Genet. Psychol.,* 1927, 34, 72-76.
[3] McDougall, Wm., *Introduction to Social Psychology,* pp. 117-119.
See also:

Appleton, L. M., *A Comparative Study of the Play Activities of Adult Savages and Civilized Children,* 1910, pp. 8-73.
Marshall, Helen, "Children's Plays, Games, and Amusements," being chapter 15 of the first edition of Murchison's *Handbook of Child Psychology.*
Smith, P. A., "Some Phases of the Play of Japanese Boys and Men," *Ped. Sem.,* 1909, 16, 256-267.

children made such collections. Another comparable study published in 1927 revealed but 10 percent of children making such collections. As it is unthinkable that an instinct could die out that rapidly the obvious conclusion must be that there was a change in social circumstances. Perhaps the method used might in part explain the difference but still there is a large falling off to account for.[1] Other studies have shown that time, place, opportunities afforded by space and weather and equipment, and climatic conditions influence play preferences and also the frequency of participation in different plays.[2]

Sex differences in the play interests of adolescence can be easily exaggerated. There are sex differences; but it is fairly well established that the time of greatest sex difference is not in adolescence. It is in childhood. Lehman and Witty place it in the ages 8½ to 10½ years. Early adolescent boys especially prefer running and the heavily muscular sports and plays, those which involve strength and dexterity and skill. Many girls like such plays and participate in them, but apparently not to the same extent as boys. Girls seem less inclined to favor plays which involve competition and strict conformity to many rules and regulations. Curiously enough boys seem to enjoy watching sports better than do girls. This may be a carry over in the form of "inner imitation" from their own periods of participation. As adolescence progresses and maturity approaches, there is an increasing tendency toward activities in which young men and women may both participate. Here may be seen the influence of sex attraction no doubt and probably also some influence of the social pressures of approaching maturity.[3]

[1] Burk, C. F., "The Collecting Instinct," *Ped. Sem.*, 1900, 7, 179-207.
  Lehman, H. C., and Witty, P. A., "The Present Status of the Tendency to Collect and Hoard," *Psychol. Rev.*, 1927, 34, 48-56.
  —— "Further Studies of Children's Interest in Collecting," *J. Educ. Psychol.*, 1930, 21, 112-127.
  Whitley, M. T., "Children's Interest in Collecting," *J. Educ. Psychol.*, 1929, 20, 249-261.
[2] Lehman, H. C., and Witty, P. A., *The Psychology of Play Activities*, chaps. 8, 9, 10, 12.
[3] For material on sex differences see the following:
Croswell, T. R., "Amusements of Worcester School Children," *Ped. Sem.*, 1898-99, 6, 314-371.
Lehman, H. C., and Witty, P. A., *The Psychology of Play Activities*, chap. 7.
McGhee, Z., "A Study in the Play Life of Some South Carolina Children," *Ped. Sem.*, 1900, 7, 459-478.

With these general considerations of theory and adolescent play characteristics in mind, it is now possible to look more intelligently at the different specific forms of play which interest adolescents:

1. *Athletics and organized games.* The appeal of these to the youth of both sexes has led to a vast development of organization and administration and equipment. So extensive and so expensive is this development that not a few thoughtful educators have feared that it was detracting from the fundamental purpose of educational institutions and establishments. Social settlements, Christian Associations, boys' clubs, and welfare agencies of many kinds have found it necessary to acquire the facilities for athletics and organized play. And there is a vast literature on this subject, books and technical journals and magazine articles; but unfortunately for psychological purposes this literature is largely non-psychological. It is primarily concerned with management, rules and regulations, history, physiology, instructions for leaders, moral and economic problems, and educational implications on a theoretical basis.[1] Of experimental and systematically inductive studies on the psychology of athletics and group games, either of the player or of the observer, and of their effects upon the growing personality there are extraordinarily few [2] and the best of these are concerned with the cognitive processes and the relationship of athletic participation to intelligence and scholarship.

That athletics and athletic games arouse pleasure is accepted as too obvious for question. Problems arise however when one seeks a reason for their agreeableness. From Spencer to the present there have been many who have thought that this pleasure was primarily due to the enhancement of satisfaction with the self. The player is supposed to be pleased by the exercise of his own skill, and especially pleased whenever he does something a little better than usual, or better than some one else, be he partner or opponent. The successful athlete is applauded and decorated and accorded social deference. And this applies

[1] Ryan, W. C., Jr., *The Literature of American School and College Athletics,* Carnegie Found. Adv. Teach., 1929, Bull. 24. (This report contains an excellent general summary of the literature and an annotated bibliography of 1030 titles.)

[2] Griffith, C. R., *Psychology and Athletics,* New York, 1928.

to a vastly larger number than those whose names appear on the sporting pages of national newspapers. The boy who makes the team and a letter in some small rural high school likewise thrills with success and distinction in his world. Many, especially those who like to follow in the wake of thinkers like Hall and Patrick, see in these plays the presence of pleasure because the functional patterns involved are old racial patterns. For them the player is happy because he is reliving the activities of his primitive ancestors. Our ball games are thus looked upon as rehearsals of the activities of primitive fighting and hunting. But it must be pointed out that our modern games require also the utilization of the highest mental processes. They cannot successfully be played without close and constant attention, much thought and study, and the utilization of all those functions involved in quick interpretation and adjustment to complex situations.

Freedom of action and expression, that freedom mentioned by Schiller and now being actively revived under the psychoanalytic influence,[1] is generally accepted as a significant factor in the appeal of these plays. Reaney thinks that the increase in popularity of athletics in recent years is due to the increasing complexity and demands of our civilization which is in consequence placing ever more demands upon human nature, demands which hamper and balk the expression of the older and possibly instinctive impulses. There may be much truth in this. Certainly true play is free from domination by the social pressures which are so constantly influential in the ordinary business of living. And it is worthy of note that the period of greatest interest and participation in athletic plays is in the earlier years of adolescence.[2] This is a time when both boys and girls are rapidly becoming conscious of social pressures and are frequently longing for freedom therefrom. Release is temporarily achieved in athletics, and usually with full social approval.[3]

[1] Reaney, M. J., "The Psychology of the Organized Group Game," *Brit. J. Psych.,* Monog. Supp., 1916, No. 4.
[2] Lehman, H. C., and Witty, P. A., *The Psychology of Play Activities,* chap. 5.
[3] Professor Stern has lately pointed out that some people never grow up beyond this stage. They remain forever "pubiles," as he has happily termed them. Possibly this explains some of our adult "sports." See Stern, Wm., "'Ernstspiel' and the Affective Life," chapter 28 of *Feelings and Emotions* (Wittenberg Symposium), 1928.

But a consideration of athletic interests of youth would be most incomplete, or for any period of life, if it did not include some attempt at interpretation of those who look on as well as those who participate. Some have said that we are fast becoming a nation of bleacher athletes, who get their exercise by proxy; and our physical education enthusiasts have long been bewailing the vogue of the varsity team and promoting intramural athletics in order to force more youth off the bleachers into personal participation. As was mentioned above, the Lehman and Witty studies show a decline through adolescent years of preference for participation and a rise of preference for watching athletic sports. This change may itself be a consequence of the growing influence of social pressures, and a responsiveness to them which makes the individual feel that he no longer has time for participation. Then, too, there is the interesting possibility that many youths retire from participation because they are no longer able to obtain the desired thrill of superiority feeling. They have tried themselves out and know that they cannot achieve a sufficient degree of skill for self-satisfying participation. So they confine themselves increasingly to handball or tennis or pool and billiards or to enough walking and calisthenics to keep themselves in good condition. When they go to a ball game or athletic meet they are participating through inner imitation and doing thus by implicit action what they would perhaps have liked to have done explicitly and could not.

Practically all observers agree that this participation by inner imitation is an important feature in the psychology of those who watch athletic competitions. One may be justified in suspecting also that there are many degrees and kinds of this inner imitation. One observer may follow every move and play of some friend or hero with actual movements of his own limbs and body sufficiently great to be an annoyance to his neighbors on the bleachers. Others may likewise follow the play, but with their movements so restrained or minimized as to make them unnoticeable to their neighbors, although an acute observer might notice them. From these more extreme degrees of inner imitation there may be gradations all the way down to those who know little if anything about the nature of the game, and respond imitatively only to spectacular plays or runs where individual action makes the play readily perceptible. One often sees also the notion expressed that no inconsiderable part of the appeal of our great athletic contests is the pageantry appeal. And this may be said of most minor contests as well. The sight of the crowd, the players, the costumes, the bands, the marching, and other items as occasions may supply—all furnish that which is entertaining to most human beings. It is pleasurable to be so stimulated. Here the reader who followed the opening discussion of this chapter will quickly realize that the more the pageantry appeal supplants inner imitation of the game, the more observation of the game takes on the form of amusement rather than of play. Probably for some people attendance at an athletic event is much more a matter of amusement than of play. They go because they like to be agreeably stimulated.

There is the possibility also of yet another motivating factor in some attendance at athletic events. There is the "desire to be in on it," however this should be technically expressed. There may be no great actual interest in the game; but "everybody else is going" and most people, especially young people, do not enjoy being different because it is so often accompanied by feelings of inferiority. And there will be the hours after the game when it is necessary to make the disagreeable admission of not having been there. To be at the game, to meet one's friends there, to be seen there by one's friends, and to be able to talk about it all afterward from first hand observation probably produces no little enhancement of self-feeling. The contrary would be disagreeable.

If, in addition, the observer at the game feels free to shout and yell and pound his neighbor on the back, throw his hat and cane in the air, and do even more undignified things, he is experiencing no little freedom from the ordinary restraints of social pressure. Thus it is possible for the observer at a game to experience, in a small way, all of the essential features of the play experience. There is some purposeful activity (noisy assertions that we are going to win, must win, play the game, etc.); there is no little release from the restraints of ordinary life; and there is the agreeable feeling of superiority (being present oneself, being well dressed, supporting the best team, and if the team loses of asserting exactly what should have been done, or what should now be done, to make a winning team for the school or community).

Of the effects of athletics upon the growing personality, we actually know practically nothing. For many years it has been confidently, and one might say noisily, asserted that athletics give youth a valuable training in the formation of habits indispensable to their successful adjustment in human society. We have been told that athletics and group games provided training in courage, determination, decisiveness, enthusiasm, loyalty, self-initiative, perseverance, determination, self-reliance, self-control, aggressiveness, ambition, reliability and a long list of other equally attractive trait designations.[1] The argument presented is based upon that which is familiar to all students of psychology as the transfer of training. The contention is that these desirable habits are trained into the personality through the experiences of the gymnasium and playing field, and that these habits will then function in a similar manner in the actual situations of real life. It is also contended, with less enthusiasm to be sure, that undesirable traits may be acquired through the experiences of organized play and that these may also be transferred into real life. Wrong standards may be so taught and the players may be trained in habits of dishonesty, of trickery, and the attitude that anything is "all right if you can get away with it." [2]

Systematic studies in proof of these contentions are, however, unfortunately lacking. It is quite true that habits acquired in one activity may be transferred to another if they are useful in the other activity. But the experimental studies upon which this conclusion is based involve situations and functions which do have much in common. There are large and conspicuous differences between the situations of the playing field and the situations of the business world. Would habits of honesty or dishonesty established by the experiences of the playing field be aroused by the situations of the business world? Do those who

[1] See for example Curtis, H. S., *Education Through Play*, New York, 1915, chaps. 3, 4. Also Bowen, W. P., and Mitchell, E. D., *The Theory of Organized Play*, New York, 1923, chap. 16.

[2] Professor Berry has presented a rather typical athletic leader's discussion of this. While he admits the possibility of transferring wrong standards and habits, he believes that the normal tendency is toward the building of good character. Berry, Elmer, *The Philosophy of Athletics*, New York, 1927, p. 52.

persevere in athletic contests later manifest a like perseverance in the face of business or professional or domestic adversity? These are questions which need to be answered by careful systematic study with control groups before conclusions are made. And there is also the troublesome possibility that in many instances the traits mentioned were fully present before the participation in organized games. Perhaps it is those who have self-control and perseverance and courage and decisiveness and the like that are selected for such participation. Those who lack these traits may be eliminated by those who have them; or they may eliminate themselves through recognition of their own unfitness for such activities.

That athletic play may provide the interests necessary to a normal functioning of the physiological processes of the body has been well established. Such functioning is of course necessary to the most normal form of personality development. Physical deficiencies and defects may be and are overcome by compensatory developments, but they are not the most desirable form of personality growth. Calisthenic exercises might produce the same physiological effects as the athletic plays [1] but they ordinarily lack the consciousness of freedom and achievement which makes play agreeable. Calisthenics are in consequence likely to become quickly disagreeable and unattractive.

2. *Dancing* exemplifies every item presented in the discussion above as essentially characteristic of play. It is mildly purposeful activity; there is a consciousness of freedom from the obligations of school or business or professional life; and there is much to contribute to the enhancement of the ego feelings (demonstration of personal grace and skill in the dance steps, effective clothing, charming partner, and so on). For these reasons it is pleasurable. Perhaps, as some think, it is also pleasurable because of its accentuation of that rhythm which is characteristic of all physiological processes; perhaps it is pleasurable because it rehearses racially old patterns of activity; perhaps, too, the intimacy of contact between the sexes contributes to the pleasure of dancing as a sort of satisfaction of sex attraction. All of these

[1] Dowd, C. E., and Arlitt, A. H., "The Relative Transfer Effects of Supervised Play and Formal Gymnastics," *J. Appl. Psychol.*, 1925, 9, 215-224.

features have been proposed and accepted by thoughtful observers.[1]

In the consideration of dancing it is important to observe that modern social dancing is but one of many forms. Dancing has a very long history indeed. Perhaps it is as old as the race itself. There have been very simple dances which involved little more than a shuffling of the feet, and perhaps a clapping of the hands; and there have been highly complicated dances looked upon by those who knew them as of so great an importance to their welfare that mistakes in their presentation were punishable by death. In comparison with the elaborate steps and movements of the Highland fling, the sword dance, the bolero, the tarantella, the horn-pipe, and the fandango, our modern ballroom dances are very simple and are not infrequently looked upon as degenerate forms. In many religions, for a long time in Christianity, dancing has been used with religious ceremonial significance. Folk dances are still current and attempts at their revival or introduction appear from time to time. And in addition to the dances of the ball-room, most young people in this country are familiar to some extent with gymnastic and esthetic dancing, some forms of which permit quite unhampered expression of the feelings aroused by the music and allow for individual inventiveness.

Obviously the psychology of dancing must vary not a little from form to form. If highly complicated and involved with important social and religious meanings, their character as pure play must be largely lost. In some there is obviously more opportunity for the manifestation of personal skill than in others. In some there can be no factor of sex attraction and satisfaction; while in others all else seems to have been subordinated to it. Dancing thus must vary greatly in the amount of pleasure which it produces and the means by which it is produced. One must first know and consider the details of any particular dance before its psychology can be appreciated.

Lehman has shown that there is through the years of adolescence a steady rise in the interest expressed in social dancing as

[1] Hall, G. Stanley, *Adolescence*, Vol. 1, pp. 212-215.
Hollingworth, L. S., *Psychology of the Adolescent*, p. 122.
Patrick, G. T. W., *Psychology of Relaxation*, pp. 73-76.

compared with other plays and amusements. The interest of girls in social dancing rises earlier and is in all of their figures constantly higher than for boys.[1] Studies of many sorts have indicated the progressively rising interest of the sexes in each other as adolescence progresses. There is the anticipation of matrimony and the consciousness of the sex urge. Social life becomes more and more a matter of association with the other sex. There is the normal and proper desire to meet and to know many and to test out congenialities. By later adolescent years this appears to overwhelm and submerge the dancing itself. The few movements used are simple and easily learned. The circumstances of the modern social dance (size of room, illumination, number of dancers, and so on) rarely provide much opportunity for demonstration of skill. It is not expected, nor ordinarily sought for. The dance as a pattern of muscular movements becomes quite subordinate to the social attractions connected with it.

Thus the contribution of the modern social dance to the development of the personality must be very slight indeed, and whatever does appear must be through the social life and customs which rest upon it. The degree of skill in dancing or the amount of awkwardness might easily aid or prevent some desired social relation and hence bring experiences of happiness or distress which might be of lasting influence. Those who do not learn how to dance would not have certain kinds of opportunities for social contacts with the other sex. More than this as a contribution of dancing is difficult to conceive.

But the customs and conventions surrounding the social dance may be of more significance. They may afford training in courtesy, special conventions, and the art of making oneself attractive. It is, however, to the morally degenerating influences that most attention has been given. That social dancing as commonly practiced is often morally corrupting there can be no doubt; but the reason for this does not lie in the dance itself. It is to be found rather in the consequences of bringing together intimately two characteristically different fields of human activity, dancing and the social contacts between young people who

[1] Lehman, H. C., "The Play Activities of Persons of Different Ages," *J. Genet. Psychol.*, 1926, 33, 250-272.

are consciously seeking a possible partner for a future marriage. It must be obvious that these are not necessarily associated. Acrobatic dancing is isolated from the social-contact field of activity; and so also is esthetic dancing, as are many of the famous dances of history. And the field of social-contact activity is not confined to the dance hall. It may occur quite apart from dancing. But when the two are brought together, as we commonly have them today, the field of social-contact activity of adolescence is confused with dancing, which it will be recalled is a form of play. And it will be further recalled that one of the salient characteristics of play is freedom from social pressure (from conventions, duty, prudence, etc.). When this attitude of freedom, of abandon, spreads to the social relations, then is there moral danger.[1] Then intimacy may be freed from the restraints of moral and social conventions, and the delinquencies of the dance hall, so often lamented, are the consequence. Where there is further complication through the introduction of alcohol, the tendency to abandonment of ideals and restrictions is aided by the depressant effect of the alcohol upon control through the higher inhibitions.

By itself dancing is just as moral, or unmoral, as bag punching or acrobatic stunts on the high bar or any other form of motor skill, and may contribute as much to personality development. It is only when its performance becomes confused with social relations between the sexes, and the play spirit of freedom from restraint spreads to these social relations, that moral dangers are to be faced. The dangers of such a confusion may obviously be minimized by all that helps to maintain the influence of personal ideals, and by those social conventions which aid in maintaining the social relations between young people on a safely moral level.

3. *Sport, travel, adventure.* It is a rare youth who does not feel the lure of elsewhere and of the adventures which elsewhere may bring. Travel to remote places and among strange peoples brings a thrill that is enjoyed and sought for. Travel in less conventional ways, by hiking or "hopping freights," or the more modern "hitch-hiking," has a powerful lure for many youths

---

[1] In modern dancing this is especially easy because the dance steps are so stereotyped as to require little or no attention. Thus the play attitude may easily turn to the partner and the social relations.

quite apart from the ability or inability to afford the luxury of "riding the cushions." Hunting, fishing, camping, living out in primitive fashion, venturing into dangers large and small and somehow escaping therefrom—all are fascinating to many, perhaps most, young people. While systematic studies are curiously lacking, the attraction of these forms of activity is a matter of everyday observation.

Why should young people, and adults as well, seek such experiences is of course the first question the psychologist raises. Why should any one wander and suffer discomforts? Why should any one go fishing when as good or better fish may be bought in the open market at far less cost of time and money? Why should one hunt at so great an outlay of time and trouble? Certainly it is not for the amount of fresh meat that is obtained. The first answer is naturally that these activities are enjoyed, that they are pleasant, and that human nature always seeks that which is known to stir agreeable feelings. But when one asks why such experiences are agreeable the answer is not so easy to find. It is difficult to apply the doctrine of conditioned learning. To be sure a few children are brought up by their parents to the experiences of travel and the out of doors; but the longing for such experiences and the pleasure in them appears with extraordinary ease in young people who apparently have not been so conditioned in childhood.

It is possible also that there is an instinctive drive or urge toward such activities. Many very able minds have thought so. Professors Hall [1] and Patrick have written brilliantly on this form of interpretation. They contend that because our ancestors lived in caves in the river banks and in the tree tops, wandered through the hills and the forests, ventured on the lakes and rivers, hunted and fished and survived by the use of fire, we who are their descendants find pleasure in those same forms of activity. Hall goes even farther and discusses at length the curious feelings and overt forms of human behavior in responses to the clouds, the wind, the storms, the changes from daylight to dark and back again, the moonlight, the hills and the trees and open water whether it be the lake or the ocean or the babbling

[1] Hall, G. Stanley, *Adolescence*, Vol. 2, chap. 12.
Patrick, G. T. W., *Psychology of Relaxation*, chap. 2.

brook. To all these things man feels in ways that he cannot understand. And these feelings have been the motivations for much of poetry and song and story and of meditation that has led to much of the finest in human achievement. Youth is living again through these periods of early racial experience when man lived close to nature and is thus more responsive to the things of nature. So Hall thought, and so many still think, although the evidence in support of such thinking has dwindled greatly since the days when Hall wrote so fascinatingly.

But, whether or not there be an instinctive basis for them, these activities of the forest and the field and of travel do very well fit into our conception of play. It is clearly purposive activity and it is done with much freedom from restraint. Indeed it would be easy to think that a prime motivation in many youths was the possibility of so escaping from the necessity of dressing-up daily, being clean shaven, and the other conventions and requirements of life at home under social pressure. Going into the woods or off on a long hike means freedom from school and parental domination and the cares of soon becoming a wage-earning adult. And these activities provide much for the exaltation of the self-feelings. The little adventures and especially the escapes from them by cleverness give thrills of self-satisfaction. The catch and the kill in fishing and hunting bring like feelings of satisfaction—and stories of how it was done, the good judgment and the skill that was involved. Certainly all these activities can be classed as play. They do not have the formulated regulations of athletic games; but, at the same time, hunting and fishing, the highway and more formal modes of travel are not without their ethics and their conventions, their notions of good sportsmanship and the like.

What the effects of all these forms of activity are upon the growing personalities who enjoy them we do not know from any careful studies, but there are some things which we can safely infer and there are others which many have thought to be important. Whatever values there may be in the occasional release from the consciousness of social demands, sometimes the conflict with them, must be found here. The self-exaltation must be useful in the stabilization of the personality, for there is danger of too much trouble in adolescent years with inferiority feelings.[1] Studies of delinquency have revealed that the urge for feelings of achievement is strong in youth and unless provided for in wholesome ways will break out in ways that are undesirable. If habits acquired in one field of activity are transferred to others, then the habits of independence, of self-reliance, acquired in the experiences of these out-of-door and away-from-home activities should be of lasting value. Hall further added, and with this the present author is in hearty agreement, that the thrills of the hunt and the chase, the curious feelings in response to wind and rain and sunset and dawn and open fire and babbling brook and all the rest are characteristic features of human beings and that he who grows to maturity without experiencing them is by so much less human. He who has never known these feelings is incapacitated for a full and sympathetic understanding of the ways and feelings of those other human beings who have had them. He is incapable of responding properly to much of the best in music and song and poetry and painting.

4. *Gambling.* Although textbooks and researches in the field of genetic psychology rarely mention this subject, every one who has had associations with young people knows perfectly well that many youths gamble and find pleasure enough therein to want to do it again and again. They also know of the troubles that grow out of it.

Pure gambling is the wagering or betting of money, or something of value, upon that which is governed purely by chance, as the fall of a tossed coin for example. Ordinarily, however, the wager is placed upon the outcome of that which involves both chance and the intellectual cleverness of the one who gambles. Betting upon the outcome of a game of cards or of football are examples of this. There is chance in the shuffling of the cards; but in the estimation of the hand and player, there is opportunity for the use of reason. Football games provide a like combination of circumstances and functions. In the outcome of any such game there are many factors of pure chance involved; but there is also opportunity for reasoning in terms of the history of the team and of the coaches, of the styles of play used and so on.

[1] See chapter IX.

Interpretations of the lure of gambling are all offered in terms of the psychology of play, but not all who have psychologized about play have attempted to interpret gambling. Patrick dismisses gambling in a few lines, yet they are interesting ones.[1] It will be remembered that he was the ardent advocate of play as relaxation to old racial functional levels, and of the need of such relaxation. Gambling for him is also reversionary, a reversion to primitive morals along with the reversion to primitive forms of action. This moral reversion he emphatically condemns. Woodworth explains gambling in terms of the same fear and escape motive which he used for play.[2] The pleasure comes from risking and escaping. Groos emphasized the effect which gambling has of increasing the intensity of the whole play experience.[3] This last statement deserves most serious consideration, for it will apply both to the play of the participant and the play of the observer (note psychology of the athletic observer given above). There is an intensification of the feeling of freedom. Notice for example the expressions of daring and recklessness among those who gamble. The feelings of self-superiority are enhanced by the faith placed in the gambler's own judgment; and, whenever he wins, this confidence in his own judgment is still further enhanced. And when he loses, or the team he has believed in loses, the consciousness of loss is likewise intensified.[4]

All authors agree that the effects of gambling are bad. It is looked upon generally as an excrescent development upon play. All the loyalties and ethics of good sportsmanship can be quickly undermined by gambling.[5] While systematic studies are here also wanting, practical experience reveals that friendships and group loyalties are easily broken up by gambling debts, with their often attending suspicions of dishonesty. Actual dishonesty is often stimulated. Boys who have acquired gambling debts which they are unable to pay out of their allowances may misrepresent the facts to their parents or others in order to obtain

[1] Patrick, G. T. W., *Psychology of Relaxation*, p. 64.
[2] Woodworth, R. S., *Psychology* (3rd ed.), p. 493.
[3] Groos, K., *The Play of Man*, pp. 201-217.
[4] On the intensification of the ego feelings involved see France, C., "The Gambling Impulse," *Amer. J. Psychol.*, 1902, 13, 364-407.
[5] This has been especially stressed by W. P. Bowen and E. D. Mitchell in their *Theory of Organized Play*, pp. 359-360.

more money; and in stealing cases most persons in positions of responsibility have formed the habit of looking for gambling as a possible cause. In all probability, gambling also leads to the use of alcohol. The youth unable to endure the strain of suspense until the end of the game shall determine if he wins or loses, drinks to quiet his tension. And when in trouble from accumulated losses beyond his power to pay, the depressant effects of alcohol may again be sought as a means of temporary escape from the disagreeable reality. Gambling may also contribute to a socially undesirable attitude toward money. Instead of being looked upon as the just compensation for labor and skill it comes to be that of something which may be obtained without effort and at the expense of the other fellow. No doubt there is also a false enhancement of the estimation of the self when the gambler wins or has a run of good fortune.

General effects of play. Before turning to amusements there are certain general effects of play which have been pointed out and which deserve attention by all who study adolescence. It is said that an eighteenth century Methodist church discipline complains that "those who play when they are young will play when they are old." Our notions of what is desirable have so changed since that time that we now hope that the eighteenth century Methodist disciplinarian was right. Many think that Hall never said a truer thing than his expression "zestless endeavor is the tragedy of life." [1] Adults now have so much leisure that one great problem of education is to prepare people for a wholesome and happy use of that leisure time. But, even though it should turn out that not many of the habits of childhood and youth are effective in the leisure hours of maturity, there is still the problem of the wholesome use of leisure during childhood and youth. Thus play in adolescence is important for the adolescent period. If there be in addition contributions to character and personality development and preparation for the leisure of maturity so much the better.

Of the immediate effects, so far as they are known, of some of the more important forms of play, a little has already been said in connection with the discussion of each. In addition it should

[1] Hall, G. Stanley, *Adolescence,* Vol. 1, p. 233.

be observed that there are certain general effects which are about as true of one form of play as of another, allowing of course always for individual differences of preference and attitude and skill. For one thing play can wholesomely serve as a means of escape. The school and social and family trials and troubles of youth are often acute and depressing. In the abandon and absorption of play these can be for a time forgotten. And it is more than possible that after such a period of release and relief the troubles can be faced more thoughtfully and with a calm which makes for better judgment. The contribution to the health of the growing boy and girl of a judicious amount of play is everywhere recognized. And in many places the old-time formal gymnasium requirements of regular exercise have been supplanted by play participation. That play can also contribute much to the development of nervous organization and control of movement is also generally admitted, and the importance of the development of nervous organization and control is stressed in almost every chapter of this book.

There is general agreement also that much of value in the form of social adjustment can be contributed by play. Here all that has been said about gang life and its contributions is applicable. Probably there is something more contributed by the training for participation in organized play which is not obtainable from mere running with a gang and participating in its social activities. The rules and the ethics of the game must force a training in self-control that is of value, and also a training in consideration of others and the merits of fair play and good sportsmanship.[1] The changes in estimation of self, particularly, and in the understanding of the self, are not to be underestimated; and the better understanding of others and how to get along with them must also be of value. But there is a difficulty here in the matter of the social contributions of play that remains to be cleared up. Lehman and his associates have shown [2]

---

[1] On this general subject see the following:

Carr, H. A., *The Survival Values of Play* (Univ. of Colorado, 1902), pp. 17-27.
Lehman, H. C., and Witty, P. A., *Psychology of Play Activities*, pp. 4 and 5 and chaps. 13 and 15.

[2] Lehman, H. C., and Anderson, T. H., "Social Participation Versus Solitariness in Play," *J. Genet. Psychol.*, 1927, 34, 279-289.
Lehman, H. C., and Witty, P. A., *Psychology of Play Activities*, p. 208.

that children who are pedagogically retarded have higher indices of social play participation. And when he set up a rating scheme by which teachers could rate the standing of their pupils in a series of socially desirable traits, he found that lower ratings were associated with more social play participation. The meaning of this is not yet clear. It is not yet known if this means that much playing with others retards the child in school and produces undesirable traits, or if it means that children who are retarded in school and have these undesirable traits in excess tend to much social play participation as a consequence. It may be of course that they merely parallel each other and are symptoms of some basic condition rather than a cause of each other either way. But their findings certainly present a problem which urgently calls for solution and suggests that all who work with young people be cautious here both concerning their theory and their practice.

In other studies [1] there is indicated a possibility that boys who have many play interests have more powerful drives and perhaps poorer self-control, while boys of fewer play interests have more self-control. Does this mean that the many play interests are interfering with the development of self-control? Or does it mean that boys who have developed self-control manage themselves and their time better, and thus find it necessary to limit themselves to a few play interests? In either case the implication is that play is not contributing much to the development of self-control.

[1] Lehman, H. C., and Michie, O. C., "Extreme Versatility Versus Paucity of Play Interest," *J. Genet. Psych.*, 1927, 34, 290-298.

Witty, P. A., "A Study of Deviations in Versatility and Sociability of Play Interest," New York, 1931.

CHAPTER V

INTERESTS OF ADOLESCENCE *(Continued)*

AMUSEMENTS (MOVIES, READING, CONVERSATION), VOCA-
TIONAL INTERESTS

Amusements. In turning to a discussion of the amusement interests of adolescent years, the reader should keep in mind that the difference from play is not so very great. As was pointed out in the preceding chapter, amusement is a much more passive experience. It is pleasure obtained by being stimulated and about all the purposive activity involved is that which is necessary to bring the self into the presence of the amusing stimuli. Attendance at movies, vaudeville shows, the legitimate theater when such is available, reading, and social conversation is probably in large part more in the class of amusement than of play. But it is quite possible, even probable, that many young people so identify themselves with the characters of screen and stage and book that there is no little of purposeful mental activity involved, in which case the character of pure amusement subsides and the experience becomes more like one of play. They are playing the game of the stage and screen and book much as the vociferous, excited observer of a football game plays the game in his imagination.

1. *Movies.* What knowledge we have about adolescents and theatrical attendance is confined almost wholly to movie attendance. An extensive study of the movie show experience of more than ten thousand children in the city of Chicago made by Alice Miller Mitchell [1] revealed that boys and girls of high school age attend movies considerably less frequently than do the children of the fifth, sixth, and seventh grades. This decline in attendance is attributed to the greater amount of social activity in high schools in the form of clubs and committee duties which leave

---

[1] Mitchell, Alice Miller, *Children and Movies,* Chicago, 1929.

young people with far less unoccupied time. The same sort of influence is still more evident from her comparisons of the frequency of attendance of children who belong to boy and girl scout organizations with those who do not. Those who belong to such organizations attend much less than others. Attractive as the movies appear to be, it is of importance to observe how easily they seem to be displaced in the interests of youth by organizations providing group activity.

Movie attendance of both grade school and high school children is very largely at the week-end. This means Saturdays and Sundays for most; but with advance into adolescent years and the beginnings of romantic attraction, "dating," there is a rising frequency of attendance on Friday evenings. Surprising as it may seem, children of all ages attend more in the evening than in the day time. Proximity to theaters, or the lack of it is apparently a matter of no consequence. Mitchell presents an instructive comparison between two areas, one of which has many theaters and another very few; but the average attendance in these two areas is practically the same.

The attractiveness of the movies in comparison with other amusement and play interests may best be judged from the following table abstracted from the material presented by Lehman and Witty: [1]

	Age	11	12	13	14	15	16	17	18	19	20
Rank in frequency of statement as most commonly engaged in by boys		6	5	6	4	4	4	4	4	3	2
Same for girls		12	9	6	8	5	5	4	5	5	6
Rank in frequency as liked best by boys		5	6	5	5	7	6	6	8	6	4
Same for girls		1	1	2	1	1	2	3	3	6	6

The reason for the comparatively lower place of movies in the preference lists of boys is because they so commonly place athletic interests above the movies. With girls, however, athletic interests fall much below. The interests which displace movies in the later years of adolescent girlhood are dancing and having "dates."

[1] From Lehman, H. C., and Witty, P. A., *Psychology of Play Activities*, pp. 51-57. (Copyright 1927 by A. S. Barnes and Co., publishers. Reproduced by permission.)

An examination of the Mitchell tables reveals some significant things about the kinds of movies which are preferred at different ages. The following table is based on the Mitchell figures [1] and shows not only the differences in percentage expressing first choice for the particular kinds of movies listed, but also the rank order of preference for the different age groups and for the sexes.

FREQUENCY OF SELECTION OF SPECIFIED TYPES OF MOVIES AS FIRST CHOICE

	Boys				Girls			
	Grade school		High school		Grade school		High school	
	per-cent	Rank order	per-cent	Rank order	per-cent	Rank order	per-cent	Rank order
Adventure ..	13.7	2	13.7	1	7.2	5	6.1	8
Comedy	11.4	3	13.0	2	16.5	2	10.3	3
Educational .	1.3	10	2.8	10	1.4	10	2.1	10
Historical ...	2.0	9	12.9	3	4.6	7	10.6	2
Mystery	6.3	4	8.9	5	6.8	6	8.8	5
Romance ...	4.7	7	7.0	7	13.3	3	22.8	1
Sport	5.3	5	11.9	4	3.7	8	8.0	6
Tragedy	2.1	8	5.6	8	7.7	4	9.9	4
War	5.1	6	3.8	9	2.2	9	2.2	9
Western	34.0	1	7.5	6	20.2	1	6.5	7

Order of rank correlations figured from this table give the following results:

Grade sch. and high sch. boys ....r   .49
Grade sch. and high sch. girls ....r   .52

Grade school boys and girls ....r   .58
High school boys and girls ....r   .35

These correlations clearly indicate the tendency for the preferences of boys and girls to become different in adolescent years. The low correlation between the rank order of preferences for boys and for girls in high school ages makes this plain. They are less alike in their preferences than are either boys or girls of the grades when compared with their own sex of adolescent ages. These sex differences in the preferences of high school boys and

[1] Mitchell, A. M., *Children and Movies*, p. 167. (Reproduced by permission of Univ. of Chicago Press.)

girls come out even more prominently when one looks at the particular differences in preference. A few of the more conspicuous ones can be isolated as follows:

Adventure pictures come 1st for H. S. boys, 8th for H. S. girls.
Romantic pictures come 7th for H. S. boys, 1st for H. S. girls.
Tragedy pictures come 8th for H. S. boys, 4th for H. S. girls.

The changing of preference as growth progresses into adolescent years is clearly revealed by such comparisons as follow:

Western pictures come 1st for grade school boys, 6th for H. S. boys.
Historical pictures come 9th for grade school boys, 3rd for H. S. boys.
Western pictures come 1st for grade school girls, 7th for H. S. girls.
Historical pictures come 7th for grade school girls, 2nd for H. S. girls.

Concerning the effect of movie attendance upon the growing personality we have much theory but only a few facts so established as to justify generalization. A group of extensive investigations known as the Payne Fund studies [1] points toward many possible influences of importance. These studies are in part based upon lengthy autobiographies of movie show experience, written under careful direction, by many hundreds of college and high school students and by some young people not in school. They clearly indicate that the thought world of modern youth is largely furnished with material obtained from the movies. Influences upon dress, gestures and mannerisms are frequently reported. Notions of etiquette, how to act in given situations, of the ways of love (sometimes termed the "technique of loving"), concepts of how people in more or less favored social and economic situations live, and also of how crimes are committed—all these and many other items are contributed by the movies to young people's knowledge of the world.

There is ample evidence, too, that the movie acquisitions are not limited to mere knowledge. There is much evidence that

[1] These will be given as referred to above. A summary of them designed for popular reading will be found in the following: Forman, H. J., *Our Movie Made Children*, New York, 1933.

seeing movie presentations of life stirs longings or impulses to act, which not infrequently emerge in overt action. Impulses to criminal actions are reported, impulses to run away from home, desires to love and be loved as they do in the pictures, and impulses to be good and generous and loyal all appear in these reports of personal experience. It is thus amply evident that the movies are exerting a very large influence for good or for bad, or perhaps for both.[1]

Whatever the nature of the effects of movie attendance, it is certain now that they may be of remarkably long duration. An extraordinarily high percentage of the material seen in the pictures is remembered, and much of it is still recallable two or three months afterward.[2] And emotional effects are far from being as transitory as casual observation might lead one to think. That the sleep of a child should be disturbed during the first night after seeing a movie is not surprising, but these studies have shown that there may be a measurable effect of the movie upon the quality of the sleep for several nights following attendance. Apparently the greatest disturbance of sleep by movies comes at about the age of pubescence.[3]

By use of a scheme for the measurement of social attitudes, Thurstone and his associates have shown that seeing a single movie may have a considerable effect upon some particular social attitude, toward the Chinese for example, and that enough of this attitude effect remains after a period of nineteen months to make it still demonstrable by his attitude tests.[4] This bit of fact raises many possibilities. Perhaps the general attitudes toward life and its institutions are largely molded by the movies as well as by home and school and church and playground contacts. But it is also pointed out that the attitudinal influence of one movie may be cancelled or compensated for by seeing another of different na-

---

[1] Blumer, Herbert, *Movies and Conduct*, New York, 1933.
   Holaday, Perry W., *Getting Ideas from the Movies*, New York, 1933.
[2] Holaday, P. W., *ibid.*
[3] Renshaw, S., Miller, V. L., and Marquis, D. P., *Children's Sleep*, New York, 1933.
[4] Peterson, R. C., and Thurstone, L. L., *The Effect of Motion Pictures on the Social Attitudes of High School Children*, New York, 1933.
   Thurstone, L. L., "A Scale for Measuring Attitude Toward the Movies," *J. Educ. Res.*, 1930, 22, 89-94; "The Influence of Motion Pictures on Children's Attitudes," *J. Soc. Psychol.*, 1931, 2, 291-305.

ture. And yet, if the individual sees movies of but one general type, or if the movies in general stir only a limited range of attitudinal responses, the attitudes of youth may be largely contributed by movie influence.

An arresting item in the Payne Fund studies is the frequent mention of what is termed "emotional possession" (Blumer). By this term is indicated a complete abandonment, relinquishment of self-control, to whatever emotion may be aroused by the particular movie. This may be of many kinds, anger, thrill of danger, sympathy for suffering, horror, sorrow, love, passion, anything. Apparently such effects are quite common among younger adolescents while present before a movie. In later adolescence more and more control appears apparently through the development of more critical reactions. Later adolescents become movie-sophisticated and with it the emotional abandon declines or even disappears.

That the intensity of the emotional reaction to movies varies with age, interests, and habits of perception was skilfully determined by Dysinger and Ruckmick [1] through the use of the psychogalvanograph, an instrument which measures the emotional reaction in terms of its electrical effects within the body. Scenes of tragedy, conflict, and personal danger had their most intense effect upon children under twelve years of age. The reactions of adolescents was less and those of adults least in comparison. But the reactions to love scenes were most intense in the middle adolescent group. For these the children gave least response. And there was much evidence that errors of perception radically affected the reactions of the children.

With these studies before us we can no longer doubt the high possibility of adolescents acquiring decidedly false conceptions of life. With their world so filled with notions acquired from the movies, there is grave possibility that many young people may develop the notion that life is a round of thrills and excitement and so find much disappointment both in their present surroundings and their prospects for the future. As so many impulses to action, and also overt acts, are traceable to movie suggestions, it is quite possible that movie attendance may produce

[1] Dysinger, W. S., and Ruckmick, C. A., *The Emotional Responses of Children to the Motion Picture Situation*, New York, 1933.

decidedly unwholesome directions of personality development. Growth may be molded into immoral and anti-social ways. The demonstrated duration of movie impressions but makes this all the more worthy of serious consideration. Even more alarming are the possible consequences to youth of the practice of abandonment of self-control into that "emotional possession" already described. This is diametrically opposite to the whole course of adolescent growth toward more and more self-control, toward better and better personality organization. Complete abandon to emotional experience is thus hygienically bad no matter whether the picture itself be morally good or bad, and no matter what the kind of emotion be to which the youth abandons himself. Unless reductives to all these influences were in sight the movie interests of adolescents would be an almost hopelessly dangerous influence.

But of such reductives there are not a few already observed. While some young people may acquire false conceptions of life and develop undesirable impulses, many others do not. The reason appears to be in the influence upon their perceptions of other environmental factors. This was observed in the Blumer and Hauser study where they found that children in low rate delinquency areas were far less susceptible to criminal influences of the movies than were children in high rate delinquency areas. It is also more than likely that many children and adolescents do not think of life as presented in the movies as anything more than an entertaining and highly artificial conception. The world of the movies may be perceived as a world apart, as one to be observed for amusement only but not for actual participation. As such the movies serve in a compensatory fashion, as does so much of play activity. Impulses and desires which would not be tolerated or permitted in the world of reality find satisfaction in this artificial world of the imagination aided by the pictured activities.[1] Certainly for some reason a vast amount of the undesirable is witnessed and enjoyed by thousands of ado-

---

[1] On this compensatory theory of movie experience, see the following:

Lehman, H. C., and Witty, P. A., "The Compensatory Function of the Movies," *J. Appl. Psychol.*, 1927, 11, 33-41.

See also Robinson, E. S., "The Compensatory Function of Make-Believe Play," *Psychol. Rev.*, 1920, 27, 429-439.

lescents with no discoverable consequences that are in any way serious.[1]

Reductives to the ominous dangers of continued abandon to "emotional possession" are presented along with the descriptions of that behavior. The Blumer study points out that this is largely a phenomenon of early adolescence and that with growth and further development such behavior normally subsides. There is a progressive change in the direction of viewing the movies with "emotional detachment." Continued experience with them, supplemented by reading and a better knowledge of life, brings a wider range of interests and of knowledge. The result is that the movie presentations are received far more critically in the later years of adolescence. Details of excellence in acting, direction, photography are considered. Apparently the habitual movie attendant comes to react more through an elaborate cortical organization and less directly through second or emotional level patterns. Support for this was found in the Dysinger and Ruckmick study, which showed that the emotional reaction was governed by the way in which the presentation was perceived, and, also, that the subjects of nineteen years and more reacted with emotions of lesser intensity than those of adolescent ages. Training for movie interpretation might thus contribute largely to off-set the baleful influence of this tendency to react with "emotional possession." [2]

2. *Reading for pleasure.* Concerning the reading habits of children and adolescents there have been a very large number of studies. Many of these concern the psychology of the reading process but here we are interested in reading as it is done for relaxation, for entertainment, for amusement. Practically all the studies of leisure time reading agree that the amount of such reading rises steadily to about the dawn of adolescence. Then there is a decline through adolescent years. This falling off is ordinarily attributed to preoccupation with extra-curricular school activities and the increasing amount of required home study. After an extensive survey of the literature, Terman con-

[1] For the place of the movies in the psychology of delinquent conduct see also the discussion in chapter XV of this book.

[2] See the excellent handbook for such training which is also one of the Payne Fund Studies: Dale, Edgar, *How to Appreciate Motion Pictures*, New York, 1933.

cludes that the climax of the intensity of reading interest is reached in the 12th and 13th years. From Lehman and Witty's tables of preference for and amount of reading the following figures have been abstracted: [1]

Most Commonly Engaged In

Rank position in list of play activities most commonly engaged in held by item indicated.

Age		12	13	14	15	16	17	18	19	20
Reading books	M	4	7	5	5	8	9	13	13	12
Reading books	F	3	3	3	2	5	8	13	15	21
Reading short stories	M	7	8	8	8	9	9	10	11	10
Reading short stories	F	5	5	6	3	4	5	7	10	10

Liked Best

Rank position in list of play activities liked best held by item indicated.

Age		12	13	14	15	16	17	18	19	20
Reading books	M	10	8	8	8	9	12	9	8	9
Reading books	F	2	1	2	1	1	1	4	5	7
Reading short stories	M						9	9	9	9	9
Reading short stories	F			7	9	9	10	7	9	9	8

The rapid falling off in frequency of participation after fifteen years of age is clearly indicated in this table; but the liking for reading in comparison with other play activities holds its own relative position (except for two curious and unexplained drops). The decline in reading then is apparently more a matter of lack of time than of loss of interest.[2]

What adolescent boys and girls like and dislike in their reading appears to be about as varied as the likes and dislikes of

[1] From tables published by Lehman, H. C., and Witty, P. A., *The Psychology of Play Activities*, pp. 51-57. (Copyright 1927 by A. S. Barnes and Co., publishers. Reproduced by permission.)

[2] The interested student should see also Additon, H., "And What of Leisure?" *J. Soc. Hygiene*, 1930, 16, 321-334.

adults. Terman thinks that by the age of sixteen years adolescent reading interests have become as fully specialized and individualized as those of adults. In early adolescent years girls turn to fiction more readily than do boys. In fact it is possible that girls generally achieve maturity of reading interest ahead of boys. And another item of no little significance is that boys are rarely found reading the books commonly listed as girls' books, whereas girls are not infrequently found expressing an interest in the boys' books. Through pubescent and early adolescent years boys are still more interested in travel and adventure and technical literature. It is fairly well established that boys and girls of higher mental ability read more than do others.[1]

The Lehman and Witty studies [2] also revealed that reading the "funny papers" was an extraordinarily common and frequently preferred form of amusement. It was reported as the most common activity at all ages up to fifteen and then in second place up to twenty years for the boys. For the girls it was the most common form of amusement up to fifteen years and then fell off gradually to ninth place at twenty. They think that this is a compensatory activity. If they are right, then reading the funnies is far more a form of play than it is of amusement. Through them they believe that children and young people find complete freedom from the restraints of the home and social conventions; through them they can in imagination "defy every law" and do so with impunity. Perhaps they are right, but the author is inclined to think that a change takes place up the age scale from compensatory play to amusement. Younger children may participate in the activities of the characters in the comic strips and thus enjoy a playful freedom from constraint; but it seems likely that older children and adults enjoy them because of their clever criticism of society, for much the same reason that much literature is enjoyed. (It would be instructive to discover age differences in the preference for different kinds of comic strips.)

On the contribution of leisure reading to the development of personality much the same must be said as was presented above

[1] Stoke, S. M., and Cline, W. F., "The Avocations of One Hundred College Freshmen," *J. Appl. Psychol.*, 1929, 13, 257-265.
Terman, L. M., *Genetic Studies of Genius*, Vol. 1, chap. 15.
[2] Lehman, H. C., and Witty, P. A., "The Compensatory Function of the Sunday 'Funny' Paper," *J. Appl. Psychol.*, 1927, 11, 202-211.

concerning the contribution of the movies. Probably most readers will agree, however, that there are at present more possibilities of valuable contributions to come from reading than from the movies. Books are even more readily available, and are often read over and over again. The very habit of reading itself is ordinarily looked upon as a most desirable feature of any personality pattern. Ideals can be and no doubt are influenced by what is found in books, although systematic measurements of such have not been made. Vocational ambitions are known in specific instances to have been stirred by the reading of books.[1]

A wide range of reading can not only add to the range of information but can also expand the vocabulary. The habit of resorting to entertaining books as a means of passing leisure time is a habit which may come to be highly valued in later years. If reading leads to a perception of excellencies in literary style, that may lead to improvement in the reader's own English. From reading, too, it is possible to gain a range of information, a fund of knowledge, which can be used for the entertainment of others in conversation. Not infrequently such abilities contribute much to the attractiveness of a personality in later years.

That there are possible dangers in reading all students admit. The adolescent girl may become too much absorbed in extremely sentimental trash of low moral standards and her own character be endangered thereby. Boys may be led into false conceptions of life and false standards of conduct by too intensive a reading of literature designed for the pleasure of the immoral and the indecent. But there is also the possibility, as was suggested for the movies and some forms of play, that the reading of literature which adults consider unwholesome may serve as a compensation or a harmless release of otherwise inhibited impulses. Whether a boy or girl in any particular case is finding a compensation or release in the reading of certain books and magazines, or is in the process of being corrupted, must be determined as best one can from what knowledge is available of the particular individual concerned.

Some have been much disturbed by the waste of time in the

---

[1] A distinguished physical educator says that he found his ambition through the reading of Frank Merriwell stories. Some will recall that these stories were once considered odious.

reading of useless literature. No doubt there is much time
wasted; but it is not easy to determine when reading is wastage
and when not. There are no doubt occasional instances of
young people who become too much absorbed in their reading.
These are individuals who have difficulty in getting along with
others, who are backward in their social adjustment. Such may
find it much easier to withdraw into the fantasy world of literature than to make their way in social contacts. Obviously such a
reading-aided withdrawal from the realities of life bodes ill for
the future and must be watched and handled with the utmost
care; not of course by forbidding the reading, but by aiding to a
social adjustment which will weaken the impulse to retreat into
the fantasy world of books.[1]

3. *Conversation.* Complete records of the conversation habits
of young people over a significant period of time should prove a
most effective means of revealing their interests and the relative
positions of prominence of these interests. Some beginnings
have been made in this direction. Apparently young women
converse more about persons and personalities than do young
men. One study conducted on a university campus revealed that
5.8% of fraternity house conversations were about personalities;
while of sorority house conversations, 10.4% dealt with personalities. Out of their setting these percentages look small, but because of the long list of miscellaneous conversation topics reported these percentages are comparatively very large.[2]

Approximately one-quarter of such student conversations concern sex interests in some form. Religion is also a frequently

[1] The reader will find an excellent introduction to literature on reading
through the following:

Gray, W. S., *Summary of Investigations Relating to Reading,* Chicago, 1925.
—— "Summary of Reading Investigations," *Elem. Sch. J.,* 1930, 30, 450-467,
    496-509; 31, 531-546.
Hall, G. Stanley, *Adolescence,* Vol. 2, pp. 474-480.
Hilton, E., *Junior College Book List,* Univ. Calif. Pub. Educ., 1930, 6, No. 1.
Jordan, A. M., *Children's Interests in Reading,* New York, 1921.
Lehman, H. C., "Reading Books 'Just for Fun,'" *Sch. Rev.,* 1926, 34, 357-364.
Terman, L. M., and Lima, Margaret, *Children's Reading,* New York, 1925.
Washburne, C., and Vogel, M., *Winnetka Graded Book List,* Chicago, Am.
    Lib. Asso., 1926.
[2] Stoke, S. M., and West, E. D., "Sex Differences in Conversational Inter-
ests," *J. Soc. Psychol.,* 1931, 2, 120-126.

recurring topic in student conversations.[1] As these topics, sex and religion, are more carefully guarded by educators, instruction concerning them is often limited and inadequate. Not infrequently young people reach later adolescent years with but very childish concepts concerning both. In the face of this lack of proper instruction, social pressure and physiological urge combine to arouse curiosity. The consequence is much questing for information through the means of conversation. The experiences and observations (and too often speculations) and the incidentally picked-up bits of knowledge which each may have are pooled for the benefit of all in these conversations.

The preferences already mentioned, as indicated by the Lehman and Witty studies of play and amusement interests, are also of significance here. Boys are interested and have much to say about athletics and athletic episodes in their conversations. Girls are likewise interested and give much attention in their conversations to "dates" and romantic experiences or the prospect of them. But the range of conversational topics extends far beyond the subjects of most frequent inclusion. Almost anything may come in for consideration and little if anything is tabooed.

The possibilities of contribution to the personality development by conversation are almost as varied as the topics of conversations themselves. Attitudes may be molded, new ones developed, and old ones more firmly established. Much information may be acquired which is questionable and even harmful, and at the same time it is possible to acquire through conversation not a little information which is of lasting value. The attitudes and prejudices of others are revealed in conversation; if the group is an intimate one, perhaps more freely than at any other time or in any other way. By such means much information concerning others is acquired even though it often be unformulated. Ideals and hopes and ambitions are talked over. Talking about them forces formulation. In the conversational situation they are subjected to the comments and criticisms of others. Sometimes this is a severe test, for youth is rarely as tactful and considerate of

[1] Stoke, S. M., and West, E. D., "The Conversational Interests of College Students," *Sch. and Soc.*, 1930, 32, 567-570.

the feelings of others as the more restrained and judicious adult is likely to be. Friendships grow and flourish through the intimacies of conversation, and they not infrequently break down under the same circumstances. Residence groups with mutual interests are often encouraged by school and college and university administrators because of the belief that there is much of educational value to be obtained, when those with similar study problems see much of each other.

Studies of learning have revealed that recitation adds much to the efficiency of learning, that one learns more rapidly by the use of some recitation than one does by merely giving all of the time to reading. So, to a certain limited extent, conversation can serve in the form of recitation, as one may explain to another his idea of a subject which both are studying. That misinformation is by such means often acquired must also be admitted; but misinformation is also acquired from textbooks and classrooms as well. How far conversation and leisure may be used for its educational and cultural effects in personality development no one knows. Many are beginning to suspect that it has extensive possibilities.

Vocational Interests. One of the most conspicuous evidences of response to social pressure is the large place which future occupation has in the thought and life of the average adolescent. What am I going to do, or what I am going to do when I get through school is a never-exhausted subject for conversation, reading, day-dreaming, letter-writing, and serious seeking of advice. Those who have decided are often a bit envied by those who have not. Those who have decided and seem to know how they are going to find an opportunity to make a start in the desired direction when school is over are still more likely to be envied. And then there are those who have selected a vocation and are becoming dissatisfied with their choice. There are those who have had a decision made for them by their parents, and want to do something else but feel under obligation to comply with their parents' wishes; and there are those who do not know what they want to do for a living and cannot seem to discover any one thing which interests them enough more than something else to justify their considering it as a selection. Perhaps it should be added that there are those who do not know what they are going to do and are not concerned about it, but they are a small minority. Circumstances may make it unnecessary for them to give thought to a vocational future, or it may be that their indifference is an indication of physical insufficiency or of serious maladjustment. By far the majority of adolescents, male and female, are concerned by the problem of their vocational futures.

The notion is still widely current that every individual is destined by nature to be especially fitted for some one vocation in life and that the task for each youth and his counsellors is that of discovering the one particular vocation for which each is predestined. Thoughtful consideration and some investigation, however, long ago dispelled this notion from scientific thought. People are not born carpenters and plumbers and druggists and life insurance salesmen and teachers and bankers and lawyers and preachers and so on. They are born with a native endowment of health and intelligence and possibly of certain other mental abilities and aptitudes. But these are general and not vocationally specific. A given degree of intelligence may be equally useful in any one of many different vocations. An aptitude for the manipulation of tools may be equally useful in any one of many different trades. Persistence of effort and application may be a native trait;[1] but it is useful, if not indispensable, in every trade and profession.

Recent years have produced many schemes for the classification of personality types which not a few have thought should be helpful in the matter of vocational adaptation. There has been much interest in the isolation of those who are introverted and those who are extroverted. Others have distinguished the mechanically inclined from the socially inclined. Then there are those who prefer to think in terms of the cyclothymic and the schizothymic (Kretschmer). Much has been made, in Germany

---

[1] For an excellent compilation of the available evidence on this matter of native traits and special abilities the reader should see *The Abilities of Man*, by Carl Spearman, 1927. A careful and exhaustive study made under the direction of E. L. Thorndike indicates that abilities as measured by school grades, intelligence tests, mechanical and clerical aptitude tests at age fourteen are a poor basis for predicting what degree of success, happiness and income will be achieved by the age of eighteen to twenty-two. See Thorndike, E. L., and others, *Prediction of Vocational Success*, New York, Commonwealth Fund, 1934.

especially, of several eidetic types (Jaensch).[1] Ordinarily the extremes of these differences can be easily recognized. Their interests characterize them; and, as these are notably different, it has been thought that through the interests which a person manifests his type could be determined. And, then, with the type determined and its characteristics known, it would be a relatively simple matter to decide what general kind of vocation or profession any young man or woman should enter. One who had the character interests of an introvert, for example, should hesitate long before undertaking to sell washing machines or life insurance; and in like manner one whose interests revealed a predominantly esthetic type (Spranger) would be far better suited for some profession involving the constant use of artistic judgments.

But while such type concepts as these are far better than the notions of plumber and carpenter and lawyer and banker types they are also subject to serious criticism and their use in the practical affairs of life is surrounded with many difficulties. Even those who feel most certain of them recognize many gradations and mixtures. It is also important to question if the interest differences which are so often said to characterize these types are not actually a matter of acquisition through the developing years. If they are, then the alleged types are the product of the interests which the circumstances of life develop. The type would then be made by the interests rather than the interests being motivated by the intrinsically determined development of a type. In adolescence, especially in its earlier years, there is often a very wide range of interests, vocational and otherwise. It is out of these that specializations and special attractions come with the passing years.

[1] The literature here is extensive but a good introduction may be had through the following, especially if the reader will use also the references which they contain:

Conklin, Edmund S., "The Definition of Introversion, Extroversion, and Allied Concepts," *J. of Abn. & Soc. Psychol.*, 1923, 4, 367-382.
Freyd, Max, "The Personalities of the Socially and the Mechanically Inclined," *Psychol. Monog.*, 1924, 33, Whole No. 151.
Jaensch, E. R., *Eidetic Imagery*, New York, 1930.
Jung, C. G., *Psychological Types*, New York, 1923.
Kretschmer, E., *Physique and Character*, New York, 1925.
Spranger, Ed., *Types of Men* (Niemeyer, Halle), 1928.

An intrinsic type difference, if there be such, would at most only determine the general direction of interest development.[1] It would lead to interest in certain general kinds of vocations but not to specific vocational interests and choices. Specific vocational interests and choices appear, however, in adolescent years; and adolescents not infrequently say why they find such and such a vocation the most interesting and attractive of all. And in addition to such reasons given, insightful persons may also observe yet other motivations of which the person making the vocational choice may be quite unaware. These reasons for vocational interest and preference deserve closer attention.

It is easy to believe that the actual number of factors influencing a vocational interest in any given case may be too numerous for discovery and itemization. Many of them may appear to be minor and of short duration. Sometimes a single brief episode is the determining factor in the choice of a life work. Complicated, however, as the problem usually is, there are a number of motivations of vocational interest which have been isolated and commented upon.

Family Influence (1) is always listed as an important factor. The reaction to this influence varies, however, with the age of the individual. In childhood and very early adolescent years a much larger percentage of young people express a preference for the vocation of one or other of the parents than is reported for later adolescence. This is in harmony with what is known of the general tendency to break away from home domination with progress toward maturity. But to what extent occupational choices made by parents for their children are accepted by the children we know little. Case studies do reveal that in individual instances some young people passively acquiesce to selections made for them by their parents; and yet, in other instances, there is rebellion and the choice of almost anything but that which the parents prefer. From this and also from our knowledge of the effect of the family situation and family relation-

[1] This general direction might of course have been started in childhood or even in infancy. Note the following:

Bingham, W. V., "Personality and Vocation," *Brit. J. Psychol.*, 1926, 16, 354-362.

Marston, L. R., "The Emotions of Young Children; An Experimental Study in Introversion and Extroversion," *Univ. of Iowa Stud.*, Stud. in Child Welfare, 1925, 3, No. 3.

ships[1] there is justification for thinking that the nature of the family influence upon vocational interest in adolescence will vary not only with the degree of progress through adolescence but also with the motivations of the parents' own attitudes toward the vocational interests of their children.[2]

The belief is growing that the *escape motive* (2), so often found in personality adjustment problems, is also a not infrequently significant factor in the selection of vocation. What attracts and interests is that which offers escape from a disagreeable reality, or from the prospect of reality situations which give promise of being disagreeable. Perhaps this is the reason why some accept the preferences of their parents. It is easier to do as they wish, for by so doing the problem of selecting and of making one's way against parental desires is avoided. This seems to be especially true of many who select the teaching profession.[3] The life of the school and the campus is familiar. The world beyond presents many difficulties which may be escaped by continuing in the ways of the school and the campus. The escape motive may be strong or it may be weak; and it may be soon forgotten (or repressed), especially as interest in the chosen field grows; but it is in all probability a very significant factor in directing the course of much vocational interest development.

That the degree of *social esteem* (3) in which certain vocations are held is an influential factor in the development of vocational interest and preference is an interesting revelation of some of the studies in this field. This should not be surprising. Every one knows that, whether justifiably or not, some professions and some occupations are looked upon as being socially superior to others; and this is curiously not entirely a matter of amount of compen-

[1] See Chaps. XI and XII.

[2] For literature on the parents' occupation see the following:

Anderson, W. A., "Some Social Factors Associated with Vocational Choices of College Men," *J. Educ. Sociol.*, 1932, 6, 100-113.

Cunliffe, R. B., "Why This Career? Significance of Vocational Information in Decisions of College Students," *Person. J.*, 1929, 7, 376-384.

—— "Whither Away and Why: Trends in Choice of Vocation in Detroit," *Person. J.*, 1927, 6, 25-28.

Valentine, C. W., and Ritchie, F. M., "An Inquiry as to Reasons for Choice of Occupation Among Secondary School Pupils," *J. Nat. Inst. Indus. Psychol.*, 1928, 4, 211-223.

[3] Austin, F. M., "An Analysis of the Motive of Adolescents for the Choice of the Teaching Profession," *Brit. J. Educ. Psychol.*, 1931, 1, 87-103.

sation. The teacher or the professor may actually be paid less than the janitor and yet the position of the teacher ordinarily has more social prestige than that of the janitor. And it will be recalled also that adolescents are especially conscious of social demands and pressures and customs. Lehman and Witty have shown that the degree of social esteem [1] in which particular occupations are held by children and adolescents of different ages varies not a little with the age. What is considered most estimable at one age is not so highly esteemed some years later, or the change may be quite the other way. Where this is influential, the tendency seems to be to select some occupation which stands high in the assumptions of social esteem.

The extent to which *vocational advice* (4) influences the permanent vocational interests and endeavors is problematic. That there is a vast amount of vocational advice being given every teacher knows very well. Adults seem to find much satisfaction in telling young people what they should do in the world; and many young people appear to crave such advice. Sometimes the advice is good, but it is certain that much of it is based upon little actual knowledge and far too frequently reflects the dissatisfactions and maladjustments of the adviser. One systematic study of the effects of expert vocational counselling [2] indicates that the advice is most likely to be followed if it conforms to the ambitions and plan of the person advised, and if it is given to persons under fifteen and a half years of age. Apparently vocational advice given to young people of the middle and later adolescent years is more likely to be taken with reservation and independence of consideration. Perhaps this is as it should be. Certainly this finding conforms to all else that we know of the maturing personality.

It is well known that in certain exceptional cases the motive of *compensating for some defect* (5) has been of large influence. Those who have a speech defect seem often to be attracted to vocations which involve public speaking. They appear to hope

[1] Lehman, H. C., and Witty, P. A., "Further Study of the Social Status of Occupations," *J. Educ. Sociol.*, 1931, 5, 101-112. See also Counts, G. S., "The Social Status of Occupations: A Problem in Vocational Guidance," *The Sch. Rev.*, 1925, 33, 16-27.

[2] Arnold, C., "Social Factors: Their Influence on the Success of Vocational Guidance of Adolescents," *Welfare Mag.*, 1928, 19, 85-96.

for compensation in maturity for the troubles of childhood and youth. Anatomical and sensory defects which cannot be directly overcome must be determining factors in the selection of vocational interests. They direct the person toward those forms of occupation which are possible for one so handicapped. Studies of inferiority feelings and complexes have also revealed that many of these troubles are based upon false beliefs concerning the self and its capacities. Consequently it is more than likely that some vocational interests are motivated by compensatory trends for defects which are imaginary rather than actual.

A number of other motives appear also in the studies of this subject. The salary prospect appears a motive with varying frequencies. Sometimes the percentage of young people reporting this runs as high as twenty-five. That the vocation is attractive because it appears to be an "easy job" also appears. And there are those who mention teaching as attractive because of the vacations available. Others speak of the degree of security, the philanthropic opportunities, the demand, and so on. Any or all of these may be factors in determining the vocational interest in any given case.

The *evaluation of a vocational interest* is not infrequently a matter of no little importance. Should one for example enter upon a pre-medical program of studies because one is interested in medicine? Is the vocational interest of a young man or woman a safe guide to vocational choice? The presentation of interest motivations above might be in itself sufficient to make one hesitate to answer these questions in the affirmative. Perhaps the interest preference is motivated by a rebellion against parental domination. Perhaps it is motivated by a desire to compensate for imagined inferiority. Or it may be motivated by something else equally misleading. Interests so motivated may for these very reasons have no relationship whatever to the ability of the person making the choice. And yet the contention has long been made, and is still held by many, that interest is the best basis for vocational selection because it is the best indication of ability or talent.

Of this relationship between interest and ability there have been many studies. Thorndike started the experimental work and much of the discussion by discovering a positive correlation of .89 between interest in school subjects and ability in them.[1] But the amount of interest in these subjects was self-estimated and many have thought that such was an unreliable method of procedure. It is quite possible that these students were biased in their estimation of interest by the grades which they could recall; and it is also possible that the interest and the grades earned might both have been influenced by some other factor than ability, the personality of the teacher, for example. Later studies have in part sustained Thorndike's findings, but have considerably reduced the correlation figure. Consequently it is not safe to predict ability from interest in school subjects in individual cases, although there may be some significant relationship between the two. Fryer who has made a careful survey of these studies concludes that a vocational prediction from interest manifested has no better than a 50-50 chance of being right.[2]

Vocational selection by interest is unsafe also because so many young people have so little knowledge about the vocation in which they express interest.[3] In fact, their interest is not infrequently based upon very gross misinformation. It has been frequently demonstrated that the vocational interests of high school pupils are such that a very large percentage will be forced by the circumstances of life to change later on, whether they want to or not. An example of this is represented in the following table taken from a study made by W. M. Proctor[4] on the vocational choices of 930 high school pupils:

	Percentage of H. S. Pupils Choosing	Percentage so Gainfully Employed in United States
	Percent	Percent
Agriculture, mechanical and industrial arts	8.8	61.1
Business and clerical	29.7	14.1
Professional service	61.7	4.4

[1] Thorndike, E. L., "The Permanence of Interests and Their Relation to Abilities," *Pop. Sci. Mo.*, 1912, 81, 449-456. "Early Interests: Their Permanence and Relation to Abilities," *Sch. and Soc.*, 1917, 5, 178-179. "The Correlation Between Interests and Abilities in College Courses," *Psychol. Rev.*, 1921, 28, 374-376.

[2] Fryer, Douglas, *The Measurement of Interests*, New York, 1931, chap. 6.

[3] Cunliffe, R. B., "Why This Career? Significance of Vocational Information in Decisions of College Students," *Person. J.*, 1929, 7, 376-384.

[4] Proctor, W. M., "Psychological Tests and Guidance of High School Pupils," *J. Educ. Res.*, Monog. No. I, 1923 (Rev. ed.), p. 71.

Obviously, under such circumstances as those represented in this table, there are many who will be forced to give up their vocational preference and seek other forms of occupation. To advise any pupil in that group to study for a profession because he manifested an interest in that profession would have been rash indeed. It would have been a direct means of contributing to disappointment and distress and possibly maladjustment later on.[1]

Much attention has been given to the problem of permanency of vocational interests and as a consequence it is now possible to be fairly certain of some conclusions. The following table represents the findings in several significant studies:

PERMANENCY OF VOCATIONAL INTERESTS [2]

	No.	Percent	
Franklin	260	73.8	same choice through 3 yrs. jr. high school.
Willett	218	24.7	same choice through 3 yrs. of high school.
Alberty	679	30.0	same choice through 2 yrs. of high school.
Douglas	2844	54.6	H. S. srs. say formerly had other preference.
Crathorne	2083	50.0	changed during four years of high school.
McHale	133	24.8	changed during last two years of college.

From these sample studies alone it is clear that vocational interests are both permanent and changeable. Apparently some young people make up their minds early and continue with that choice, while others choose and change. To some readers this may be a fact so obvious that it scarcely required systematic vali-

[1] See also Sears, J. B., "Occupations of Fathers and Occupational Choices of 1039 Boys in Grades Seven and Eight of the Oakland Schools," *Sch. and Soc.*, 1915, 1, 750-756.

[2] Taken from:

Franklin, E. E., "The Permanence of Vocational Interests Three Years After," *Sch. and Soc.*, 1926, 23, 438-440.

Willett, G. W., "Permanence of Pupil Interests," *Sch. and Soc.*, 1919, 9, 334-338, 365-368.

Alberty, H. B., "The Permanence of the Vocational Choices of High School Pupils," *Indus. Arts Mag.*, 1925, 14, 203-207.

Douglas, A. A., "Vocational Interests of High School Seniors," *Sch. and Soc.*, 1922, 16, 79-84.

Crathorne, A. R., "Changes of Mind Between High School and College as to Life Work," *Educ. Adm. and Super.*, 1920, 6, 274-284.

McHale, Kathryn, "An Experimental Study of Vocational Interests of a Liberal Arts College Group," *J. Appl. Psychol.*, 1924, 8, 245-255.

See also chapter 5 of Douglas Fryer's *Measurement of Interests*.

dation. Others will see in these figures support for their belief that young people should not hesitate to change their choice as maturation and increasing knowledge bring better understanding of self and society. There is also ample justification in these tables for abandoning the notion that the appearance of a vocational interest is the evidence of the maturation of a vocational type.

There is some reason for thinking that less able minds tend to an early fixation of vocational choice and that they select some vocation from their immediate environment; while abler minds delay longer in coming to permanent decisions, change more easily and seek a wider range of experience for their selection.[1] Young people who fear to change may profit by knowing this and also that a study of the names in *Who's Who in America* has revealed that of these people who have achieved some degree of distinction for their work 16 percent changed their vocation at least twice. One-third of these changes came before twenty-five years of age.[2]

From these many considerations it must be clear that the psychogenesis of a vocational interest may be a very complicated matter indeed. It may be the product of a very large number of different influences. Developing talent may be a factor, but it is quite as likely to be influenced by friendships, casual incidents, parental desires, rebellions against parental domination, escape motives, compensatory trends, notions of vocational esteem, financial gain, and other influences. Relatively uncomplicated choices of interests may be permanent; while other choices may change as the motivations for them are outgrown or dissipated. Family troubles often smooth out, the necessity for escape motivations and compensatory trends disappears, and changes in notions of vocational social esteem are likely to come with increasing knowledge. A better adjustment to life may bring very different motivations and consequently different vocational interests and preferences.

[1] Mackaye, D. L., "The Fixation of Vocational Interest," *Amer. J. Sociol.*, 1927, 33, 353-370.
[2] Kitson, H. D., and Culbertson, L., "The Vocational Changes of One Thousand Eminent Americans," *Nat. Voc. Guid. Bull.*, 1923, 1, 128-130.
Kitson, H. D., and Kirtley, Lucile, "The Vocational Changes of One Thousand Eminent American Women," *Sch. and Soc.*, 1924, 19, 110-112.

While vocational counselling and guidance in terms of interest alone is thus quite unreliable, this must not be interpreted as meaning that vocational interest is not of value. Interest in an activity accounts for much of the difference between work and drudgery; and, if sufficiently strong, may give to the work activity much of the character of play. But the absence of interest does not mean that an interest may not be developed. Interest it will be recalled (see discussion at the beginning of the preceding chapter) means both a background of knowledge and the experience of pleasantly held attention. The reason why some things do not interest is often because of the lack of that background of knowledge. When an interest in some activity is desired or appears to be wise or even necessary, it can frequently be obtained first by patiently acquiring a background of knowledge of the field. Frequently the lack of interest in some vocation indicates merely that the person who lacks the interest knows nothing about that vocation.

Finally, it should be pointed out that a pattern or group of interests may be more indicative for vocational counselling than the presence or absence of particular vocational interests. Strong,[1] in a series of studies, has shown that the characteristic life interests of successful adults differ measurably from profession to profession. And, on the basis of this, he has devised a method whereby the pattern of interests, likes and dislikes, of young people may be determined. From a knowledge of this interest pattern it may be possible to discern with better chances of success in what vocations a particular young man is most likely to find himself associated with people like himself. If people with a particular pattern of interests are happy in that type of work, it is reasonable to assume that a young man with about that pattern of interests is likely to be happy in that type of work.

With this matter of interest pattern we come back to the problems of personality development. What vocational interests and vocational choices contribute to personality is not yet known. On this there have been practically no studies at all. One can

[1] Strong, E. K., Jr., "A Vocational Interest Test," *The Educ. Rec.*, 1927, 8, 107-121.
See also: Fryer, D., *Measurement of Interests*, pp. 122-142.

infer or guess a few things tentatively. The selection of a vocation which does not subsequently bring disappointment and a desire for a change may contribute much to the systematization of choices in other things. As it brings a definite purpose into the life, it ought to contribute not a little to the personality integration and to those habits which commonly characterize self-control or consistency. Changing of interests on the other hand should contribute not a little in the way of increased range of information. Sometimes a long-delayed vocational determination brings unrest and dissatisfaction with the self; and, if many immediate associates have chosen, there is the possibility of notions of inferiority in this regard. The roots of vocational selection and interest spread wide, their psychological connections and possible influences reach out into many phases of growth and therefore justify still much further study and thoughtful observation.[1]

[1] In this connection see Douglas Fryer's suggestions for the study of vocational interests by a genetic or autobiographic method, *The Measurement of Interests,* chap. 11.

For general literature on vocational counselling and on vocations see:

Brewer, J. M., *The Vocational-Guidance Movement,* New York, 1918.
Bureau of Vocational Information, *Training for the Professions and Allied Occupations,* New York, 1924.
Fryer, Douglas, *Vocational Self-Guidance,* Philadelphia, 1924.
Kitson, H. D., *The Psychology of Vocational Adjustment,* Philadelphia, 1925.
Myers, G. E., *The Problem of Vocational Guidance,* New York, 1927.
Parsons, Frank, *Choosing a Vocation,* Boston, 1909.
Proctor, W. M., *Vocations,* Boston, 1929.
Rosengarten, Wm., *Choosing Your Life Work,* New York, 1924 (2nd. ed.).

CHAPTER VI

IDEALS

NATURE OF, SOURCES, RELATION TO INTELLIGENCE, SELEC-
TION IN FORMATION, DAY-DREAMING EFFECTS, INFLUENCE
OF OBJECTIVE IDEALS, AS STANDARD OF JUDGMENT, ADULT
IDEALS, PERSISTENCE AND PERVASIVENESS, LOYALTY ATTI-
TUDE, PSYCHOANALYTIC CONCEPTION OF, RELATION TO SO-
CIAL COMPLEXITY, EXTRA-FAMILIAL INFLUENCES, CONCRETE
IDEALS, CHANGE TO ABSTRACT, MASCULINE IDEALS IN FE-
MALES, PERFECTIONISTIC IDEALS, CONTRIBUTION TO PER-
SONALITY

From the first years of research in genetic psychology there has
been no lack of awareness of the importance of ideals. In the
earlier years, interest was centered primarily upon the conduct
and development of children; and there were a considerable
number of studies made of children's ideals.[1]

The method was simple. Children were asked to write little
papers on what they would like to be when they became adult;
or in an imaginary new city, what would they like most to be.
Sometimes they were asked more directly to state whom they
most desired to become like. Since those early years there has
been no lack of recognition of the importance of ideals; but there
has been an unfortunate lack of systematic studies of them, and
of how they function in the lives of growing boys and girls. Consequently it is impossible to make any very certain statements
concerning the subject.

Nature of an Ideal. Strangely enough, there has been little attention given by research in general psychology to the nature of
an ideal and its operation. But it is possible to bring together
the available material and the observations of thoughtful minds;
and it is also possible to apply the results of some experimentally

[1] See Barnes' *Studies in Education*, Vol. 2.

established facts of general psychology in such a manner as to throw some light upon the probable nature of the ideal and of its operation.

Turning to the contemporary textbooks one finds that many authors have failed to include the topic entirely. Others, who have considered it, fail to agree, probably because the best they can do is to give their own observations. Warren says that it "consists of a vivid image or thought, together with an intense feeling and a strong tendency to act." [1] Pillsbury mentions ideals but only as they are related to will and action, quite without analysis or definition of the ideal itself.[2] Perrin and Klein say that an ideal is "essentially a plan of action formulated verbally." [3] The tendency to act, sometimes more specifically described as an impulse toward the realization of the ideal in the person's own life, seems to have been uppermost in the minds of most of those who have written of the subject.[4] But this certainly cannot be characteristic of all ideals, and perhaps it is characteristic of but a comparatively small number of them.

There are vast numbers of ideals which could not be accompanied by an impulse to emulate. A little observation will reveal that mature adults, well and happily established in life, have ideals which they do not seek to realize in themselves. They would make themselves absurd if they sought to do so. One may have his ideal of motherhood without any impulse whatever to become a mother; and in like manner one may have his ideal of what a soldier ought to be, of what a preacher should seek to be, and so too, one has one's ideal of what a college, a home, a school, a boy, a girl, should be. But all of these are ideals for people or institutions in which the one who holds the ideals may have no part whatsoever. The psychological accompaniment of these, which are here called objective ideals, is an attitude of acceptance or approval. They may even be accompanied by very positive assertions of the desirability of such ideals being more seriously considered by others, by those so involved; but they cannot by their very nature be accompanied by an impulse

---

[1] Warren, H. C., *Elements of Human Psychology*, p. 282.
[2] Pillsbury, W. B., *Essentials of Psychology* (3rd edition), pp. 368-369.
[3] Perrin, F. A. C., and Klein, D. B., *Psychology*, p. 374.
[4] Brooks, F. D., *Psychology of Adolescence*, p. 325.

toward realization in the lives of the individuals who experience them.

Doubtless the emphasis upon impulse came from consideration primarily of the self ideal. When one thinks of what one would like to be, or of what one ought to be, there is probably a pattern of impulses, even though faint and fleeting, toward action in the direction of realizing that ideal in one's own personality. Conversations of everyday life, as well as expressions of human experience in prose and poetry, reveal how considerations of an ideal self stir longings—and longings are apparently incipient tendencies to action. Sometimes the impulses to emulate become overt and obvious, even amusingly so. The young girl conceives of her ideal self as a school teacher, remarkably like the one under whom she is now studying, and soon her associates observe that she is imitating that school teacher in dress and speech and manner. The boy sees in some prominent athlete the personification of his ideal for himself, and is soon walking and talking like the athlete. So, even though systematic inductive studies are lacking, it is probably safe to assume that self ideals are accompanied by impulses to appropriate action; but one must not make the mistake of generalizing about all ideals from what seems to be characteristic of the ideal for the self.

A working definition would then be that *an ideal is a concept of the most desirable in some trait, or skill or type.* That may be individually desirable, or personally desirable, or socially desirable, or institutionally desirable, depending upon the particular ideal and its reference. Ordinarily the ideal is accompanied by an attitude of acceptance or approval; but, in the case of the ideal for the self, the attitude of acceptance or approval if present is submerged in the pattern of impulses toward realizing action. Thus considered, there may be many ideals at any given time in the life of any adolescent or any adult.

In thus defining the ideal as a concept, a relationship is established at once to the general psychology of thinking. The term concept indicates that there is nothing about it to involve the difficult problem of inherited traits or patterns. The concept is an acquired pattern. Its sources are sensory and perceptual experience. It is thus dependent originally upon the environment in which the individual lives. Many of those who have studied the ideals of children and adolescents have commented emphatically upon this close relationship to the environment. Children's ideals are limited in their scope. Many studies have indicated this and there is a tendency to think that the ideals cannot, or, at least in most cases, do not rise above the level from whence they come.[1]

Sources of Ideals. Most readers will no doubt have observed the manner in which children pick up ideals for the self from their immediate contacts. The small boy wants to be a carpenter or a lawyer because his father is, and later he wants to be a football player or an aviator or a prize fighter according to what for the time being has captured his attention. So, too, the girl wants to be a school teacher because her mother was, or because she happens to have an especially attractive teacher in her school; or, she wants to be a dressmaker because she has watched the work of one with admiration; or, she wants to be a missionary because she has heard a returned missionary speak most charmingly. Welfare workers and moralists point out that herein lies the source of much that is lamentable as well as much that may be fortunate. If the associations are such as to suggest no socially desirable ideals, then the ambitions of the child are most certain to be such as to eventuate in socially undesirable conduct, in delinquency and criminality, or, at best, in useless mediocrity.

It would be a serious mistake, however, to conclude that the ideal for the self or that objective ideals cannot rise above their source. Concepts, it is true, grow out of sensory and perceptual experience; but the material obtained through sensory and perceptual experience may be worked over by an active able mind into a great variety of patterns. Imagination and the selective dissociative processes commonly termed attention can result in the production of concepts very different from the immediate experiences of sensation and perception. Hence, while the ideal

[1] For useful material on ideals see the following:

Barnes' *Studies in Education,* 1902, Vol. 2.
Study of Children's Hopes, Rep. State Supt. Instruction, New York, 1896, 2, 977-1042.
Barnes, E., "Children's Ideals," *Ped. Sem.,* 1900, 7, 3-13.
Darrah, Estelle, "On Children's Ideals," *Pop. Sci. Mo.,* 1898, 53, 88-98.
Hollingworth, L. S., *Psychology of the Adolescent,* p. 178 et seq.
Moxcey, M. E., *Psychology of Middle Adolescence,* chap. 6.

may find its source in the immediate environment it need not necessarily be limited to that which exists in the environment.

Intelligence and Ideals. Moxcey, in a discussion that is hortatory rather than inductive, observes that ideals are dependent in large part upon the intelligence of the individual, and also upon what she calls moral and esthetic insight.[1] Mackaye's study of vocational ambitions (see preceding chapter) revealed that those of higher mental ability showed less tendency to early fixation of vocational ambitions for the self and a greater willingness to change. And it was the abler minds in the group he studied which selected vocations from a wider range of possibilities than those perceptible in the immediate environment.[2] While obviously limited in numbers and to but one type of ideal, nevertheless this study does lend support to the contention that the rise of the ideal above the level of what can be produced by direct observation is related to the mental ability of the individual.

This influence of intelligence upon the development of the ideal is a matter of no little importance to the student of adolescence who is primarily interested in the interpretation of individual behavior problems. In any given case, if the intelligence is at the average or above then it is possible that the ideals have varied greatly from their content in childhood years. If, however, the intelligence be lower than average, one may suspect that there has been far less development of the ideals beyond their childhood sources, that they are more closely representative of the early social situation. Hence a knowledge of both the early environment as well as of a reliable psychological test score will be of service.

Selection in Formation. It must also be obvious that all of the contacts of any given individual boy or girl are not absorbed into the ideals constructed. There is some sort of selective process operative. Why is it that two boys, brothers even, in apparently the same environment, should select out of that environment such very different material? Of the motivations here psychology is unfortunately ignorant. One can suspect the influence of inferiority feelings, perhaps superiority feelings, the influence of

[1] Moxcey, M. E., *Psychology of Middle Adolescence*, chap. 6.
[2] Mackaye, D. L., "The Fixation of Vocational Interest," *Am. J. Sociol.*, 1927, 33, 353-370.

physical health upon behavior, disciplinary relationships, the health and interests of the parents as it affects behavior toward the children, in fact, all of those more obscure motivations of conduct which are admittedly so influential in the molding of the personality.

Day-dreaming Effects. That day-dreaming, especially in adolescence, contributes largely to the molding of ideals, both of the self ideal and of the objective ideals, has been often recognized.[1] Perhaps this is the greatest service which day-dreaming can render. Here, if the individual has the capacity for constructive imagination, old ideals are broken up and new ones are constructed. Especially do these day-dreams concern the self ideal. The day-dreamer sees himself in a great variety of situations and occupations. New material is introduced and old dropped out. Perhaps the result may be a rather extravagant self ideal, but with youthful minds there is always the prospect of yet further reconstruction.

The exalted nature of ideals so developed has often caused comment, and sometimes called forth no little unjustified decision. Frequently, perhaps ordinarily, the ideals of adolescents are far beyond the realizable. He who hopes to become a physician dreams of being a Mayo or an Osler; he who dreams of becoming a lawyer imagines himself in the rôle of a Taft or a Root; she who sings sees herself as a future grand opera star; and the day-dreams of greatness in the movies our cartoonists keep constantly before us. Absurd as such ideals may appear to the sophisticated adult to be, they have their value and so must be seriously considered. Such dreams furnish in a short time a range of experience far beyond what could be perceptually possible. The knowledge gained thereby may lead to comparison with known or supposed abilities and disabilities, and in turn bring about yet further reconstruction, perhaps on a more conservative basis, of the self ideals. That such day-dreaming is motivated by desires and hopes and longings, efforts to escape and to compensate and the like, but makes these day-dreams in

---

[1] Pruette, Lorine, *Women and Leisure,* chap. 8.
Moxcey, M. E., *Psychology of Middle Adolescence,* chap. 6.
Hollingworth, L. S., *Psychology of the Adolescent,* p. 190.
Varendonck, J., *The Psychology of Day Dreams.*

relation to the ideals and the personality as a whole all the more significant.

Influence of Objective Ideals. While here again inductive studies are unfortunately lacking, one may nevertheless feel fairly confident of security in asserting that the contents of the objective ideals not only influence judgments and hence behavior and the personality pattern (see next paragraph); but that they also contribute, perhaps, indirectly, to the content of the self ideal. What the girl thinks a father ought to be must have some reflex effect upon her ideal of what she should herself become. The boy's ideal of motherhood must have some influence upon his behavior in the presence of women, upon his conversations about them, hence upon his relation to them, his thoughts of himself in such relationships and therefore affect the content of his self concept and his self ideal. So, through the effect of thoughts about or actual behavior toward the institutions for which the individual has ideals, may those objective ideals influence the conduct of the individual, his self concept, and his self ideal. Hence it is of importance morally and educationally that consideration should be given to the molding of ideals for the school, the city, the state, the nation, society, industry, business, home, welfare work, professions, etc., etc. And conversely, the effort to understand the ways of any individual youth will be greatly aided by discovering not only the self ideal, which may be rather carefully guarded by a wealth of rationalizations and defense mechanisms, but also the ideals for others and for institutions which may appear superficially to be unrelated to himself. The latter may be the more easily discovered because of the apparent lack of personal relationship.

Ideals and Standards of Judgment. In its operation, the ideal functions as a standard of judgment. The ideal of artistic excellence, for example, serves as a basis of comparison and evaluation of particular examples of art as they are presented. Here the effect of differences in the ideal becomes quickly evident. Where tawdry calendars and cheap crayon portraits are hung in the living-room and looked upon as delightfully beautiful, one has a right to suspect that the standard of excellence, the ideal, is very crude. There are likewise trained artists who quickly reject what many of ordinary culture accept as beautiful, indicating that in these artists the ideal has become so specialized as to set its possessor apart from the rest of mankind by the individuality of his judgments.

Concerning this influence of the ideal or standard upon judgment one may fortunately learn much from the studies of experimental introspective psychology.[1] These have revealed that judgments may be determined by what is present in the consciousness of the individual; or, that they may also be quite as effectively determined by what has formerly been conscious and which has through much repetition gradually become merely a set or determining tendency in the central nervous system. One makes many judgments which are first carefully considered. Gradually a standard of judgment is established, and after much use one makes judgments of such matters without stopping to think. The standard operates apart from consciousness, and quite efficiently. So the artist rejects without hesitation or consideration that which is far from conforming to his standard. Hesitation arises only when the work of art approaches the ideal.

The significance of this for adolescent psychology lies in the influence of the various ideals upon behavior. Their influence may function quite apart from consciousness, without the individual stopping even to think about relationship to an ideal. If a boy's father is his ideal and that father has always used alcoholic liquor, then that boy's anti-prohibitionistic behavior and conversational judgments can be readily understood. Daydreaming, reading, study and the experiences of social relations can bring rapid changes in the nature of ideals. Along with such changes one may properly expect that judgments may change. In the eyes of the consistent slowly changing adult, such changes appear as mere instances of adolescent inconsistency. But from this it must not be assumed that all judgments, all decisions, made by adolescents are determined by ideals. This depends upon the degree of pervasiveness of the influence of ideals which has been achieved, a subject which is considered in greater detail below.

Ideals in Adult Life. As has already been pointed out, adolescence is always studied and considered with maturity as a stand-

[1] Titchener, E. B., *Textbook of Psychology*, pp. 532-537; and also his *Experimental Psychology of the Higher Thought Processes*, Lecture IV.

ard. But when one turns to the literature on ideals for information about the functioning of ideals in adulthood, in order
to determine the direction in which adolescent changes are moving, one is surprised to discover that there is little available.
One might even be led to think that ideals were matters primarily for youth and the philosophers. Of course, after a man
dies, or resigns after a long period of service, the words of adulation spoken are quite likely to stress the fact that he was a man
of fine ideals. But the thoughtful often wonder if the man so
praised could have formulated those ideals had he been called
upon to do so. When adults of achievement are challenged by
an inquiring reporter with a thirst for news or an itch to do
magazine writing, they find themselves forced to formulate their
ideals. The product of such efforts, when we read them in print,
appear strained and unnatural, and are probably in large part
rationalizations.

We are driven to the conclusion that the average adult thinks
comparatively little about his self ideal. The adult has learned
to live and does live by certain well-established principles, so
habituated that there is little if any thought about them. They
are not concepts of that toward which there is a struggling to
attain. If there is awareness of them at all, there is awareness of
them as the ways in which things with him have always been
done. The adult may not have realized the ideals of his youth,
but he has come to live in a socially acceptable manner. The
ideals have brought about the establishment of determining
tendencies which dominate his behavior. They are merely habit
patterns. Unless something serious occurs to disturb them, he
will be lauded as a man of fine ideals, although the clergyman
may have to hunt out those principles and formulate them into
concepts, ideals, for the purposes of the funeral address.

These indications concerning the functioning of the self ideal
in mature years present a psychology quite different from that of
early adolescent years, where there is so much conscious consideration of ideals. It means that the whole course from the conscious ideals still undergoing development and formation in early
adolescence to the domination of life by habituated principles of
conduct, must take place between early adolescence and the
middle years of life. Perhaps the change may take place in some

individuals in a far shorter period of time. Others may live to a good old age without completing the change. They may live always with the adolescent consciousness of ideals. Every youth must be thought of as being somewhere in the course of this change. And he may be making the change rapidly, growing into an early maturity; or he may be making the change slowly, a prolonged adolescence.

Persistence and Pervasiveness. Not infrequently the lack of correspondence between the ideals and the conduct of youth is commented upon, sometimes with undue severity. That this lack of correspondence exists, those who are acquainted with youth admit freely. Warren has pointed out that the persistence with which they are followed and the pervasiveness of their influence [1] are the measure of their importance in the personality. Pillsbury thinks that the persistence with which ideals are followed in any individual is an intrinsically determined trait; [2] and for the present that may be as good an explanation as any, at least until we know more about individual differences in temperament. Certainly it is true that many have fine ideals and make little effort to realize them; others make a conspicuously persistent effort, struggling through or over any and every obstacle.

Of the pervasiveness of the effect of ideals held, there is perhaps a little more explanatory knowledge available. What is meant by the term is doubtless the extent to which a given ideal influences the whole range of the individual's responses. If the whole personality of the individual is influenced by a given ideal, then one would say that the influence was highly pervasive. One thinks he knows such youth, where decisions about the most insignificant as well as the most important items are made in terms of some long-sought goal. Others have such goals in mind and may select their school or courses accordingly, but for some reason the ideal fails to influence other features of their lives. The effect is not pervasive. Perhaps this is related to the intelligence of the individual. It is conceivable that individuals of the lower ranges of intelligence may fail to perceive the relationship to their ideal of many situations. They may have a professional

---

[1] Warren, H. C., *Elements of Human Psychology*, p. 283.
[2] Pillsbury, W. B., *Essentials of Psychology* (3rd. ed.), p. 368.

ideal for the self and fail utterly to perceive any relationship between their participation in athletics and the realization of that ideal. But one also finds such a lack of pervasive effect among those of higher ranges of intelligence. And here one turns for explanation to all that has been presented concerning the synthesis or integration of the personality.

Where the personality is well integrated one may expect a pervasive influence of the ideal, but where the personality is loosely organized one must expect that many responses will take place in an impulsive fashion quite without being influenced by other response patterns. For proof of this one may turn to the numerous interesting cases presented in recent years on the effect of encephalitis lethargica (sleeping sickness) upon the personality organization. Its characteristic effect is the break-up of what is here termed the personality synthesis. This break-up is usually manifested by the presence of both satisfactory ideals and a conspicuous lack of pervasive effect of those ideals, a lack which was not manifest prior to the illness. The personality seems to have lost much of its integration and to have become in large part a mere congregation of poorly associated functional patterns, of which the ideal is one.

Progress through adolescence then should normally manifest a progressive increase in the pervasiveness of the ideal, as the various functional patterns become linked up with that for the ideal. Theoretically it would be possible for a very considerable amount of integration to be achieved with the ideal remaining a largely isolated pattern, and perhaps this does occur in some instances. Certainly wherever disciplinary measures are used they should not fail to include efforts to bring the undesirable conduct in question into full association with the ideal, in the hope that such a linkage may eventually give the ideal a chance to inhibit such actions in the future.

Loyalty Attitude. Where the ideal is highly pervasive in its influence upon conduct the individual is often said to be loyal to the ideal, or to his ideals. But, as the term loyalty is used in everyday life, it seems to be quite as often used for the designation of an attitude. Some people appear to manifest an attitude of loyalty toward their ideals, as others most certainly do not. An attitude, it will be recalled, is a rather widespread pattern, or neuromuscular set, involving many preparatory movements. It is then quite within the range of possibility, even of probability, that such an attitude of loyalty might be of very large influence upon other response patterns. Where there is an attitude of loyalty toward an ideal, there might be more possibility of interference with the completion of response tendencies not in harmony with the ideal. The consequence would then be that associations, interconnections, between the ideal and other response patterns would be further established and reinforced.

So, through the influence of the loyalty attitude, the ideal may become more and more pervasively influential within the personality organization. Perhaps much of that described above as persistence in following an ideal is essentially the influence of loyalty attitude. Leaders of youth have long laid heavy stress upon ideals and the practice of loyalty to those ideals. They have apparently found that stress upon loyalty is effective. Here is a possible explanation for what these leaders have discovered through practical experience. But such interpretations as these are inevitably speculative in the present state of our knowledge.

Psychoanalytic Conception of the Ideal. Because the peculiar thinking of the psychoanalysts has achieved so extensive an influence, it is wise for the student of these problems to know how this matter of the ideals and their development fits into psychoanalytic thinking about the personality organization. Today the psychoanalysts conceive of the individual as growing from a psychologically very simple organization into one which is very complex. The infant, lacking differentiation, lacking what the behaviorists would term verbalization, manifests psychically only that which the psychoanalysts now term Id. There are all the familiar animal impulses and responses of infancy. There is no clear consciousness of these impulses as being impulses and desires; and there is likewise no control or inhibition. There are no ideals, no standards. Each Id impulse reaches satisfaction unless blocked by the environment or opposed by some other impulse of the same order.

With growth, perceptual and conceptual experience develops; and this means the gradual achievement of the consciousness of the self, the Ego. As this continues, the individual arrives eventually at a concept of what the self may become and of what it should be and do. This is the Ego Ideal. The effect of this Ego Ideal upon behavior is the inhibition of many of the unconscious, Id, impulses. Thus do conflicts within the personality, between the Ego and the Id, come into being. Then has the long program of life's adjustments and maladjustments been entered upon.

But there is yet another step in the growth progress which is here of equal significance at least. It is allied to that which experimental psychologists discovered many years ago and called a determining tendency. As the Ego becomes well developed and there has been much repetition of its effect upon the responses of the individual, there is gradually established a sort of precipitate into the unconscious. Much of the Ego continues to function without being present in consciousness. This the psychoanalysts term the Superego. This Superego, they point out with interest, is unconscious and yet at the same time frequently in conflict with the original, Id, content of the unconscious. Consequently, conflicts may take place in the unconscious as well as between the unconscious and the conscious.[1]

It must be almost immediately apparent that what has just been said of the psychoanalytic system and what has been said above concerning the psychology of ideals are in no functional sense in opposition. They are but two ways of systematically conceiving the same facts of human behavior. One may think if he prefers in terms of the Id and Ego-ideal and Superego, or one may think in terms of the ideal, the determining tendency, habits, etc. The result should be the same.

Relation to Social Complexity. It should also be observed that interpretations of youth in one social setting must not be too hastily applied to youth developing in other and different social settings. Where growth occurs in a complex civilization, where many ideals, customs, mores, traditions, standards, and the like have been established, and where there is no universal agreement upon what every one should do, there the development of ideals is forced and they are certain to be much in conflict with the simple basic generically-human drives or urges of the individual. As there is more to live up to, so there is more

[1] See Sigmund Freud's *The Ego and the Id.*

reason for ideals and more conflict and more effort. But where society is comparatively simple, where customs are relatively few and the ideals of the group not far above the satisfaction of simple desires, there the development of the ideals of the individual (of the Ego-ideal and the Superego) is not likely, except perhaps in the rare instances of moral geniuses, to rise much above the nature and content of the basic urges or drives.

Hence the effect of ideals may be much more conspicuous in the lives of youths in a civilization where there is much to be struggled for that is far above the simple beginnings of life, than is the effect of ideals in a civilization where ideals are few and simple and easy to achieve. For most students of the subject the importance of this will appear chiefly when they come to read some of the older literature on adolescence and growth changes. In the earlier years of genetic psychology, the prevailing method was to study youth in some highly civilized country and then, in terms of the findings, to make sweeping generalizations concerning the inherent nature of the individual. Traits appearing at various stages of development were assumed to be universal, and hence to be inherent and generically human. Differences due to the degree of social conflict were largely ignored. If one reads such books as G. Stanley Hall's stimulating volumes on adolescence and the wealth of magazine articles on youth and child life which appeared during the last years of the nineteenth century and the first decade of the present, one must keep in mind the mistake which was thus made, probably in large part because of the too dominant influence of the evolutionary concept recently taken over from the biologists.[1]

Extra-familial Influences. Numerous studies have indicated the large place which the father and the mother, sometimes other older members of the family, have as sources for the ideals of childhood. The small boy wants to be like his father and the girl like her mother. Sometimes this family source of ideals is a much older brother or sister, or some other adult member of the family circle. But with the dawn of adolescence and all the many changes in life experiences which comes with it, the sources

---

[1] In contrast with this and for a good example of adolescence in a simple social situation, see Margaret Mead's *Coming of Age in Samoa*, New York, 1928.

of material for the content of ideals are less and less frequently found in the home. More and more are they found outside of the family.

The boy now finds his ideal in the person of some popular local athlete, or prizefighter, or engineer, or club leader, or what not; and the girl finds hers in some attractive teacher, scout leader, Sunday School worker, or other young woman of the community. When asked about their ideals, adolescents often report also the names of famous characters in history; but these, it should be observed, likewise indicate the drift to extra-familial sources. The day of idolization of parents has passed. Some students of youth have even gone so far as to say that if parents wish to maintain their influence through the adolescent years of their children they must do it through the habits of thinking established in their children before adolescence is reached. This also places a heavy moral responsibility upon all who are placed in positions of influence with boys and girls coming into adolescence, upon any who are likely to be used as personal ideals.

Here one must not make the mistake of assuming that the frequency of this change means that it is intrinsically determined and therefore inevitable. Individuals do grow up through adolescence into a normal maturity with some parent as the continuing source of their ideals. And this does not mean that there is any abnormal dependency upon the parent. It simply means that the family circumstances were such, that the usual influences pressing toward extra-familial ideals did not operate in the more usual way. Whether or not a swing from the familial to the extra-familial is desirable must depend upon the individual circumstances, upon the nature of the parents and their relationships with the child, and also upon the broader general social situation. The failure to seek extra-familial ideals might in some instances be definitely associated with undesirable parental fixations of attachment; and it might in other instances be not properly characterized as a failure at all, but rather as a development through the changes of adolescence in a thoroughly wholesome manner aided by the guidance of unusually astute and tactful parents.

The motivations for the shift to extra-familial sources have never been well worked out. One may, with propriety suspect, however, that it is but a phase of that progressive emancipation from parental domination which is a part of normal adolescent development. It is also true that children frequently overestimate their parents' abilities as well as the value of their parents' ways of thinking and doing. The accumulation of knowledge and increasing social experience is bound to bring a re-valuation of the parents. As a consequence, they may, in the estimations of youth, for a time fall far below what they were once supposed to be. They come to appear far less desirable as ideals, and others are looked to for the purpose. As the stage of the concrete ideal has not yet passed, there must be in such instances a seeking outside the family circle.

Period of the Concrete Ideal (Hero worship). It is noteworthy, also, that the ideals of early adolescence, and frequently during the whole of adolescence, are in the concrete form. It is some concrete person who is taken over and substituted for the father or mother in the rôle of the ideal. Abstractions are always more difficult to follow with constancy, and the early adolescent has had little experience with ideals in other than personal form. When, however, the abstraction is the principle advocated by some flesh-and-blood person, loyalty is easier and far more attractive. Sometimes even the person appears to be more important than the principle advocated—the principle being accepted because it is advocated by the admired person. And, perhaps, as is often the case, there may be no principle involved at all. It is merely that the person taken as a concrete ideal manifests traits and achievements that are intensely alluring.

This is popularly referred to as "hero worship." Certainly it is devotion to a person as an ideal, and if devotion constitutes worship, then this is a stage of hero worship. But the modern student of religious behavior would be properly critical of such a use of the term. Worship means more than devotion. What is really meant here is loyalty to a hero rather than worship.

There seem to be many differences of degree of accentuation or prominence of this adolescent loyalty to a concrete ideal. Sometimes this devotion to a single person is so prominent as to be known to many associates. If the person taken as a concrete ideal is physically present, and participating in current social activities, the devotion may approach the proportions of a "crush." Often, however, the person serving as a concrete ideal may be at a distance and totally unaware of the use to which his name and reputation are being put. The concrete ideal may even be a character in history, which has somehow attracted attention and is found to satisfy and inspire. In these latter instances the fact of the devotion to the concrete ideal is likely to be less conspicuous and may not be known to other than the most intimate associates. But there are milder degrees of devotion even with the ideal person actually present. There may be less feeling about the matter. The whole thing may be taken quite casually. Frequently, too, the persons selected as heroes are not kept long in that class. Interest shifts; and with it there is a shift to now one and now another person. Some youths appear to have many different concrete ideals in the course of a few years, or in even a shorter time.

It is well, also, to observe that some people never outgrow this stage of development, at least in so far as ideals are concerned. One need not look far to find adults in the middle years of life who are still living, as they have always lived, with concrete ideals. They are "hero-worshippers" even though they can number the years which ordinarily see growth away from devotion to a concrete ideal. Others grow away from this period of the concrete ideal for a time, and then, as a consequence of some period of stress, it may be, slip back or regress to the ways of their youth.

Change to Abstract Ideals. The ordinary course of events seems to be in the form of growth away from the influence of a concrete ideal to the development of abstract ideals. As maturity is approached and there is more knowledge of the world and a greater degree of self-reliance, loyalty to some person as an ideal tends to give way. The person once taken as an ideal is better known or differently judged. Faults are recognized, even in the person once idolized. The self is no longer dreamed of as growing into the pattern of the concrete ideal. The self ideal has become emancipated from such limitations; and that emancipation makes possible the inclusion in the self ideal of any trait or principle abstracted from any person known actually or by reputation. It can even include traits or principles entirely new. Day-dreaming need no longer be in terms of seeing the self in the part of another; it can now be in terms of a self ideal constructed out of the best from any source.

This shifting from the concrete to the abstract ideal is most often met in later adolescence and may properly be thought of as characteristic of that period; but it may be found much earlier in some individuals. Sometimes also it may be delayed until after adolescence, even on into maturity. Where this is the case there is danger of a shocking disillusionment when the person taken for the concrete ideal is discovered after all to be merely human, suffering the weaknesses of humanity.

That the stage of abstraction is not the last in the course of development of behavior with relation to the ideal has already been indicated. Many adults in the course of time find that the self ideal has largely disappeared into formalized habits or ways of doing things.

Male Ideals in Females. A generation ago there was much lament over the alleged fact that girls were far too much influenced by the masculine in the formation of their ideals.[1] The studies then made did seem to indicate that girls had more male ideals than female, but today we are doubtful of the validity of the methods used. The direct questions and the writing of essays about ideal persons may have served more to reveal the range of knowledge of historical characters than it did the nature of the girls' ideals. The history texts of those days had very little in them about great women.

Since that time a notable change has taken place in the writing of histories for school use. Most of them today contain far more about distinguished women. There are special occasions given over to the celebrations of the memory of great women. Much more stress has been placed upon the achievements of womanhood. One can suspect that these changes in educational influences, and with them the many changes which have taken place in the social status of women, may have brought about no little change in the nature of the concrete and abstract ideals of adolescent girlhood, but of facts we have none yet that are satis-

[1] Hall, G. Stanley, *Adolescence*, Vol. II, pp. 387-392.

factory.[1] It may still be that the ideals of adolescent girlhood are much influenced by men and masculine ways. Perhaps this might persist even though history texts were saturated with material about women. Selection of ideals is not merely a matter of that which is available. There are also selective factors within the individual.

Romantic influences are known to be prominent in the motivation of day-dreaming in adolescent girls.[2] Perhaps then when an adolescent girl is asked about her ideals in the course of a research by questionnaire methods she responds in terms of an ideal which has been influenced by romantic motives. She may be giving information about her ideal man, the kind she would like to have fall in love with her. Her self ideal might be somewhat different, if information about it could be obtained without confusion with the romantic motive. It might be much more feminine than her answers make it appear to be; and yet the romantic influence might bring into it much from masculine sources.

If the concrete ideal is always but a step in the course of development soon to be followed by the abstract ideal, the temporary concrete ideal would be a matter of little consequence. The character traits of the person so chosen would be of far greater significance, because it is those traits which might later be abstracted and used in the molding of the abstract self ideal. Many character traits are quite as desirable for the female as for the male. Possibly it might be contended that the long period of masculine concrete ideals for girls has eventuated in the "feminist" movement toward masculinity, as a consequence of the ideals constructed under that influence representing a pattern of traits more commonly found in the male than the female. But this is highly speculative, and there are other and probably more significant motivations for the changes which have come about in the lives of women.

[1] One study does show a falling off in the number of male characters chosen as ideals by girls, but the numbers of cases at ages above 15 years are few. See Macaulay, Eve, "Some Social and Sex Differences Shown in Children's Choice of Ideals," *Forum. Educ.*, 1925, 3, 105-114. It is also interesting to observe that when Lorine Pruette asked her adolescent respondents to name their preferred heroine, several gave the names of male characters. See her *Women and Leisure*, chap. 8.

[2] Pruette, Lorine, *Women and Leisure*, chap. 8.

Perfectionistic Ideals. Indispensable as ideals certainly are for the healthy personality they are at the same time not infrequently the cause of no little distress, and even indirectly of distortions in development. These troubles come through what has been so happily characterized as perfectionistic ideals.[1] These may be of either the concrete or the abstract variety.

In concrete perfectionistic ideal cases, we have first the familiar story of the adolescent who has been strongly attracted for some rather vague reason by the apparent personality of one who appears to be quite worthy of emulation. This person becomes the hero, the concrete ideal; and for a time all goes well. The influence may appear even to be desirable. Then, usually because of the lack of sufficient personal contact, phantasy thinking enters in. The products of the phantasy thinking are projected upon the hero. This may be most complimentary to the person so selected, but it is emphatically misleading. A highly exalted and largely fictitious conception of the personality of the concrete ideal is developed. Perceptions are so falsified by this idealization that the true individual is wholly unknown. He is looked up to as little less than perfection itself.

With increasing knowledge of life and other growth changes, especially the development of greater self-reliance, there comes a time inevitably when the hero is discovered to be no more than human, to have faults or imperfections which make the actual, after all, far below the false perfectionistic conceptual ideal that had been constructed. Such a discovery may be a crushing experience. The disillusionment, the discovery that the hero has feet of clay and is not nearly so godlike as supposed, may bring acute disappointment, disgust and depression. It may be a thoroughly bewildering experience. There may be that which is best described as a "loss of faith in all mankind." To say that the youth should have known better helps little. There are many things youth does not know and frequently one of them is the necessity for caution in the judgment of others. Such experiences are obviously the product of normal functions and normal growth changes taking place without proper control from within or without. That they can ever be entirely prevented is doubtful.

---

[1] Elliott, G. L., *Understanding the Adolescent Girl*, pp. 76-81.

The acuteness of the emotional upset in such instances must be dependent upon the degree of the contrast between the actual and the assumed, and the suddenness with which the discovery is made. Where the contrast is great and the disillusionment sudden, the emotional reaction will be intense. Many, however, experience a more progressive alteration in their perception of the hero and so avoid the worst features of the change. The reconstruction then takes place as merely a part of that experience already described of shifting from a concrete to an abstract ideal.

Perfectionistic ideal troubles may come quite as well from exalted abstract ideals for the self. If the conduct is impulsive and erratic, as adolescent conduct is so likely to be, there will be many occasions for observing the contrast between the ideal and the actual. Judgments of the self made in terms of the exalted ideal may be highly disparaging to the self. The difference between the actual conduct and the ideal may be very discouraging. Perhaps herein lies one explanation for the periods of melancholy so often observed in adolescence. Much meditation about these failures to live up to the ideal can produce not only inferiority feelings, but also the development of inferiority complexes. The discouragement may even develop into hopelessness.

The educator and counsellor is here confronted by a rather delicate problem. One hesitates to say that the ideal is too high, or that the ideal should be scaled down nearer to that which is possible, although in some instances it might be better so. The trouble may, however, turn out to be not so much in the exalted nature of the ideals but in the expectations of the youth. He may be judging himself, and disparagingly, because he expects to achieve the ideal too soon. Some ideals can only be approximated through a long period of years. This young people are prone to overlook in their haste. So solutions of the troubles from perfectionistic ideals may often be found in a broader outlook upon life and a better understanding of the self, to the end that too much may not be expected of the self too soon.

Attention has also been called to the possibly unfortunate effects upon the person selected by young people as a concrete ideal. The psychology of the person selected as hero by the hero-worshipper deserves more thoughtful consideration than it has probably ever received. Such a person is often also still in the changes of adolescence. Early adolescents frequently pick on some older adolescent as the personification of all they consider desirable and worthy of emulation. Scout leaders and other young workers with youth are thus forced into awkward situations. Realizing that he is being idolized and conscious of the responsibility involved, as well as of the fact that he is really not so ideal a person as his followers assume him to be, there is the almost inevitable feeling in one so selected of obligation to play the part expected. This pretense aids of course in maintaining, or even in the further development of, the false conception of the hero in the mind of the hero-worshipper. Thus is cultivated that which is certain to end in the disaster of disillusionment. But the effect of "acting a part" upon the actor may be equally disastrous. It constitutes essentially a maladjustment to life. The person who attempts to live a life of pretense has immediately the consciousness of guarding against slips in conduct and the possibility of embarrassing discoveries. Here is exactly the sort of psychic soil upon which conflicts and complexes and their kind grow and flourish. It is very different from an honest effort to live up to a self ideal. The leader of youth thus has his own way complicated by his commendable efforts for the welfare of others.

Contribution to Personality. Probably few features of adolescent behavior have the possibilities for contributing to the healthy development of personality that the right kind of ideals may supply. To whatever extent the ideal determines judgments of value in human affairs and influences choices between impulses, to that extent does it contribute to the integration of the personality. The youth with a well-established ideal for the self who is seeking the realization of that ideal in his own life must pick and choose accordingly among the many possibilities for activity, for study, for social relations, and so on. As this continues through the years it makes for coherence of selection and habit formation, which is obviously the best course toward integration.

It is conceivable that some kinds of ideals might not make much contribution in this direction. If the dream of a youth were that of becoming like some unstable, erratic, impulsive person possessed of what is popularly termed the "artistic temperament," it is not likely that such an ideal would contribute much to personality integration. Rather would it aid in the cultivation of the opposite condition.

The integrative influence of an ideal might, as has been suggested above, be not a little aided by an accompanying attitude of loyalty. An associated ideal of being persistent in the effort to realize the ideal for the self should also contribute much in the same direction so far as we now know. All these features appear to function in the direction of orderly living, selection in terms of a purpose, constancy in preparation and steadiness of application, the values of which are beyond question. Ignorant as we still are of much of the psychology of ideals and their functioning, we are nevertheless able to bring together enough to fully justify the long-standing emphases which have been placed upon the importance of ideals, and of the right kind of ideals, in the life of the adolescent.

CHAPTER VII

FACTORS IN SOCIAL ADJUSTMENT

Students of genetic psychology as well as of abnormal behavior
have in recent years thrown an ever-increasing emphasis upon
the importance of social adjustment and maladjustment. The
complete psychology of any social adjustment or maladjustment
has, however, never been entirely worked out. Perhaps it never
can be. As one seeks to disentangle the various factors involved
in any such experience, one finds it impossible ever to reach an
end to the task, because every adjustment when traced back into
its roots is found to involve all that has gone into the making
of the particular personality. What an adolescent personality is
at any given moment is the product of all that has gone before.
And this means not only all of that with which the individual
was endowed by nature, but also all of that which has been produced through response to the many social pressures encountered.

By the time adolescence is reached the social influences have already forced the establishment of certain ideals, as was presented
in the preceding chapter. But the social pressures to which every
child and youth is subjected effect also the building of a concept
of what the self is, a concept which has frequently much to do
with the present behavior of any adolescent. Somewhat more is
known about the earlier development of the self concept and that
must be reviewed because it gives a valuable glimpse into the
content of the self which is carried over into adolescence. Experiences with the self in social situations stir many emotions.
Habits concerning these become established which for convenience are designated as self-regarding sentiments. They must
be as well understood as is at present possible. So, too, do the

138

social experiences of growing up build into the personality a great number of social attitudes which factor largely in all reactions to social situations, in all social adjustments. From time to time much has been made of the so-called altruism of youth. Unless one prefers the dubious interpretation in terms of instincts, this must also be a product of the social experience, perhaps in part indirectly through the content of the self concept and the self-regarding sentiment and the social attitudes earlier established.

It is these features of the personality, which appear to have been molded by the social experiences of life, that are to be considered in this chapter. Others will be presented in the following chapters.

Self Concept. It may be necessary to remind some readers that this discussion must be confined entirely to that concept of the self which has grown out of individual personal experience, sometimes called the empirical self. There is also the concept of a metaphysical self. Some philosophers and some philosophically minded psychologists believe that it is necessary for the clarity of thinking to posit the existence behind all experience of an ego or metaphysical self. But by definition this ego or self is outside of experience and is therefore not describable. If it exists, it exists; and the psychologist can do nothing more about it. If it does not exist, well, then the suspicions of some psychologists and some philosophers are justified.

It is the empirical self with which we are here concerned, and it will be ordinarily designated as simply the self or the self concept. Like all other concepts it has grown out of sensory and perceptual experience; and like all other concepts it is subject to change, as the concept is affected by new sensory and perceptual and imaginary experiences. The origins, the influences which have affected it, and the present content of the self concept cannot be easily underestimated in their importance. What a youth thinks of himself influences his interpretations of present situations, and thus in turn affects the course of his imagination, his emotional reactions, and his overt responses. Some insight into what a youth thinks of himself is indispensable to the interpretation of his present personality; and such knowledge contributes not a little to the possibilities of predicting the course of future development.

It is assumed that every self concept began very early in infancy. Where it changed from isolated sensory or perceptual experiences into a genuine concept no one knows for sure. That its first content involved primarily the physical person is also generally accepted. When the baby amuses his parents by discovering and examining carefully his hands and feet and ears and eyes and hair and so on, the baby is laying the basis for a self concept. No doubt also organic and kinesthetic sensations contribute a very large part of this early core of the self concept.[1] Then follow quickly many other influences. The possession of material things, clothing, and toys, and pets, and so on, the being talked to and addressed by pet names and expressions of affection, and as soon as the beginnings of ideals appear they must also contribute largely to the molding of the meaning of the self concept. The joys and sorrows of childhood and such climactic experiences as being taken on journeys or staying with others for a time, and, above all, of starting school with all its new world of adventure and revelation—all of these and the myriad of associated events must likewise contribute their share to the self concept.

The many changes through which the developing and changing self concept must pass before adolescent years are reached have not only never been mapped but they have been barely even guessed at. Only two significant phases or episodes in the development of the self concept have been revealed and neither of these has been very thoroughly studied.

It is certain that a very large percentage of children, some are daring enough to say all, pass through a period of thinking, and sometimes believing to a considerable degree, that they are not the children of those with whom they live and call their parents. The questioning of over nine hundred high school and younger college students revealed that twenty-eight percent of them could immediately recall having had experience with such a fantasy.[2] There are good reasons for thinking that this obtained percentage is much smaller than the true percentage of frequency. The

---

[1] Hall, G. Stanley, "Some Aspects of the Early Sense of Self," *Amer. J. Psychol.*, 1898, 9, 351-395.
[2] Conklin, Edmund S., "The Foster-Child Fantasy," *Amer. J. Psychol.*, 1920, 31, 59-76.

respondents were asked for their immediate recall only; no time was allowed for recollection and investigation. Many subsequently reported that by one means or another they had discovered that they had had experience with the fantasy, although they had at first been unable to recall such and had answered no to the question. Also, there is the probability, as psychoanalysts have pointed out, that many who had had experience with the fantasy had suffered a repression of all memory of the experience by the age when they were asked about it. Therefore the true frequency is probably very large, how large no one knows on the basis of any carefully conducted study; but of the twenty-eight percent one may feel certain in so far as the group studied is representative.

When asked for the age at which they had experienced this foster-child fantasy the respondents reported variously but the central tendency was somewhere approaching the twelfth year. A few reported it in the years which might be termed early adolescent, and a very few said that it still troubled them; but the evidence points to its being primarily a pre-adolescent experience.

By far the largest number described it as a mere passing fancy, but it must be noted that it could not have been very lightly passed by because it was still remembered several years afterward. Fifteen percent imagined themselves to be foundlings or orphans, to have come from an inferior social status; three percent imagined themselves to have come from homes of a like social status to the one of their imaginary adoption; and eighteen percent had thought of themselves as having come from a superior, sometimes very superior, parentage. Some had believed, and had believed it thoroughly. A little over twenty-five percent of the group reporting experience of the fantasy said that they had believed it. More girls (31.6 percent) than boys (19.5 percent) reported this experience of belief. Many said that it had a very definite effect upon their conduct. These conduct effects varied all the way from mere investigation, seeking of proof and inquiry, to instances of actual running-away from home. Recollections of the duration of the fantasy experience varied greatly. Many of course said that so far as they could recall it was of very brief duration, and yet forty percent reported the experience as continuing for two years or more.

Thus when one is attempting to achieve some understanding of the conduct of a particular adolescent boy or girl it is necessary to keep in mind the possibility that the self concept may have just come through the foster-child fantasy experience or that it may still involve some lingering remnants of the belief or suspicion. Of how this may affect the attitudes toward parents and the conduct in relationship to them we know little that is positive; but it is safe to guess that it might be the cause of an otherwise puzzling alienation from the parents, or of a marked devotion to them, according to the nature and degree of the remnants of the fantasy remaining, probably also to the nature and degree of the experience when at its height. It is equally safe to guess that the patterns established by the experience with this fantasy may have their effect upon the direction and content of the day-dreams of adolescence, although the subject has never been systematically studied to that extent. That it is one of the roots or influences coming before and influencing the adolescent stage of the self concept development in a very large number of young people is now beyond question.

The other growth phase or feature of the self concept to which some attention has been attracted is even less known by systematic study. It is only known that some children, perhaps more girls than boys, pass through a period of considerable duration in which there is a sort of duality of the self. The classical presentation of this is to be found in a little book entitled *Una Mary* and written by Una A. Hunt (New York, 1914).[1] In this book the author tells the story of the development of her own self concept. As a child she apparently had two rather distinct empirical self concepts. One was composed of external experiences, those with her parents and the maid and the other people and things of her little world. The other was built out of her thoughts and feelings related thereto and also the many experiences with the people and things of her imaginary play world. The two selves were so real to her that they bore different names.

[1] G. Stanley Hall, in a moment of characteristic enthusiasm, said that he would rather have been the author of this book than of his two huge volumes on adolescence. A literary use of this feature will be found in H. G. Wells's *The Bulpington of Blup*.

This went on for a number of years and then as puberty approached a fusion gradually took place into the one self concept such as all ordinary adults experience.

No one knows how frequently this occurs in the development of self concepts. It would be worth knowing. Of three hundred and nine college students interested in psychology who were asked about this, eighty-one, or 26 percent, could immediately recall an experience which they said was quite like that of Una Mary. There was apparently no significant sex difference. Of these, fourteen, or more than 4 percent, said that it was not a matter of history with them, but that the fusion into a single concept had never yet taken place. Twenty-eight percent of the above group reported that they had observed the same phenomenon in others. In general it was attributed to pubescent or immediately pre-pubescent years.

Is this the way the self concept ordinarily develops? Does it always begin by the traces of perceptual experience constellating first around two, or perhaps more, focal items? And do these gradually fuse into one constellation or pattern? Are these who can recall the Una-Mary-like experience of it merely the children in whom the development of a single constellation has been for some reason delayed into a longer process? And do the others know nothing of it because the fusion took place too early for present recollection? One would like to know. It seems possible. And if such were the facts these few cases which do come now and then to our attention would be much easier to understand.

It is certain, however, that this experience of duality in the course of the development of the self concept is a fact in the lives of not a few children, and that occasionally the fusion is delayed until some time in adolescence or even later. That means then that we have here another item which must be kept in mind in attempting to understand the behavior and peculiarities of any given personality problem. The lingering duality may be the cause of otherwise puzzling inconsistencies of conduct. Awareness of this duality may cause the possessor to feel queer and different; and these feelings may motivate peculiar conduct. Perhaps the duality has but recently passed and there are lingering recollections of the days of the duality. Such might motivate

self-protecting behavior; and again it might be the cause of peculiarly free and uninhibited behavior, depending upon the attitude toward the experience which had been set up.

Self-regarding Sentiment. For this useful concept we are
largely indebted to McDougall.[1] No one knows for certain that
there is such a thing as that designated by the term self-regarding
sentiment. No experimental studies have demonstrated its existence. But the behavior of human beings in situations which involve that which has been called the self concept above, as this
behavior is observed by thoughtful people in the contacts of
everyday life, leads easily to the acceptance of McDougall's self-
regarding-sentiment concept as a very useful interpretative
device.

Caution should be exercised here against permitting the term
sentiment to imply the designation of a conscious feeling or emotional experience. Such to be sure is the meaning ordinarily
conveyed by the term sentiment in everyday life, but such is not
the technical meaning of the term as it is here used. In Mc-
Dougall's thinking the term sentiment designates a complicated
neurone pattern, the product of much stimulation and response,
which connects the self concept (probably cerebro-cortical) with
certain emotional response patterns (probably thalamic). As a
consequence of the establishment of the pattern, it is very easy for
anything which arouses the self concept to arouse by way of the
sentiment pattern these associated emotional reactions.

The emotions so easily aroused in connection with the self
concept, because of the presence of this self-regarding sentiment
or pattern, are, ordinarily, elation (positive self-feeling) and feeling of subjection or inferiority (negative self-feeling).[2] And the
degree to which each is aroused or the ease with which each is
aroused, goes back to the content of the self concept and to the
sort of experiences the self concept has had with the world of
the personality's social contacts.

In the abstract this may appear somewhat vague; but, when
translated into the concrete, it quickly becomes no more than a
formulation of the everyday experience of most thoughtful ob-

---

[1] McDougall, Wm., *Social Psychology,* chap. 5.
[2] The emotional terms here used are those later presented by McDougall
in his *Outline of Psychology,* chap. XI. The older terms appear in paren-
theses.

servers. Every one knows the youth who is annoyingly self-
satisfied. He is really more than merely satisfied with himself.
He is positively pleased, delighted, elated over himself. All this
is commonly attributed to his "thinking so well of himself." But
the student of psychology knows at once that it is far more than
mere thinking. To such a person it is obvious that this cocky
youth has a concept of himself which has grown out of such contacts in life as to make it rich with meanings of his own superiority and high abilities. Of course, such a concept presents a
background for perceptive experience as will force the interpretation of anything and everything which happens into a mold that
is favorable to himself. And all this has long been associatively
connected with pleasant emotions. Now and then some one may
"break through his tough hide" with remarks or actions which
will be perceived as questioning his assumptions of high ability
and superiority, and so long as such perceptions or thoughts
linger there may be the unpleasant feeling or emotion of inferiority. But the nature of the habitual interpretations of life has
been such that the habit pattern established, the sentiment, will
arouse elation far more easily and in greater intensity than inferiority.

Again every one knows the opposite kind of youth, the kind
that annoy by their hesitancy to use the abilities we know they
have. They seem to be constantly apologetic for living, and so
lacking in self-assertiveness that they seldom even give expression
to their apologetic tendencies. One suspects immediately a very
different sort of self concept. Here the concept must have grown
out of experience which has supplied a meaning content of incapacity, ignorance, inexperience, social inacceptability, inferiority, lack of opportunity, and the like. Such a self concept must
inevitably color the perceptions of life in like manner. And living with such a concept and such perceptions will have established an associative pattern to the emotional reactions which
will easily and intensely arouse the unpleasant feeling or emotion
of inferiority, the negative self-feeling. Now and then something
will happen which will force a more favorable interpretation of
the self and this would stir the other self-regarding emotion, elation; but such instances are comparatively few, and such emo-

tional reactions give little coloring to the general flow of emotional experience.

Between these two extreme forms of self-regarding sentiment there are obviously a vast number of possible gradations. Most of the people we meet are somewhere in between, if classified in terms of their self concepts and their self-regarding sentiments. Perhaps some day a measure will be developed by which a person may be scored for his position on such a scale; but at present our notions about these extremes and the gradations between are but tentative and still await experimental verification and measurement.

That most self-regarding sentiments tend to the arousal of yet other emotions than elation and inferiority seems highly probable. Recall again the two extreme forms just described. The cocky, prideful, self-assertive youth often displays no little anger. Apparently the world does not always appreciate him at the value of his self-estimate and the perception of such failure or neglect stirs anger. Such experiences seem to have altered the self concept but little. They have merely had the effect of establishing in the self-regarding sentiment pattern such features as are necessary to the easy arousal of anger.

It is further conceivable, especially as one moves down the line a little and thinks of other youths whose self concept and associated patterns are not quite so exalted, that the experiences of life might be such as to bring some fear into the experiences of the self. Perhaps there are thoughts of possible failure and the distressing contrast which such would produce; perhaps associates are harsh and unappreciative and there may be touches of fear lest the proper opportunities be not forthcoming; and perhaps there may be a good many other kinds of situations which when related to a self would stir more or less of the fear reaction. Thus it is more than likely that many if not most self-regarding sentiments tend to the arousal not only of elation and inferiority but also of anger and fear. At the other extreme of the self concept the sentiment would in all probability have features which would stir more and more prominently the fear reaction.

If the day ever comes when these sentiments can be classified and graded and described with differentiating terms, we may feel certain that a vast number of differences will have to be handled.

The many different possibilities of combination of tendencies to the arousal of these four different emotions, the possibility that there may be self-regarding sentiments which involve yet other emotions, and the influences upon these sentiment patterns of the many differences possible in the self concept—all force upon one the conviction that there may be an almost infinite number of differences in the self-regarding sentiments in adolescence. How these change with social experience, and how they change as the content of the self concept changes, must some day be worked out in detail; but for the present, one can at least recognize the existence of such differences and the possibility of such changes, and use the concept tentatively both for the interpretation of individual personalities and for the setting up of programs for the modification of these personalities in desirable growth directions.

Attitudes. The attitudes are another class or group of functional patterns which contribute largely to the present nature of any personality. After a prolonged controversy over the way in which the term attitude should be defined there is now a tendency to think of it as meaning a neuromuscular set. It involves all that was formerly meant by the term determining tendency, and somewhat more. When one responds with, or assumes, or falls into, a certain attitude toward something, there must be a nervous pattern involved. There is certainly a demonstrable pattern of overt muscle tensions; and there is ample reason for thinking that in addition to these overt muscle responses there are also many incipient or preparatory tensions or movements of the skeletal muscles.

Many examples are to be found, for human beings from childhood up are constantly manifesting attitudes. Suppose, for example, that some one says, What do you think of so-and-so as a candidate for the Presidency? Immediately we respond by a shift in body posture, a change in the positions of the arms and hands sufficient sometimes to be called a gesture and to convey considerable meaning, and by carefully watching one's self under such circumstances one quickly becomes aware of many muscle tensions and relaxations much too slight for any observer to perceive but which we recognize as being preparatory movements. If they went out into overt action, they would constitute an emphatic pantomimic expression of approval or disapproval of the person proposed for the candidacy. With these of course are our thoughts and our tendencies to speech. The whole thing constitutes a huge neuromuscular set toward the question and the questioner.

Such an attitude may be a very complicated response indeed. Perhaps it may really be the fusion of two attitudes, or soon become such. Perhaps the first attitudinal response was favorable to the name proposed; but then comes the thought that the questioner is probably opposed and that his political affiliations are such that a frank expression of opinion would be unwise and with those thoughts another attitude, of guarding carefully, is aroused and displaces the first, or modifies it, or is perhaps fused with it. Certainly our expressions in speech at any given time may not be a direct expression of our attitude. We may be most courteous to some one in speech and be aware of the attitude of wishing them anywhere but in our personal presence.

It soon becomes clear that an attitude is but a certain kind of habit pattern, and as such it is the product of learning; and that means in turn that our psychology of learning is applicable to their formation. New attitudes must be at first combinations of old ones, with slow accretions from newly acquired possibilities of response. Old attitudes are modified by the gradual loss of some parts or features and the addition of others. They are the product of social experience. Doubtless they are at first largely a matter of parental training. Subsequently they become modified and added to by all that manifold of experiences arising outside of the home. Our prejudices, preferences, religious and political judgments, and most of our opinions are determined in very large part by these attitudes. Men of science and philosophy in whatever field constantly seek to avoid them and their influence upon their conclusions; but it is an open question if they ever entirely succeed in doing so.

The relationship of attitudes to emotions is not entirely clear although it might help greatly to think of the attitude as involving primarily and predominantly the striated or voluntary musculature of the body. The term emotion might be reserved for the responses which involve primarily or predominantly the unstriated muscles and the glandular functions. Perhaps an attitude is but part of that which will become an emotion when the unstriated muscles and the glands join in with their telling effect. But whatever this relationship turns out to be, the fact remains that we have these experiences, which under ordinary circumstances we would not term emotional, which appear to us to be primarily cognitive and muscular (striated). It is these which are now designated as attitudes.

That these attitudes must be influenced in their building by the nature of the self concept and the emotions aroused through the self-regarding sentiment seems to be certain. Surely the attitudes toward life in its various presentations would be very different in the youth whose self concept is that of a very superior person from the attitudes which would be influential in the personality of the youth who constantly and habitually thinks of himself as inferior. Hence it becomes necessary to add attitudes to the self concept and the self-regarding sentiment as factors within the personality which may be used for the explanation of the behavior of the personality.

It should also be recognized that our attitudes may be influenced by other constellations as well. Memories of books we have read, of lectures and sermons we have heard, of pictures we have seen, of conversations to which we have listened or in which we have participated, of our travel experiences and a host of others constitute memory constellations which influence not only our perceptive and attentive behavior, but also the attitudinal responses at any given time. Some may prefer here to call such constellations complexes, as do the psychoanalysts,[1] and say that our attitudes are influenced by our complexes. In that case we should find ourselves interpreting the attitudes of the personalities we meet in terms of their complexes, and we might be right in doing so. But there are those who think that the term complex should be reserved for those constellations which cause trouble within the personality, which lie behind the more serious and chronic maladjustments. They think that for the sake of clarity of thought and expression the term should be reserved for the abnormal constellation. For our present purposes, however, it is far more important to keep in mind the fact that

---

[1] On some of the difficulties involved in the use of this term see the symposium on the complex in the *British Journal of Psychology* for 1922.

these constellations, or complexes, or both, frequently determine the special nature of particular attitudes. As such they are important.

In recent years a number of systematic attempts have been made to develop measures for the determination of degrees of individual differences in certain chosen attitudes. It has been observed that an attitude toward any given subject must vary between two extremes, that of complete acceptation and approval and that of complete rejection and disapproval. The attitudes toward war may, for example, vary between the extremest form of pacificism and the most jingoistic form of militancy. Attitudes toward the church may vary from the most complete approval and support to an equally complete rejection of it as an utterly outworn and worthless institution. Attitudes toward the law, the tariff, the Democratic party, the Republican party, censorship, the Chinese, the Japanese, the Germans, the negroes, athletics, fraternities, a college education, and a host of others may be similarly considered and measured.[1]

So far the work here has been largely directed toward the development of tools with which to measure attitude differences. The use of them for the study of how attitudes change through adolescent years remains to be made. The few reports now available indicate very slight changes from year to year. Thurstone and Chave found with their measure of attitude toward the church that there was very little change from freshman to senior year in the groups which they studied. Lockhart's study revealed a most interesting progressive approximation toward those of expert lawyers in attitudes toward the law from the fourth grade up into the high school; but high school seniors, especially those of higher mental ability, manifested a notable deviation. Others

[1] Lockhart, E. G., "The Attitudes of Children Toward Law," *Univ. of Iowa Stud.*, Stud. in Char., 1930, 3, No. 1.

Neuman, G. B., "A Study of International Attitudes of High School Students with Special Reference to Those Nearing Completion of Their High School Courses," *Col. Univ. Contrib. to Educ.* (No. 239), New York, 1926.

Thurstone, L. L., and Chave, E. J., *The Measurement of Attitude*, Chicago, 1929.

—— "Attitudes Can be Measured," *Amer. J. Sociol.*, 1928, 33, 529-554.

Vetter, G. B., "The Measurement of Social and Political Attitudes and the Related Personality Factors," *J. Abn. & Soc. Psychol.*, 1930, 25, 140-189.

have revealed marked race prejudice, and the very familiar willingness to base opinions upon very little knowledge.[1]

It is further important to recognize that while comparisons of
different age groups by these tests are valuable, the mere fact that
averages do not change much from year to year does not mean
that individual personalities may not undergo much attitudinal
change. Large numbers of individuals must be followed by measurement methods from year to year in order to discover the characteristic group changes of attitudes, but for the understanding of
the growing of personality it will be necessary to understand how
these attitudinal changes are related to changes in the self concept, in the self-regarding sentiment, and in the constellations of
memories. In other words, the relationship of any given set of
attitudes must be seen in terms of its relationship to the residua
from former experiences of all kinds in that individual. The student of adolescence is called upon to interpret and to prescribe
re-educative training for particular behavior problems. Consequently general changes of groups must be kept in the background as bases for interpretation in special individual cases.

It must also be true that attitudes are influenced in their pattern and in the cause of their formation by whatever instincts or
drives or urges there may be within the personality. If there be
such a thing as a collecting instinct, then the attitude which a
given personality manifests in the presence of some unusual foreign stamps, or the eggs of some rare bird, must be an attitude
which has grown out of instinctive behavior. The attitude toward the stamps and the attitude toward the birds' eggs may be
in some details slightly different. Perhaps the person involved
has been giving more attention, due to the accident of environmental circumstances, to stamps than to birds' eggs. But in each
case they are the attitudes of a collector; and if he began life
with a collecting instinct then these attitudes must be traceable
to that instinct in their growth history. One may of course, and
with much reason, reject the concept of a collecting instinct in
the human being; but if one admits the existence of any instincts

1 Carlson, H. S., "Information and Certainty in Political Opinions: A Study
     of University Students During a Campaign," *Univ. of Iowa Stud.*, Stud.
     in Char., 1931, 4, No. 1.
   See also the extensive study of college student attitudes by Katz, D., and
     Allport, F. H., *Students' Attitudes*, Syracuse, 1931.

or drives or urges these must be looked to as the roots of attitudinal responses. Attitudes in one sex toward all persons of the other sex and perhaps also of the same sex before and after pubertal development illustrate very well the fact that an instinct or an urge has its influence upon the nature of the attitudes. Much that has been called rivalry in the later years of childhood and through much of adolescence and which for a long time was attributed to the maturation of an instinct may be far better interpreted as an attitude established through the motivation of conduct by a will-to-power drive.

As the reader must already know, it was for a long time customary to interpret adolescence as a period when many instincts came to maturity. It was even thought desirable and to some extent possible to determine the modal age for the nascence, as it was called, of each instinct. But as the instinct concept fell into disrepute and our knowledge of attitudes began to grow, psychologists found it far more satisfactory to interpret in terms of attitudes much that had formerly been attributed to specific instincts.

Thus the appearance of altruistic tendencies in the last years of childhood and the early years of adolescence can be better comprehended in terms of the acquisition and growth of attitudes. The finding of one's satisfactions and the outlet for one's interests primarily in the activities of life, in the outside contacts, is described as extrovertive. Some attribute this to the maturation of inherently determined tendencies. But they can quite as well be interpreted in terms of attitudes. And the converse likewise. The finding of satisfactions within one's self and the satisfactory outlet for self-expression through the things of the mind may be called introversion and be attributed to intrinsic determination; but it may also be interpreted as the development through the vicissitudes of life of a set of attitudes so different as to make them, or the personality within which they are growing, conspicuous and characterizable by them. Vocational interests, also, as they grow and become established, build attitudes. These may not all be attitudes of approval. They may be attitudes of disapproval and rejection. And there may be many degrees of partial approval and partial rejection.

Birth of Altruism. In the language of Hall, every individual is normally born twice: once as an individual, and once as a member of the species.[1] Hall had been attracted by the self-centered behavior of childhood; and in contrast with that he had also observed the instances of magnificently self-sacrificing conduct so often observed and so often described in memorials. He liked to think of these as a birth and a rebirth of the self. Hall had had a theological training before he went into physiology and psychology, and the lingering influences of that training are to be seen here, as often elsewhere, in the language which he chose for the expression of his ideas. In likening the change to a sort of second birth or blossoming, there is a biological implication as well; for Hall, that almost invariably meant intrinsic determination. While he attributed much to the influence of the environment, it is easy to see that he was also fond of thinking that there was a push from within whenever he sought to explain adolescent behavior.

This notion of new urges or pushes maturing within the personality dating back to germ-plasm determination still lingers in the minds of many. Perhaps this is due in large part to the vagueness of our knowledge of these growth changes. We can see changes taking place sometimes suddenly under our very observation, yet we are unable to detect the nature of what is going on, and it is then easy to think in the vague terms of instinct and emergence.

But today we do have some means by which it is possible to push the analysis of these growth changes somewhat farther. First of all it should be observed that the re-birth figure does not work out very well. Hall himself had recognized that the fine altruistic impulses and actions of adolescence were not the dominant traits of even those personalities in which they were manifest. These same personalities frequently manifested surprisingly inconsistent selfish actions. In one and the same adolescent, then, as every one who lives with adolescents knows very well, one may expect to see both selfish and altruistic conduct separated by but the briefest of intervals. It is here that the re-birth figure breaks down. If the individual has been born anew, into a new sort of self and social conduct, then why the inconsist-

[1] Hall, G. Stanley, *Adolescence*, Vol. 2, p. 304.

encies? Is the second birth incomplete or recurrent? Is there some sort of return or regression? Obviously the figure is inadequate. It does not fit either the facts of psychology or what we know of the growth of the nervous system and its functioning.

The psychology of attitudes fits the facts far better, and fits more of the facts. The world in which the average child grows up is a child-centered world. The life of the home centers pretty largely, especially if there are but one or two children, about the health and the growth and the achievements and the happiness of the child. The child is praised and rewarded in a myriad of ways. As soon as the child is old enough to go out, even a little, into the institutions of society there is at first little other than a continuation of this emphasis upon individual achievement. In Sunday School and public school and playground, there is a like stress upon rewards for having learned this or recited that or achieved this grade or that rank. Stars and honors and marks—all kinds of rewards center on the child's own achievement. And at the same time all of this child-centered activity is establishing attitudes toward the self and toward others which characterize the general course of the child personality as one of self-centeredness. Even the little altruistic acts, the little kindnesses of childhood behavior, in so far as they are recognized at all are recognized as commendable and praiseworthy of the child himself. The attitudes must all be so patterned in consequence as to be intimately related to the growth and achievement and satisfactions of the individual self.

But, by the dawn of adolescent years, the seeking of individual satisfaction and achievement drives the growing boy or girl more and more out of the home into life with other becoming-adolescent boys and girls. Then social pressures begin to operate strongly, and in a direction quite different from the acts which would dominate if the attitudes acquired in earlier years should regularly result in overt action. The social situations are becoming such as to demand self-subordinating if not self-sacrificing conduct. The social situation puts the group first and not the individual. Survival in the group, self-realization in extra-familial situations, forces the establishment of many new patterns of response and the inhibition or suppression or neglect of old ways of responding. The inevitable consequence is the gradual establishment of new attitudes toward the situations and contacts of life; and these attitudes are such as to denote a considerable change in the dominant features of the personality. Through these attitude changes the personality is becoming much more other-centered and much less self-centered.

In terms of such attitudinal changes the *inconsistencies of adolescent social behavior* are much easier to understand. The inconsistencies are manifestations of the transition. New ways of acting are being acquired. Old ways are still present and occasionally function. Sometimes the youth behaves in terms of the new and sometimes in terms of the old. Hence in one adolescent personality there may occur within a short time a very wide range of actions, some that are laudable in the highest degree and others that are puerile and childish and self-centered to the point of being disgusting. With the progress of adolescence and the gradual achievement of a social adjustment in the larger world outside the home, the extent of the inconsistency subsides. It may be reduced to a minimum by the achievement of full maturity, in which case we have the fully socialized adult living with a fine consciousness of his responsibilities to his family, his community, his state, his nation, and the world of mankind. Many, perhaps most, never achieve that completely. They carry over into maturity some of the incompatible attitudes of adolescent years, and so remain to some extent inconsistent in their social relations all their lives. They may even go into maturity dominated by the carry-over of many attitudes and ways of action from childhood. Such will be met with frequently in the discussions of delinquency, of parental attachments, and of abnormalities.

Since the pioneer studies of Hall and those whom he inspired there have not been many in this special field of investigation. Such as there are indicate the same altruistic impulses manifested by the earlier ones. H. H. Moore in an investigation published in 1920 [1] reported the responses of nearly a thousand junior and senior high school students to a simple questionnaire. Of these respondents, scattered through sixteen different cities, 59 percent reported experience with such altruistic impulses or urges. Some

[1] "Altruistic Impulses of Older High School Students," *Educ. Rev.*, 1920, 59, 271-295.

had been impressed by the pathos of vice and had been inspired to devote themselves to its elimination. Others had been touched by the dirt and filth in which the poor they had seen lived, and were inspired to activities which would bring cleanliness within the easy reach of all. Others would abolish strikes and the consequent suffering; others would care for sick babies; and so on and so on through a very familiar list.

These are all highly philanthropic, as is obvious, and thus must be the more extreme manifestations of the newer attitudes which are in process of establishment. If the census had included a collection of the less spectacular as well, the new group loyalties and the little sacrificial acts for the sake of the team, the club, the fraternity, the school, for friends and associates, and so on, there would no doubt have been produced a percentage far in excess of the 59 percent reported. These highly philanthropic impulses must then be looked upon as but symptomatic of the change of interests and attitudes which is in process.

This is further supported by the evidences in the study that these philanthropic impulses vary greatly in duration and in strength. Of those reporting, 38 percent said that they were soon abandoned. Perhaps they were in the haste and ignorance of youth unwisely conceived and increasing knowledge may have brought greater wisdom and a further modification of social attitudes. It is possible, too, that such impulses may have in some cases indicated the highest point of social achievement, from which there was a rapid regression back to that which was more in harmony with the rest of the attitudes functioning. But it is wise to observe that the percent of such is comparatively small. There were the remaining 62 percent who at the time of the inquiry still retained more or less of this highly philanthropic impulse or urge. So long a duration must, according to all that we know of habit formation, result in the establishment of a rather permanent attitude toward social welfare and the individual's responsibilities toward it.

The wide range of sources of influence in the establishment of the new social attitudes of adolescence is indicated well by his discovery that in the opinion of the respondents only 4 percent could attribute these extreme philanthropic impulses to school sources. This fact should make any reader pause. Educators may feel chagrin and seek to moralize; but the student of psychology will merely be forced away from that dangerous pitfall of thinking that most of the social influences of adolescence come through the school. One must look far and wide when seeking the influences which have given the peculiar twists to the growth of any personality.

Further evidence of the existence of these altruistic attitudes in adolescence may be found in the vocational selections and preparatory activities. By far the most of these are the conventional ones of teaching, business, law and medicine and do not, superficially at least, reveal very much that could be identified as a highly altruistic or philanthropic motive. But upon more intimate investigation some of these will be found to have been chosen as a means for the highest social devotion. And then, too, there are those who with high consecration select the ministry, missionary careers, deaconess work, religious education, and the great variety of vocations involved in social reform, social welfare, and settlement work. Nursing is sometimes selected, also, as a means to a life of high devotion, to the relief of suffering, to the welfare of the poor, to the evangelization of some foreign and non-Christian land.

As Moore's study has indicated, there appears to be, in a large number of adolescents at least, a progressive decline from the heights of altruistic ambition, as maturity and its problems come into fuller consciousness. Satisfactory figures on this probable change of social attitude are unfortunately lacking, but of its frequent appearance there can be no doubt. Wm. DeWitt Hyde, long experienced in collegiate student contacts, wrote out his impressions of the characteristic changes of social attitudes of college students in a series of letters purporting to have been written by a college boy.[1] These letters, written more than a generation ago, show that the author had in his experience observed not only this same development of highly philanthropic social attitudes; but, with approximation to maturity, he had also observed their gradual decline from the extreme forms of mid-adolescent years.

What effect experience of these extreme forms of altruistic atti-

[1] Hyde, Wm. DeWitt, *The College Man and the College Woman*, Boston, 1906.

tude has upon the development of the various features of the personality pattern cannot yet be stated in any general terms, for the simple reason that large masses of data upon which such generalizations could be safely based are not yet available. But out of his many years of constant contact with student life and from any other informative associations the present writer is convinced that, whatever the general tendencies may some time be revealed to be, there will always be the fact of great individual differences in the effects of experience with such attitudes. Some individuals who have been through such experiences relate in their mature years the great regret with which they look back upon that period of what they now term hare-brained devotion to absurdly impossible causes. Sometimes one gathers the impression that they are not even yet well adjusted to life. One suspects that the subsequently enforced relinquishment of the impossible goal brought out feelings of inferiority, which in turn affected the content of the self concept and of the self-regarding sentiment in such a manner as to be very disagreeable, and to make a long and unwelcome struggle for peace and adjustment necessary. On the other hand there are those who achieved a satisfactory adjustment in maturity after a period of such grandiose ambitions and attitudes, who look back upon their adolescence with only the happiest of recollections. They seem to feel that the change was a normal, natural, gradual re-adjustment with the greater wisdom of maturity, and that the extremes of their youth left behind only a wholesome socialized attitude toward life.

Here one must be working with a very large number of unknown factors, and with factors which force the consideration of every instance as an individual case. The circumstances, internal and external, which brought out the extreme social attitudes, the nature of the ideals, of the self concept, of the self-regarding sentiment, and perhaps even of the basic temperament or personality type must all be important factors. And there must also be the effects of the environment, social and otherwise, in which the individual chances to be during these critical years. Doubtless also the native mental capacity and the special abilities with which he is endowed will have to be included in the consideration.

For a full understanding of these changes we should also some day know how these attitudes affected the course of development in the personalities of those who continued their devotion and really did become missionaries, religious workers of the many kinds, social welfare workers, anything in fact which, as a vocation, might be considered a logical outcome of the extreme altruistic attitudes of adolescent years.   In the meantime it is not only possible but wise for every student of personality growth changes to take these experiences with altruistic attitudes in adolescence into consideration in any effort to understand any given personality.

CHAPTER VIII

FACTORS IN SOCIAL ADJUSTMENT *(Continued)*

PUBIC INITIATIONS, CLOTHING, SOCIAL STATUS, GROUP AND GANG ACTIVITIES, FRIENDS AND CHUMS

Growth into social adjustment means that the adolescent is confronted by many established social customs and institutions which may be unpleasant and undesired, or they may be welcomed as aids to self-realization. Or, they may be accepted thoughtlessly as a matter of course. But these customs and institutions do operate as social pressures molding the personality, and so must receive careful consideration.

Practically all peoples have some sort of ceremony of initiation through which every pubescent is expected to pass in order to be acceptable as an adult. While in our civilization only remnants of such exist, they are nevertheless adhered to with a curious persistency. What are the effects of these ceremonies and what are their motivations? Race and religion and economic conditions and other factors produce very different social situations in which growth takes place. These differences must produce profoundly significant, and sometimes trying, differences in self concepts, social attitudes, and emotional responses.

Clothing is a highly formalized institution which frequently has profound effects upon the concept of the self and upon associated feelings. Growth away from the home is characterized by participation in the activities of gangs and clubs of a great variety. Some of these are spontaneous, but a vast number of them are adult-sponsored and the youth is practically forced to participate in one way or another. Then, as interest in the group activities subsides, the influence of friendship comes into prominence. So, in the course of adolescent social adjustments, there arise questions concerning the influence as well as the motivation of clothing customs and reactions, of the effects of growth in one social situation as compared with another, of the effects of changes in social situation, of life in the gang and the social group, and of friendship experiences. It is to these questions that this chapter is devoted.

Pubic Initiations. The achievement of sexual maturity has been almost universally recognized as a period of some great significance in the growth changes of the individual. Practically all peoples signalize it by initiatory ceremonies of some form. The primitive or savage customs of the sort have attracted much attention and have been described at length by anthropologists. As one turns from people to people, from tribe to tribe, and from time to time, one finds much difference in the details of these initiatory practices. Sometimes it is the girl who receives the maximum of attention, and sometimes it is the boy, while yet other tribes give about the same attention to each sex. Sometimes the period of initiation is as brief as a few days or hours, while at others the period of initiation is prolonged over three or four years. Here and there one will find reports of peoples or tribes which have two such initiatory periods, one at the dawn of puberty and another toward the close of the teen age.

A reading of any considerable number of these descriptions soon reveals certain features in common. There is usually a period of isolation of the initiate. There is much abasement of the individual, through the clothing worn or the lack of it, or through other bodily ornaments and insignia, through the filthy and indecent food which must be eaten or through the isolation and other enforced practices of the period which suggest the inferiority or the untouchableness of the person subjected to them. There is much infliction of pain which the initiate is expected to bear without flinching. Sometimes this is by actual direct physical torture, as by cutting and laceration of the body; sometimes it is more indirect through fasting and the repulsive stuff substituted for food. Circumcision is a not infrequent part of the ceremony. There is more or less emphasis upon instruction. The secrets of the tribe are imparted by some of its older members. The responsibilities of maturity are stressed. There is coaching in the arts of the chase and of war; and, with the girls, there is instruction in what we would term the domestic arts. And, finally, with the conclusion of the ceremonies, there are much rejoicing, congratulation, praise and reward.

Hall [1] was so much impressed by these ceremonies that he included lengthy abstracts of the descriptions of many of them. But he seems to have been attracted chiefly by the older and more primitive practices. L. S. Hollingworth [2] added to her description of the savage pubic ceremonies a very instructive description of the "coming-out" ceremonies of the modern girl of wealthy parentage. In this one sees some few remnants of the ancient practices. The isolation appears in the utilization of segregated education in finishing schools. And the highly formalized or regularized steps or phases of the process suggest its ancient origin or relationship. The emphasis upon clothing might also be looked upon as a remnant of the old customs.

Yet other remnants are to be found in the religious practices of confirmation, first communion, joining the church, or whatever be the name preferred for the custom. Herein one can see manifest a very strong emphasis upon the fact that the growing boy and girl are now passing into another stage of life, that they are now entering into and beginning to share with the adults of their faith the knowledge, the privileges, and the responsibilities of group membership. Sometimes these customs call for a rather rigorous preparatory period. Usually they include some impressive ceremony, for which new or even special clothing is provided, and after which, there are much praise and congratulation.

Commencement exercises now so frequently experienced, preceded by examination periods and involving more or less elaborate ceremonies with their flowers and special costumes and instruction and congratulation, partake also to a considerable extent of the features described in the stories of primitive initiatory practices. Perhaps something comparable may be seen as well in the more recent practice of freshman-week welcoming ceremonies, especially if surreptitiously accompanied by some hazing. There is in them, or is supposed to be, that which is instructive and that which emphasizes the change from one social status to another.

But, in this country at least, the best examples of the retention

---

[1] Hall, G. Stanley, *Adolescence*, Vol. 2, chap. 13.
[2] *Psychology of the Adolescent*, chap. 2.

of savage initiatory practices are to be found in the initiation ceremonies, formal and informal, prescribed and carried out by our high school and collegiate secret societies. If one combines pre-initiation periods, or Hell Weeks as they are colloquially termed, with the formal initiation, one will find that one has before him all the essential phases, and some even of the details, of the savage pubic initiation. There is the isolation, the abasement, and the obligation to endure fatigue or bad food or even actual pain. There is the instruction, the impartation of secrets, the advancement to a new status signified by the privilege of wearing special clothing or special insignia. And there are the congratulation and praise.

Why such apparently useless and savage practices should continue in the face of much opposition is a question which has not infrequently been raised. It is not so many years ago that genetic psychologists, dominated by the recapitulation method of interpretation, would see in them but the rehearsal of ancient racial practices and imply thereby that there was something about them which was intrinsically motivated, that there was some instinctive basis for them. And while we now know better than to be satisfied with such an interpretation we have not for it a substitute which has been satisfactorily worked out and substantiated. One may say of course that they are but the continuation of racial practices in a more or less modified form; but the question remains why so much that is undesirable and so widely condemned, even by many of those who have been through the experiences and subsequently put others through them, should persist in spite of the strong social pressure against them.

Practices that are approved by society or certain groups within it because they are considered desirable are probably continued not because they have any racial background but because they are wanted for what appear to be good and sufficient reasons. If, as in the case of confirmation and first communion, they are believed to have some divine sanction, then the whole psychology of religion enters into the illumination of their motivation. But with the undesirable there is neither a strong social pressure in favor of them nor the presence of belief in a divine sanction.

The reason for the continuation of the undesirable initiatory features must lie in the effects which they have made upon something within the personality of a majority of those who go through them. That this effect is far from being permanent, as is evidenced by the many who subsequently reject and oppose them, is but one of the facts to be noted by the psychologists. And it must also be that socially approved initiatory practices, aside perhaps from those believed to have a divine sanction, are maintained in large part because of the recollections of the effects experienced by those who, having been through them, continue to advocate their maintenance and use. Thus, whether considered good or bad, the continuation of initiatory practices for the pubescent must rest in large part upon the influences which they have upon the personalities subjected to them.

We come then to the question, What are the effects upon the growing personality of subjection to initiatory customs? This would seem to be the most important question concerning them so far as the genetic psychologist is concerned; but they seem not to have been carefully studied from this point of view. Hall had much to say about the nature of the ceremonies themselves as practiced among primitive peoples and a little more about the more civilized practices; but of the effect of them upon those who were initiated he suggests practically nothing. Brooks [1] reviews them briefly and expresses the opinion that they taught the virtues of obedience, freedom from maternal domination, bravery, observance of tribal customs and morals, and liberality. L. S. Hollingworth [2] sees in them a social recognition of certain adolescent needs, abilities and growth tendencies. She mentions the necessity for emancipation from the family, recognition of the fact that the adolescent is now facing the selection of a vocation and the responsibility for becoming an earner in the community, recognition of the arrival at sexual maturity, and, finally, of the need for such an attitude toward life or a philosophy of life as will provide a working interpretation of both life and death.

But the vigorous way in which society down through the years and throughout most of the races of mankind has gone about the business of pubertal initiation would seem to indicate something more than a mere recognition of needs. There appears to be not

---

[1] Brooks, F. D., *Psychology of Adolescence*, p. 3.
[2] Hollingworth, L. S., *Psychology of the Adolescent*, pp. 34-35.

only a recognition of needs, but also an active effort to do something about it, and that active effort has taken the form of doing something to the adolescent. Brooks has apparently seen this as is evidenced by his emphasis upon the teaching features of pubic initiations. There was an effort to teach certain socially desired virtues. If one can assume that by these ceremonies the virtues mentioned were actually taught, then one might say that the effects upon the growing personality included the establishment of meaningful concepts of obedience, self-reliance, bravery, conformity to social customs, and liberality and perhaps such attitudes toward them as would result in a greater or less degree of practice. But this does not seem to be all that was accomplished, whether by design or not. One suspects from reading descriptions of the ceremonies that there would be many other effects; and there is sufficient evidence to justify a tentative enumeration of them.

The time of life at which these ceremonies are placed and the content of so many of them, always excepting of course the attenuated contemporary remnants, force us first of all to mention the large change in the adolescent's concept of himself which must take place with regard to his or her own body. Every adolescent knows for himself by the anatomical changes taking place, by the new physiological processes which appear, and the wide gamut of new sensations which are experienced for the first time, that maturity is being reached. Then he finds himself forcibly subjected to a vast number of experiences manifesting a general social recognition and emphasis upon this fact. The effect of such ceremonies must be the insurance of very large and significant changes in the self concept. If the experience is sufficiently prolonged, there must be corresponding changes effected in the self-regarding sentiment. Many new emotional experiences must be aroused, and the beginnings at least of not a few new attitudes toward life and toward other human beings old and young. The childish attitudes are to be abandoned as rapidly as possible and the new ones substituted.

Secondly, there is ample reason for thinking that many other concepts are considerably altered by the experience, and new ones may be established. Brooks has pointed out the teaching aspects of the ceremonies with regard to virtues. Perhaps these were all known before the ceremonies began; but certainly the instruction associated with the rigors of the ceremonies would serve to enrich the meanings involved. As Mrs. Hollingworth has indicated, there is also the recognition of a need for some sort of religion or philosophy of life. And the descriptions of the initiatory ceremonies frequently include the initiation into tribal secrets and teachings by the wise men of the tribe. Thus it is fair to assume that many new ideas are added to the store of knowledge already achieved.

Thirdly, there must be the development of the consciousness of a new social status, with its accompaniment of new attitudes.[1] The taking away from the mother, the assumption of the clothing of the mature adult, the changed attitude on the part of adults toward them, the changed attitude on the part of their former companions among the children not yet initiated, the new privileges and obligations, must all have a profound effect upon the social attitudes and the feelings of self-estimation.

In the fourth place, there must be much, even though temporary, satisfaction of the will-to-power drive. If the ceremonies have included privation, the suffering of pain, tests of self-control, and the like, and if the initiate has gone through them without overtly flinching, then there must be a heightened self-confidence, there must be a new consciousness of one's own capacity to endure, a new consciousness of self-power. And there must be some similar influences from all that has been mentioned as contributing to the development of a consciousness of a new social status and to the new consciousness of one's self as sexually mature.

Then, too, fifthly, there must be listed the achievement of a new world adjustment. Not merely does this mean the new social adjustment, but an adjustment to the world as it is known to the individual, the world of life and death and unseen powers. The instruction in tribal mysteries must have achieved much in this direction and certainly in the religious pubertal ceremonies of today, of confirmation and first communion and the like, this world adjustment of the self is paramount.

[1] Hutton Webster, in *Primitive Secret Societies,* mentions ceremonies having the effect of establishing a caste feeling, consciousness of tribal solidarity, and strong feelings of brotherhood.

So far the personality effects of pubic ceremonies have been presented here in terms of those who go through them with a full measure of success. But from this there must have been many gradations, and even in the contemporary forms and remnants there must be those who receive the lesser praise and the lesser satisfactions. In discussing the psychology of the ceremonies in general one may properly concentrate upon the general effects as listed above; but when one confronts the problem of interpreting the behavior of some particular adolescent it becomes necessary to think of the possibilities of individual differences. Perhaps there was some flinching at some time and some degree of social disapproval; perhaps there was a partial failure to pass the examinations required, and a consequent postponement of the time of full social acceptance. Then one could expect some self-dissatisfaction and some cautious, even suspicious, attitudes toward others. The attitudes of the new social status might be somewhat marred by the doubts and suspicions of the degree to which the acceptance should be estimated.

Then there may be those who came up to the pubic ceremonies with such ideas and attitudes toward them as to result in no little conflict, perhaps some open rebellion, and an eventual achievement of social acceptance flawed by disbeliefs and disapprovals and the recollections of treatment still believed to be unmerited and unjustifiable.

Following down through these various degrees of partial achievement of the desired effects of the pubic ceremonies one must come at last to the fact that there must have been and there must still be, even with our attenuated remnants of pubescent ceremonies, those who for one reason or another fail completely. With these the effects of the ceremonies must be very different, but far more difficult of generalized statement and estimation because of the still smaller amount of available information.

From this point of view, of the effect of the ceremonies upon the growing adolescent personality, more illuminating interpretations and sounder evaluations of contemporary adolescent initiatory practices are likely to develop. When so examined the ceremonies, ancient and modern alike, will be found to include many items of little discoverable value. It is reported that savage peoples frequently insisted upon the use and impartation of words and phrases the meanings of which they themselves had long since lost. A contemporary correlate may be seen in the ignorance of Greek manifest in modern Greek letter society initiations, an ignorance which might both astonish and bewilder the founders of those societies. Perhaps such items have value by adding a mystical touch to the whole; and perhaps they are utterly useless because they have none of the desired initiatory ceremony effects upon the adolescent subjected to them. Perhaps Hell Week and all forms of pre-formal initiatory practices should be abolished; perhaps all Greek letter society initiations should be abolished, as many now advocate; but the wiser procedure should be to make a systematic psychological investigation of their effects upon growing personalities before jumping to the conclusion that they are all bad. That some who have been through them are now opposed to them means merely that for some reason yet to be determined these personalities were not desirably affected by them, or that in the years since they have come to a greater wisdom and a new valuation of the various features of the ceremonies they once approved. If such a study of the effects of the ceremonies as a whole, and of the parts, upon adolescent personalities has ever been made the present writer has sought in vain to find it. And when it is made it should include all contemporary forms of pubic ceremony, religious and social and academic included.

Clothing. The wearing of clothing is a custom so firmly fixed in most human societies it must be looked upon as constituting one of the social pressures at work upon the growing personality. Every human being is born into a clothing-habituated world and wear it he must in some form whether he desires to or not. And, among most peoples, the custom has become highly differentiated into special clothing customs. It is not merely that the growing personality is subjected to the necessity of wearing clothing; but it is forced into the wearing of certain kinds of clothing at certain times and stages and other kinds at other times and stages. Certain clothing is proper in infancy, other kinds in childhood, others in maturity, and yet other kinds are reserved for the aged and infirm. And, at any age, some kinds of clothing are reserved for special occasions. They would be improper and socially frowned upon at all other times.

Unless one is still much interested in the comparison of growth changes with racial history the origin of clothing is not an acute problem of students of adolescent psychology. Perhaps this is fortunate because of the great diversit⁓ of opinion still current on this subject.[1]

What the first effects of clothing are upon the human infant no one knows. If Watson is right in his assertion that confinement is an original stimulus to anger, then the early experiences with clothing might be thought of as exercising the anger reaction. And this, through the combined effects of primacy and frequency, might start a development of the anger reaction which could in large part explain the bad tempers of some of the youth and adults whom we meet.

On the other hand, if the psychoanalysts are right in positing an instinct for the familiar, an urge to return to the comforts and the protection of the former state, then the first effects of clothing should be highly pleasurable, because, through the warmth and wide distribution of contact stimuli and confinement which they supply, they reproduce to a considerable extent the prenatal environment. In this case, the early effects of much use of clothing should exercise the retreating tendencies, the snuggling, comfortable, quiescent reaction; and if by primacy and frequency these were given an early and active development, we should expect to find them a prominent personality trait in later years.

Perhaps the timid retiring personality in adolescent years can be traced back likewise to the early effects of clothing. And then when one thinks of the differences in child handling and children's clothing, one suspects the possibility of there being some truth in both propositions. Perhaps the handling of some children's clothing experiences develops a tendency to quick anger arousal; while the handling of other children's clothing experiences perhaps develops a tendency to the timid, retiring, introvertive personality.

[1] Summaries of these theories may be found in the following:

Dunlap, Knight, "The Development and Function of Clothing," *J. Gen. Psychol.*, 1928, 1, 64-78.
Hurlock, E. B., "Motivation in Fashion," *Arch. of Psychol.*, 1929, No. 111.

The content of the self concept appears to be easily molded by clothing satisfactions and dissatisfactions. If the child wears peculiar and unusual clothing, if the clothing be exceptionally rich and varied, if it be poor and ragged, all these items must affect the concept of the self and all the perceptions and feelings which are related to it. The few studies which we have, however, reveal little about this effect upon the self and associated patterns; but they do reveal a rather prolonged struggle with or against clothing. Rusling has stressed the recklessness of childhood toward clothing.[1] Macaulay has reported much intolerance in childhood of tight clothing, and rebellion against clothing conventions.[2] She also, as had Hall,[3] found that the decorative feature of clothing is active in childhood.

To the student of growth changes this decorative interest can only indicate that the content of the self concept is still closely related to the physical body, from which its earliest meanings came, and, at the same time, that a shift is taking place from the body itself to its ornamentation or covering. This shift from the skin to the artificial coverings has been much emphasized. Hall saw in it a progressive translation of the primitive body consciousness into a clothes consciousness. Macaulay mentions a progressive sublimation of body interest into clothes interest, which in her judgment continues on into adolescent years. This may in turn be articulated with the views of the more extreme psychoanalytic thinkers who see in all adult clothing customs a great variety of sex symbols.[4] They think of libido as being sublimated from the autoerotic, or purely bodily, attachments to the higher attachments to clothing, which, because its forms are racial in origin, is already supplied with items that symbolize different parts and functions of the body.

This brief review of pre-adolescent experience with and effects of clothing upon the growing personality should prepare the reader for the adolescent problems with clothing. The indi-

---

[1] Rusling, L. A., "Children's Attitude Toward Clothes," *Ped. Sem.*, 1905, 12, 525.

[2] Macaulay, E., "Some Notes on the Attitude of Children to Dress," *Brit. J. Med. Psychol.*, 1929, 9, 150-158.

[3] Hall, G. Stanley, "Some Aspects of the Early Sense of Self," *Amer. J. Psychol.*, 1897-98, 9, 351-395.

[4] Flügel, J. C., "Clothes Symbolism and Clothes Ambivalence," *Int. J. Psychoanal.*, 1929, 10, 205-217.

vidual comes into adolescence with a background of infantile experiences with clothing, which may have been either those of struggle or of comfortable retreat or of both; and with memories of childhood's struggle with clothing that confined disagreeably, and of clothing customs that irritated. A considerable shift has also taken place from skin or body interest to clothing interest, although this shift is far from complete.

In this one thing, all students of clothing seem to agree, that *adolescence is the period of highest clothes consciousness.* Hall saw this as especially prominent in girls, of whom he says that nearly half develop a great desire to be dressmakers or milliners. They manifest taste for the loud and attention-attracting, and love to try on and exchange clothing with others.[1] Fictional literature and biography has long made much of the adolescent boy's sudden interest in his own appearance. The boy who shortly before rebelled at ties and jackets and the shining of shoes suddenly becomes disturbingly particular about all of these. He seems to be embarrassed and distressed if not appearing in a manner which will merit the approval of his associates, if not attract attention to his virtues. Of Hurlock's more than fourteen hundred respondents 52.5 percent of the males and 59.9 percent of the females reported that adolescence was the time in their lives when their happiness was most affected by matters of clothing.[2]

It is evident then that by adolescent years the battle between the growing individual and the clothing customs of society has been won by society. But it is more than that. In adolescent years youth has not only submitted to the social practices of wearing clothing, but also has laid hold of the practice as a means of satisfying certain desires or urges now either just emergent or just coming to prominence. Clothing is now capable of providing the wearer with a great thrill of self-exaltation, or with the most intense embarrassment and feelings of disgrace and inferiority. A great change has taken place since childhood's struggle with the physical restraint and the physical discomforts of style.

Students of the psychology of clothing have often pointed out

---

[1] Hall, G. Stanley, *Educational Problems*, Vol. II, p. 2.
[2] Hurlock, E. B., "Motivation in Fashion," *Arch. of Psychol.*, 1929, No. 111; see also her *Psychology of Dress*, New York, 1929.

that the customs of clothing at once satisfy two conflicting tendencies in the human being. They satisfy the desire to be like others and they satisfy the urge to be different, to be individualistic. If clothing is so prominent a concern of adolescent years it can only mean that these two desires, to be distinctively different and at the same time be like others, are prominent features of adolescent motivation; and that in satisfying them one effect of the social practices of wearing clothing is that of establishing these traits in growing personalities in an undistorted manner. But should economic conditions, parental attachments, or what not, prevent the normal satisfactions of these desires, through the use of clothing, there arise all the possibilities inherent in those psychological situations which we describe as conflicts between drives and the blocking or inhibiting or repressing tendencies. Inferiority complexes may easily be born of unsatisfied clothing desires. Unsatisfied and repressed desires may break loose into the occasional wearing of eccentric clothing; or they may so distort selection as to result in the chronic wearing of that which is eccentric; or these repressed and unsatisfied desires may make themselves manifest in distorting the behavior in some phase of life quite other than that which concerns clothing.

The only extensive survey of adolescent behavior with regard to clothing which the writer has been able to discover is that of Hurlock's just mentioned, and this was of necessity a pioneer study by a simple questionnaire method. Nevertheless it contains much that is instructive. Many items indicate the influence of these motives of imitation or conformity and of differentiation. The following table reproduces some of her items in an abbreviated form.

Substance of the Question Asked	*Percent*	
	M	F
Dressing for the approval of own sex	66	64
Dressing for the approval of the other sex	32	33
Dressing to escape criticism of own sex	58	66
Dressing to escape criticism of the other sex	42	34
Care most about personal appearance when with friends	84	62
Choosing clothing to cover defects	37	63
Choosing clothing to bring out best qualities	84	94
Dressing with effort to appear prosperous	33	37

	M	F
Seeking appearance of equality with higher social status	16	28
Dressing to give the impression of having much leisure	8	14
Willing to sacrifice if necessary to be in style	42	34
Changing style if socially inferior copy it	25	63
Usefulness considered in selection of clothes	92	90
Cost considered in selection of clothes	92	83
Willingness to adopt a fashion even though disapproving	8	17
Choose clothing to be conspicuous	8	25
Refusing to wear styles that are immodest	92	85
Admitting that dress affects manners and behavior	92	89
Can work better if feeling well dressed	84	93
Saying that dress affects their happiness	92	92
Self-confidence increased by consciousness of being well dressed	92	100
Admitting that estimate of others is affected by the clothes they wear	100	99
This influence of clothing on estimate of others is confined to the first impression	67	89

Doubtless few will read this table without being impressed by the many indications of eagerness for the approval of others. It is more than a seeking to be like others in clothing worn. It is an effort to merit and to win the approval of friends, associates, strangers, and not only of the other sex but also of the same sex. When around ninety percent of this large number of respondents admit that clothing affects their happiness, that they can work better when they feel well dressed, and that it affects their manners and behavior in general, one sees that the factor of clothing deserves a large place in the thought of all administrative officers who have to do with youth as well as a much larger place in the literature of genetic psychology than it has hitherto achieved.

It is natural to look for sex differences in such a study. There are some which will arrest the attention. If these figures are reliable, then girls are much more concerned with the concealment of defects and with dressing to bring out their best qualities. The effort to dress with the appearance of a higher social status appears also to be more conspicuously female; and they also seem to be more troubled at finding the styles they wear imitated by those who are thought of as socially inferior. And the answers to the question about the effort to make one's self conspicuous indicate that this also is more frequently evident in the female adolescent. There is here manifest a somewhat greater effort on the part of the girls to be distinctive, to be different, than there is among the young men.

Long before this study of Hurlock's was made, George Van N. Dearborn [1] published a monograph on clothing in which he contended that the basic motivation in the selection of clothing was fear. When one is well dressed and properly dressed, he contended, one feels at ease. One feels then that one is safe and there is a relief from the danger of being wrong, a relief from the possibilities of experiencing the disagreeableness of fear. Doubtless Dearborn was right but the analysis needs to be pushed a little farther. One does not fear if one knows what is the proper thing to wear on some occasion and has the proper clothing in one's wardrobe. Also, one does not fear if one is entirely indifferent to what others think about the clothing worn, nor does one fear if one is dressing according to some religious or philosophical conviction even though it be quite different from current social conventions. Where fear is there is much consciousness of social pressure. Hurlock's long list of replies indicates a conspicuously keen consciousness in these adolescents of the pressure upon them of the social situation. And this is far more true of adolescents than of adults. They are seeking to be right, to be just right, not to make mistakes; they must manifest no ignorance, and there must be no evidence of inexperience even though they be inexperienced. Mistakes here would be embarrassing and would stir feelings of inferiority. The prospect of such a possibility is unpleasant and fear arousing. Likewise society urges youth to struggle upward, to merit the approval of superiors, to merit the approval of a desirable girl, to merit the approval of a desirable young man. To achieve in this regard one must be distinctive as well as proper. To fail, even temporarily, is an unpleasant fear-stimulating prospect.[2]

---

[1] "Psychology of Clothing," *Psych. Rev. Monog.*, 1918, Vol. 26, No. 112.

[2] In the light of this dynamic psychology one sees how limited in scope was the old psychology of clothing presented by Herman Lotze (*Microcosmus*, pp. 592-595 of 4th ed.) and since his time so often quoted. Lotze based his psychology of clothing on the simple perceptual phenomenon of eccentric projection. Thus things like hats and canes which added to one's height or reach increased the scope of the perceptions and made one feel larger. In like manner one is said to feel one's self to the end of all waving and hanging drapery. Close, stiff or stoutly binding garments added, Lotze thought, to the size of ourselves by forcing a tall erect bearing.

Periodically students of adolescence are confronted by some one who wants to know if it is desirable to force all students in some school or institution to wear uniform clothing. Certainly in the light of what we now know concerning clothing and adolescence no general answer could possibly be given. Circumstances and uniforms are not alike. To force all the girls in some public high school to wear the same costume might be one of the worst possible moves for some of the girls in that school. The costume might be such as to reveal their worst points and fail to emphasize their best qualities. For others who were giving too much attention to clothing, because of their clothing fears, or because of much too large monthly allowances, the requirement of uniformity might be wise. To require by regulation that all adolescent boys wear exactly the same style of clothing might crush a budding self-respect in some just when it should be developed. But that again depends upon the uniform. To wear the uniform of a celebrated and socially distinctive military school might serve to increase the self-respect. Whenever such questions arise they must be answered after full consideration of both the psychology of adolescence and of the particular situation in which the problem arises.

Finally, there are in nearly every group a few who persist in dressing so eccentrically as to constitute a problem in themselves. These must be looked upon also as individual case problems. No general rule can be applied. They may be motivated by impulsive efforts to compensate for a conscious inferiority; or their behavior may be in the form of defense mechanisms, to aid in the repression of inferiority feelings. The eccentricity of dress may be a form of exhibitionism. This may have a genuinely sexual motivation, perhaps more or less concealed in some form of symbolism; and it may be a simple social exhibitionism resulting from a peculiar individual history which when discovered will be found to involve a course of conditioning or substitution of stimuli for the pleasures of being the center of attention in childhood.[1] It is possible, too, that these eccentric dressers are psychoneurotics in whom there are complexes and maladjustments of other kinds. The clothing peculiarity would then be

[1] Smith, S., and Guthrie, E. R., "Exhibitionism," *J. Abn. & Soc. Psychol.*, 1922, 17. 206-209.

but one feature of a larger distortion of development. And it is possible that some eccentric adolescent dressing may be an early symptom of a developing psychosis. One must use this possibility with the greatest of caution of course, but every student of adolescence should be aware of the fact that the schizophrenia (dementia præcox) and some post-encephalitic cases are likely to attract attention by their peculiar habits of dress.

Influences of Social Status. Another of the social pressures in the background of all adolescent behavior is that of the social status in which infancy and childhood years have been spent. The rigidity of this as a persistent social pressure and the struggles which many adolescents experience with the effects of it justify a serious consideration. Unfortunately our studies of attitudes and of emotional conditionings have not yet proceeded far enough to be of much use here. It is therefore necessary to fall back upon general observations and literary presentations for support and elaboration of the few hints available from experimental studies.

A sharp contrast often serves best to bring out features of psychological significance. Compare for example the training received by a child growing up in a New England city in the home of one of the old families with the training received by a child in the same city but in the home of immigrant parents. The child of the old New England family would grow up in an old-family atmosphere. Associations would be with other old-family homes. Residence would be in a different section of the city; and, even if public schools were attended, it would be with the children from the same section. There would be much family pride instilled. Perhaps an ancestor came over on the *Mayflower;* and perhaps another signed the Declaration of Independence. The customs, the attitudes, the ideas, the opinions, and the beliefs acquired would be those characteristic of the old-family home. In the home of the immigrant, while the family history might be cherished, it would nevertheless be a foreign history and the consciousness of that would be unavoidable. Language difficulties and the struggles to achieve in a new country would create an atmosphere certain to produce very different ideas and attitudes in the growing children. Schooling would bring to the children, as our social workers have often stated, an easy mastery of the English language which the parents could never achieve. This in itself must produce a most significantly peculiar environmental influence. The schools are pressing for Americanization, and the parents may be also, as best they can; but their roots are in the old country from whence they came.

When children from two homes so different, from two social situations so different, reach adolescence, it is to be expected that their attitudes toward country and family and ancestry and customs should be different. It must also be that the content of their concepts and the range of their knowledge must be different. Their emotional reactions have been conditioned to different patterns of stimuli; or, to put it otherwise, their emotional affections and attachments must be different.

To realize how extensive these features are in life, it is but necessary to think for a moment upon the many different social situations which serve as patterns of social pressure upon growing children. In addition to the contrast already mentioned there are the children who grow up in Roman Catholic homes, in Roman Catholic communities; there are the children who grow up in Jewish homes, in Jewish communities; there are the children who grow up in Mormon homes, in Mormon communities; and the vast number of other racial and religious community differences available. There are the children who grow up in Negro homes in Negro communities; and the children who grow up in Negro homes in white communities. There are the children who grow up in white homes in white communities where the only knowledge of Negro life is acquired through reading and hearsay; and there are the children who grow up in white homes adjacent to large Negro centers. There are children who grow up in occidental homes with little if any knowledge of life and attitudes in an oriental home; and there is the reverse of this. And there are the children growing up in American communities where there are both oriental and occidental groups.

The achievement of adolescence ordinarily means shifting scenes, and thus to some extent a relaxation of the pressure of the social status in which infancy and childhood years were spent. There is the gradual breaking away from the home domination, the feelings of independence and the impulses to be independ-

ent; there are the fruits of further education in the form of new
ideas and new ideals; there may be actual moving to other communities or the going away to school and college where it is
necessary to live with other adolescents from most or all of these
many different social-pressure backgrounds.

One effect of such shifting about in adolescence is that these
earlier acquired attitudes, and ideas, and opinions, and standards
of judgment, and emotional attachments are brought out into
strong relief. They become noticeable by contrast with those
who have quite different patterns. The pressure of the old social
status has done its work; now a new social status and a new
pattern of pressures is to be faced. The result is sometimes a
marked change in the basic patterns within the personality.
Sometimes this change takes place easily and happily, but often
it is accompanied by distress and all the distortions which the
facing of a disagreeable reality may involve.

New standards of evaluation are an almost certain consequence. Reactions which had formerly been looked upon as
quite right and proper are now classed as prejudices. Attitudes
toward people of other social classes and of other races and of
other religious preferences, which were once looked upon, if considered at all, as matters of course, now come to be thought of
as social and race and religious prejudice which may or may not
be approved. Sometimes a disapproval is masked by a rationalization which makes the disagreeable task of changing and of
admitting that one was wrong appear to be unnecessary.

But the shifting situations of adolescence force also a change
in the attitude toward the self, and in what has been termed the
self-regarding sentiment. From being a social light among the
young people of a small town, the shift may be to comparative
obscurity in the city; or from the comparative obscurity of the
city, the shift may be to the small town, where by virtue of a few
abilities and skills not conspicuous in the city, the youth so shifting finds himself in a position of prominence. When the youth
with Catholic or Jewish or Mormon or oriental training moves
into a community where there are few of his kind and many of
some other kind, the differences become conspicuous. Perhaps
racial and religious prejudice must be faced. Many cases are

reported where such a change produces so great a change of self-evaluation as to cause feelings of inferiority, with all of the well-known disturbances consequent to such feelings about the self. Some, in such situations, merely feel queer or different. While yet others feel superior, are proud of their position and their heritage. Just why there should be such differences is not entirely clear; but, if our psychology so far is sound, the cause must be sought in some differences of emphasis in the early home and home environment.

A third form of reaction to the shifting situations of adolescence is the development of rebelliousness against the past, or against the new, environment. Doubtless this is often motivated by the new valuations developing and also by experiences of inferiority; but, as all changes of standards of valuation and all experiences of inferiority do not produce this rebelliousness, it is worthy of separate comment. Some youths rebel against their past completely, would do away with the traditions and customs and beliefs under which they were raised. Others rebel against the new environment which fails to appreciate their past and all of its values.[1]

With regard to these rebellious reactions, some have thought that there was discernible the influence of some intrinsic personality difference, that there was a temperamental difference between the radical and the conservative. Vetter studied a large group of college students with a multiple choice attitude test and found that those who manifested markedly peculiar attitudes, what Vetter wisely calls marked "atypicality" of attitude, did not give evidence of being mentally abnormal. While Vetter is cautious, he apparently suspects that behind typicality and atypicality of attitude there may be something as basic as an intrinsic determination.[2] Washburne and her associates in a careful study failed to reveal any evidence of the two types which

[1] Perhaps it is the influence of this rebelliousness which caused the adolescent downward trend in the curve of development of attitudes toward law which Lockhart found. See Lockhart, E. G., "The Attitudes of Children Toward Law," *Univ. Iowa Stud.; Stud. in Character*, 1930, 3, No. 1, p. 61. A thought-provoking paper in this connection is that by W. T. Root, entitled "The Psychology of Radicalism," *J. Abn. & Soc. Psychol.*, 1925, 19, 341-356.

[2] Vetter, G. B., "The Measurement of Social and Political Attitudes and the Related Personality Factors," *J. Abn. & Soc. Psychol.*, 1930, 25, 140-189.

Moore's earlier work seemed to indicate.[1] So, until some one can demonstrate the probable existence of intrinsically determined traits of conservatism and radicalism, it will be necessary to seek explanations for such traits in the influences of past training combined with the effects of the present situation. Why some should rebel against the old, and some against the new, must be determined in terms of the individual history and present situation.

Influence of Group Activity. Our studies of social activities agree fairly well in indicating the appearance of some qualitative change coming into group, club, or gang life in adolescent years. During childhood there is play in groups to be sure, but it is the play of individuals in the presence of others rather than co-operative group activity. Children do not participate easily nor well in such games as baseball and football which require co-operation and the frequent subordination of the self to the success of the team. In adolescent years, however, the opposite is notably present. Adolescents do participate in group activity requiring team play; in fact, such seems to be the characteristic of adolescent group life. This will be found to be true not only of sports or athletics but also for dramatic, literary, social, religious or any kind of group activity. Cooperative participation in clubs and societies and gangs may be looked upon as a distinctive feature of adolescent life.

In this country, at least, the youth who is not subjected to the influences of some group life belongs to a decided minority. High schools and junior high schools now provide a vast array of so-called extra-curricular activities of this sort. They are literally too numerous to mention. One study presents a list of 848,[2] and attempts to classify them as literary, forensic and declamatory, journalistic, dramatic, foreign language, historical, geographical, mathematical, scientific, musical, arts and crafts, industrial, home economics, commercial, physical and athletic,

---

[1] Washburne, M. F., Kepler, H., McBroom, N., Pritchard, W., and Reimer, I., "The Moore Tests of Radical and Conservative Temperaments," *Amer. J. Psychol.*, 1927, 38, 449-452; see also Moore, H. T., "Innate Factors in Radicalism and Conservatism," *J. Abn. & Soc. Psychol.*, 1925, 20, 234-244.

[2] Koos, L. V., "Analysis of the General Literature on Extra-Curricular Activities," *25th Yearbook* of the Nat. Soc. for the Study of Educ., Part II, pp. 9-22. This entire volume is devoted to a collection of papers on such activities.

and lastly, civic-social-moral which in itself includes a vast array of committee, club, council, and other groups. Participation in these seems to vary from nearly every pupil in a school down to half of the students, doubtless depending upon the attitudes and policies of the school authorities. And in addition to all these numerous and somewhat formal organizations, there are the many formal and informal organizations which exist quite apart from the school life and its occupations. There are the church, the Y.M.C.A. and the Y.W.C.A., the Boy Scouts and the Girl Scouts, and similar groups (although these may come under the head of extra-curricular school activities in some instances), the dancing classes which sometimes take on many of the features of the social group, organizations fostered by lodges such as the De Molay societies, and the very large number of local gangs and clubs which develop quite apart from adult leadership. Among the latter of course are to be found the gangs which Thrasher has demonstrated to be predominantly an adolescent phenomenon.[1]

The success of adult-fostered organizations for adolescents, as well as the vast number of spontaneous social organizations of youth, led the earlier students of genetic psychology to interpret them in terms of a gregarious instinct, sometimes less appropriately termed the gang instinct.[2] It was assumed that in every normal person there was an innate determination which eventuated in the propensity to participate in group activity, an urge from within to seek the society of others in the limited fashion of the club or group or gang. Today we are less certain that such activity of later childhood and youth can be wisely attributed to the maturation of an instinct.

It is safer to think of gregariousness as a habit, or conditioned reaction, which has been trained into a person from infancy.[3] Our earliest satisfactions and comforts are brought about by the presence of others. We are brought up with others, in a family group ordinarily. Thus the presence of others becomes essential to peace and happiness. Without the presence of others we shortly,

---

[1] Thrasher, F. M., *The Gang*, Chicago, 1927.
[2] Good examples of this are to be found in Puffer, J. A., *The Boy and His Gang*, Boston, 1912. See also Hall, G. Stanley, *Adolescence*, chap. 5.
[3] Cason, H., "Gregariousness as a Common Habit," *J. Abn. & Soc. Psychol.*, 1924, 19, 96-105.

with certain exceptions of course, become restless, uncomfortable and unhappy, and go seeking that which we know from experience will bring contentment. But, if this were all, we might grow up continuously satisfied by the family group. Our social organization, however, is such that we are not allowed to remain indefinitely in the family situation. We are in early childhood thrust out of it for an increasing number of hours of the day to attend school and to play with others of approximately the same age. For a time, we are much too self-centered in our habits to cooperate well, are too thoroughly conditioned for our pleasure to the praise and applause of others, and have not yet developed a sufficient degree of intelligence to be much influenced by ulterior motives. Thus, at first, only the characteristic individual-in-a-group type of social activity is manifested.

By the dawn of adolescence the enforced association with school- and play-mates has partially erased the self-centered habits, and has begun the establishment of habits of cooperation. A re-conditioning is also taking place which links the happiness of the individual to the achievements and rewards and praises of the group. And it must also be remembered that intelligence is reaching a degree of development which makes it possible to think in terms of ultimate goods, in terms of principles, goals, ends, purposes, and the like.[1] It is such changes, rather than the maturation of a specific instinct, to which we now prefer to look for the explanation of the appearance of cooperative group life.

Group or gang activity is predominantly a pubescent or early adolescent characteristic. In this country it continues on well into middle adolescence and only gradually gives way to friendships and romantic love. The range of group or gang phenomena in the age scale appears to be somewhat dependent upon the general social setting. A European study indicates that for the individuals there studied it is largely a pubescent or even pre-pubescent phenomenon.[2] Thrasher has convincingly demon-

---

[1] Hartson, Louis D., "The Psychology of the Club; a Study in Social Psychology," *Ped. Sem.*, 1911, 18, 353-414. (In this paper there is an admirable presentation of the influence of the consciousness of ends or purposes.)

[2] Vecerka, L., "Das soziale Verhalten von Mädchen während der Reifezeit," *Quell. u. Stud. Jugendk.*, 1926, 4, 49-121. See also summary of such studies by Charlotte Bühler in her chapter entitled "The Social Behavior of Children," in C. Murchison's *Handbook of Child Psychology* (Chap. 9, of 2nd rev. ed).

strated the evanescent nature of the gang. His thesis, now generally accepted, is that the gang is essentially a form of group-life coming between the family group-life of childhood and the group-life of the new family established by marriage in early maturity. The new urges and desires of pubescence combining with many social pressures push or drag the early adolescent out of the home group, but immaturity prevents the establishment of a new family group for several years. This gap in social development is supplied by the gang or club or whatever the temporary adolescent group behavior may be called. That gang interests subside somewhat in later adolescent years in no wise invalidates Thrasher's thesis. This shading off is associated with the rise of intimate friendships and especially of romantic love interests which are the preparation for matrimony. To some degree the formation of the new family-group interest is taking shape before marriage and the establishment of a new family becomes a full reality.

So much effort has been expended upon the task of interpreting the appearance of gang and club phenomena in adolescent behavior, there seems to have been little left for any careful study of the effects of such social relationships upon the adolescent himself. But it is only natural, and from our point of view most important, to ask, after the motivation has been discovered, to know what may be the effects of gang and club and society membership upon the adolescent boys and girls who participate.

Puffer contends from his study of gangs that they train in loyalty to the group, establish habits of obedience, of self-sacrifice and of cooperation. From Thrasher's study of delinquent gangs [1] one learns of the training in struggle for social position within the group, which the member of the gang undergoes. There is the possibility of training in habits which may be transferable to other groups and the larger group life of adulthood. Thrasher is of course thinking in terms of the delinquent gang; but the well-organized and well-led social group in a high school or a Y.M.C.A. may accomplish a similar kind of training. In the gangs there is also the establishment of life in a different social world, or, perhaps better, the development of a new social world in which the gang member lives. The home has been dis-

[1] Thrasher, F. M., *The Gang*, chap. 19.

placed by this gang social world; and it should be further observed that it is a very limited world. It is one in which there is
little thought or consideration for the welfare of the community
in which the gang exists. Undesirable traits, such as being a sissy
or a braggart, are condemned by the members of the gang; and
those who manifest such traits are either laughed down or subjected to rough handling. Capacities for certain skills, such as
singing or dancing, are often cultivated by the gang. Instances
are reported of such cultivation eventuating in sufficient development of the skill to bring to its possessor the means of earning a
comfortable living.

From the collective life of the gang the members also acquire
many habits. In the delinquent gangs studied these are habits
of vulgarity, obscenity, drinking, and other vices, as might be
expected; but the principle is thus made clear that habits hitherto often unknown may be acquired from the collective group
life of adolescent years. Thrasher also points out that the members of these delinquent gangs acquired a sort of philosophy of
life which involved attitudes toward others, especially toward
the established authorities of the community, and an interpretation of life in terms of a simple fatalism from a criminalistic
point of view. Undesirable as this all is, without doubt, it
nevertheless is important because of its exemplification of the
principle that the adolescent is acquiring a philosophy of life.
One is reminded here of the custom of savage peoples to impart
such a philosophy in the course of their initiatory pubic ceremonies.

What the effects are upon the growing personality of the adolescent of participation in the vast number of guided social or
extra-curricular activities, providing a socially more desirable
form of collective experience, has yet to be determined. Statistical studies on the frequency of participation in such groups are
available and a number of studies have been made of the relationship between such participation and the degree of excellence
in formal school work. But unfortunately instruments with
which to measure the effects of such participation upon personality traits are too few, too new, or else totally lacking. Consequently we really know very little of their effects. Of opinions
about these effects there is no lack. Koos's study of forty dif-

ferent books and articles on the subject as a means of discovering
the consensus of such opinion revealed that thirty-seven of them
stressed the values of training in some civic-social-moral relationship; twenty-three emphasized the socialization which resulted
from such participation, twenty-two mentioned training for leadership; twenty-one gave improvement in discipline and school
spirit as an important value; nineteen mentioned cooperation;
sixteen gave training for citizenship in a democracy; fifteen gave
training for recreational and esthetic participation; and there
were many other items mentioned.[1] Sometimes students in high
school have been asked for their opinions about such participation. Stanforth[2] in such a study revealed that out of 240 students responding, sixty-two said that such participation taught
social conduct, fifty-two how to meet others, twenty-six promo-
tion of friendliness, twenty-four ease in manner, and twenty-one
that it taught poise. All of them agreed that high school pupils
were in need of social training.

At the University of Minnesota an extensive study was made
of participation in collegiate extra-curricular activities which revealed that there is a marked tendency for students who in college years were active in such social affairs to carry those habits
of social activity over into the life after college.[3] There is in
this the hint that possibly the training in other habits afforded
by the group, whether they be desirable or undesirable, may be
carried over into mature years.

In Hall's discussion of club life in adolescence, there is the
interesting suggestion that such collective experience may contribute much to that change of habits or attitudes here described
as the shift from the self-centered life to the socially centered life.
Hall thought that membership in one group began the process
by its forcing the establishment of habits of loyalty to that group
and also by forcing actions of self-sacrifice for the good of the
group. But Hall went further. He contended that membership

[1] Koos, L. V., "Analysis of the General Literature on Extra-Curricular Activities." This is chap. 2, of Part II of the 25th Yearbook of the Nat. Soc.
for the Study of Educ., 1926. See also Reaney, M. J., "The Psychology of the
Boy Scout Movement," *Ped. Sem.*, 1914, 21, 407-411.
[2] Stanforth, A. J., "Study in Social Attitudes of a Group," *Sch. & Soc.*,
1927, 26, 723-726.
[3] Chapin, F. Stuart, *Extra-Curricular Activities at the University of Minnesota*, Minneapolis, 1929, especially chap. 8.

in one adolescent organization alone was far from being ideal because it merely started the shift of loyalty from the individual outward. There was in that the danger of the individual becoming circumscribed in habit and attitude and thought by the limits of that particular group. Hence he thought it far better that the growing boy and girl should belong to many such groups. Thus would the loyalty be successively spread out to more and more people. Thus presumably would the limited loyalty to the single group be broken up and a larger loyalty to the good of mankind be established.[1] If Hall was right in this contention then the existence of many societies and clubs in high school and college life and the membership of individuals in several of them each would have to be considered, other things being equal, a desirable condition.

There is plenty of evidence, also, for saying, although the evidence is of a rather unsystematic nature, that the collective group life of adolescent years builds in the growing personalities many new sentiment patterns. Sentiments grow concerning the school, the team, the group, perhaps also for individual leaders within the group, the club, the society, the institution within which the society exists; study clubs develop a sentiment for the subject studied; athletic groups develop sentiments for their particular sports; religious groups develop sentiments for their particular causes and purposes; social-fraternity organizations develop sentiments for their particular chapters and for their national symbols and ideals; and so on through a very wide range of possibilities. Doubtless, also, the development of these sentiments is aided by what McDougall has termed active sympathy. In the collective life of the adolescent group it is easy for the individual to find another in whom he can easily arouse feelings and emotions like his own. Seeing such would by passive sympathy intensify his own feelings and emotions; and, according to McDougall's thesis, it is out of the recurrence of emotional experience with an object that sentiments arise. Hence by living in a group of those who can easily feel alike there is an interplay which assists in the formation of the new sentiments.

Lastly, it should be added that in the group there is provided

---

[1] Hall, G. Stanley, *Adolescence,* Vol. 2, p. 430.

the means for satisfying many of the urges or desires of the youth. There is opportunity for display, for activity, for thrill, for leadership, for the consciousness of power, and for the observation of approval of one's own acts and achievements. As an opportunity for the satisfaction of human desires one might think that the group should not be listed as an important feature in the molding of the personality. But those who are familiar with the distortions of personality which occur as a consequence of the lack of proper opportunity for such expression, for such achievements, and for the desired approval, know very well how important such opportunities are for the development of a normal, balanced, poised personality. Hence, in providing such, the group life is a very important factor in growth experience.

Not infrequently the contention is raised that group life, especially the resident groups in college years, are undesirable because they limit the development of individuality, that by their systems of social pressure they force the growth of the personalities of its members into a common mold. Certainly there is ample evidence that group life does develop certain attitudes and sentiments and interests and ideas in its members that are alike. Thrasher found this in his study of the gangs, but he also found that gang life tended very definitely in the direction of the development of individual traits and capacities. A considerable portion of his chapter on personality [1] is devoted to the many individual differences developing within the gang. And in Angell's study [2] of personality problems among students in the University of Michigan there is much emphasis upon the wide range of individual differences found. Presumably those students had been much subjected to the alleged standardizing pressures of collective experience.

Friends and Chums. Perhaps chumming or friendships should be looked upon, as Thrasher does, as merely a very small gang; but the permanency of many friendships, the degree to which they are cherished, and the distinctive nature of many of them, justify the special attention which they have received. Certainly, as they often exist within the gang or club, they must exercise in some fashion some form of special influence upon the

[1] Thrasher, F. M., *The Gang*, chap. 17.
[2] Angell, R. C., *A Study of Undergraduate Adjustment*, Chicago, 1930.

adolescent personality and the changes which are taking place within it.

Published investigations on the subject have been devoted very largely to the determination of the degree to which similarities, especially of intelligence, characterize chum or friendship pairs and to the social sources of friendships. These studies agree very well in their indication that, by and large, friendships are between youths of approximately the same degree of general mental ability.[1] Also, they come from much the same social status, frequently from the same neighborhood and school. Furfey found that correlations for age and size and intelligence averaged a little higher than .30; but when he correlated for degree of general development he obtained a higher figure (.41). A study of Columbia college freshmen[2] produced a positive correlation for scholarship between friends of .62, but for intelligence (.21) and for social intelligence (.27) the correlations were much lower. There is the interesting suggestion in this that those who were making good grades would be attracted to each other, and that in turn the friendly association might contribute to the scholarship. Giddings and later Loukas, much influenced by their concept of the "consciousness of kind," sought to discover to what extent similarities of physical appearance, color of hair and eyes and skin, factored in the selection of friends. Their investigation, however, covering many hundreds of cases, failed to reveal any tendency to select friends of like physical appearance. But when Loukas extended the investigation to a consideration of manners, morals, ideas, beliefs, tastes for food and amusement, and appreciation of the arts, he found very marked evidence of likenesses.[3] This investigation supports the

[1] Almack, J. C., "The Influence of Intelligence on the Selection of Associates," *Sch. & Soc.*, 1922, 16, 529-530.

Furfey, P. H., "Some Factors Influencing the Selection of Boys' Chums," *J. Appl. Psychol.*, 1927, 11, 47-51.

Warner, M. L., "Influence of the Mental Level in the Formation of Boys' Gangs," *J. Appl. Psychol.*, 1923, 7, 224-236.

Wellman, B., "The School Child's Choice of Companions," *J. Educ. Res.*, 1926, 14, 126-132.

Williams, P. E., "A Study of Adolescent Friendships," *Ped. Sem.*, 1923, 30, 342-346.

[2] Garrett, H. E., "Jews and Others: Some Group Differences in Personality, Intelligence, and College Achievement," *Person. J.*, 1929, 7, 341-348.

[3] Loukas, Christ, "Consciousness of Kind Among University Students," *Social Forces*, 1929, 7, 385-388. See also Flemming, E. G., "Best Friends," *J. of Soc. Psychol.*, 1932, 3, 385-390.

casual observation that youths of like interests and habits tend to chum together.

Of the influences which friendships have upon the traits of those who participate, a few are fairly clear. Certainly the friendship contacts must contribute much to the development of organization within the personality, to stabilization as a consequence of the greater organization, to the better integration of that which has here been so often mentioned as the personality synthesis. There are many things which would contribute to this. As friends think and talk together, with little or no reservation, of the most intimate affairs of life, new relationships, new meanings, new associational connections must be established. Things are not merely meditated about. In friendships, thoughts find overt expression. The good and the bad are externalized and looked at objectively, with all of the changes of values which such experience is likely to bring. It is not merely an interchange of thought and opinion; but, according to McDougall's principle of active and passive sympathy, there is much development of feeling reactions. In the friend, one is most certain to find a person who will respond with like feelings and emotions and thus satisfy the active sympathy desire. And, as a consequence, one's own feelings are somewhat increased thereby. Without a friend in whom to confide, there must inevitably be much repression with tendencies to those distortions of personality which repression may effect. Friendship thus provides a means of expression, of catharsis. There is in it the possibility of all of the psychological values of confession. To the friend, one may talk in confidence, and find the release and satisfaction of such expression. Talking into a diary or journal can do this to some extent; but the friend supplies a much more natural mode of confession or catharsis.

Friendships also develop loyalty of attitude and of conduct. The mutual consciousness of intimate confidence stirs and emphasizes the loyalty attitude. The consciousness of confidence stirs a consciousness of responsibility to protect. Perhaps herein lies the reason for, or at least a very large factor in the production of, the well-known permanency of youthful friendships. This permanency came out prominently in Bonser's study of over two thousand high school students.[1]   Williams,[2] studying the friendships and attitudes toward them in a group of delinquent boys, found loyalty stressed in a variety of ways. Loyalty was emphasized as an important trait in selection and again as a necessary feature in one's own behavior toward a friend. In this loyalty and consciousness of responsibility because of the confidence of the other, there is both the possibility of developing desirable character traits and also the possibility of perversion into the undesirable. Students of delinquency have frequently found this living and acting together a stimulus to the rapid development of criminal conduct, under certain contributing circumstances. And, in like manner, the intimacies and loyalties of friendship may serve to enhance and establish tendencies in one to lead and to dominate and in the other to submit and to follow. Mutualization of habits and traits may sometimes occur.

While studies of the sources of chums and friends indicate that they come from community and school groups of those who are already much alike and that out of these there is a tendency for those of like traits to chum together, still it must be observed that the percentages are not high.[3]   There are many instances thus of friendships in which both the physical and character traits studied are different. This checks with common unsystematic observation. We all observe the friendship pairs which startle us by their difference. We wonder why they should find each other mutually attractive. Certainly this possibility merits investigation and serious consideration. It may be that such friendships grow out of the consciousness that the other has what the one lacks, and perhaps desires to have. One may suspect that in such friendships the compensating traits develop con-

[1] Bonser, F. G., "Chums: A Study in Youthful Friendships," *Ped. Sem.*, 1902, 9, 221-237.

[2] Williams, P. E., "A Study of Adolescent Friendships," *Ped Sem.*, 1923, 30, 342-346. The reader should see also F. A. C. Perrin's study, "Physical Attractiveness and Repulsiveness," *J. Exper. Psychol.*, 1921, 4, 203-217. This study of a small group of advanced college students reveals sincerity and consistency and affectionate disposition ranking high in reasons for being attracted to a friend. Physical features rank high in lists of items marked unattractive.

[3] The highest percentages in Loukas's study was 70 percent for likeness in morals and also for tastes in amusements.

fidence and some satisfaction in the one who lacks and perhaps contributes something to the development of such traits where they are weak, but at present one dares to do little more than to suspect and watch for possible verification.

Concerning the psychology of friendships in the later years of adolescence a few interesting suggestions appear. Terman reports that the group of gifted children whom he and his associates studied showed a declining interest in friendships with progress through adolescence.[1] In Vecerka's study of girls, made in Europe, there is the indication that in pubescence the meaning of friendship is not well understood, but that this understanding grows with progress through adolescence.[2] Thrasher, it will be recalled, demonstrated the temporary nature of the gang and that individual professional or vocational interests along with the attractions and demands of romantic love tended to displace the lure of the gang. There is evidently a period between the high-tide of gang interest and the age of entering upon married life. This appears to be the blossoming period for adolescent friendships. Gang interest shades over into friendship interest. Vecerka's study supports this as well as Thrasher's. The declining interest in friendship reported for gifted children may be but an indication of more rapid progress toward maturity.

Perhaps, then, friendships of later adolescence should be looked upon as a temporary development to be later supplanted by matrimony. Certainly many friendships are displaced by the attractions of companionship of the other sex. Just as gang interests shade over into friendship interests, so it may be that friendship interests shade over into friendships with the other sex, into romantic love, and finally marriage. Certainly many love affairs grow out of such boy and girl friendships. As the gang socializes and prepares the way for friendship, so friendship may prepare the way for love and marriage. The friendship experience may train in habits and attitudes which are subsequently re-conditioned into the responses of marriage compan-

[1] Burks, B. S., Jensen, D. W., and Terman, L. M., *The Promise of Youth*, chap. 9, Stanford, 1930.
[2] Vecerka, L., "Das soziale Verhalten von Mädchen während der Reifezeit," *Quell. u. Stud. Jugendk.*, 1926, 4, 49-121.

ionship.   While such an interpretation of friendship must be considered as wholly tentative, it seems to be worthy of serious consideration.

Note.   In addition to the references given in the text, the student will also find the following items useful:

Furfey, P. H., *The Growing Boy*, New York, 1930.
Sheldon, H. D., *Student Life and Customs*, New York, 1901.

CHAPTER IX

EFFECTS OF THE SOCIAL CONFLICT

INFERIORITY TROUBLES, THEIR CAUSES, AND BEHAVIOR EFFECTS; HOMESICKNESS (NOSTALGIA)

The struggle for social adjustment in a social order filled with institutions and customs which function both as social pressures and as obstacles to the developing adolescent results in many disturbing reactions. Sometimes these are but temporarily discouraging; sometimes they are permanently disastrous. Inferiority troubles (feelings and concepts and complexes), and homesickness (nostalgia), as frequent effects of the struggle to achieve in this complex social situation, are presented in this chapter. Others will be found in the next chapter.

The Inferiority Reaction. Feelings of inferiority are a frequent consequence of the adolescent's struggle with the social situation. From childhood up the social pressures of the home, the school, the play group, of clubs and friendships are such as to establish a forward-looking attitude. It is an attitude of seeking, preparing for, and expecting achievement. But, in childhood, the number of things that can be done as well as the number of things expected of the child are few in number. In adolescent years, however, the number of things which may be done, which may be achieved, of which the individual is aware as possibilities, increase enormously and at the same time there is an ever-increasing consciousness of social demands. Adulthood is not many years off. The youth knows that he will soon be expected to marry, to have a vocation, to succeed in life, to be able to play the game, to realize something of what the family and friends expect of him, to approximate somewhat the ideal which he has for his own life. Associations with other adolescents bring knowledge of the intensity of the competition in all of this, and of the great individual differences in capacity. The contrast between what one is and what one is expected someday to be is never quite so great. As a consequence, boys and girls in the teens are often troubled by feelings of inferiority.

Before proceeding further it is probably wise to point out the distinctions prevailing between the terms inferiority feeling, concept of inferiority, and inferiority complex. The inferiority feeling is that which we often experience when we perceive that we are smaller, weaker, less capable, less impressive, less attractive, or less influential than something or some one else. There is nothing abnormal about it nor is it necessarily reprehensible. It is just one of the disagreeable feelings which every human being experiences more or less.

The concept of inferiority is, as the term indicates, a purely cognitive process. It is a concept of one's self which includes the well-established meaning that one is weaker or smaller or less impressive or less capable or less attractive. Such a concept when aroused may easily stir feelings of inferiority, but there is ample reason for thinking that one may have a concept of inferiority without feeling inferior. Many people know their limitations very well. They know that they are not as big, not as able, not as strong, as some other people; but they know these things just as they know a lot of other items. A young man may know that as a baseball player he is inferior to many others. Nevertheless, he gets a lot of fun out of playing, and so does not feel inferior. A girl may know that she cannot golf or swim as well as some other girls; but she likes to do these things, and is not troubled by feelings of inferiority because she is not the world's champion in one or both. Whether or not a concept of inferiority habitually arouses feelings of inferiority will depend very much upon the individual experience with that concept and what feeling associations have been established with it. It will also depend upon the individual's ideal for himself.

An inferiority complex is produced by much experience both with notions of inferiority and with feelings of inferiority. Unsuccessful struggles to adjust to the fact of certain inferiorities, too much attention to those who are greater and more powerful and more highly privileged, too much meditation and phantasy thinking about what one longs to do and cannot—all these gradually build a habit pattern, a constellation of memories, which can be easily activated by any one of many different cues because of its wealth of associations. However it is activated, it promptly arouses the feeling of inferiority. Probably it is better to think of the complex as apart from consciousness. It is primarily a mass of habit patterns. Portions of it may be recalled and thus be conscious; but, by and large, it operates apart from consciousness and is a straight and easily functioning path to the arousal of inferiority feeling and all of the disagreeable consequences of chronically feeling inferior.

Every adolescent, as, likewise, every adult, has feelings of inferiority and has them often. A person in whom a feeling of inferiority could not be aroused would be decidedly abnormal. But it is not the mere occasional feeling of inferiority with which we are concerned. Such a feeling does not produce conduct that attracts attention by its peculiarity. Young people do not ordinarily seek counsel because they occasionally have feelings of inferiority. But the people who have well-established concepts of inferiority and inferiority complexes frequently do become problems to themselves and not infrequently carry their problems to those who are supposed to know something about human nature.

Just how frequently the more troublesome form of inferiority phenomena appear in adolescence no one yet knows with any degree of certainty. There are those who are inclined to state that practically all young people are at some time troubled with them. Out of a mixed class of 297 typical college students 125 (42 percent) reported immediate recall of trouble with inferiority experiences. In another study of 512 college students, 48 percent could immediately recall such troubles.[1] There is some reason for thinking that it is to be found more frequently among certain social classes than among others.[2] And it has been further contended that it occurs more frequently among girls than among boys. Sometimes this sex difference has been based largely upon theoretical considerations; but, more recently, experimental stud-

[1] Gardner, G. E., and Pierce, H. D., "The Inferiority Feelings of College Students," *J. Abn. & Soc. Psychol.*, 1929, 24, 8-13.
[2] Faterson, H. F., "A Study of the Minnesota Rating Scale for Measuring Inferiority Attitudes," *J. Soc. Psychol.*, 1930, 1, 463-493.

ies furnish support for the contention.[1]   Whatever be the frequency of appearance, the fact remains that individual adolescents are often seriously troubled by inferiority notions and complexes, and it is also true that difficult and peculiar and undesirable modes of conduct can frequently be traced to such notions and complexes even though the possessor be unaware of their existence.

Originally, the cause of inferiority complexes was attributed to *organic defects*.   Alfred Adler [2] was responsible for this and through his efforts it was brought to light that many could be traced to such defects as smallness of stature, delayed or defective physical development, bad digestion, a crippled condition of any sort, or to poor health in general.   In order to explain why these physical defects should stir inferiority disturbances Adler posited the existence of a will-to-power drive,[3] a drive or urge toward power or wholeness or normality of development and achievement.   As achievement or satisfaction of the drive was blocked, or appeared to be blocked, by the physical defect, the inferiority complex developed.

Both clinical experience and systematic study [4] support the early contention of the large contribution to inferiority troubles made by the awareness of physical defects; but it is also becoming clear that imagined physical defects often function in the same manner.   Not infrequently one meets young people who suffer inferiority disturbances because of a belief that they are incompetent in some way.   They may have been unnecessarily coddled by unwise parents and thus the notion of defect became established.   They may have read quack medical advertisements, or even reliable medical literature which they were not able to

[1] Heidbreder, Edna, "The Normal Inferiority Complex," *J. Abn. & Soc. Psychol.*, 1927, 22, 243-258.   See also the Gardner and Pierce study mentioned above.

[2] The essentials of Alfred Adler's thinking will be found in the following volumes: *The Neurotic Constitution, Study of Organ Inferiority and Its Psychical Compensation, The Practice and Theory of Individual Psychology, Understanding Human Nature.*

[3] This was at first termed the "masculine protest" on the assumption that girls ignorant of anatomical differences thought themselves sexually defective in comparison with the male and thus rebelled against their state.   Gardner and Pierce (see above), however, found no evidence of a sex difference in the frequency of inferiority feelings attributable to physical causes.

[4] Faterson, H. F., "Organic Inferiority and the Inferiority Attitude," *J. Soc. Psychol.*, 1931, 2, 87-101.

understand properly; and, as a consequence, developed beliefs in their own defective nature. Not infrequently the lack of adequate instruction concerning sex anatomy and sex physiology, and of the physical phenomena which normally appear in pubescence, leads to misinterpretations and false beliefs in the supposed existence of a physical defect or functional abnormality which incapacitates for normal living. Some believe themselves so homely as to be repugnant to others. Here, again, one may see not only the effect of the will-to-power drive, but also the effects of the many social pressures leading to ideals and standards and specific desires which obviously cannot be responded to and achieved if the person is as defective as he believes himself to be.

Without doubt there are instances, also, where a defect of native intelligence, or at least a degree of mental ability below that necessary for the achievement of what is desired, does function, as do physical defects, in producing inferiority feelings and concepts and even complexes. The possibility of this should always be watched for in any problem case; although one must, also, keep always in mind the possibility of an adolescent boy or girl presenting notions of limited mental ability as a rationalization for their own failure, when the true cause was something much less honorable. With the rapid spread of the use of mental tests in schools and colleges, the advisability of revealing to students the scores which they made on the tests has frequently been questioned. There has been the fear that a knowledge of a comparatively low intelligence rating would discourage and tend toward the establishment of an inferiority complex. On that ground there are those who urge the concealment of the scores as a measure in mental hygiene.

By the time adolescent years are reached, however, most students have had sufficient competitive experience to create a fairly correct idea of their own relative ability, and so there should not be much disturbance from similar information determined by more accurate methods. It must be true, to a considerable extent at least, that individuals in the lower ranges of ability do not have the capacity to think as ambitiously for themselves, and so are less liable to the more acute forms of inferiority disturbance. Also, it is contended that boys and girls should know their mental limitations, if they have been accurately measured, as soon as possible, so that adjustments may be made before hopes and anticipations develop for that which can never be realized. The few attempts at systematic investigation of the matter are all too inadequate. What we do have indicate that students are not much affected in general by knowledge of their test scores. Instances of discouragement are reported but they are relatively few in number.[1] Obviously care should be used in giving out test score information in order that it be properly interpreted. Misinterpretations might cause distress, and unnecessarily.

Most students of the subject, even Adler himself, are now placing the emphasis heavily upon social causes of inferiority disturbance. One study of American college students attributed 32 percent to social causes.[2] Preparation for the socially developed inferiority reactions probably goes far into childhood, or even into infancy. Life with the parents who are so much more powerful may serve in many instances to establish the first patterns of inferiority reaction. Growing up as a younger brother or sister is also responsible for not a few inferiority disturbances. Especially is this true where the older brother or sister is distinguished for certain abilities or talents or achievements. In such cases, far too often, the achievements of the older are held up to the younger as models which they should emulate; and that quite without regard for individual differences in ability and opportunity. The studies of foster-child fantasies reveal that lack of family resemblance, notions of improper or discriminatory treatment, and the like, lead to fantasies of being a foster-child and that many of these fantasies are coming from some socially inferior origin.[3]

In school life the emphasis placed upon grades and the various pressures used to force grade achievement, coupled with the possible assumption or misinterpretation that all should do as well as the best, may easily contribute to the development of inferi-

---

[1] Allen, C. M., *Some Effects Produced in an Individual by Knowledge of His Own Intellectual Level*, New York, Columbia University, 1930. Fenton, Norman, "Mental Test Scores and Self-Regard," *J. Educ. Adminis. & Supervision*, 1924, 10, 103-108.

[2] Gardner, G. E., and Pierce, H. D., "The Inferiority Feelings of College Students," *J. Abn. & Soc. Psychol.*, 1929, 24, 8-13.

[3] In the author's study of this he found that 15 percent of 224 cases having detailed recallable experience with the fantasy thought of themselves as orphans or foundlings. See "The Foster-Child Fantasy," *Amer. J. Psychol.*, 1920, 31, 59-76.

ority troubles among those of lesser ability or lesser achievement.

Differences in educational and cultural and social advantages and training constitute a constant source of inferiority disturbance. Faterson has experimentally demonstrated a relationship to social status; [1] and behavior problem clinics reveal the same in a less systematic manner. Many homes as a matter of course provide training in customs of dress, of conversation, of etiquette, of manners and practices that are socially approved; while others, for obvious reasons, do not supply much of that sort of training. Young people who lack such experience when suddenly forced into circumstances where it is needed are often at great disadvantage. The social embarrassment which follows is the start of their inferiority disturbances. No doubt this is often exaggerated by them unduly. Young people from the less wealthy homes or from the smaller towns are prone to exaggerate the advantages of their fellows who came from the more privileged homes and from the cities; but this in no wise minimizes the serious effects of the notions and feelings aroused. It does, however, make the removal of them by a wise counsellor a much simpler matter.

The apparently insurmountable barriers established by social prejudice easily develop not only inferiority feelings but also concepts of personal inferiority and even inferiority complexes. Sectarian religious prejudices often operate in this manner. Jewish adolescents in a largely non-Jewish group, Catholics in a group that is largely Protestant, children of Mormon training when thrown into almost any group unfamiliar with Mormon life and ideals, and so on, all constitute unhappy sources of inferiority troubles. Racial prejudice and ignorance function in like manner. Children of Negro or of Indian or of any foreign origin which gives a conspicuously different physical appearance, when with groups of other than their own kind, feel the sting of the social prejudice. Now and then, too, there will be found those who must face the old social prejudice against illegitimacy of birth. Even though this be so effectively concealed that associates are quite ignorant of the fact, if the adolescent himself is

[1] Faterson, H. F., "A Study of the Minnesota Rating Scale for Measuring Inferiority Attitudes," *J. Soc. Psychol.*, 1930, 1, 463-493.

aware of it there is the fear of its becoming known, the knowledge of the prejudice which could be so easily aroused, and hesitancy about accepting normal courtesies from the other sex, all of which contribute to the production of inferiority phenomena.

Sometimes the source of trouble lies in the establishment or acceptance of ideals which are so far beyond the possible that inferiorities are accentuated and aggravated. The exalted ideals fostered by some religious movements and the corresponding emphasis upon the unworthiness of the individual human being are known to have had such effects. With the best of intentions religious leaders have made the mistake of exaggerating the contrast between the actual and the ideal to the distress of the boy or girl. The consciousness of inexperience and the uncertainty about personal abilities and capacities in the face of social pressure to realize their ideals, or to achieve what is supposed to be expected of them by the adults with whom they associate, again makes a contrast which is easily interpreted in terms of inferiority.

For reasons which should now be obvious the adolescent does not deliberately advertise the existence of his inferiority complex or his disturbing belief in his own inferiority. It is kept concealed, sometimes so effectively that the most careful students of adolescent behavior may not at first suspect its presence. Thus it is necessary to know what in general are the kinds of behavior which may be used as *indicators of the existence of inferiority* disturbance. Of these there are many which may be mentioned; but it must always be kept in mind that any form of conduct listed as an inferiority effect may also at times be caused by other factors.

Outstanding among them is an irritating *self-assertiveness* (1). There is an overly eager seeking of office and distinction and social recognition. The person talks too much and too loudly, and often in ways which appear to others as unmannerly if not immodest. Privacies are disregarded and cherished proprieties trampled upon. The clothing may not be in harmony. It may be extremely and conspicuously stylish; or it may be noticeable for its roughness, uncouth, and untidy. In its more extreme forms all associates are treated in an overbearing manner.

Closely allied to the self-assertiveness is the appearance of intense *self-consciousness* (2). In such cases there is complaint of embarrassment, inability to speak or otherwise perform in public, and a persistent self-criticism. Everything is brought up and thought over and interpreted adversely to the self. This may so disturb self-control as to result in conduct regarded by others as silly, brainless, and muddle-headed. Here, obviously, there is the familiar disturbance of thought and of control by emotion, but it is not the social situation which is directly stimulating the emotion. It is the inferiority complex which is activated by the social situations. The ineffectiveness or impropriety of the conduct is also perceived by the inferiority sufferer himself and this perception in turn still further aggravates troubles which are already bad enough.

A bad temper (3) needs always to be watched. It may be motivated by inferiority disturbance. When an adolescent boy or girl is too easily stirred to anger, and by situations which associates look upon as far from being so provocative, one may properly suspect that there is something in the situation which is stirring latent notions of inferiority or an inferiority complex. Where there is such a complex in the background, little things will excite the feelings of inferiority through the complex. There will be instantly the attitude that social prejudice is rising as an obstacle, that every one else has a better chance; and the situation will be maddening. Where everything blocks the normal will-to-power drive, or whatever it may be called, the normal reaction is to fight. Sometimes it appears in what is called insolent habits or it may be in mere touchiness.

The youth who chronically complains that he *never has a chance* (4), that it is always some one else who gets the "break," may also be properly suspected of inferiority. Unfortunately, most people are familiar with this sour, disgruntled, irritable, and irritating sort of behavior. It is not of course confined to adolescence. It may even become chronic and a permanent feature of the personality. Out of such notions, ideas of persecution easily arise. Meditation upon one's lack of opportunity and the belief that the chances and the favors all go to some one else can all too easily become focalized into the belief that some particular person or institution or group or organization is really responsible.[1]

A noticeable *lack of social grace and ease* (5) should also be watched as a possible indication of inferiority disturbance. Of course the degree of grace and ease in social situations to be expected of adolescents must not be too high. Too much poise cannot be expected for their lack of experience, of well-established habits. But when, by comparison with others of the same age, there is a conspicuous embarrassment in social situations and a persistent avoidance of them, then one may be properly suspicious of the possibility of inferiority motivation. Such cases may desire very sincerely to come and go as others do, or as they believe others to do; but it is only with the exertion of much effort and the summoning of much courage that they can force themselves into social situations. When there they are intense, strained, and unnatural. They may be quite unable to mix with others, and seek the quiet corners and out of the way places. For this McDougall has happily suggested that in such behavior we may observe the conflicting effects of uncontrolled stimulation of both the impulse to self-assertion and the impulse of self-submission. Now one and now the other predominates.[2] In the more serious instances of this sort it is the impulse to self-submission which dominates, and is only now and then for a little time conquered by the much-stimulated but little-active impulse to self-assertion.

Enviousness (6) may be stirred by almost any sort of inferiority experience. The mere existence of envy implies at once the judgment of the self as somehow inferior, or lacking in opportunity or power or achievement. Again it is important not to generalize hastily. The occasional experience of a little envy is not serious, and may be a valuable stimulus to worthy achievement. It is only when the enviousness becomes pronounced and

[1] Here the counsellor of young people must be especially careful. Such notions of a persecutory nature may be merely the consequence of inferiority notions and complexes, and may by proper guidance be eliminated. But it is also possible that persecutory ideas may be a symptom of a more serious condition that is developing, schizophrenia (dementia præcox), and · unless they respond promptly to the adviser's guidance the assistance of a psychiatrist should be sought.

[2] McDougall, Wm., *Social Psychology*, chap. 5.

appears to be taking the place of effortful seeking to achieve for one's self that one may properly suspect inferiority motivation. Such enviousness finds expression in disparaging remarks about others, which, if true, would tend to lower their general esteem. In thought and in expression the tendency is toward a sort of neutralization of the supposed difference. The motive seems to be that of seeking to bring the envied person down to the level of the one who envies. In extreme instances this can even eventuate in malicious acts. Such behavior can be thought of as a rationalization of the inferiority or it may be thought of as defensive behavior. In any case it is evidence of maladjustment.

Timidity (7) should also be considered in this connection. It is manifest in a curiously significant manner. The person developing this trait appears to be chronically afraid to put himself to any test. He apparently does not dare to enter into competition with others, often even when he knows perfectly well that he is practically certain to win. His inferiority complex stirs feelings of inferiority so intensely that he is unable to convince himself that he has the ability or the social approval sufficient to achieve in any sort of competition or approximation to a competition. He does not try because of the chronic fear of failure, the prospect of which even though remote is unendurable. In extreme cases such people cannot even play simple social games because of the distressing effect of losing. Losing but accentuates their feeling of inferiority, already too much and too easily aroused.

What is coming to be called *perfectionistic behavior,* or simply perfectionism (8), must also be listed as a possible product of inferiority disturbance. Here nothing ever satisfies. A letter must be re-written again and again and even when it appears to the author to be phrased as well as he is able to write, there is nevertheless the hesitation to mail because there is the thought that it may not perhaps be after all correct in every detail. Every task undertaken must be completed in every item even though before completion and perfection have been achieved the completion may have become unnecessary. Such a trait quickly becomes in itself a handicap to achievement. It blocks progress and absorbs time and energy unnecessarily and unwisely. The person manifesting it may become aware of the unfortunate handicap which he suffers, and, failing to understand its real motivation, looks upon it as another defect in himself. Thus is the inferiority complex, the real motivation, still further reinforced.

When *sex* (9) is looked upon *as a disadvantage* and a handicap, one may with confidence look for notions of inferiority. In the early days of Adler's work he believed that the female was frequently disturbed by inferiority complexes because of a mistaken belief that she was sexually abnormal. It was assumed that only the fully-developed male was normal and that all others were abnormal, defective, inferior. Later, as emphasis came to be placed more upon social causation, there was still reason for assuming that sex differences were the source of much inferiority trouble. The female was supposed to be limited, confined, denied the great achievements of life because of her sex; and she was thus supposed to long for the achievements and opportunities open to the male, and, finding herself thus blocked, to develop inferiority complexes. It is a pity that we do not have systematic studies of the frequency of inferiority feelings among women and girls of two or three generations ago, for comparison with the studies available today, made in a period when women have much more freedom and much more opportunity.

The few studies which we do have are contemporary, and, while they do indicate a slightly greater frequency of inferiority responses among females, the difference is not very significant. Gardner and Pierce found 42 percent of their male respondents indicating inferiority feelings, and of their females, 52 percent. Aikins in a study of a very small number of cases found the inferiority experience very frequently present in young women, but he also found that sex had comparatively little to do with it. Race and color and class and social customs were far more distinctive causes than the mere difference of sex.[1] But, after all, it is not the relative frequency that is of most importance. Rather it is the fact that some individual adolescents feel that because of their sex they are handicapped in life, that they are inferior. As a consequence they may develop any of the many

---

[1] Aikins, H. A., "Woman and the Masculine Protest," *J. Abn. & Soc. Psychol.*, 1927, 22, 259-272.
　　Gardner, G. E., and Pierce, H. D., "The Inferiority Feelings of College Students," *J. Abn. & Soc. Psychol.*, 1929, 24, 8-13.

effects of inferiority complexes. This every student of adolescent behavior should be aware of, especially when he seeks to understand the behavior in any particular instance.

One must be always watchful of *compensatory trends* (10) in behavior. They may be often traced to inferiority troubles. Of them there are many. Almost any form of skill, knowledge, art or vocation may be resorted to as a means of compensation for inferiority. Vaughan,[1] in a most entertaining and useful volume, has summarized a large number of life stories of people who have achieved as a consequence of the effort to compensate for inferiority, actual or imagined. Sometimes this is intelligent, wise, balanced devotion to a selected field of endeavor as a deliberate effort to compensate. As such, it can only be commended. It is in this form an adjustment which most adolescents must make, because most people are handicapped in one way or another. It is only when the compensatory behavior is unduly intense, and is of such a nature as to lead to the suspicion that there is something rather blindly impulsive about it, that one should suspect an ill-adjusted relationship to inferiority.

When there is intense and exaggerated application to the development of physical strength for no very apparent reason, then one may suspect an inferiority motivation. Frequently, a persistent and irrational seeking of thrills, so often seen among adolescents, is really a compensatory trend for inferiority. Instances of petty stealing, where there is no apparent need for the objects stolen, have been convincingly traced to this same seeking of a thrill as a means of giving the person the longed-for feeling of superiority. In like manner, one is often safe in applying the same interpretation to a passionate devotion to the reading of thrilling tales of daring adventure. Excessive devotion to the clothing, to physical appearance, to the enhancement and effective use of all the beauty one can command is of a like nature, and often of like motivation. Believing that one's body is not beautifully formed, and that one's face is not attractive has been the cause of no little inferiority distress in many adolescent girls.[2]

[1] Vaughan, W. F., *The Lure of Superiority*. New York, 1928.
[2] A pathetic instance of this is the famous case of Charlotte Brontë who was much influenced by the belief that she was ugly and unattractive. See Mrs. Gaskell's *Life of Charlotte Brontë*.

Lastly, there is always the possibility that the *introverted personality* (11) is so because of an inferiority complex. Perhaps there is introversion that is due to some basic temperamental peculiarity, actually a psycho-physical type; but there are many case studies which indicate the tendencies of people to withdraw into themselves as a consequence of the struggle with inferiority. They find in their fantasies of greatness and achievement, in their day-dreams, some satisfaction of their will-to-power drive, of their conscious desires to achieve as they believe others are doing and as they believe that they are prevented by the nature of the social situation from so doing. When an adolescent boy or girl is reported to be spending much time alone with no apparent activity but that of probable day-dreams, one has at least a right to suspect that the content of these day-dreams is compensatory for inferiorities actual or believed.[1]

When one turns from such a survey of inferiority effects to think again in terms of the growing personality, it is easy to appreciate how significant for the future such experiences may be. In them many traits which are to characterize the personality throughout life have their birth. Case studies of abnormal adults, of people who have arrived at a distressing degree of maladjustment in life, frequently go back to these troubles of adolescent years for their explanations. Studies in social psychology which seek to explain the peculiar behavior of certain groups or kinds of people often reveal the lasting effect of adolescent struggles with inferiority feelings and complexes.

It is perfectly safe to say that any of the traits just mentioned may not only be the immediate product of inferiority disturbances, but also that, unless something happens to dissipate the inferiority factor, the trait may readily become established as a permanent and perhaps salient feature of the personality. Allport traces radicalism in the adult to inferiority troubles; and to the same factor he attributes the persistency and over-intensity of

---

[1] Here again persons in positions of responsibility must be cautious. Such a withdrawal from activity and finding of satisfaction in day-dreams may be a symptom of a more serious condition, schizophrenia (dementia præcox). If it becomes chronic or manifests a tendency to become chronic, or even if it does not respond readily to counsel and guidance, the assistance of a psychiatrist should be obtained.

many chronic social reformers.[1] And there are many case studies which supplement and support the experiences of everyday life in tracing the timidity of adults, the self-consciousness, the over-assertiveness, the social awkwardness, the enviousness, perfectionism, the soured personality and the other items mentioned to the inferiority troubles of their youth from which they have never recovered.

But such an habituation of the trait is not always the case. Sometimes a sufficient degree of compensation is achieved for the inferiority, actual or imagined, so that most or all of these disagreeable manifestations disappear. But that does not mean that the inferiority is not still in the background. It means only that so much has been achieved in life that the inferiority is no longer disturbingly and conspicuously influential. Vaughan and Swift[2] have both presented long lists of those who have achieved more or less distinction in life as a compensation for their early inferiorities. Indeed, from a reading of such reports, one might almost be inclined to generalize that success in life could be more easily achieved when the individual was pricked into energetic effort by the sting of inferiority. But it is true, also, that many adults who have achieved and tell of their life-long struggle with inferiority troubles believe that they have achieved in spite of their inferiority rather than because of it. And possibly there are large numbers who never achieve much in life because of inferiority complexes, or their inferiority-motivated traits. Here, unfortunately, our knowledge is still far too limited; but we know enough to be certain that the presence of much struggle with inferiority trouble in adolescent years does not always mean an unhappy outcome.

Sometimes the inferiorities of adolescent years are completely dissipated. This may take months, or even years, and they may at times be dissipated very quickly. A better knowledge of the self and individual capacities often works wonders. The discovery that large numbers of other young people, all of whom are falsely supposed to be free of such troubles, likewise struggle against feelings of inferiority sometimes works like the magic of

[1] Allport, F. H., *Social Psychology*, pp. 372-373.
[2] Vaughan, W. F., *The Lure of Superiority*, New York, 1928.
  Swift, E. J., *Mind in the Making*, 1909, chap. 1.

a great revelation. So often the youth does not know that others have the same struggles, and that those who have achieved went through exactly the same experiences in adolescent years. Sometimes correct information actually removes the cause. Where there has been the belief in mental inferiority the discovery of a mental test score proving the contrary may be enough. Sometimes it is a matter of false social standards or of total misunderstandings of social customs and attitudes. More knowledge has the effect of changing the estimation of the self, of changing the meanings which accrue in many of the perceptions in life, and there is no longer the stimulus to inferiority feeling. Where the cause is an actual physical inferiority, the cause cannot of course be removed; but the increased knowledge of the self, of social customs, and the knowledge of one's own capacity which comes through successful achievements in life, may very greatly minimize the earlier assumed significance of the physical deficiency.

It is always important to keep in mind that where behavior is disturbed by inferiorities there are habits to be dealt with, and that habits are not quickly altered. Also, that the alteration of habits depends much upon how thoroughly they have been established. Often much effort is necessary and much practice indispensable, before new habits of self-interpretation and self-evaluation can be brought to dominate. Even then scars of the experience may last throughout a lifetime. There may be unpleasant memories which, try as one may, cannot be forgotten. The desperate efforts which many parents make to give their children every possible advantage are doubtless often traceable to the lingering influences of these unhappy memories.

In many instances a religious faith has done much to efface the inferiority trouble.[1] Religionists have pointed out time and again that man's abilities and disabilities in the sight of God have a very different evaluation than in the sight of men. Obviously what man is to God is of far greater importance than what man is to men. Where these divine evaluations are dwelt upon and accepted, there will be found in them a powerful aid to the elimination of many inferiority interpretations. When thought of in terms of a lifetime, or, even better, in terms of some

[1] Allport, F. H., *Social Psychology*, pp. 404-407.

vast universal design, the disabilities and inferiorities of adolescence are frequently belittled into harmlessness.[1]

The Homesick Reaction (Nostalgia). Homesickness, or nostalgia, is a common adolescent reaction; and it is an important adolescent reaction. As it is ordinarily found among young people
in school and business, it is complicated in a way which makes
both its handling and its interpretation not quite the same nor
so simple as that of the old-time textbooks.[2] It is not simply a
longing for the familiar sights and sounds of home.

Systematic studies of the subject are extraordinarily rare and
such analyses as are available seem to the writer to be decidedly
inadequate; but such as we have agree pretty well upon certain
general features of the homesickness upset. All stress the effect
of being in a strange environment; and some point to its being
different from a genuine nervous or mental disease. There is to
be sure a more or less aggravated emotional depression; but this
depression or melancholy does not behave like an ordinary melancholia. It will clear away rapidly upon the return of the sufferer to the old environment. Cases in illustration of this are
usually presented from the observation of soldiers far from their
homes, or from the experiences with refugees who, through war
or flood or fire, have been forced to leave their normal places of
residence. In grave instances, marked physical symptoms appear.
There is loss of appetite, digestive disturbances, vomiting, and
disturbances of heart action and respiration. Instances are reported in which these physiological disturbances so depleted the
individual sufferer that death came as an inevitable consequence.
Suicides also are reported.

Of mental symptoms the descriptions are less detailed and satisfying. Hallucinations are generally mentioned as of occasional
appearance although the special nature of these is not known.
Kline [3] speaks of a "shrivelling of the ego," without amplification

---

[1] For practical purposes the reader will find many useful hints in W. S.
Walsh's *The Inferiority Feeling*, New York, 1928. An elaborate attempt at
the measurement of inferiority feelings will be found in Smith, R. B., "The
Development of an Inventory for the Measurement of Inferiority Feelings at
the High School Level," *Arch. of Psychol.*, 1932, No. 144.

[2] Modern textbooks of nervous and mental diseases almost uniformly ignore
this subject.

[3] Kline, L. W., "The Migratory Impulse *vs.* the Love of Home," *Amer.
J. Psychol.*, 1898, 10, 1-81.

of his meaning. Others mention a fixation of thoughts upon home. Those who seek to relieve the distress of the homesick sufferer find it annoyingly impossible to get his thoughts upon anything but those of his home and his longing to be there again. And, as is characteristic of depressed conditions, there is the belief, more or less profound, that the whole situation is helpless, that there is no way out, that the beloved homeland will never be seen again, and the like. In rare instances nostalgic disturbances appear in the form of explosive, or uncontrollable, criminal actions, arson, and even murder.[1]

Marbe[2] suggests that homesickness is in all probability a far less frequent occurrence today than it was a century or more ago. This opinion is based upon the greater amount of travel and shifting of places of residence occurring in modern civilization. The earlier studies have reported homesickness to be much more frequent among people of rural origin than of urban, and the interpretation offered was in terms of greater variety of experiences in city life which better prepared them for changes than did the constancy and simple regularity of life in the country. As variety has come into the rural communities and modern conveniences, especially those of travel, have come even to the more remote dwellers, the assumption may be well founded that homesickness is declining in frequency.

Féré[3] states his belief that homesickness is far more likely to trouble those of the lower grades of intelligence. Unfortunately, however, we have only Féré's opinion on this. He may be right; but until there are some controlled studies of the subject, one should be cautious about accepting the statement as anything more than the opinion of an able observer.

Marbe[4] appears to believe stoutly in the existence of a special form of personality organization which is more susceptible to disturbance by homesickness. He marshals some experimental evidence in support of his contention that there are marked individual differences in adaptability. Some people can adapt

---

[1] Gross, Hans, *Criminal Psychology*, Boston, 1918. See especially pp. 77-78.
[2] Marbe, K., "Ueber das Heimweh," *Arch. f. d. ges. Psych.*, 1925, 1, 513-524.
[3] Féré, Ch., *The Pathology of Emotions*, London Univ. Press, pp. 407-408.
[4] Loc. cit. The same idea is hinted in one of Southard's war case descriptions. See Southard, E. E., *Shellshock and Other Neuropsychiatric Problems*, p. 440, Case No. 320.

themselves quickly to new situations and new subjects and new kinds of activity. Others do so only with difficulty. It is these people who adapt or adjust themselves slowly whom Marbe believes to be more liable to the troubles of homesickness.

And then there are those who glibly interpret homesickness in terms of instinct motivation. There is said to be a homing instinct at the base of the trouble; but there is no explanation of why it should not always produce homesickness.[1] G. Stanley Hall resorted to the positing of two instincts, one leading the individual toward home (oikotropic) and the other away from home (oikofugic), and attributed nostalgia to the conflict between these two without much attempt at further analysis.[2]

It must quickly come to the attention of any thoughtful observer that the occurrence of homesickness in adolescence today is comparable in only a general way to the homesickness aroused among conscripted soldiers far away from home, among refugees who have fled from their homes to escape the disasters of warfare, or among boys sent away to school against their will by parents or legal guardians. Most of the adolescent problems which we confront are among young people who have left home by their own desire to find the better opportunities which they believe to lie elsewhere, for the fun of seeing other sights and hearing other sounds, or to obtain a higher education not available in their own communities. Whatever of instinct or drive there may be in their going away from home, there is certainly a very large influence of social pressure. They have grown up in an environment which has built in them ideals of achievement, expectations of obtaining an education, desires to enjoy the pleasures of seeing other places and other peoples, beliefs in their own capacity to achieve, and beliefs that they should strike out for themselves in order to satisfy both themselves and their associates who expect so much of them. The content of the self and the nature of the self-regarding sentiment are all such as to lead to residence away from the scenes of childhood. This makes a more complicated psychogenesis of homesickness; and, at the same time, makes it impossible to relieve the distress by merely returning to

[1] Guthrie, L. G., *Functional Nervous Disorders in Childhood*, Oxford Press, pp. 56-63.
[2] Hall, G. Stanley, *Adolescence*, Vol. 2, pp. 380-382.

the old home sights and sounds. To return against the pressure of all these long-established desires and beliefs about the self would be as distressing as to stay away.

Behind all this there may be the push of an instinct to wander, as so many thoughtful people have believed and still believe. Davenport [1] contends that he has demonstrated in those who are feebly inhibited the clear manifestation of a nomadic instinct. Certainly, as a race, man has done much wandering, and there are those among us today who wander so constantly as to lead to the suspicion that they may be the victims of an instinct to wander which has never been controlled or which has undergone a perverted development. As the studies of maturation indicate the possibility of structural patterns coming to their full development at periods of different length after birth, there is the possibility that this propensity to wander, to respond to the lure of elsewhere, is an instinct pattern which in adolescent years is coming into the full maturity of development. But even though the reader prefer to accept the instinct to wander as a motivating factor in leaving home, it must always be kept in mind that the desires and beliefs and self-expectations mentioned above still remain as complicating factors in the psychogenesis of whatever cases of homesickness may arise.[2]

The classical studies of nostalgia all stress the significance of the absence of familiar environmental features as a causative agent. It is said that the German term for homesickness (Heimweh) came from a Swiss dialect and that as late as the 17th century it was referred to in Germany as the Swiss disease (Schweizerkrankheit).[3] The inference is that, whenever the Swiss left their homes, the change in the landscape especially was so great as to work more of a hardship on them than upon other people. Mention is also made of the absence of familiar foods, familiar faces, familiar voices, the familiar language, and even of the accustomed dialect of that language. Today we see more in this than

---

[1] Davenport, C. B., *The Feebly Inhibited: Nomadism, or the Wandering Impulse,* Carnegie Inst. of Washington, 1915.

[2] It is also probable that in specific instances rebellion against the repressive discipline of the parents may be a factor in leaving the home. For a discussion of this see chap. XI.

[3] For an excellent presentation of the early medical history of the subject with a bibliography of 86 titles see Jaspers, K., "Heimweh und Verbrechen," *Archiv. f. Kriminal-Anthropologie,* 1909, 35, 1-116.

the mere absence of certain patterns of stimuli. We see that the adolescent who goes away from home abandons that pattern or those patterns of stimuli to which his peaceful, comfortable, quiescent reactions (controlled by the cranial division of the autonomic system) have been conditioned by all the experiences of infancy and childhood.

When thought of in this manner, one realizes at once that there must be involved more than the mere absence of that pattern of stimuli to which the quiescent reactions have been conditioned. There must be that which is activating the emergency emotions (the sympathetic division of the autonomic system), fear, distress, and inferiority especially. And one does not ordinarily have to look far for it. The homesick youth finds himself in a very different social situation. In the new town and in the new job, at preparatory school or college, he is no longer looked upon as superior in any respect. His abilities and talents are not known. In the new place he is looked upon by his fellows as another stranger, perhaps even as an intruder. If he is welcomed, it is more or less formal; and then he is left to show what he can do. From being a big frog in a little puddle he often finds himself suddenly a very little frog in a very big puddle. This lack of appreciation, as he may term it, may stir a little anger for which there appears to him to be no adequate opportunity for expression. Certainly it may arouse much feeling of inferiority, and very probably no little fear that in a place so big and so different, in which there seems to be so little appreciation and willingness to give him a chance, there may not be much possibility for success. When difficulties arise, as come they must at school or in the business world, these raise serious questions about his own ability. There are disagreeable thoughts about the possibility of having over-estimated his powers, and all that train of thinking so often associated with feelings of inferiority and the fear of personal failure.

At home it had been possible to tell others of his troubles and of his achievements and by so doing stir in them emotions like his own. In seeing them so aroused, he found some satisfaction, perhaps through the reinforcements of his own feelings and convictions. But now, away from home, in a new environment, there may be no one with whom he can talk, in whom he can stir a sympathetic response. There is a blocking of what McDougall terms the tendency to active sympathy. As the youth faces his troubles alone, he is prone to wonder if perhaps he has not over-estimated himself, or if others have not led him into mistaken expectations. The situation appears to be hopeless, or nearly so. There is in it much to stir emergency emotions, which are asthenic and depressing, and there is little or nothing of that to which his comfortable, quiescent reactions have been conditioned.

To all of this the natural human reaction is that of seeking a way of escape. There is much thinking about home, the friends there, what they are doing, and all the familiar sights and sounds. There he was appreciated; there he was comfortable and happy; while here all is miserable. It is the simple psychology of desire. He has been happy. He is now unhappy; and he can recall what it was that made him happy. And so there is the desire to return to that pattern of stimuli which, from experience, he knows will arouse the agreeable feelings he longs for. Actions to avoid the disagreeable and to approach the agreeable are accepted by even some of the most severe critics of the instinct hypothesis as probably native reaction patterns.

But here unhappily the normal impulse to escape, to go back home, is blocked. To give up and go home would be admitting defeat; and, to a self (and a self-regarding sentiment) trained as these have been, that is most disagreeable. To go home and have all those who have praised and encouraged know that he had failed is a prospect quite as disagreeable as is that of remaining in the present miserable situation. Such thoughts stir inferiority feelings intensely. It is the home situation as it used to be that is attractive, not the home situation as it would be if he went back to it an avowed failure. Thus the impulse to escape by going back to the familiar and comforting pattern is an impulse to seek that which he knows no longer exists. Thus is action inhibited. Both to stay and to go home are equally distressing and depressing prospects. Both stir emergency emotions, activations of the sympathetic division of the autonomic nervous system with their well-known physiological effects. Digestion is disturbed. There is loss of appetite, and all the rest. And in turn there is the limitation of the range of thought usually present in depressed states. The homesick boy seems unable to think about much but the home (as it was) situation, and interprets everything in a hypochondriacal manner. He is overwhelmed by the miserableness of his present reality.

The way out must be through whatever means will bring quiescence to his emergency emotional apparatus, and for a time at least a domination by the cranial division of his autonomic nervous system and all its allied functions. Whatever pressure may effect in his behavior a preoccupation with his work will contribute most to the solution of his conflict. Preoccupation with work means exclusive attention to the present situation and the exclusion of thoughts that arouse conflict. And, furthermore, hard work is the best way to achievement. Through working hard he may accomplish something which will satisfy his desires concerning himself, bring a little praise from some one in authority, begin the process of establishing self-confidence in the new situation, achieve some indications of respect from his fellows, and provide opportunity for the display of whatever abilities he may actually have. Thus the process of developing in the new situation items which will stimulate, as once did the old home situation, the agreeable self-satisfying reactions. Idleness was early recognized as one of the factors contributing to the development of nostalgia among soldiers, and Papillon [1] contends that in his time sailors were kept so busy with work, or diversions of one sort or another, that there was far less homesickness among them than among soldiers. Certainly, work, facing the present situation actively, is the best way out for the homesick adolescent youth.

Other reinforcements or aids are possible, but they all lead back to work and active preoccupation with the present. Sometimes those who would assist the homesick do that which will make them angry. They make scornful remarks which stir the I-will-show-you-what-I-can-do attitude, with all of its possible dynamogenic effects or accompaniments. But this is merely a means of getting the youth back to his work. Some try to stir courage. There is the re-emphasis upon the youth's ideals. There is a re-arousal of all the old ambitions, and possibly some

1 Papillon, F., "Nostalgia," *Pop. Sci. Mo.*, 1874, 5, 215-220.

efforts to utilize or develop the youth's philosophy of life. This again is merely a means of leading him back to work with a new zest, and of getting him out of the distorting effect of his depressed state.

Some recommend a short visit home. For obvious reasons this may have the effect of aggravating the situation and bringing the contrast between what was and what is yet more vividly to mind; but there is also the possibility that it may renew the determination to work hard. Other aids to the development of the new adjustment will be found in the development of new friends; and, to some extent, through the association where possible with people from the same home town who have gone through the struggle and won. Their achievements as well as their community of interests help to bring about comfortable and comforting reactions. The goal is the conditioning of the comfortable reactions to the new pattern of stimuli, the restoration of self-confidence, and gradual achievement of such alterations in the concept of the self, and of the self-regarding sentiment, as may be necessary for successful living in the new environment.

If Marbe is right in his contention that there is a decline in the actual frequency of nostalgia, that alone would suggest the possibility of a further reduction by intelligent preventive measures. If the interpretation in terms of conditioning of reactions, the content of the self concept and the nature of the self-regarding sentiment, and the effects of the various social pressures brought to bear upon the growing boy or girl, proves to be acceptable and justifiable, then prevention should be clearly possible. And there are those today who are thinking in these terms.[1] It is possible that through an early training in independence and self-reliance, through much changing about, through occasional absences from home at summer camps and the like, through a careful avoidance of that excess of petting and coddling which develops parental fixations, the conflicts which produce homesickness with all of its distressing effects might be avoided.[2]

[1] Hollingworth, L. S., *Psychology of the Adolescent*, pp. 41 and 50.
[2] For a suggestive new formulation of nostalgia and its possible social significances see Ruml, B., "Theory of Nostalgic and Egoic Sentiments," *Psychol. Bull.*, 1933, 30, 656-657.

CHAPTER X

EFFECTS OF THE SOCIAL CONFLICT *(Continued)*

DAY-DREAMING, SELF-CONSCIOUSNESS, DEVELOPMENT OF SELF-CONFIDENCE

Inexperienced youth forced into social situations for which they are not well prepared frequently escape into day-dreams, a reaction which has been much discussed and deserves even more attention. Self-consciousness is of such common occurrence it is in danger of neglect, but may be subjected to careful analysis. These reactions to the social conflict are presented in this chapter as a continuation of the discussions of the preceding chapter which should be read first. Out of these troubles the normal development is into an adjustment which brings self-confidence. Not much is known about this but a few suggestions are possible.

Day-dreaming. This is one of the most familiar of adolescent traits. It has long been recognized and celebrated in song and story.[1] Descriptions of adolescence abound with such terms as reverie, introspection, brooding, wool-gathering, building castles in Spain, musing, inner absorption, mental involution, absent-mindedness. That children day-dream, and adults as well, is usually recognized; but the notion has always been that youth was especially given to such behavior.

Of systematic studies we have not so many, and what we have are frequently far from satisfactory, especially in the light of contemporary methods of research. T. L. Smith [2] obtained returns from 1,475 persons of ages ranging from seven to adult years. She found that all but two or three of these could report experi-

---

[1] For an incomparable description see G. Stanley Hall's *Adolescence,* Vol. 1, pp. 311-313.
[2] Smith, T. L., "The Psychology of Day-Dreams," *Amer. J. Psychol.,* 1904, 15, 465-488.

ence of day-dreams. Pruette [1] questioned over three hundred adolescent girls and found only a very few indeed who could not at once report their day-dreams. The writer asked a mixed class of 295 college students to state, among other things, if they day-dreamed frequently. Of these 201, or 69 percent, responded immediately that they did. Thus there is ample support for the belief that day-dreaming is a common adolescent reaction; but details concerning the relationship of this reaction to age and intelligence and personality and so on have yet to be discovered.

Especially since the advent of the psychoanalytic movement it has become increasingly the custom to think of day-dreaming as being in most respects psychologically similar to nocturnal dreaming. The same psychoanalytic mechanisms are used in its interpretation.[2] Perhaps it has been a bit easier to slip into the psychoanalytic way of thinking when day-dreams have been under consideration, because the wish-fulfillment feature appears a little more reasonable, a little more obvious, here than in the vagaries of the nocturnal dream. Perhaps the day-dream may be a little more simple, a little more like the Freudian descriptions of the dreams of childhood, a much more direct expression of some thwarted wish. Most people are willing to admit that in their day-dreams the realization of some wish, even though it be a rather absurd and fantastic one, is a feature often observed. For this reason it is difficult to think of the day-dream as entirely purposeless thinking, as some appear to have done. Certainly, also, it is not purposeful, at least it is not dominated by any serious purpose which is intimately related to the actualities of the present situation in life.

Whatever interpretation of the dreams of normal sleep one may prefer, the day-dream must be looked upon as a form of fantasy thinking. The very terms which have been used for it, musing and wool-gathering and reverie and the like, all indicate a withdrawal from the present perceptual situation. Of course there may have been that in the perceptual situation which provoked or stimulated the withdrawal, for the day-dream is not infrequently associated with an escape from a disagreeable present;

[1] Pruette, Lorine, *Women and Leisure,* chap. 8, entitled "Day Dreams of the Adolescent Girl."

[2] Varendonck, J., *The Psychology of Daydreams,* London, 1921.

or there may have actually been nothing in the perceptual field of sufficient attention-compelling influence to command attention. But the withdrawal should be noted as a psychologically distinctive feature. And then, too, the content of consciousness at the time is never exactly that which is characteristic of serious problem-solving.

While problems of life may be solved temporarily in the day-dream, the attitude toward the experience and the attitude toward the product of the experience are quite different from the attitudes toward purposeful or problem-solving thought. The solutions of problems arrived at in day-dreams may be pleasurable and satisfying; but they are pleasurable and satisfying only so long as the individual remains in the introverted, withdrawn, shut-in state of mind, only so long as he is abstracted from the present actualities of the life situation. As soon as the day-dreaming reaction is passed, there is, in the normal personality, a full realization that the solutions just arrived at were purely in the realm of fantasy and are quite useless and ineffectual in the world of present reality.

Day-dreaming then is a form of problem-solving, although an impractical one. For that reason it cannot be said that day-dreaming is a process of free association, unless by free association one means merely a freedom from the constraints set up by awareness of the present situation of the person involved. From that, to be sure, the process is relatively free; but it is not free from the influence of the person's wishes and hopes and desires and urges and even of instincts.

Where productive imagination leaves off and day-dreaming or fantasy thinking begins has never been agreed upon; and it cannot be until we have some means of measuring degrees of difference in this function. But it is instructive to observe that the two, productive imagination and day-dreaming, are very similar states or reactions, that they shade over into each other as the degree of influence by present reality or social actuality waxes and wanes in dominance. The more the present dominates the more thought takes on the form of productive imagination and serious problem-solving; the less it dominates the more freely is thought influenced by wishes and desires and urges, and the more the thinking takes on the form of fantasy or day-dreaming. In either state, one may appear to be indifferent to others and even to rather strong sensory stimuli. If one could get at the patterns of muscle tensions and relaxations in two extreme forms of these states, one might find there also a very great difference, now unobserved.

Of what people dream about in their day-dreams, we have many reports. Apparently the ideational content is as varied as are the hopes and wishes and longings and desires and urges of those who day-dream. There are dreams of travel, of high adventure, of thrilling and praiseworthy achievements in many fields of endeavor, of love and of being loved, of peace and security and happiness achieved, of revengeful acts, of illness, of death, of one's own funeral, of being an orphan, of being the child of the great, of sexual desires and satisfactions, of things probable and of things utterly improbable, of marriage, of the having a home and children, of religious privileges and realizations, of almost anything in fact or fiction. It is a matter of common observation that adolescent day-dreams are characteristically of the future, not of a happy past as is so often true in the later years of life.

Some of these content items have been isolated for special consideration. The notions of great achievement which will win the applause of the multitude are often designated as the "conquering-hero" dreams; while fantasies of illness and death and funerals and the like are designated as "suffering-hero dreams." Of these it has often been noted that, although the content differs in logical nature, there is an essential similarity. In the suffering-hero dream, the sufferer (the day-dreamer) is at last the actual center of interest and achievement and is thus actually the conqueror. The fantasy of not belonging to one's family, the foster-child fantasy, has been subjected to a little study. While so far as we know this is more frequently a day-dream of later childhood than of adolescence there is nevertheless sufficient evidence for recognizing its occasional appearance still in adolescent or even later years. Of this day-dream there are a number of forms. The dreamer may fancy himself as the child of inferior parentage, an orphan, a waif, a foundling; or, he may have fantasies of himself as of high social origin, of being the lost or sequestered child of wealthy or even royal parents.[1]

Occasionally a student of the subject has noted some features of the day-dream content which are thought to be especially characteristic of the adolescent period. Smith [2] in examination of a very large number of day-dreams saw many more in adolescent years about the achievement of fame and also about love and marriage. Children's fantasies were more about plays and games, of good things to eat, of wealth, of out-of-door life. Adolescent day-dreams in comparison with those of children showed much greater variety and complexity of content. Green [3] finds day-dreams of team or group activity more conspicuous in the early years of adolescence (an interesting similarity to the course of development of group play), and in later adolescence the rise of romantic dreams. Pruette [4] found in the adolescent girls of her study that day-dreams of personal success and of romance were far more frequent than those of any other classification. The definitely sexual has received scanty consideration at the hands of those who have made this census type of study. That it is present is evident, but it has been largely buried in the general classification termed romantic, or dreams of love and marriage. Individual studies of delinquents and the psychoanalytic literature, however, reveal much fantasy life of a definitely sexual nature; and in all probability this feature becomes a prominent one in adolescent years because of the newness of sexual development, the curiosity aroused concerning things sexual, and, above all, because adolescence is the period of enforced sexual restraint.

Of sex differences in the day-dream content we may suspect much, but we really know little. McKaye,[5] from a study of 244 high school students' papers on day-dreams, has concluded that sex differences were well indicated. He thinks that subjectivity (egocentricity) is the dominant note in the day-dreams of the

[1] See Conklin, Edmund S., "The Foster-Child Fantasy," *Amer. J. of Psychol.*, 1920, 31, 59-76.
  Lehrman, P. R., "The Fantasy of Not Belonging to One's Family," *Arch. Neur. & Psychiat.*, 1927, 18, 1015-1023.
[2] Smith, T. L., "The Psychology of Day Dreams," *Amer. J. Psychol.*, 1904, 15, 465-488.
[3] Green, G. H., *The Daydream,* Univ. of London Press.
[4] Pruette, Lorine, *Women and Leisure,* chap. 8.
[5] McKaye, D. L., "Recording Emotional Qualities," *Psychol. Clinic,* 1929, 17, 234-248.

adolescent girl, and that this is comparatively infrequent in the day-dreams of boys. Boys day-dream about things, and girls about the self. Boys day-dream about travel as a means to some end that will be thrilling, while girls dream of travel for itself, for the pleasure and distinction which they themselves find in the experience. Whether or not this difference be ultimately substantiated, certainly we may properly expect that sex differences will be established. The differences in the life experiences and the differences in the hopes and desires and ambitions which traditions and customs force upon the two sexes must produce differences in the frequency of some items in the content of the day-dreams of adolescent boys and girls.

Causes of day-dreaming have been largely inferred from their content. And here it is pleasant to record that there is little conflict of judgment among those who have written on the subject. Differences are largely a matter of emphasis, largely a matter of how much of the psychoanalytic system it is necessary to accept. Even the more critically minded see in day-dreams a functioning of imagination motivated by urges or desires which are strong and yet are blocked by the immediate circumstances of life.

The combined effect of the social pressures upon the adolescent and the urges or drives with which nature endowed him is the establishment of many hopes and expectations to be realized. But the intellectual and economic and social situations confronted prevent their early realization. The consequence is that many find a temporary and substitute realization in the make-believe world of the day-dream. Society expects boys and girls to marry, to establish homes and to have children. But social conditions force a postpostment of the realization of the desire. The resulting conflict finds some temporary resolution in the day-dream of marriage and home and children. Youth in the teens is developing a consciousness of independence, the attitudes of self-reliance, and is beginning to think of activities which will bring a full satisfaction of the desires for independence and self-reliant activity. Thus dreams of travel and thrilling adventure are motivated.

Mrs. Hollingworth [1] has wisely stressed the dangers of a plan of life in excess of the capacity to perform. But it must be recog-

[1] Hollingworth, L. S., *The Psychology of the Adolescent*, pp. 166 and 190.

nized that every normal adolescent has a plan of life, even though its details be crude and sketchy, which is beyond the possibility of immediate achievement. Some of the most alluring features of that plan depend for their realization upon circumstances and possibilities nearly if not quite beyond the conscious control of the youth who has formulated the plan. The consequence is a sort of anticipatory realization in the day-dream form. The desire to become, the urge to become, supplemented by the social pressure to become, is temporarily blocked by age or ignorance or social circumstance or belief.[1] The fantasy of realization is thus anticipatory achievement.

The psychoanalytically inclined find this interpretation often much too simple and to their way of thinking inadequate.[2] For them it is necessary to assume the sex instincts, the ego instincts, the Id, the ego and the superego; and to find behind the day-dream a motivating conflict among these. Perhaps there has even been the development of a complex. And the mechanisms of the dream work, dramatization and secondary elaboration and displacement and condensation, may also be found in the formation of the manifest day-dream content. All of this means that the apparent content of the day-dream, as of the nocturnal dream, is very different from its real meaning, which may be found in many cases only by the elaborate process of psychoanalysis. The psychoanalysts thus see in the motivation of the day-dream a maladjustment, a conflict and possibly a complex, all of which means a disagreeable reality from which the individual is seeking to find some escape, and it is this escape which the day-dream process or state provides.

It must be further recognized that day-dreaming is in all probability related to systemic differences between individuals. There has long been a general supposition among psychologists that in day-dreaming is the germ of a reaction pattern which may all too easily develop into abnormality. The shut-in per-

---

[1] There is some evidence that adolescents of the higher degrees of mental ability are more given to day-dreaming. Unfortunately this information is based upon the study of a group of delinquents only. See Ackerson, Luton, *Children's Behavior Problems*, Chicago, 1931, pp. 137-138.

[2] The best presentation from the psychoanalytic point of view is J. Varendonck's *The Psychology of Day-Dreams*, but there is much of psychoanalytic influence to be seen in G. H. Green's *The Daydream*, Univ. of London Press.

sonality has been thought to day-dream more than others. Hysterical disturbances of the more severe and less common form, especially the monoideic and polyideic somnambulisms and the hysterical narcolepsies, have been explained as comparable to a forceful intrusion of a dream mechanism into and dominating the waking consciousness.[1] Day-dreaming has been thus often looked upon as very closely related to abnormalities of personality. The quick and sometimes very complete abstraction in the day-dream state from the present sensory situation, the apparent loss of awareness of what is going on in the world about, looks very much like dissociation. It looks to the observer as though the day-dreamer's personality was loosely put together, as though parts of the personality could readily be activated into isolated functioning. This loose organization is known to be true of the hysterical and has already been presented in this text as characteristic, although to a lesser degree, of adolescence. Youth has not yet achieved the full integration of personality to be found in the normal adult. Hence day-dreaming might be expected with some considerable degree of frequency, and of a frequency which might also be expected to vary from individual to individual as individuals differ in the degree of personality integration to which they have achieved.

If this reasoning is correct, much day-dreaming could be looked upon as an indication of a poorly developed personality synthesis. And, likewise, if one found in any given youth the presence of much day-dreaming, he would have ground for suspecting the probable presence of other forms of behavior known to be traceable to a weak synthesis, impulsive and erratic conduct, poor emotional control, and the like. While this is in general current thinking among many psychologists, we unfortunately have very little collected evidence for it and practically no systematic studies. The writer submitted the Thurstone personality schedule to a group of 295 college students under conditions which would guarantee privacy and concealment of identity. This schedule includes questions concerning day-dreaming. The following table presents some of the results isolated and arranged for the present purpose:

[1] See Janet, P., *The Major Symptoms of Hysteria.*

DAY-DREAMING FREQUENCY IN RELATIONSHIP TO SCORES FOR PSYCHONEUROTIC TENDENCY

Class	Thurstone classification Score	No.	Day-dream frequently No.	%	Day-dreams of improbable occurrences No.	%
A	0-14	11	1 or	9	1 or	9
B	15-29	49	23 or	47	10 or	20
C	30-59	156	107 or	69	67 or	43
D	60-79	48	43 or	90	36 or	75
E	80-	31	27 or	87	28 or	90

The group described as Class A and having the lowest scores on this personality schedule are the students who are the best adjusted to life, who presumably have the best organization of personality, and who also, presumably, have the fewest conflicts and repressions and emotional distresses. Class E on the other hand includes those whom the Thurstones think are so badly organized and whose personalities are so much disturbed by maladjustments of one sort or another that they are in need of skilled psychiatric advice. The other classes present gradations in between these extremes.

Looking down the columns in the table one quickly sees that the frequency of day-dreaming does increase rapidly with the rise in the personality schedule score, that in so far as this is a reliable measure it looks as though there was ample support for the current notion that day-dreaming is really related to the nature and degree of the personality synthesis.

This relationship raises at once the equally interesting because important question, if these who day-dream much do so merely because they are experiencing for some reason a rather delayed development of their personality synthesis, due perhaps to somewhat unusual difficulties arising in the course of achieving a satisfactory adjustment to the circumstances of life, or, if their day-dreaming should be attributed to a weakness of synthesis which is intrinsic and unchangeable. Perhaps they are conspicuously day-dreamers because they are by nature loosely organized and always will be. Perhaps there is some systemic peculiarity of their nervous organism which makes any high degree of integration impossible. Certainly we all know from our everyday experience some individuals of mature years who while far from being insane are nevertheless chronic day-dreamers.

Day-dreams are ordinarily thought of as being agreeable. But it is almost certain that there are also disagreeable day-dreams, which have largely escaped consideration. There are day-dreams of fantasied disasters, not of the suffering-hero variety. There are day-dreams of difficult examinations, of teacher prejudice, and failure. These border on the field of worry or are perhaps a genuine part of worry. Here the day-dream is the amplification of a vague possibility rather than the realization of a wish. Probably the vigorous healthy youth is not much given to this sort of thing, as he is not much given to worry; and so this type of day-dream might wisely be thought of as a feature of the excessively fatigued, the nervously weak. Their existence, however, needs to be recognized. Their causes and nature and relationships need to be better known.

A few French specialists have in recent years been much attracted by people whose day-dreams have a peculiarly large place in their lives. They note a marked lack of self-criticism. The day-dream states become so elaborately developed and occur so frequently and so extensively that the whole life of the individual is influenced by them. In extreme cases such people apparently project much of their day-dream content upon the world in which they live, until it becomes a very fanciful place indeed. They seem, through their lack of self-criticism, to get their world of fantasy and their world of perceptual reality badly confused. For this condition, the special term of Bovarism (Bovarysme) [1] has been coined. Where knowledge of reality checks the flow and development and degree of influence of fantasy thinking there is full normality; but the less the fantasy thinking is checked by reality, the less there is of self-criticism, the more the fantasy thinking runs free and tends to dominate. The degree of this these authors are terming the "index bovarique." [2] Where this index is large the personality is also thought of as

[1] Obviously this has been taken from the justly famous fictional description of this type of personality by Gustave Flaubert in his novel, *Madame Bovary*. A more recent utilization of the same feature will be found in the latter part of H. G. Wells' *The Bulpington of Blup*.

[2] Readers will find the best introduction to this literature through the following reference: Levy-Valensi, J., "Bovarysme et Constitutions Mentales," *J. de psychologie*, 1930, 27, 289-299.

being weak and poorly organized. And the assumption appears to be again that in such cases we are dealing with a constitutional defect. This brings from another point of view yet other evidence for thinking that day-dreaming, especially when it is excessive, cannot perhaps be entirely attributed to the conflicts presented between ambitious youthful life plans and the dragging, delaying demands of society.[1]

From these three causes or groups of causes the writer is much inclined to the opinion that no specific choice can be made. Many youthful day-dreams, especially those of achievement in some field, can be quite adequately explained in terms of the ambitious life plan and the obvious obstacles which prevent an immediate realization. At the same time one can easily think of day-dreams which are not easily explained in terms of a theory so simple. Where the content is quite bizarre, recurrent and perhaps even annoying, one may be inclined to turn to the psychoanalytic system of thinking for a more adequate scheme of explanation. Behind such there may be a complication of repressions and conflicts and very likely also a complex. The same may be true of compensatory dreams where there has been much trouble with inferiority feelings and ideas, and very likely also of many, although certainly not all, of the sex fantasies.

[1] Students of psychoneurotic conditions have made much of the loss of a consciousness of reality, the feeling that things are not real. A consideration of Bovarism brings this at once to mind and with it the question if frequency of day-dreaming be related to the degree of this loss of the consciousness of reality. While unfortunately we do not have at present any measures of the individual day-dreaming frequency and amount nor of the degree of the loss of the feeling of reality, we nevertheless can approximate an answer to the problem by asking if the frequency of reports of much day-dreaming is at all related to the frequency of positive answers to a question concerning this loss of the feeling of reality. This may be done by referring again to the responses made to the Thurstone personality schedule. The following table is derived from a re-examination of those same returns mentioned above:

Class	Thurstone classification Score range	No.	Day-dreaming frequent No. %	Day-dreaming frequently, losing feeling of reality also No. %
A	0-14	11	1 or 9	0
B	15-29	49	23 or 47	4 or 17
C	30-59	156	107 or 69	39 or 36
D	60-79	48	43 or 90	25 or 58
E	80-	31	27 or 87	23 or 85

This indicates at least that day-dreaming and the loss of the consciousness of reality tend to be much more frequently associated in the less well-organized personalities.

How far the conception of the notion of day-dreaming as related to some constitutional defect or delay of development may
be wisely applied is not yet clear. It is one of those concepts,
however, which every student of youthful problems should keep
always in mind. Certainly either of the preceding causes could
more readily produce day-dreaming when they occur in a poorly
integrated personality. But it would be unpardonably hasty to
dismiss any given instance of excessive day-dreaming on the mere
assumption of a constitutionally defective personality synthesis.
Such defects may indeed occur. However, it is also possible that
the frequent recurrence of day-dreaming, or the immediate
causes of the day-dreaming, might be the actual cause of the
delay in the development of the personality synthesis. A careful
investigation of the life-adjustment problems of a youth followed
by intelligent counselling and guidance might produce not only
a marked reduction in the amount of day-dreaming but it might
also remove the blockade which has delayed the integration
of the personality. Perhaps the relationship of day-dreaming
frequency to the psychoneurotic conditions mentioned above
should not be attributed to some basic systemic defect. It may
be that the day-dreaming is but an incidental feature of some
more complex disturbance of the personality organization.

Thus the writer is inclined to think that all of these interpretative points of view are valuable. Certainly there is ample
justification for the assumption that every instance of day-dreaming is not like every other. If one would understand a particular
instance of day-dreaming, it is necessary to study the setting
within which the day-dreaming occurs. When that is clearly
before the investigator, then and only then is it safe to begin to
think in terms of one or more of these conceptions of day-dream
causation.

What is the *effect of day-dreaming upon the growing personality?* Most thoughtful observers could answer this at once by
enumerating a string of undesirable effects. Certainly there are
not a few. Those who have studied industrial accidents point
out the many traceable to mind-wandering, inattention, day-
dreaming. Others stress the less serious errors of many kinds
which result. And there is always the tendency of the human
nervous system to form habits. Habits of mind-wandering, of

chronic wavering of attention are disastrous to any form of life endeavor.

Yet others have pointed out that through day-dreaming there is the possibility of developing a fantasy world which is far more attractive and interesting and satisfying than is the world of material and social reality. When such is developed the youth may prefer to live in his fantasy world and to resent all that forces him out of it into the miserable world of sensory and perceptual experience. Miss Van Waters has shown this to be the cause of some forms of delinquency.[1] Where the home is unattractive, in comparison with the world of fantasy, antagonistic attitudes develop toward the home which parents and others have often failed to understand. And it may even go farther than this. The world of perceptual reality may be by contrast so very miserable and trying and hopeless that the person feels utterly unable to continue in this life. The only way out is suicide and this some are said to have taken.[2]

That day-dreaming may distort the course of personality development has been frequently noted in a variety of ways. The satisfactions to be found in fantasy thinking are presented as leading away from a constructive and effective attack upon the problems of life and achievement therein. A bad or weakened or divided orientation is established. Thus the development of the personality pattern may be distorted. The habit of easy abstraction, of the isolated functioning of a few patterns, may, as has been indicated above, hinder the development of the personality synthesis. It might even tend toward the development of two loosely related syntheses. For this reason G. Stanley Hall spoke of the day-dream as the germ of "some ancillary personality."

More often, however, the habit of day-dreaming and the finding of satisfactions therein has been looked upon in recent years as a reaction tending in the direction of dementia præcox. Youths manifesting such deterioration apparently find high satisfaction in a sort of day-dream form of existence and are quite indifferent to the commonplace demands of life which press so

[1] Van Waters, Miriam, "I Would Rather Die Than Go Home," *Survey,* 1927, 57, 565-569.
[2] Genil-Perrin, "Les attitudes mental vicieuses—le 'Bovarysme,'" *Prophyl. Ment.,* 1929, 6, 35-37. See *Psychol. Abstracts,* 1929, No. 4454.

hard upon the normal person. Dementia præcox (schizophrenic) patients are quite content to sit day after day on a bench in a hospital ward, living in a world of their own making, indifferent to what goes on about them.

On the other hand, those who have written on day-dreaming have had almost as much to say about its valuable effects upon the personality development. Few items in normal growth have been placed above the development of ideals in importance. Many have stressed the contribution made by day-dreaming to the development of the individual ideal. The concept of the self is molded by the day-dream. In the day-dream the youth can try himself out in a vast number of ways. Through it his life acquires a purpose, a goal, and a life plan. As a consequence of such day-dreaming his life may become characterized by a planful constructive effort. He has discovered for himself what he wants most to become; and he turns from his day-dream to a more coordinated controlled effort to realize that which he has envisaged in his periods of fantasy thinking.

Longings which cannot be immediately, if ever, realized in actuality can, so some say, be realized in the day-dream. A sort of joyous satisfaction can thus be experienced and through that there is the relief of that tension which comes from blocked desires. The girl who sees no immediate prospect of love and marriage day-dreams the happiness she hopes to experience some day in reality, and finds peace through the happy dream. And this quite without any interference with the efficiency of her life in the world of present realities. The youth who hopes some day to be a great surgeon day-dreams of thrilling achievements for the good of humanity, and thus makes the long grind through medical and pre-medical years a little easier. Thus it is argued that day-dreaming actually contributes to the stabilization of personality.

Through day-dreaming, also, there is the possibility of a vast addition to the range of experience. One may stand in far distant places, one may soar the heights and plumb the depths, one may feel oneself living through the experiences of any other self from ancient times to the present, and one may thus live through types of experience far beyond that which modern knowledge and means could make possible. The limits of imagination are vague and easily overcome. What such imaginative ranging may contribute to human understanding, to human knowledge, and to the possibilities of yet further expansion of human knowledge and understanding, only those who have much capacity for day-dreaming could possibly begin to comprehend.

And in this connection must be mentioned the possible contributions of day-dreaming to the understanding of art and religion, perhaps also to further achievements in art and religion. Green has made much of this in two useful chapters.[1] The boundary between day-dreaming and productive imagination, as has already been pointed out, is a hard one to place. So, no doubt, the habit of day-dreaming may aid enormously in the constructive imagination so necessary to much artistic work, and, as well, to the understanding and appreciation of art. So, too, without such imagination, would much of religion be unintelligible.

When as good a case can be made for the values of day-dreaming as for its dangers, any sweeping conclusion concerning the effect of day-dreaming in general upon personality development becomes obviously impossible. It is certain that no one can with wisdom say that day-dreaming is definitely either good or bad. One can only say that sometimes day-dreaming contributes much of value to the developing personality and sometimes day-dreaming seems to be the rock upon which the growing personality is wrecked completely. Whether the effect be good or bad must be due to something quite other than the day-dreaming function or state itself. One must look beyond and behind the day-dream. One must see the day-dream as but an incident in a much larger and more complicated mass of growth factors. Perhaps to such factors the day-dream is merely an epiphenomenon. It may be motivated by some simple conflict in life. It may be symptomatic of some much larger disturbance within the personality. It may be related to some constitutional defect. This much only can be certain, that day-dreaming considered in isolation can be neither good nor bad for the growing personality, that the goodness or badness of the day-dream effect is to be found in the personality setting in which it occurs. It is the

---

1 Green, G. H., *The Daydream*, Univ. of London Press, chaps. 8, 9.

setting which makes it good and the setting which makes it bad.

The Self-conscious Reaction. Another outstanding effect of social pressures upon the behavior of the growing boy or girl is the development of self-consciousness. In the earlier literature of genetic psychology there was much emphasis upon the "birth of a new self," supposed to occur somewhere along about puberty. But that was in a day when the instinct concept was a popular resort for interpretative purposes, and the efflorescence or blossoming doctrine of growth was warmly advocated. At puberty or in early adolescence the growing person was thought to blossom out into a new self, or, at least, into manifestations of the self so different as to justify the application of the adjective "new."

Although there is far more caution now about using such explanatory concepts, the fact nevertheless remains that in adolescent years, especially earlier adolescent years, the growing individual manifests peculiarities of behavior which appear to be much concerned with the self, the self concept and the associated emotional reactions. No doubt it was this self-consciousness of adolescence which attracted the attention of the earlier genetic psychologists. We think now that this self-consciousness is produced not by any delayed instinctive development, but rather that like so many other reactions it is the consequence of normal growth in a social environment which brings much pressure to bear upon the course of that growth.

By the dawn of adolescence intelligence is fast approaching its maximum of development. Knowledge is expanding rapidly. The youth is being pushed by everything from within and much that is about him to an awareness that he is soon to be an adult and that much is expected of him. All those pressures and urges mentioned before operate not only toward the development of inferiority notions and homesickness and day-dreaming, but also toward the habit of thinking much about his own self. And it will doubtless be recalled that, in the foregoing discussions of inferiority and homesickness and day-dreaming, there was frequent mention of thoughts about the self, of consideration of the self and its abilities, its disabilities, its possibilities, its limitations, and what was hoped and expected of it in the future. Here it is important to drop some of those relationships temporarily and examine merely the self-conscious features of them and to look also at some of the effects of this self-consciousness upon the growth of the personality.

The magnitude of this self-consciousness of adolescence can possibly be best realized by comparing youthful ways and experiences with the ways and experiences of both childhood and the middle years of life. In childhood there is ordinarily little meditation. There is a wealth of overt sensory-motor activity. The child must be active for himself or be entertained by others. Thoughts of self are far from being so personal and intimate and prolonged as in adolescence. The self is often treated in an almost objective fashion. There is much talk to be sure of what the self is to be when fully grown; but it is talk with little evidence of the "long, long thoughts" of youth about the self and the future and possibilities of this and that and the other.

In the middle years of life, the adult has either achieved or settled down with resignation to the humdrum necessities. The business of making a living, of caring for the family, and of getting in a little pleasurable relaxation now and then have objectified the life of the average adult to the extent that precludes much meditation about the self. Adults who have arrived and are taken for granted by their associates are not only no longer so responsive to social pressures, but they are also by age and achievement exempt from many of them. Society is no longer looking to adults for great development in the future. But society does so look to the youth and does everything possible to make youth conscious of that fact. Through childhood the growth attitudes of expectancy and anticipation have been well established. So by the time adolescent years are reached the growing personality, as at no other time in life, is subject to situations and influences which persistently and frequently bring to attention thoughts about the self of many kinds.

A chronic self-inspection is brought into being. The youth gives so much attention to his personal appearance. He must be like others. He must be dressed for any occasion as custom (social pressure) demands. Every item of the toilet may come in for its consideration. There is much thought about the future vocation or profession. Behind the current interest in vocational guidance lies the fact of youthful interest in the selection of a vocation, which in turn means of course that the youth is thinking about himself and what he is to be in the future. There is, too, the more delicate matter of attractiveness or unattractiveness to the other sex. If for some reason some individual does not have as many "dates" as do his associates, or as would be considered desirable, there is cause for much thoughtfulness and self-consideration. Virtues and vices, big and little, actual and imagined, are considered. Why are other young people more popular than he? Why did she not receive this election or appointment? And so on, through an ever-growing list of details all relating to the self and the social situation.

Physical growth changes also contribute frequently to the content of this thinking about the self. Anatomical and physiological features of development, normal and abnormal, are considered and often through ignorance misinterpreted. The health is questioned and thought about. Notions of personal strength or weakness flourish. Not infrequently also there are thoughts about the mental capacity and sometimes serious considerations of the prospect for mental health. Many young people wonder if they are mentally normal and a few think of themselves as destined to become insane. Present traits and habits are mulled over in terms of these morbid notions. Serious as such thoughts may be it is also easy for the adult to treat them too seriously. Often the boy or girl will have such thoughts for a time, rather enjoy toying with them, and then lightly cast them aside for something more interesting.

Of the effects of this self-consciousness upon the growing personality we know all too little. Much of what can be said today of these effects is based upon a few case studies and much casual observation; and so must be accepted with appropriate caution. It is commonly assumed that one consequence is the molding of a more useful, effective, and desirable set of character traits; and that there is a better understanding or evaluation of the self. Bad habits of the past are examined and dropped. Better ones are substituted. There is a thoughtful, perhaps more wisely guided, selection of a vocation. Ideals are developed and established. Newer and saner standards of judgment are brought into existence. The individual's own capacities and abilities are re-appraised. A newer and wiser and socially much more desirable plan of life is formulated.

Before looking at the less desirable effects of self-consciousness, it is well to observe that the term is used to convey two psychologically different meanings. There is the self-consciousness as already discussed, which is a habit that may function quite as, if not even more, easily when the person is alone than when in the presence of others. In fact, it is in the quiet moments or hours of isolation that youth thinks the "long, long thoughts" of the poet's description. But the term self-consciousness is also commonly used to designate a form of experience or behavior which can occur only in social situations, and which does not at all imply that the person who manifests it is habitually self-conscious in the meaning described above. This other kind of self-consciousness appears to be a temporary confusion. Most people have seen an experienced public speaker or an accomplished society matron unexpectedly forced into a situation for which they are quite unprepared by their experience. The result is behavior that cannot well be described as embarrassment, although embarrassment may be a part of the reaction. There is in it much self-consciousness, with responses and possible adjustments badly disturbed by the emotions aroused. Whoever has been himself in such a situation knows all too well the unpleasant and unusual awareness of self, the confusion, the inability to act effectively for some reason that eludes one for the moment, and of the fact that one is being very awkward and making a mess of things generally.

Both of these forms of self-conscious behavior occur in adolescence, perhaps more than in any other years of life, and they are without much possibility of doubt related to each other. They must therefore be subjected to some thoughtful consideration; and it is to be hoped that they will eventually be subjected to systematic study. For our present purposes it is, however, of first importance to discover some means of distinguishing between the two by the use of differentiating terms. Perhaps the best we can do is to refer to the first presented form of self-consciousness, the habit of much meditation about the self, as *cognitive self-consciousness;* and then to use the term *emotional self-consciousness* for that other and largely emotional disturbance which may come to any one occasionally when the social situation is just right. To be sure, that which is here termed cognitive self-consciousness is not entirely without feeling or emotion, and that which is here termed emotional self-consciousness is not without cognitive features (no emotion can be that); but these terms do indicate a difference of preponderance of content in the reactions designated, and until some better terms are available they may serve to call attention to these differences.

One undesirable effect of self-consciousness appears when the cognitive self-consciousness interferes with social adjustment. The cognitive self-consciousness may become a dominating habit. The morbidly introspective youth is unfortunately not an infrequent problem. This may be merely the consequence of a combination of training and social experience which developed an excessive conscientiousness. But there is also the possibility that such disturbances are basically due to some serious maladjustment, or to some physical weakness, an organic disease perhaps, which should have professional care.

Too much preoccupation with this cognitive self-consciousness may result in the intrusion of the self-consciousness at times when the situation calls for objectivity. If youth has the habit of thinking first in terms of himself, his capacities and possibilities and possible inabilities when the situation requires co-operative action, it is quite likely that he will appear to be negative, or resistive, or at least uncooperative. Such negative or resistive or uncooperative actions can often be explained by looking for such self-conscious habits in the background. Fortunately for this there is one scrap of experimental support. Nelson has studied the appearance of such resistive behavior while testing small children, and found that it appeared far more frequently when the test aroused a consciousness of the self. Apparently then it was the self-consciousness which, when projected into the testing situation, produced some sort of blocking that was manifested by reluctance to cooperate or outright refusal.[1]

[1] Nelson, J. F., "Preliminary Report on Some Uses of the Psychological Test Situation for Studying Personality," pp. 118-149 of a book by D. S. Thomas, entitled *Some New Techniques for Studying Social Behavior* (Columbia Univ. Press), 1929.

It is at least not unreasonable to think that similar behavior may be produced in like manner in other years than those of childhood.

There seems to be no possibility of any value to the personality to be found in the emotional type of self-consciousness. It is essentially a disturbance and the sooner it can be displaced by control and self-confidence the better. But it is a disturbance of such frequent occurrence in adolescence and one so troublesome it is necessary that the student of adolescent problems should be quite familiar with its features. Examples are everywhere available. The amateur debater unexpectedly disturbed by something happening in his audience, the young man who is conscious of having committed some social blunder, the high school graduate trying desperately to walk across the platform at commencement time in a nonchalant manner—all manifest the impulsive, strained, clumsy carriage and movement of the limbs. The hands move awkwardly; and walking is transformed into a stiff and graceless gait. Speech is stumbling or wholly inhibited.

In social situations which involve the presence of a number of the other sex, this emotional self-consciousness is everywhere to be seen. Youths who with their own sex are perfectly at ease suddenly become stiff and awkward and reserved when guests of the other sex enter the room.* And all may know perfectly well what to do and how to do it; but with such a mass of conflicting tendencies aroused within themselves, including the conscious effort to maintain poise and to act properly, many mistakes and unnatural responses appear.

Where there is an actual lack of knowledge, where the youth is plunged into some social situation where he knows that he should conform to the nicest details of current etiquette but is unhappily aware that he does not know for sure just what he should do, then of course the condition of emotional self-consciousness is quickly aroused. Fatigue and any form of physical depletion are also conditions in which this disturbance appears easily. But the writer is inclined to think that the most common cause for the frequent appearance of this emotional self-consciousness in adolescent years is the frequency of that other pattern just described, that of the cognitive self-consciousness.

The youth who has the habit of thinking most about himself

is the one whom the writer believes is most likely to be troubled by this emotional form of self-consciousness. Certainly many instances of youths who are more than ordinarily troubled by emotional self-consciousness reveal when investigated a more than usually frequent practice of thinking about themselves, and often the thoughts about themselves involve things which stir shame or inferiority or hopelessness. As these troublesome notions are minimized or eliminated the emotional self-consciousness becomes less disturbing both in intensity and in frequency of appearance.

Development of Self-confidence. It is of course toward the self-confident poise of maturity that youth is presumably growing. It is that toward which he looks, for which he longs when he finds himself disturbed by these periods of emotional self-consciousness. As one watches youths growing up, one is inclined to think that from such observations and from these crude analyses of the disturbing reaction patterns it is possible to outline some of the changes which contribute most to the establishment of self-confidence. A very little, but unfortunately only a very little, experimentally obtained evidence is available.

The development of self-confidence must be at base a process of learning to which much of what we know of the psychology of learning may be applied. Effective adequate response patterns must be established. This means practice, but it also means imaginative as well as actual practice in social situations. The youth can do much of the preparation through reading and thinking about what to do, and about what should have been done. This means then, curiously enough, that the habits of thinking about the self, cognitive self-consciousness, may be used to contribute toward the establishment of self-confident behavior. Whether cognitive self-consciousness contributes to emotional self-consciousness or the development of self-control must depend upon the governing attitude. The end must be the establishment of habit patterns which are adequate to the needs of the social situations confronted and which are so well established that they will function to the exclusion of all other and less desirable reaction patterns. Then will the conflicts and confusion and emotional excitement disappear.

Growth of knowledge must also be a factor, learning through

profiting by experience. There must be attention to the different kinds of social situations and much interpretation of them as including the self. For this and for a few other factors we have some significant indications from a study made under the direction of W. H. Hughes of a very large number of high school students.[1] In the course of this investigation he found that self-confidence when correlated with an intelligence test score produced a coefficient of $+.33$ ($\pm.018$). If intelligence is thought of to any considerable extent as a capacity to learn, then there is here indicated the probability that those of higher native ability are those who achieve self-confidence a little more easily than others. The correlation is not high to be sure, but the measurement of self-confidence was of necessity by a rating scale technique which is likely to involve many of the difficulties of subjective standards of judgment. The fact that it is not very high may also be taken to indicate the presence of many other factors in the acquisition of self-confidence.

Hughes' correlation between self-confidence and initiative which he found to be $+.80$, is even more interesting. After allowing for all of the difficulties involved in using a trait rating method, it must still indicate that there are many factors in common between self-confidence and what is commonly termed initiative. If it should turn out that this high correlation was due to an inability of his judges to distinguish between the two traits clearly, then that also would indicate the presence of many factors in common. But initiative is ordinarily described as being the combination of a highly active imagination with well-established habits of action. The person of initiative is one who thinks quickly and much beyond the immediate perceptual situation, and is also accustomed to put his thoughts into action. On the other hand, it was the absence of these very traits which was considered above to be a salient characteristic or feature in the production of the emotional self-conscious form of behavior.

1 Hughes, W. H., "A Rating Scale for Individual Capacities, Attitudes, and Interests," *J. Educ. Method*, 1923, 3, 56-65.
—— "Organized Personnel Research and its Bearing on High School Problems," *J. Educ. Res.*, 1924, 10, 386-398.
—— "General Principles and Results of Rating Trait Characteristics," *J. Educ. Method*, 1925, 4, 421-431.
—— "The Relation of Intelligence to Trait Characteristics," *J. Educ. Psychol.*, 1926, 17, 482-494.

Consequently, the youth who would develop self-confidence must practice through imaginative preparation and through actual experience in social situations those habits which he would eventually have dominate at times of stress.

Hughes also presented a correlation coefficient which he obtained between judgments for self-confidence and judgments for control of attention. This was +.58. Again it is evident that there must be many factors in common. And concerning the psychology of attention control we are much better informed.[1] It is basically a matter of developing well-organized habits which influence the selection of responses for the focal point of consciousness, what Pillsbury has termed the subjective conditions of attention. If there is confusion of response to any situation and a rapid shifting of attention from one thing to another, it is because these conditioning habits have not been well developed. The confusion which appears in emotional self-consciousness is exactly this. The avoidance of emotional self-consciousness and the development of self-confidence means the training of those habits which control attention so that there shall be a coordinated adjustment or response to social situations. It is the person whose attention is clear and steady whose responses are without internal conflict, who is looked upon as the person of self-confidence.

It is obvious that all of this is pointing in the direction of the establishment of response patterns such that attention shall be primarily if not exclusively upon the objective situation and not upon the self concept and its relations. So often we find that young people who are much troubled by emotional self-consciousness are quickly relieved from the more serious features of their trouble by the simple trick of interesting them in the behavior of others. Developing an interest in the way others are acting, observing their posture, carriage, voice and so on, and of how they may be led and controlled, bringing about what is commonly referred to as an objective attitude of mind, is often a sure road to the development of self-confidence, because it eliminates many of the causes of emotional self-consciousness.

It is doubtless true that self-confident behavior may not in-

---

[1] See Pillsbury, W. B., *Attention*, and also Titchener, E. B., *The Elementary Psychology of Feeling and Attention.*

frequently be due to ignorance rather than to knowledge and experience. But this does not at all change the nature of self-confident reaction to any situation. Whether attributable to knowledge or ignorance, it is in essence a response to a social situation which is coordinated, in which there is little if any conflict of impulses, in which consciousness is clear and in which the attention is not being distracted by a welter of possibilities. One sees this often in childhood, and not infrequently in adults who are plunging into fields of thought and action in which they are not expert. But the whole trend of adolescent development is in the direction of knowledge rather than of perpetuating ignorance and so while this ignorant form of self-confidence should be known and be recognized it is not a feature which any one could wisely seek to maintain.

Another sort of self-confidence appears in those individuals who are apparently not only at ease but who genuinely enjoy being in situations which attract the attention of the group. They are people who enjoy being before the public. They like to speak, to act, to see their names in the papers, to wear conspicuous clothing, to do anything in fact which will give them the consciousness of being looked at and talked about. They enjoy and are at ease in exactly those situations which are the torment of people much given to emotional self-consciousness. In recent years it has become customary to term this trait exhibitionism. This term came out of the psychoanalytic psychology and was originally associated with a sex perversion; but as it is used here, in the wider contemporary sense, it designates a form of behavior which may or may not involve a sexual factor.

The simplest and most satisfactory explanation yet proposed for exhibitionism is in terms of conditioned behavior.[1] In infancy individual comfort is brought about by the presence and the attention of others. Being looked at and talked about in those years is definitely associated with comfortable reactions. The inevitable consequence is that being looked at and talked about becomes substituted for the originally effective stimuli, that the comfortable reaction becomes conditioned to the pattern

[1] Smith, S., and Guthrie, E. R., "Exhibitionism," *J. Abn. & Soc. Psychol.*, 1922, 17, 206-209.

of stimuli designated as being looked at and talked about. This goes on through the years. Those individuals who in adolescence and maturity still have their most happy reactions aroused by social situations of attention to the self are those who have never been subsequently re-conditioned. They carry over into adolescent years and the years of maturity the habits established in infancy and early childhood.

While we have here also few studies to go by, it is probably true that comparatively few of those who manifest self-confidence in later adolescent and mature years are manifesting a self-confidence based upon an exhibitionistic conditioning. Most people have been to some extent exhibitionistically conditioned for a while in childhood; but, through the many social pressures effective in later childhood and adolescent years, they have had that conditioning quite effectively broken up. Then through experience and training they have developed that synthesis of personality, that pattern of effective habits, which is manifest in their self-confident behavior. And the writer is inclined to the opinion that the self-confidence based upon an exhibitionistic conditioning is a self-confidence that can be all too easily disturbed into emotional self-conscious behavior when everything does not go just right.

From the point of view of personality development one must always consider the possibility that troublesome experiences with both cognitive self-consciousness and emotional self-consciousness may grow into habits which distort and prevent the eventual development of a balanced integrated personality pattern. There are individuals who never get beyond the heavily introspective habits of adolescent years. Their unhappy ineffectiveness is notorious. And there are individuals who never achieve much self-confidence. They have never worked out effective coordinated patterns of response. Putting it in other words, they have never developed the most effective kinds of self-control. They continue through life with habit patterns which are conducive to the easy arousal of emotional self-consciousness. And their ineffectiveness is well known. Not infrequently such people develop rather marked distortions as a consequence of their efforts to get along somehow. They may become very suspicious of others, may live much to themselves as a sort of self-protection, and there is a high possibility of such failures developing inferiority disturbances with all the inferiority effects already described above.[1]

[1] Useful suggestions for the prevention or cure of self-consciousness will be found in the following:

Riggs, A. F., "Nervousness, Its Cause and Prevention," *Ment. Hyg.*, 1922, 6, 263-287.

Roback, A. A., *Self-Consciousness and Its Treatment*, Cambridge, 1933.

CHAPTER XI

INFLUENCES OF THE FAMILY

FAMILY CONSCIOUSNESS, EFFECTS OF FAMILY CONSCIOUS-
NESS, PARENTAL INFLUENCES THAT DISTORT, JEALOUSY,
PARENTAL INFLUENCES UPON LOVE DEVELOPMENT

In recent years much emphasis has been placed upon the significance of the family situation in the formation of personality. Those who seek to trace out the history of any given bit of human behavior find constant reason for stressing the influence of the parents, or of the brothers and sisters, or of all taken together. This seems to be equally true in all schools of psychological thought, be it behavioristic or psychoanalytic or what not; and as true also in the studies of normal as of abnormal forms of behavior. It is even possible that attitudes toward the family, habits established by family contacts and emotional responses cultivated by family situations, underlie all adolescent and mature forms of conduct. Perhaps in these family contacts are to be found the roots of behavior once attributed to instincts.[1]

Our sources of information on these matters of family influence are unfortunately varied and frequently quite unsystematic. Much of what we know has come from the study of delinquent behavior, and it is not always easy to read back from such magnifications or distortions to the probable nature of parental influences in the life of the ordinary and more law-abiding adolescent. From those whose business it is to counsel with parents upon their problems in the guidance of youth has come yet other information; but this is even more unsystematic and casual than are the studies of delinquency. There is also a vast literature

---

[1] In this connection it is worth noting that where the usual family situation is no longer possible, as among girls isolated in correctional institutions, an urge appears which is strong enough to bring about and to maintain pseudo-familial patterns. See Selling, L. S., "The Pseudo-Family," *Amer. J. Sociol.*, 1931, 37, 247-253.

available from the studies of the genuinely abnormal, the psychotic and the psychoneurotic, especially those studies which are frankly psychoanalytic or are largely influenced by the psychoanalytic point of view. This, too, must be handled with care lest one carry over distorted notions into the life of the normal family and the healthy individual. And yet there is to be found in all of these studies, as also in the convictions of those who work with adolescents in trouble but without making systematic records, a sufficient uniformity of finding and of thinking to merit a very serious consideration. Of systematic inductive studies on the effects of different family constellations, there have been a few, and these will be referred to in their proper place.

Through all the discussion which follows, the peculiar position of the adolescent in the family setting must be kept constantly in mind. This position is quite different from that of the preadolescent child in what might be otherwise an identical family situation. By the time pubescent years are reached the capacity of any family to establish attitudes and habits and emotional patterns has been pretty well exhausted, or at least such is the trend of current thought on the subject. Youth is more and more attracted and apparently influenced by that which is without the family circle. What others do and what others think constitutes a strong pressure upon their conduct. And there is often the tendency to assume that the parents are a little uninformed, backward, or narrow-minded. With this there is also the influence of that which has been described in preceding chapters as the consciousness of social pressure, to grow-up, to be adult, to have a profession or vocation, and the like. But, curiously enough, as most will at once recall, the very content and nature of this social pressure to grow up, to be adult, to have a vocation, to make a home for oneself some day, and the rest, has come from that very family situation from which there is now a tendency to seek emancipation. The family situation trained the individual as a child into habits of submission and into similar ways of thinking and feeling. And it was that same family situation which trained the child into the notions and attitudes of some day becoming independent. In youth the process of becoming independent is taking place in the presence of the same parents, and, aside from some shifting of ages all along the line, in much the same general family situation.

The attitudes which the parents take toward this process of emancipation and maturation are of profound significance for the changes which are taking place within the personality of the adolescent. Many of the peculiarities of adolescent behavior, especially those which have come to be known as behavior problems, are traceable to the conflict between the tendencies of this emancipation process and the attitudes of the parents. Sometimes the attitudes toward, and the relationships with, other members of the family, especially of the brothers and sisters, may also be of no little significance. But the family relationship features of adolescent life are primarily outgrowths, directly or indirectly, of the conflict between matured habits and attitudes established by the parents and the present attitudes of the parents themselves.

Hence no one can hope to achieve a satisfactory understanding of an adolescent's family setting and its influences until one knows much about the personalities of the parents who dominate that family. Are they happily mated? Are they dissatisfied with life? Are they disappointed with each other? Are they disappointed with what they have achieved in life? Are they disillusioned about life and its possibilities, and have they become adjusted to the realities of life? Are they suffering the anhedonia [1] which to some degree comes to so many people in the later forties or thereabouts? Are they seeking to realize in their children what they wanted to be and have never become? Is it that the mother is thinking that the period of her usefulness as a raiser of children is nearly past and that there is nothing in the future for her to do? If the parents are troubled by any of these, or any other form of maladjustment to life, it will in all probability be reflected in one way or another in the behavior of the adolescent or in the pattern of his personality.

Then, too, the family influences are determined in nature by the family pattern. Are both parents living? Are they old or young? Is one quite old and the other rather young? Is one

---

[1] This is the term with which A. Myerson designates the loss of pleasure in life, the loss of zest in living, which characterizes certain years of so many adults. See his able little book, *When Life Loses Its Zest,* Boston, 1925.

parent dead? Is there a step-parent in the home? How many other children are there? And what are the relative ages of the other children? What is the intelligence of the parents? Are they about alike in mental ability, or is one distinctly more able than the other? And the same for the children. Is the individual child in question brighter or duller than the others? Many other questions of importance could be raised but these are doubtless sufficient to give the necessary orientation for the material of this chapter.

Family Consciousness. There is much reason for thinking that a basic family influence in adolescent years is a rising consciousness of the family itself in the thought of the adolescent. He may for the first time come to a full appreciation of the distinctive status of his family.[1] Its long history, its famous members, and other items of genealogical lore may be a source of pride, and possibly of inspiration to excel. Recognition of the achievements of his own parents and their own social standing may add to that family consciousness, and contribute to his family loyalty. There are many indications of a new influence through a better understanding of the actual family income, of what allowances are possible, and of how soon the youth must do his part to contribute to that income. And here enters also the matter of individual allowances, the propriety of their size, their sufficiency, and the like.

Of course one must also recognize here that not infrequently this increased interest in the status of the family does not lead to a discovery of greatness either in past or present. There may be the discovery of "skeletons in the closet." There is ordinarily the gradual admission of the growing boy and girl into a more confidential relationship concerning all matters of family standing and support. This may mean a sort of initiation into the secrets of the family. For the first time there may come the knowledge of some hitherto carefully guarded secret, the revelation of which, or so it is believed, would bring disgrace upon the household. Perhaps there is a wayward older member of the family. Perhaps some relative committed suicide, perhaps there has been

---

[1] G. Stanley Hall somewhere expressed the opinion that this is more true of and more influential in the life of the adolescent girl than in the boy, but without adequate statistical support.

insanity in the family, or there may be a criminal relative; and along with these there may be a well-established belief that such traits or tendencies are inheritable.

Other revelations concerning the family may come more from without than from within. The progress of education and the growing range of personal acquaintance may precipitate a considerable change in the concept of the family status in the community. Instead of pride or secret shame, there may come knowledge which will stir inferiority feelings and embarrassment with regard to the family relationships. Sometimes it is realized that the parents are foreigners and that they do not speak the language of their adopted country with nicety and precision. Again the youth may discover that his parents are really very ignorant people, that they are poor, rough, ill-mannered, uncouth, uncultured. The tragedy possible in all this for both parents and children, the consequence of separation by education, has not infrequently been observed and described.

Effects of Family Consciousness. So far as we know, the effect of this new knowledge and new intimacy within the family circle apparently depends not only upon the nature of the new knowledge itself but also upon the attitudes of the parents toward the children. Taken alone such new knowledge might stir either alienation or greater loyalty to the family group. Discoveries of actual social inferiority and lack of culture, making the home and many of its members a source of embarrassment, may easily turn the youth away from the home, make him ashamed of it and lead him to avoid its contacts, and even at times avoid admission of any relationship to it. The discovery of dark family secrets hitherto carefully guarded may stir resentment against what may be interpreted as a long and deliberate process of deception. But it is also possible that the admission into family affairs, the discovery of the facts of which the family is fearful or ashamed, may stir a far greater loyalty than has hitherto been experienced. The consciousness of intimacy, the possession of knowledge not known to outsiders and which must be guarded from outsiders, the awareness that the parents are now trusting them as adults, a new feeling of sympathy or pity or pride or of shame that must be shared and concealed,—any or all of these would ordinarily stir loyalty to the group. Trust begets trust. And, as these things, and others related or unrelated, are talked about within the family circle each learns that it is in the family that one may most easily find sympathy and the easy arousal of like feelings which reinforce and satisfy (McDougall's doctrine of active sympathy in relation to passive sympathy).

But along with this loyalty reaction tendency must be considered the many parental effects upon the growing children which alienate and distort to such an extent that the loyalty reaction may be not merely minimized but not infrequently overlaid completely. To these distorting influences we must now give our attention.

Parental Effects Which Distort. Many instances are reported of parental practices and attitudes and purposes which have the effect of cultivating or establishing features in the personality of the adolescent that are undesirable and unfortunate because they interfere with both success and happiness. But it is insufficient today merely to list these. It is inadequate merely to say that parents are excessively dominant, or that they are too lenient, that they cultivate in their children their own fears and timidities and inferiorities, or that they persist in forcing their children into vocational selections that satisfy the parents but which are repugnant to the children. The student of psychology wants to know why the parents behave in such ways, and then he is at once on the trail of the psychogenesis of these troublesome family factors.

Where it has been possible to look behind the tendencies of parents to *excessive leniency* with their children, there has frequently been found an influential recollection on the part of one or both parents of their own bitter childhood and adolescent experience with parents that sought to dominate completely. This recollection lives as a determining tendency to avoid strictly the mistakes which they believe their parents made, with the consequence that they go too far in the other direction. A psychologically similar influence may be found in parents who have fought all their lives against devastating inferiority beliefs and feelings. They do everything for their children which will guard against such inferiority troubles and thus develop the almost equally disturbing influence of superiority notions and superiority feelings.

In like manner must one look behind the efforts of parents to *dominate* the *vocational selections* of their children. Every one is familiar with this as an actuality. There are parents who consecrate their children in infancy to the ministry, the law, medicine, business, or what not, quite without regard for the latent aptitudes and capacities of the children. Childhood in such homes is spent in an atmosphere of expectancy governed by these vocational selections made by the parents. By adolescent years, when more serious thoughts are given by adolescents to the matter of life investment, youths so brought up discover to their distress that they apparently have no more liberty of personal selection than has the senior prince in a royal household. All seems for them to have been determined in advance. And what has been determined may be the path of least resistance. To follow it would please the parents to whom there is a growing consciousness of obligation. To insist upon any other course would not only distress and disappoint them, but it might also bring an open rupture. And to follow in the way of parental desires might also mean ample financial support.

With adolescent years, however, comes not only a better understanding of one's own capacities and interests, but there also comes that tendency to strike out for one's self, to be independent and self-reliant, to satisfy the will-to-power drive. The parent selected vocation may be looked upon as a very good one, perhaps quite suitable in many respects; but it is parent selected and not self selected and in that fact lies often much of the trouble. Such circumstances bring into the lives of many young people a situation which is the source of much tension and distress.

It has made many people wonder why parents should be so insistent, and when they seriously seek an answer they often find it in the life experiences of the parents themselves. The vocation which they are forcing upon their children is that which they wanted to have for their own, in which they had in their own youthful years dreamed of becoming happy and successful, but which for one reason or another (perhaps the insistence of their own parents in turn) they were obliged to relinquish. What they gave up they never forgot. Through the years their own aborted careers haunted them, and when children of their own came there came with them the determination to realize their own lost hopes vicariously in the lives of their children.

Many a boy has been forced into the vocation which his father wanted for himself and could not have. Many a boy has been subjected to the necessity of seriously disappointing his parents in order to do that for which he believed himself best fitted. This parental human reaction of projecting upon the children what the parents wanted to become and could not is a frequent cause of personality alteration if not of distortion in adolescent years. In the train of this struggle, however it be solved by the youth, follow regrets and notions of inferiority and resentments and a host of other unpleasant lingering influences.[1]

The readjustments of adolescence bring to the front many *parental influence effects* which were really *established* long *before adolescent* years were achieved. Attitudes and fears of the parents become the attitudes and fears of the children. Notions about social and racial and religious differences and inferiorities with their accompanying attitudes and emotions of submission, hopeless rebellion, resentment, fear, and the like, are not infrequently reproduced in the children. And where there are fears of the possibility of inherited disease tendencies, the children are frequently brought up with so much caution and with so many warnings as to establish timidities of a like nature. The writer once knew an adolescent girl who from her earliest recollections had grown up with the constant admonition at home that she must not do this or that or something else because she might "go insane like her father." Through childhood years all these may be accepted as facts with little consideration of their consequences. But in adolescent years, when the new outlooks upon life become prominent and there is the rapidly increasing consciousness of becoming a new and independent personality, all these fears and inferiorities appear as handicaps to the achievement of success and happiness in life. Especially do they annoy because they apparently prevent the individual from doing and achieving as his associates appear free to do and to achieve.

While such disturbances may not often be the sole cause of the

[1] For an excellent discussion of this see Young, K., "Parent-Child Relationship: Projection of Ambition," *Family*, 1927, 8, 67-73. See also E. R. Groves, *Personality and Social Adjustment*, chap. 12.

troubles and stresses of adolescent years, they are not infrequently contributing causes. The degree of their influence will also depend upon their particular nature, how they are evaluated by the particular individual involved, and also by the social situation in which they occur. What would be a serious disturbance of a youth in one social level or social setting may not be considered a serious matter in some other social level or setting.

Some parents seek so persistently to *maintain absolute control* over their children as to lead one to the suspicion that they would if possible continue their habits of domination so long as they live. In rare cases that is actually achieved, and the children, although mature in years, never arrive at full self-determination. Ordinarily, however, the healthy youthful desire for freedom sooner or later prevails. Why parents should so seek to continue their domination has frequently been considered. A number of motivations are possible. Perhaps the parents are coming into those years of life when so many adults are markedly disinclined to change their ways. Perhaps they are timid about the product of their own efforts at child raising, and dare not trust their children to fend for themselves in the struggles of life. Perhaps they fear a moral breakdown and would protect indefinitely, never letting their children achieve character by overcoming. Perhaps there is a more or less repressed disinclination to give up a position of authority so long held. It has satisfied their desire for power and if it is relinquished they must give up and "take a back seat," for there is to them no other visible opportunity for the satisfactions which come through the domination over other human beings.

And perhaps there is a tendency to hold on to the children for business reasons. The family may possess a large business or professional practice; and the parent may have long built his life and his business around the expectation of bringing his children into it. The business or professional practice may actually offer an exceptional opportunity; but the prospect of submitting to the parent and becoming a cog in the family machine may fail to satisfy the desire for self-selection, for self-determination, and the pleasure of exercising one's own initiative. The parent may be earnestly seeking the best for his children in such instances; or, his efforts on their behalf may be colored by a greater devotion to the welfare of the business than to that of the children.

In instances of parent-child distress in adolescent years, one may expect to find one or more of these motivations operative. There may be modifications and shadings and combinations in a great variety of ways, but these are the sort of motivations which students of behavior problems have been revealing. Sometimes the negative aspect of them is also mentioned. Along with these efforts to continue parental domination there is also a corresponding degree of indifference to the fact that the average adolescent is much attracted by, much influenced by, the ways of those outside of the family. It will be recalled that ideals, as adolescence is approached, are likely to come more and more from extra-familial sources. It is obvious that the struggle with parental domination will be more acute where the appeal of any and all that lies beyond the family circle is especially strong.

The effects of continued parental domination and of the struggles to overcome it are not well known. There is a growing suspicion that there may be many of them, and there is a tendency to look more and more frequently to this feature of parental influence for bases of explanation. For a long time students of behavior problems have been aware of the frequency with which rebelliousness in adolescence could be traced to the struggle with parental efforts to dominate, a rebelliousness which was manifest not only in purely family relations but also in many other social situations. It can be seen in such youths in the rebellious reactions to any one in position of authority, and in extreme cases they react in like manner against any sort of authority even though it be in the impersonal form of laws or of institutional regulations. Sometimes this apparently becomes, as a consequence, a permanent trait of the personality. Chronic agitators and rebels of all sorts, people who seem never able to live peaceably in the presence of any sort of constituted authority, are now often interpreted as being the product of such parent-adolescent conflicts.

Perhaps some less conspicuous traits are determined or molded or established by parental efforts at prolonged domination. Perhaps the degree of one's social adaptability is influenced by it. Perhaps introvertive and extrovertive growth twists are given to

the personality by it. Of these we today know little but are beginning to suspect much. Chassell,[1] in a study which needs much
amplification and repetition by better methods, found notable
evidence of a possible sex difference in the reactions to parental
discipline. Parental domination seems to be associated with introverted tendencies in daughters; while it seems, in sons, to be
associated with extrovertive behavior.

Jealousy. Practically all studies today assume that jealousy is
a product of family life. There seems to be no inclination to
deny the possibility of its developing in adolescence or in maturity without previous experience and without any family influences involved; but, at the same time, it is quite clear that
recent writers on the subject favor the opinion that jealous behavior is ordinarily the product of early family situations and
impressions.

All students, whatever their special preferences in psychological thinking, agree that jealousy in human beings does in one
way or another involve the concept of the self and the feelings
concerning that concept. The struggle for vocational adjustment
and the beginnings of romantic love throw special emphasis
upon the self and social relations. The efforts at financial independence and to achieve self-determination, emancipation from
parental control, likewise force attention to the self and its situation. Relationships to others within and without the family are
accentuated. Desired privileges may be denied. The favors of
loved ones may not be forthcoming. In all these efforts and
struggles to be and to become it often seems as though others enjoyed that which is the right, or the longed-for privilege, of the
self. The disappointments, the disheartening embarrassments,
and the feelings of injustice which so often arise in these struggles for self-achievement are the immediate causes of jealous
behavior.

Little is really known about the *essential nature* of the experience and the mode of behavior called jealousy. It has often been
pointed out that animals manifest a form of behavior which is
commonly thought of as jealousy. For that reason jealousy has

[1] Chassell, J. O., *The Experience Variables* (pub. by author, 1928, Univ. of
Rochester).

not infrequently been looked upon as an instinct, especially in
the older treatises of the subject.[1] A most thoroughgoing although non-experimental attempt at a psychological analysis is
that made by Shand and McDougall.[2] While there are slight
differences in their conceptions, both insist that the appearance
of jealousy first depends upon the presence of a love sentiment
of some form in the individual. This means of course a relationship between two persons. Then the behavior of a third person,
or the behavior of the loved one toward a third person, prevents
a satisfactory expression of the love emotions, and above all, prevents self-satisfying responses from the loved person. There is
both the blocking of impulses to action and the injury to the
self. These are the normal stimuli to the arousal of anger and
of inferiority feeling. The response may be yet further complicated by fear that the situation may become worse for the self
or that it may become dangerous to the loved one; and there may
be ideals or social pressures which prevent any adequate expression of the anger aroused.

McDougall also suggests that jealousy may sometimes arise
where there is little if any tender emotion for the object of the
sentiment, that the object may be perceived as a part of one's
property and thus in a way a part of the self. When that object
is lost or some one is apparently guilty of preventing its full and
proper possession, then there is a comparable blocking with like
arousal of anger and injured self feelings. Such experiences may
occur over items of privilege within the family, over the amount
of allowance permitted by the parents, the clothing provided,
and so on.

The psychoanalysts have much the same idea although they
have placed rather more stress upon the child's love for an individual parent and the effects of this upon the relationships with
the other parent.[3] White briefly formulated the idea when he

1 See Gesell, A. L., "Jealousy," *Amer. J. Psychol.*, 1906, 17, 437-496. See
also Hall, G. Stanley, *Adolescence*, Vol. 1, pp. 357-358.
2 Shand, A. F., *The Foundations of Character*, pp. 256-262.
  McDougall, Wm., *Social Psychology*, pp. 142-144.
3 Flügel, J. C., *The Psychoanalytic Study of the Family*, Internat. Psychoanal. Press.
  Jones, E., "La Jalousie," *Revue française de psychoanalyse*, 1929, 3, 228-
242.
  White, W. A., *Mechanisms of Character Formation*, pp. 167-168.

said that jealousies between children of the same family are but expressions of "attachment to the parents once removed." They, the psychoanalysts, believe that they have demonstrated a marked, and possibly instinctive, tendency for girls to develop a near-romantic love for the father and in boys that there is a tendency toward a like reaction to the mother. Then the girl who so loves her father finds in the mother that third person who is in her way, a competitor for her father's love and attention. And in like manner the boy becomes jealous of the father's intimacy and love relationship with the mother. Brothers and sisters may enter into the picture either as other contenders for the love and attention of the loved parent, or they may serve as substitutes for the loved parent. A boy may be jealous because his mother showers too much attention, or so he believes, upon the brother or sister; or an older sister may be the center of affection in place of the mother and then jealousy arises if any brother or other sister appears likely to supplant him in her affection.

But it should also be observed that the psychoanalysts do not place the blame entirely upon the impulses or urges within the child. They have also observed that parents may show special preference for one or another child, and that a parent may even be jealous because the other parent seems to be giving the child too much attention and affection. Thus jealousy may be carried on from generation to generation. A child grows up in a home where thoughtless parental habits develop jealousy. The reaction pattern thus established colors his attempts at a romantic love life, and continuing spoils his marital life. As a jealous parent he turns to one of his children for solace, only to stir jealousy in other members of his family. He may be driven to sulks and favoritism through jealousy aroused by the belief that his wife is showering attention and affection upon a child in preference to himself. Thus are his children contaminated by the love distortions established in him by his parents. And so on from one generation to the next.

In any given case of jealousy it is evident that, if one would think psychoanalytically, one must think in terms of the interplay between the drives and tendencies from within the child on the one hand, and, on the other, the unsatisfied longings, the repressions, the conflicts, the maladjustments, and so on, within the personality of either or both of the parents.[1]

Unfortunately the only systematic studies which we have at present upon the development and manifestations of jealousy are those which have been made upon children considerably under adolescent years. It is possible, however, as many already believe, that the jealousies encountered in adolescence are really carry-overs of traits established long before; and thus, while one must be properly cautious about generalizing concerning adolescence from studies made upon young children, it is wise to note the trend of these studies of childhood jealousy.

In all of these the *prominence of parental maladjustment* and the effects of it upon disciplinary methods and the general management of the child are most notable. Other items, such as sex and degree of development and age difference between children, seem to be of far less significance, and on these the studies show conflicting observations. Perhaps a considerable difference in native mental ability is an important contributing factor. Smalley found in her study of pairs of children that the older and the duller child was most likely to be jealous.[2] Certainly this difference in native ability continues on into adolescent years, and all who have had much to do with youth are aware of the troubles which come to the boy or girl who is following through school in the wake of a brilliant older brother or sister. Ross[3] found some relation of jealousy to intelligence, that bright children were more likely to develop the trait than dull. She also found that a larger proportion of jealousy cases were first-born, a fact which checks well with traditional notions of the effects of a younger child coming into the home. These family settings

[1] Perhaps the most readily accessible presentation of this will be found in J. C. Flügel, *Psychoanalytic Study of the Family*, pp. 17-20, 158, 167, 178, and 209.

[2] Smalley, R. E., "The Influence of Differences in Age, Sex, and Intelligence in Determining the Attitudes of Siblings Toward Each Other," *Smith Coll. Stud. Soc. Work*, 1930, 1, 23-39. The reader should see also a companion study, Sewall, M., "Some Causes of Jealousy in Young Children," *Smith Coll. Stud. Soc. Work*, 1930, 1, 6-22.

Similar work will be found in Foster, S., "A Study of the Personality Make-up and Social Setting of Fifty Jealous Children," *Ment. Hyg.*, 1927, 11, 53-77.

[3] Ross, Bertha M., "Some Traits Associated with Sibling Jealousy in Problem Children," *Smith Coll. Stud. Soc. Work*, 1931, 1, 364-376.

which produce jealousy in childhood may continue to be an irritating background in adolescent years even though growth changes, especially the progress of emancipation from family domination, may tend to obliterate the traces of childhood experience.

Burnham apparently thinks of jealousy in adolescent years as always a retention of a childhood trait, and thus something approximating an abnormality. It is a distortion within the personality which is the product of circumstances surrounding the growth of the self. In essence it is defensive, a defense reaction which is a somewhat aberrant effort to protect the self.[1] As such it must be placed in that large and ever-growing class of maladjustments.

Jones [2] sees jealousy as a very complicated and always more or less pathological form of behavior. He believes that the jealous person is basically defective in the capacity to love others because he has carried over into adolescent years so large an amount of narcissistic fixation (exaggerated self-love). When such a personality does manifest what superficially appears to be heterosexual love, careful examination will reveal it to be essentially a desire to be loved, a desire for adulation of the self as a means of quieting the feeling of guilt and of satisfying the narcissistic desire. This kind of personality disturbance developing in the family situation would first involve the parents. The jealous boy would be seeking the constant affection of the mother and be jealous of the father. In adolescence and later years there would be a transportation of this behavior into extra-familial settings, in which the loved girl and the disturbing rival would become substitutes for the parents.

Jones also believes that jealousy is complicated by the influence of those homosexual trends always assumed by psychoanalysts to be lurking in the background. The anger factor, which all writers on jealousy have noted, is assumed to be an impulsive effort to repress the homosexual tendency. What this really means in psychoanalytic language is that the jealous boy is identifying himself with the loved girl in her attitudes (actual

[1] Burnham, W. H., *The Wholesome Personality*, pp. 369-372.
[2] Jones, E., "La Jalousie," *Revue française de psychoanalyse*, 1929, 3, 228-242.

or assumed) toward the third person of the triangle. This would tend to release the poorly repressed homosexual trend, in this case toward the intruding third person. But the possibility of such a release of the homosexual is shocking to the ego-ideal, or super-ego, and there is a violent reaction to keep it down, in control, or repressed. This violent repressing effort takes the form of anger toward the third person; for if the third person were out of the way there would be no danger of the homosexual trend finding release.

If Jones is right in this psychoanalytic interpretation, then we shall be forced to look upon jealousy in the adolescent personality as a trait so complicated and so well established as to be removable only by a very elaborate course of re-education, if it can be removed at all. The unfortunate probability is that such a person is likely to be troubled by jealousy more or less for the rest of his life.

That adolescence brings new situations and new valuations rather rapidly into the life of the growing boy and girl must be recognized and appreciated to the full or one will be in danger of making too hasty and too general an application of the notion that jealousy is always a carry-over of a childhood habit, or that it is the product of some basic personality defect. It is conceivable that these new circumstances and experiences of life may produce jealousy in adolescence for the first time.

The only available collection of descriptions of personal experience of jealousy was made many years ago [1] and by methods which today are far from satisfactory; but, even after one allows for all of its defects, there remains an indication of the possibility of unique adolescent experience of jealousy. In these descriptions the situations and experiences which are reported as causing jealousy differ notably from those reported for childhood. Individual talents, personal appearance, personal popularity, friends, and lovers appear prominently in adolescent descriptions, but rarely in pre-adolescent descriptions of jealousy. In these one can read the influence of the parental background and influence (favoritism) to be sure, but one can also perceive the effect of those social pressures which become so large a factor in adolescence. It is wise at least to recognize the possibility of any

[1] Gesell, A. L., "Jealousy," *Amer. J. Psychol.*, 1906, 17, 437-496.

given instance of jealousy being but a passing episode in the storm of adolescent struggles with a world which is for the youth very new and bewilderingly complex.

Parental Influences on Love Development. From the studies of the psychoanalyst has arisen a belief which is gaining ever-widening acceptance that in the love life of the adolescent may be seen many influences of present and past relationships with the parents.[1] For a clear understanding of this it must be recalled that the psychoanalysts do not think of the romantic love life in adolescence as a new development. For them it is far from being an instinctive tendency just coming into appearance. Rather is it for them a late stage in a course of development which began with birth or soon after. If it really be true that the love behavior in adolescent years is the end result of such a long course of development through infancy and childhood, then indeed is it quite possible that the course of that development may have been much influenced by parental contacts.

The general nature of this growth of love forms may be briefly summarized. It presupposes the existence of a libido, or affect, or pleasure, or satisfaction, or valuation, which may be associated with or attached to different modes of response to the self and to others. And with progress up the age scale, through the course of socializing influences, this libido may be progressively shifted from older and socially less desirable modes of response to newer responses that do receive social approval. In early infancy this libido is attached to the purely vegetative functions of the body and the love life is then said to be autoerotic (sometimes but now less often called polymorphous perverse because of certain vague similarities to the many forms of sexual perversion in abnormal adults).

PSYCHOANALYTIC STAGES OF LOVE DEVELOPMENT

Autoerotic (polymorphous perverse), early infancy.
Narcissistic (self-love) up to about three years.

Parental	three up to about six years.
Sexual latency	six up to pubescence.
Homosexual love	early adolescence.
Heterosexual love	middle and later adolescence.

[1] Flügel, J. C., *The Psychoanalytic Study of the Family.*
White, W. A., *Mechanisms of Character Formation*, chap. 7.

This autoerotic period is presented as rapidly merging into a period of self-love called narcissistic from a somewhat fanciful relationship to the Greek myth of Narcissus. Then somewhere about three or four years of age comes a shifting of the libido to the parents. And a cardinal belief here is that the little girl experiences a shift of her libido normally more to the father than to the mother, the boy of course more to the mother than the father. This period manifests the first indications of a tendency toward love of others and especially toward love of those of the other sex. Then follows, or so it is claimed, a period just prior to puberty in which early eagerness for sexual information has been largely satisfied and the love reactions or urges become less prominent in the emotional life. It is therefore termed a period of sexual latency.[1]

With the dawn of puberty the libido is again thought to swing outward, but first of all to those of the same sex as the individual under observation. And this first swing outward is influenced more by remnants of the narcissistic period (some libido still remaining there attached). Consequently it is an individual most like the self that is attractive, that is of course one of the same sex. This period of homosexuality is then not to be thought of as anything abnormal but as a period in which individuals of the same sex are of greatest interest. It is the period of groups and gangs and clubs in which the segregation of the sexes has often been observed.[2] This is normally followed by the appearance of a rapidly rising interest in the other sex, of puppy love affairs, and eventually of more stable romantic love.

From the above brief statement of the theory, it is no doubt already more than half clear how the parents may influence the love behavior in adolescent years. It is obvious, if one accept this conception of love development, that behavior in the period of

[1] Doubt concerning this period of sexual latency is now much in evidence as is indicated by the tendency to omit this period in many recent descriptions of this course of development. Where this omission is made, the gap is bridged by stretching upward the period of parental love and downward the stage of homosexual attraction. For fuller presentation of love theory see chap. XIII.

[2] Hall, G. Stanley, made much of this tendency of the sexes to draw apart for a time at or near puberty. See his *Adolescence*, chap. 17. The writer also found that 54 percent of a group of over 300 college students could immediately recall such a tendency for the sexes to draw apart for a time. See chap. II.

romantic love may be much influenced by the parental love experiences of childhood. Perhaps the boy may have been very fond of his mother, and this may have been aided and developed by a special preference of the mother for this particular boy. Then when the period of heterosexual love is reached, the girl with whom he falls in love is one who appeals to him as much as his mother had formerly done. The psychoanalysts say that the parental love period experiences have established in the personality of the growing boy a "mother imago" which largely determines the selection of the girl with whom he will subsequently fall in love. Resemblances between the girl and the mother may be hard to find, and the boy may not be at all conscious of the fact that he is being so influenced by his earlier affection for his mother. Yet the psychoanalysts are so confident of this influence that they are prone to say that the boy falls in love with and marries one who stands psychologically as a substitute for his mother. In the girl it is, of course, the "father imago," or the lingering influence of her own affective relationships with her father, which causes the boy to be attractive to her.

But influences from the period of parental love may be so strong as to prevent a proper development in the period of heterosexual love. By petting and loving the boy too much, the mother can establish what is termed a "fixation of the libido." [1] This means that the boy may go on developing into full manhood in every way except in his love behavior. That remains at the childish stage, fixated on his mother.

With the passing of the years the boy would grow into young manhood and become conscious of the fact that other young men fell in love, or at least liked to "go with the girls," but that he himself not only did not feel any tendency to fall in love but had no inclination to associate much with the other sex. Such is the home boy. He is so devoted to his mother that all the neighborhood applauds and holds him up as a beautiful example of devotion to his mother, one which they wish all other boys might emulate. They are ignorant of course of the fact that he is him-

[1] There are other possible causes which involve the boy's own behavior and also the relationships between the boy and the father. These will be found in the psychoanalytic works already referred to above. They are of significance here, however, only as they would supplement the development of too much affection between the boy and the mother.

self unhappy and that his personality is being distorted in its development by this lingering childish excessive affection for his mother. And the reverse is also to be frequently observed where girls find young men quite crude and undeveloped and generally unattractive because they come so far from measuring up to their fathers whom they idolize and worship and love.

Of such fixations there may be many degrees. The fixation may be more or less slowly outgrown. It may effect merely a delay in the development of romantic love and marriage. And it may at times be seen to prevent completely the achievement of a full heterosexual love and happy marriage. According to the degree of the consciousness of the cause and the ideals and the effects of the social pressures under which the individual has grown up and continues to live will there be anxiety and day-dreaming over the situation in life. There may be almost perfect content in the love and protection of the parent, and there may be much vacillation and uncertainty and impulsiveness and unhappiness apparent to whoever will observe thoughtfully. It is probably wise to add also that there may be some variant forms of this so-called parental fixation. It is possible for a relative of the parents' generation, an uncle or an aunt for example, to be the center of this same sort of excessive filial affection and there are instances reported of grandparents and also of older brothers and sisters appearing in the life experience as a substitute for the parent.

In this connection Allport [1] has stressed his belief that such parental fixations are not infrequently the cause of introversion. Because of the inability to adjust to life as do the others of the same sex and age there is, he thinks, a tendency to withdraw and find satisfaction within the personality of the individual himself. Such introverted folk live more and more in a world of their own making, much of which is fantasy thinking, according to the extent of their introversion.

In a comparable manner it is possible for the libido to become fixated at the narcissistic stage. This is manifested in the individual behavior by an excessive self-centeredness. The individual loves himself so highly that he cannot love any one or any-

---

[1] Allport, F. H., *Social Psychology*, p. 362.

thing else well. The effects of such a failure of the love life to develop beyond the narcissistic stage might be observed prior to adolescence; but it would certainly become most noticeable in adolescent years, when normally there is not only the development of love for the other sex but also a more or less rapidly rising consciousness of responsibility for the welfare of others. The highly altruistic impulses and acts of youths at various stages of adolescence have often been commented upon and have not infrequently become of historic significance. To be interested in the other sex and to be altruistic are characteristics of adolescence so familiar one's attention is promptly attracted by the few who do not develop them. They are looked upon as queer and somehow unnatural, perhaps distorted in their development. They are all of that; and, what is more unfortunate, they are often all of that to themselves as well as others. But in spite of a knowledge of what they ought to be they cannot of their own will bring themselves to be other than they are.

Such narcissistically fixated persons may, in order to make themselves appear like others, force themselves to try to be agreeable to the other sex and to the appearance at least of interest in the welfare of others. But it is all a hollow sham. It is a defense mechanism. They may even attempt to participate like others in matters of public welfare, but ever and again the true nature of their impulses and emotional reactions is revealed and becomes the cause of no little unhappiness. While this may not all be due to the home situation and the way in which they were guided through the childhood years by their parents, far too little is known about such distortions of development at present, there is nevertheless a wide-spread conviction that much of such fixation can be traced to the type of discipline or lack of it in the home situation, to excess of provision and protective care exercised by the parents, and perhaps also to the existence of a similar narcissistic fixation in one or both of the parents themselves.

Fixations at the homosexual level may also appear through parental influences, intentionally or otherwise. This must not be construed to mean a perversion into disgusting forms of abnormality. We are here concerned only with those disturbances of adolescent development which result in a lack of interest and attraction to members of the other sex, and which are characterized by a constant preference for the companionship of members of the same sex. There is much the same sort of behavior that is so often seen in pubescent years when the other sex is rather despised and looked upon as generally useless and undesirable. Normality of growth appears to characterize the individuals in such instances up to pubescence. From then on they appear to be retarded or blocked in their love development.

Ordinarily today such fixations are attributed to overcautiousness on the part of the parent concerning the child's relation to the other sex. There are instances of mothers who cultivate a fear of the other sex in their daughters. By tales of the sins of men and by constant cautioning against the dangers of associating with them, they develop in their daughters an actual fear of the other sex. If the mother has been unhappily married, exaggerated stories of her own experience may be used to the extent of developing in the daughter an actual hatred of men. And perhaps the daughter has seen enough of the disgusting behavior of a brutish father to establish a reaction to all members of the other sex that inhibits any development of the heterosexual stage of love in herself. Disappointed fathers are known to have cultivated a hatred of all women in their growing sons. Sometimes the dramatic breakdown of this hatred in adolescent years or in early maturity, when the young man really discovers the true character of some young woman and the falsity of his notions concerning women, has been made the basis for most readable fiction.

Instances are also reported where the ideals of what kind of a man or woman will make a suitable mate have been developed so highly by misguided but loving parents that all whom their children meet are unattractive. When a girl's notion of what a young man must be to be suitable for her company, and a young man's notion of what a girl should be are so far above the actual and possible, there may be the false interpretation that their duty is to wait and in the meantime to avoid associations with those who are inferior. Doting parents, who may also be motivated by a fear of losing their positions of authority, may do their best to maintain such attitudes in their children. Such may also appear to the observer as behavior best interpreted as fixation at the homosexual level of development.

A few instances have been reported of the effect upon the love life of the discovery of delinquencies on the part of the parents. Emerson [1] has reported an instructive case wherein a child of six discovered that her parents had been married but two months at the time of her birth. The influence of this continued through adolescent years. At first she was seclusive and disinclined to mix socially. Then came a period of wild seeking of excitement. There was much social activity. Several engagements were entered into which seem to have been in many respects rather unnatural and complicated in their motivation. But even when engaged, she would never permit petting. In all probability there are many more such instances of disturbance of the development of the love life, more disturbances of orientation toward the other sex, because of discoveries or misunderstandings about the parents, than we are ordinarily inclined to assume. The psychoanalysts have often made much of these childhood "psychic sex traumas" as causes for the distortions into abnormalities of behavior in later life.

These parental effects upon the development of the love life in adolescent years have been presented largely in terms of the psychoanalytic theory because much more of the literature has been written in that language than in any other. But to the thoughtful student familiar with psychological systems it will be readily apparent that other language might have been used. The facts of development disturbances termed fixations at one or another level remain facts whether one accept the psychoanalytic libido or not. Narcissistic fixation, and parental fixation, and homosexual fixation may equally well be expressed in terms of unevenness of development, the retention and carryover into adolescent years of habits of reaction which should have been abandoned or displaced by other habits more appropriate to that stage of growth. The fears of the other sex and the distortions by impossibly high ideals may be equally well

[1] Emerson, L. E., "The Psychopathology of the Family," *J. Abn. Psychol.*, 1914, 9, 333-340.

explained in terms of conditioned learning. The girl who has been taught to fear all men has had her fear reaction conditioned by her training to all perceptions of the other sex. And the training to an impossible ideal of the other sex can be quite as satisfactorily interpreted as a form of conditioning.

CHAPTER XII

INFLUENCES OF THE FAMILY *(Continued)*

MINOR PARENTAL INFLUENCES, STABILIZING INFLUENCES OF
PARENTAL CONTACTS, EFFECT OF POSITION IN THE FAMILY
PATTERN (ONLY CHILD, OLDEST, YOUNGEST, FOSTER-CHILD),
PSYCHOLOGICAL WEANING

Minor Parental Influences. There are a number of other ways
in which parents and parental situations may be found as influential factors in the adolescent personality, but they are influences about which even less is known. Perhaps they are not
really minor at all, certainly in some instances they will be found
to be decidedly major influences, but there has been less written
about them and so they can be but briefly commented upon.

The effects of extremely stern and *severe parental discipline*
in matters of love and sex fall inevitably into this class. Fiction
and drama have for many years presented the stern father shut-
ting the door upon the wayward or merely willful adolescent
girl. Sometimes the stories are given a happy and sometimes a
tragic ending. But of the details of development within the personality of the girl herself too little has been presented. Social
workers today continue to report boys and girls turned out by
stern parents or alienated from the home by parental severity
over matters of love and the sex relation. The casual observer
may wonder at the parental severity and not be surprised to
learn that it has often been traced to the lingering effects of maladjustments toward sex in their own lives. The effects upon the
boys and girls so treated are many and various. So far as we
know they cannot well be treated in isolation but always in
connection with the ideals and attitudes already developed,
towards themselves, towards their parents, and towards others.
And, along with these, such a home would in all probability

have developed many inferiorities and repressions, as well as the disturbing effects of much misinformation.

The place of the parents in the development of childhood and adolescent ideals should also be included here. In Chapter VI it was stated that the early content of the ideal ordinarily comes from the parents; that is, that the early ideals are very concrete and in the form of what the parent now is or as the parent is childishly conceived to be. Then the ideals undergo a course of change in which they become with the progress of adolescence more and more abstract. It is quite conceivable also that the attitudes and habits and ways of parents may even in these later stages of ideal development have much influence. Where parental attachment continues through adolescent years, the nature of the abstract ideals developed may be largely influenced by the beloved parent's ideas and habits. Likewise where there is open rebellion, or even a strained relationship, between the boy or girl and the parents, the ideals developed may be much influenced in the formation of their content by this very rebellion or strained relationship.

Some psychoanalytic students of religious concepts have believed that they could see in the nature of adolescent concepts of God and of the devil the influence of parental factors in the formations of their ideals projected into these concepts. The concept of God has been presented as a reflection of the childhood conception of the father as great and good and powerful and lovely and so on. The concept of the devil has been likewise presented as a reflection of the adolescent struggle with the father as the father is said far too often to appear to the adolescent in the struggle for emancipation.[1] Whether or not such interpretations of the religious concepts mentioned will stand more critical study, these ideas well represent the trend of thinking. More and more psychologists and sociologists alike are coming to recognize the large influence which parents have, consciously or unconsciously, upon the ideals in adolescent years of their children; and this whether the relationship between the parents and the children be happy or otherwise.[2]

[1] Flügel, J. C., *The Psychoanalytic Study of the Family,* chap. 13.
White, W. A., *Mechanisms of Character Formation,* chap. 10.
[2] Van Waters, Miriam, *Parents on Probation.*

Parents are probably also responsible to some extent for the *inferiority troubles* of adolescent years. In part this is doubtless inevitable. It is their duty to initiate their children into hopes and anticipations and expectations for their own future, and to aid them into a consciousness of what society is expecting of them. All of these, it has already been pointed out (Chapter IX), contribute to the inferiority reactions often so disturbing. But there are instances of parental contributions to inferiority troubles which are far less commendable.

All through the struggles toward achievement and adjustment in adolescent years the youth needs encouragement and guidance. He needs the encouraging and stabilizing influences of successful endeavor quite as much as did the shell-shocked soldiers during the recent war. The youth is timidly struggling into life as the shell-shocked patient was fearfully making efforts on the road back to health and efficiency. Both can be seriously damaged by discouragement, the youth much less doubtless because of his basic health and vigor but nevertheless seriously. Here parents are often unwittingly to blame. They may thoughtlessly treat with derision some tenderly guarded effort to achieve. Parental ridicule of the first efforts at social relations, of the first boy and girl who appear attractive, of first efforts at dancing with the other sex, of the first shave, of the first love affairs, of the first social slights and successes, may seriously wound the youthful hopes and ambitions. Inferiority troubles are easily started by such checks and disappointments.

The first efforts of youth do indeed appear very funny to the average adult. To the thoughtless, the youth appears to be taking himself and his efforts and his troubles far too seriously; but the adult is then perceiving the youth and his experiences in the light of adult knowledge and experience. The youth perceives his efforts and troubles far differently. To the youth they are not funny. And if those whom he respects and whose judgment he values treat his efforts and his troubles with ridicule, one of two things is almost certain to follow, alienation or belief in his own inferiority, with all the troubles which follow in the train of either of these reactions.

Instances are also reported of parents who cause their children trouble in adolescent years by more or less deliberately cultivating in them traits which are highly satisfactory to themselves but which are not approved by society. The parents may approve of meanness in money matters, of shrewdness which in the child appears to be merely amusing to the parent, and of self-centeredness which the parent may really believe to be desirable. Then when as youths such children find themselves in a social order where such traits are not approved as they were at home, their social adjustment may be seriously handicapped. The groups with whom they would like to associate do not want them. Opportunities are denied to them. It is necessary for them either to capitalize their meanness and shrewdness and self-centeredness and make their way largely in social isolation, or to go through the long and distressing experience of changing these now well-established character traits. Either program involves much needless unhappiness. Turning the matter around, it becomes the responsibility of those who must interpret individual adolescent behavior to keep this possibility in mind, and to look to the home and the parents for the possible sources of such struggles with traits that result in disturbances of the personality development.

What the *effects* may be in the adolescence of personality *of the loss of a parent* little is known unfortunately. And much the same must be said of our knowledge of the effects of the loss of both parents. There is also the at-present bewildering field of the problems aroused by parental separation, still further complicated if one or both of the parents re-marry. The step-parent situation must always bring, for a time at least, new factors into the growth of personality. It is known that lost parents frequently continue to live actively in the personalities of their children in an ideal, and sometimes a much-idealized, form. Parental fixations are quite possible with such a concept or image (psychoanalytic imago) serving as a substitute for the actual presence of the parent, and sometimes these are quite as disturbing in adolescent years as any other form of fixation. Parental substitutes are well known and sometimes serve quite as well as the original parent. But divided loyalties brought about by parental separations for reasons which the children cannot fully understand or appreciate are not infrequently found as causes of emotional distress in adolescent years.

The particular nature of this distress, so far as the writer has been able to discover, seems to depend upon a vast number of other factors in the life of the individual quite as much as upon the divided loyalty itself. Probably the most outstanding influence of these family disturbances by parental defection or death is the weakening of that consciousness of security which the normal child ordinarily finds above all in the home. In adolescent years, however, the importance of finding security in the home must be of declining significance; yet enough is known about the influence of other traits to justify the belief that a loss of the security feeling in childhood years may bring the individual up to adolescence with a background sufficiently different from that of the average boy and girl to contribute some probably quite peculiar features to the adolescent course of growth and adjustment.[1]

Stabilizing Parental Influences. It must be obvious that all of the many items discussed in the preceding sections as disturbing factors in the adolescence of personality could well be presented here in the reverse form. Parents contribute a stabilizing influence who carefully abstain from permitting their own troubles and maladjustments in life to influence either directly or indirectly their manner of guiding their children. Tactful progressive efforts toward the establishment of self-reliance and independence in the adolescent in place of any attempt to retain unduly a personal domination will likewise aid in the growth of a normal personality. Avoidance of all indication of favoritism and a careful impartiality in providing for each child in a family aids in keeping out the major causes of jealousy. Encouraging the development of socially acceptable traits, imparting such information as will minimize the possibility of developing excessive notions of inferiority or superiority, the exercise of sufficient restraint in the expression of affection so as to avoid all possibilities of fixation or the disturbing carry-over of childhood habits, and much tactful care in the cultivation of adolescent concepts of the ideal may contribute largely to the development

---

[1] A thoughtful essay on this general topic is the following: Preston, G. H., "Mental-Hygiene Factors in Parenthood and Parental Relationships," *Ment. Hyg.*, 1928, 12, 751-760. See also Flügel, J. C., *The Psychoanalytic Study of the Family*, chap. 10.

of a personality which will lack most of the major disturbing factors now so often lamented.

In addition, a few other items may be stressed. Many now emphasize the contribution which parents may make who realize that as a family group they are all facing the problems of life together. The thought seems to be that those members of the family group who are in adolescence will achieve most by feeling that in their parents they may find sources of wisdom but not dictation, friends to whom they may go for counsel, friends who are after all far more intimate than friends, who can because of their deeper understanding aid in facing the problems of life adjustment.

Mention has already been made of the growing adolescent consciousness of the nature and social status of his family. Parents who are themselves proud (in the best sense of the word) of their family history and achievement can contribute a valuable stabilizing factor by making such attitudes a part of their daily life. Then will it come into the lives of their children in a casual matter-of-course manner. If there is that in the family history which might be genuine cause for shame or of fear, then that is one of the problems of life to which the adolescent members of the family circle must sooner or later make their adjustment. This may be greatly eased if the parents have long before that time comes made their own adjustment. If the parents have faced the facts squarely and have them properly evaluated, they will be able to talk of them in an impersonal fashion and to guide the course of their children's adjustment to the same facts. The habit of quietly but firmly and courageously facing the realities of life, whatever they may be, is now recognized by practically all schools of psychological thinking to be an invaluable aid in the development of a normal personality.

Parents who have themselves achieved this attitude toward the problems of living can through their longer experience and wider knowledge protect their children against the distorting burdens of a premature assumption of the responsibilities and attendant anxieties of life. In the casual literature of the day, there is much emphasis upon the importance of this easing-into the responsibilities of life. Where the responsibilities can be assumed gradually, and allowed to accumulate not too rapidly, adjustments may be made with each new problem and thus the distressing bewilderment of a sudden plunge be avoided. By such means it is evident that all of the native capacity for the development of a wholesome normal integration of personality can be capitalized.

Far too often our sociologists and social welfare workers are obliged to call our attention to the unfortunate fact that the home is often a part of a miserable reality from which youth seeks to escape.[1] Why any particular home should present such a miserable reality is usually found upon analysis to be due to some one or more, sometimes many, of the distorting familial factors presented in the earlier paragraphs of this chapter. But, so far as we can now perceive, the best development in adolescent years will be found not where there is merely the avoidance of the undesirable, but where there is the cultivation of a home situation designed to establish the consciousness of security.[2] With such security in the home, it becomes a place for refreshment and encouragement and preparation for the facing of the realities that lie beyond. The danger through excessive coddling, of making the home so attractively secure as to make retreat from the other realities too easy, is a very real danger; but there is a difference between coddled enervation and a feeling of security, a difference which most can recognize even though a complete analysis be not yet available. The security feeling implies poise and quiescence while the other implies a retained childishness. The security may contribute through rest, relaxation, and re-orientation what coddling can never supply.

For all of this, the value of maintaining a relation of intimate friendly confidence between the maturing adolescent and the parents must be obvious. Its contribution is probably first of all to the development of personality organization, through the confident talking-things-over with those of greater maturity and wisdom. It is characteristic of youth to seek such confidence and counsel. Obstacles to its development lie only within the parents

---

[1] Van Waters, Miriam, *Parents on Probation.*

[2] It is unfortunate that we do not have yet an adequate analysis of this. Certainly it is more than the absence of fear, and probably not entirely a matter of attitude.

themselves. Leonard [1] has on this contributed a valuable study of that which interferes with the development of such confidential relations; but unfortunately it is confined to the experiences of adolescent girls. From her study a number of obstacles appear among which are any undue emotionality in the mother, such as excessive fussing or nagging, any obvious lack of leisure for confidential talks, ridicule, lack of interest, misunderstanding of the daughter's attitudes or actions. Leonard also points out that the obstacle may not be entirely within the parent, but that some traits of the girls themselves may make such confidence difficult. Where the daughter is inclined to be secretive, is excessively inclined to be independent, is conscious of shame over something she has done, there the confidential relation is also difficult. But it may be also observed that these very traits in the daughters may in turn be traceable to the effects of earlier parental relations.

Effect of Position in the Family Pattern. Highly competent people have frequently asserted that the growth experience of an *only child* is a very bad preparation for the adjustments of both adolescence and maturity. It has been claimed that they are much more susceptible to the disturbances consequent to parental fixation of affection and some have gone so far as to assert that they could never have the same capacity for adjustment that may be developed by growth in a family pattern including several other children. Brill [2] contends that only children rarely marry. Blanton and Blanton [3] claim that the only child is prone to difficulties of adjustment because it grows up in an adult world wherein it can most successfully compete by the retention of infantile behavior. Hence it becomes a behavior problem. Studies made in institutions for juvenile delinquents have amply supported this belief. Levy,[4] working with vast collections of material available at the Institute for Juvenile Research in Chicago, found that only children were much more likely to be-

[1] Leonard, E. A., *Concerning Our Girls and What They Tell Us.* Teachers College, New York, 1930.
[2] Brill, A. A., *Fundamental Conceptions of Psychoanalysis,* chap. 11.
[3] Blanton, S., and Blanton, M. G., *Child Guidance,* p. 175.
[4] Levy, J. A., "Quantitative Study of Behavior Problems in Relation to Family Constellation," *Amer. J. Psychiatry,* 1931, 10, 637-654.

come problem cases, and Burt,[1] working on similar material in London, found a much higher frequency of only children in his delinquent than in his comparison group of non-delinquent children.

From such indications we would expect to find the tensions of adolescent years especially trying for all young people whose childhood experience was that of an only child in the family. But such is far from being true. In fact, more recent studies seriously question the validity of the older statements and beliefs about the troubles of the only children, both in childhood and in adolescence. A number of studies have found very little if any differences in conduct, adaptability, problem behavior, and character traits of the only child when compared with children with one or more siblings; and some have even indicated that being an only child was advantageous.[2]

It is no longer possible to make sweeping generalizations concerning only children. One cannot assume in any given instance that the individual will have a harder time than others in making the adjustments of adolescent years just because he was an only child. Being an only child may be a serious handicap, it may be a real advantage, and it may be of little significance. It now appears that other factors in the family situation are quite as important as that of onliness. And there is much reason for thinking that the rough and tumble of school and playground life may smooth out any peculiar twists in the personality started by early growth experiences as an only child.[3] But it must also

[1] Burt, Cyril, *The Young Delinquent*, p. 62.

[2] Bender, I. E., "Ascendance-Submission in Relation to Certain Other Factors in Personality," *J. Abn. & Soc. Psychol.*, 1928, 23, 137-143.

Blatz, W. E., and Bott, E. A., "Studies in Mental Hygiene of Children. I. Behavior of Public School Children," *Ped. Sem.*, 1927, 34, 552-582. See especially p. 574.

Fenton, N., "The Only Child," *J. Genet. Psychol.*, 1928, 35, 546-554.

Goodenough, F. L., and Leahy, A. M., "The Effect of Certain Relationships upon the Development of Personality," *J. Genet. Psychol.*, 1927, 34, 45-71.

Guilford, R. B., and Worcester, D. A., "A Comparative Study of the Only and Non-Only Child," *J. Genet. Psychol.*, 1930, 38, 411-426.

Hooker, H. F., "A Study of the Only Child at School," *J. of Genet. Psychol.*, 1931, 39, 122-126.

Stuart, J. C., "Data on the Alleged Psychopathology of the Only Child," *J. Abn. & Soc. Psychol.*, 1926, 20, 441.

[3] Ward, Anne, "The Only Child," *Smith Coll. Stud. Soc. Work*, 1930, 1, 41-65.

be kept in mind that there are individuals who do have difficulties in childhood and adolescence, and even all through life, which are definitely traceable to the distorting influences of growth as an only child, in a family and social setting which did not compensate for the lack of other children in the home. Surveys of college student problems reveal the influence of the only child experience as a not infrequent factor.[1] And it is further possible that certain specific personality traits may be due to the fact of onliness;[2] but unfortunately individual traits have not yet been much studied from this point of view.

In a careful comparison of one hundred only children of college age with one hundred who had grown up as intermediate children, Campbell[3] found that the effect of growth as an only child was more pronounced in girls than in boys. Perhaps the girls were more protected, and the boys more subjected to the normalizing effects of associations outside the home. Only girls were less inclined to be dominant and self-sufficient than those raised as intermediate children; while the only boys were more dominant and more self-sufficient. In scores for neuroticism, both the only girls and the only boys exceeded the scores for the intermediates. In physique and scholarship no difference of significance could be found between the two groups.[4]

Of the *effect* upon a personality *of growing up* in a home *where there are several other children* comparatively little is yet known. One may suspect with some confidence, that the effects, whatever they are, will be found to vary considerably with the number of other children, the frequencies of one sex or the other in the family group, age differences, differences in general mental ability and also in special talents, and above all with the effects of these differences upon the parents and in turn of the parental

1 Angell, R. C., *A Study of Undergraduate Adjustment,* Chicago, 1930, see p. 66.
2 In Vetter's study of social attitudes, it appeared that the atypical, reactionary and radical personalities were more frequently those who had grown up as only children. See Vetter, G. B., "The Measurement of Social and Political Attitudes and the Related Personality Factors," *J. Abn. & Soc. Psychol.,* 1930, 25, 140-189.
3 Campbell, A. A., "A Study of the Personality Adjustments of Only and Intermediate Children," *J. Genet. Psychol.,* 1933, 43, 197-205.
4 For an extensive review of this literature with bibliography see Campbell, A. A., "The Personality Adjustments of Only Children," *Psychol. Bull.,* 1934, 31, 193-203.

attitudes toward the different individual children. It is conceivable that the family pattern may be the birthplace of much that is desirable and also of much that is undesirable in personality development. The group may have a decidedly socializing effect upon its individual members. Self-confidence may be cultivated, talents brought out, and loyalties developed. On the other hand an especially petted and favored member of a group may for that reason be far from socialized. Marked differences in general and special abilities may be the source of both inferiority and superiority troubles. Age differences may have a like effect where significant differences in ability are lacking. With two or more children jealousies are always possible.

By far the most significant attempt to investigate this subject has been that by Busemann.[1] In a number of studies he has obtained the reactions of pubescents and early adolescents to their own family and social situations, the observations of the subjects concerning each other, the judgments of the teachers, and records of school progress. All these have then been distributed according to whether they applied to only children, to those in two-child families, to those in three-child families, and so on. Some sex comparisons are made possible but not for all the traits studied.

Busemann points with interest to the indication in all of his studies that the best results in bringing up children seem to be achieved where there are three or four children in the family. Children with this number of brothers and sisters seem to be happiest and least nervous. There seems to be greater individual activity in such families and hence the individuals are better prepared for the pursuit of various phases of school life. In docility or manageableness (Lenksamkeit) there appears to be a notable sex difference. Boys are apparently most docile when they have grown up with other children in the family and are least so when there is but one other child or none at all. Girls, however, seem to be least docile when there are several other children in the family. The effect upon an older sister of younger brothers

---

[1] Busemann, A., "Geschwisterschaft, Schultüchtigkeit und Charakter," *Zsch. f. Kinderforsch.*, 1928, 34, 1-52; "Geschwisterschaft und Schulzensuren," *Zeit. f. Kinderforsch.*, 1928, 34, 553-569; "Bruder und Schwester," *Zsch. f. Sex.-wis. u. Sex.-pol.*, 1929, 16, 392-400; "Die Familie als Erlebnis-milieu des Kindes," *Zsch. f. Kinderforsch.*, 1929, 36, 17-82.

in the family seems to be that of bringing out or developing a maternal attitude. As this attitude is toward the younger children, rivalry may be aroused in any still older children, if there be such. Perhaps here there is a complication of maternal affection or tendencies, instincts possibly, with the urge or drive for power and the satisfactions of domination and preference.

Brothers, because of the association with sisters in the family, are quite likely to have a guardian-protector attitude developed in them. Especially is this true when the brother is older than the sister. Separation from the parents, as when sent away to school, sometimes develops an almost marital-like comradeship between brother and sister. Rivalry among the children in a family pattern is more likely to develop between brothers or between sisters; far less likely is it to occur between brother and sister.

Busemann also thinks that his data indicate some influence of family relationships upon the development of the love life. The friends of the brothers and sisters brought into the home frequently provide the first opportunities for friendships with those of the other sex. And, in an almost psychoanalytic fashion, he thinks that affection for the parents may progressively shift from the parents to the brothers and sisters, and from them to members of the other sex outside of the family.

The indications of sex difference in reactions to the family situation as revealed by Busemann are supported by the data which Chassell [1] collected. From these it appears that boys and girls do not react alike to friction in the home situation. It tends to produce extroversion in males and introversion in females. Where older children manifest a kindly attitude toward the younger, there seems to be an association with extrovertive tendencies in the younger. This is in the same direction for both males and females but much more so for females.

The effects of growing up in a family circle of several children are in all probability not the same for each age position within the group. The experiences of the *oldest child* and of the youngest child must often be very different from those who are intermediate. Generalizations here as elsewhere in matters of

[1] Chassell, J. O., *The Experience Variables* (pub. by author), 1928, Univ. of Rochester.

family influences are dangerous because so many other influences than those of age position in the family may enter in to off-set or obscure the effects of age position; but it is necessary to recognize that many individual instances are available wherein special traits of personalities have been quite convincingly traced to the age position in the family group. The oldest child may be honored and favored and given every advantage, producing as a consequence many of those same personality features already presented as appearing in only children. The youngest, or the younger children, in such a family group might have inferiority and jealousy patterns built into them as a consequence. The oldest child, because of its greater maturity and physical vigor, may be forced to take over some of the parents' responsibilities for the younger children. And where one of the parents is lost by separation or death this forced assumption of great responsibility is often a serious matter. Fictional and biographic literature has for a very long time been giving us instances of the enforced early maturity of oldest children, whose adolescent growth was at least foreshortened by the responsibilities forced upon them through the early death of a parent.

Comparable disturbances of development may appear as the consequence of being the *youngest child,* of being the "baby of the family." Where the older children are considerably older and their achievements are perceived by the youngest child as very great, feelings of inferiority and hopelessness easily appear. Every clinical worker has tales to relate of the troubles of the younger brother or sister of a boy or girl who has made a distinguished reputation in school or college or in starting a business career. The "baby of the family" may be petted and privileged in a manner comparable to that of the traditional only child, with all of the ensuing peculiarities of personality and difficulties of adjustment in life.

Brill writes very confidently of this.[1] He thinks that many of the world's famous teachers and leaders have become such, in large part at least, because they were either the oldest child in a family or the youngest. The circumstances and necessities of family life early force upon the oldest child the habits of teaching and leading the younger, and youngest children often be-

[1] Brill, A. A., *Fundamental Conceptions of Psychoanalysis,* p. 289 et seq.

come teachers and leaders as an outgrowth of rebellion against the apparent superiority of the older child. He believes such achievement of youngest children the consequence of an I-will-show-them-what-I-can-do sort of reaction. Busemann [1] thinks that the youngest child in a family group is more conscious of its position in the group, that of being the youngest child, than are the other children conscious of their positions in the group. But if Busemann is right, it is an item worth watching for and deserving of much more investigation.[2] Doubtless all of these influences are complicated by or mitigated by economic factors, intelligence, education, social position, neighborhood circumstances, and many others.

In individual instances certain trait peculiarities in adolescent years will be found explainable in terms of growth as a *foster-child* in the family setting. Beyond this it is difficult to speak with certainty at present because of the lack of systematic studies of the life experiences of those who have grown up as foster-children. There is a growing belief that foster-children are much affected by a lessened consciousness of security.[3] If this continues on into maturity has yet to be determined; as has likewise the effect upon it of breaking away from the security of the home. Insecurity in childhood and the consciousness of being a foster-child may easily be the background for inferiority troubles in adolescent years, and it must contribute to the self concept a considerable difference of pattern. Perhaps this may ramify out into differences in the self-regarding sentiment, and even farther.

It must also be obvious that a childhood experience as a foster-child may have been so carefully guarded by thoughtful foster-parents as to completely offset the possibility of any consequent peculiarities. What the effects may be of growing up in ignor-

---

[1] Busemann, A., "Die Familie als Erlebnis-milieu des Kindes," *Zsch. f. Kinderforsch.*, 1929, 36, 17-82.

[2] In this connection R. H. Barker has reported a useful instance of inferiority troubles appearing in a family setting which involved relationships with an older brother. See Barker, R. H., "The Effect of an Unsatisfactory Relationship of Brother to Brother on the Development of Personality," *Social Forces*, 1930, 9, 85-91.

[3] Danziger, L., Hetzer, H., Löw-beer, H., *Pflegemutter und Pflegekind. (Psychol. d. Fürsorge*, Vol. 2), Leipzig (Hirzel), 1930.

ance of being a foster-child, and subsequently discovering the fact we do not yet know. It is possible, of course, that in individual instances such a discovery might be alienating and depressing, while in other instances it might be the cause of greater loyalty to the foster-parents. Much must depend upon the parents, the training received, and all the many other factors and influences in social adjustment.

·*Psychological Weaning.* This is the process of outgrowing family domination, especially of parental domination. Rarely does any person change through the years so much that all family influences are completely left behind; but the fully matured person differs conspicuously from the child in most matters that are traceable to family influence upon his growth. Normally this change takes place in adolescent years. Sometimes, however, we meet instances of adults in whom the process of psychological weaning seems never even to have been started, others in which it appears to have been arrested at some stage, and others in whom the change appears to have been delayed into later adolescent or even the early years of maturity.

Some authorities prefer to use the term emancipation instead of psychological weaning. Concerning this difference of usage there need be no quarrel and should be no confusion. Those who prefer to use the term emancipation appear to be thinking almost exclusively of the progressive change in the habits of the growing individual. From such a point of view it may be properly said that every adolescent goes through a progressive emancipation from parental control and domination. But a full consideration of all the factors involved in the course of normal adolescent emancipation reveals that there is a parallel change in the habits and attitudes of the parents as well. Where the course of emancipation is blocked or fraught with emotional distress and disturbance, it is usually found to be traceable to a failure on the part of the parents to make their corresponding habit changes. So when one is thinking of the changes which are taking place simultaneously in both parents and children, changes which are breaking up the old childhood parent-child relationships and bringing into establishment the behavior patterns of independence and self-reliance for both parents and children, then does the term emancipation become inadequate and the term psychological weaning much more appropriate.[1]

Our information here is based almost wholly upon clinical material, upon case studies of adolescents whose difficulties have brought them under the special observation of experts. Valuable as this material is, there is the usually attending danger of generalizing from it to all adolescents. Caution is thus again necessary. One must not think that all adolescents go through a serious struggle in the process of becoming emancipated from parental domination just because some do have to struggle. Nor should one conclude that all parents seek to obstruct the achievement of independence on the part of their children because experts in the analysis of adolescent behavior problems find this true in certain cases. What the various features are of the psychological weaning process in the ordinary home we know very little indeed. We suspect that they are like those features which have been revealed in the clinical case studies, although greatly reduced in degree. We are inclined to think that the clinical case studies are made on adolescents who for one reason or another have suffered an exaggeration, a magnification, of the features of the weaning process, but it is also quite likely that many of them manifest growth distortions. And it may be that the features and course of psychological weaning in homes where adolescent emancipation is achieved smoothly, without attracting public attention, are quite different because of the differences in training, in attitudes, in inhibitions, in expectations, and the like.

When one looks at the case studies of psychological weaning problems with the purpose of ascertaining the reasons for the behavior difficulties, one finds a number of factors apparent. There is first of all the effects of the social pressures to which the growing boy or girl has been subjected. These have established ideals of independence to come some day, of travel, of leaving home and setting up a home of one's own, of self-control and self-determination, and all that these involve. And then there is the urge to realize these ideals. Perhaps we shall some day discover that there is little in this urge other than the effects

[1] See the usage of this term in Leta S. Hollingworth's excellent discussion of the subject in her *Psychology of the Adolescent,* chap. 3.

upon a growing human organism of the social pressures; but there is current today the tendency to think of a growth urge, or drive, or impulse, or even of an instinct, which is pushing from within toward independence, and which realizes satisfaction through the patterns established by the social pressures. Sometimes this is termed the will-to-power drive; sometimes it is thought of as an inherent tendency to overcome and displace the father (the Œdipus complex of the psychoanalysts) if the individual is a boy, and of the mother (Electra complex) if the individual is a girl. Sometimes it is thought of more vaguely as merely the general growth impulse of a living growing human organism, and sometimes there is assumed to be the existence of a specific instinct to break away from the home ties, an instinct which is supposed to become nascent somewhere in adolescent years.

There is also visible in most of these cases the carry-over into adolescent years of the habits of submission, of obedience, of conformity to the ways of the family life, of dependence upon the parents, and especially of seeking the security and protection to be found in the parent-dominated home setting. But, along with these, it is possible often to observe also the development of a consciousness of childishness and of the desire to throw it off. There are shame or jealousy and impulsive efforts to escape the childish ways, resulting in inconsistent and often troublesome conduct. If these childish habits which still cling are interpreted as the psychoanalysts do in terms of fixation of the libido at an earlier, parental, stage of affection, and we think of the adolescent as struggling against this fixation, of seeking to repress it and to be somehow like what others are and which his ideals would lead him to be, then we have all that is necessary for the establishment of much fantasy thinking, for the growth of complexes that disturb both immediate conduct and normal achievement of the desired social adjustment.

All this may be further complicated by the tendency of the parents to cling to their children. Especially is this true in behavior problem cases. The parents have lavished an excessive affection upon them; and they persist in their habits of domination, even though the children be obviously fast growing into manhood and womanhood. Sometimes this persistence appears to be intensified by an apparent awareness in the parents that the children are becoming mature and a reluctance to admit the fact. Here there may enter in another motivation. The parents may dislike the prospect of being forced into the background, of becoming merely the parents of their children. And, with mothers especially, there is often the further unpleasant prospect of having nothing of much importance to do in the world when the period of child-bearing and child-raising has passed. The mother has given her life to her children and has acquired no other interests in life or in the community. The prospect of coming to a time when the children shall no longer need her is not a pleasant one. She does not wish to become idle and useless. Against such a prospect, but half admitted even to herself, she fights impulsively by struggling to retain her child-raising habits and activities and responsibilities.

Involved with these factors one may often observe in problem cases the failure of the individual to make that shift already described [1] as the change from an individual or self-centered personality pattern to a largely other-centered or socially centered personality pattern. While the retardation of development in this respect may be incidental to the conflicts aroused by some of the other features already mentioned, this retarded socialization needs to be kept in mind. Retraining of such cases requires not only retraining of the habits and attitudes toward the parents and toward the self, but also the development of adult attitudes toward social responsibility.

There seems to be no one particular kind of behavior which can be isolated and described and definitely classified as that form of behavior due to a failure in psychological weaning or defect of emancipation. Rather is it possible for such troubles to take many forms. So it is not the form of behavior one must keep in mind but defect of emancipation as a possible cause in any one of many possible forms of adolescent conduct. When one meets with unusual timidity in an adolescent, disinclination to go out socially at an age when much seeking of new social contacts and new experiences is ordinarily expected of youth, accompanied with occasional impulsive, if not quite er-

[1] See chapter VII.

ratic, social behavior, then one may suspect that behind it all is trouble in the course of the weaning process. Homesickness may be aggravated by delayed weaning.

When one receives frequent reports of rebellious, uncooperative conduct in a youth who is otherwise mature and promising, one may suspect delayed weaning; the father may be seeking to retain his dominance, and the boy may be rebelling against him. The mother may still be petting and aiding the boy to get what he wants as she has unfortunately done since he was a child. Where such is the case, the boy, who should now be rather a young man, is likely to rebel not only against his own father but against any one who seeks to control him, against any one in an official capacity, be it teacher or professor or dean or traffic policeman. In fact any sort of regulation or statute or law which appears to be restraining in any way, may arouse the same reaction as does sight or sound or mention of his own father. Officials and regulations thus serve as substitutes for the father.

In comparable fashion does any one or any institution appeal to him who stimulates in the same way as his mother has always done. Deans and professors and friends of all sorts who seek to guide and comfort and assist, especially assist out of trouble, thus actually serve as substitutes for the mother. They often remark with surprise, unfortunately, upon the remarkable ease with which the ordinarily rebellious and uncontrollable youth responds to a kind word, a little sympathy. He does: he takes to coddling easily, for in this respect he is still a child.

And while this description has been made in terms of the male it must of course be obvious that girls frequently behave in much the same manner. They may be rebellious against restriction, or what looks like restriction on the part of any woman, but respond readily to kindly manifestations from men in positions of authority. It should be here obvious that the degree and nature of such behavior goes back to the degree and nature of the pattern of parental relationships to which the individual has been habituated from childhood.

Instances of notable selfishness should also be watched for the possibility of their being related to defects in the weaning process. As has already been indicated, delayed development in the matter of achieving independence and self-reliance may be accompanied by delay in the assumption of social responsibilities. But selfish conduct in adolescence may have a yet other relationship to the parental influence. It may be in some instances that socialization is fairly well underway, but weaning has been delayed and is progressing with difficulty. As a consequence there may be sudden and impulsive, almost explosive, manifestations of the effort or desire to do and act for one's self. Impulsive actions are by their very nature somewhat isolated. They are not expressive of the whole of the personality synthesis. Thus these impulsive actions may be notably selfish, sufficiently so to lead to much questioning and bewilderment on the part of friends and counsellors. Their selfishness may be conspicuously different from the general trend of the individual's behavior. They are so because of their impulsive nature, and because the impulse behind them is a part of the effort to be self-assertive, self-controlling, self-dominating. They may be traced back to a struggle to break away from excessive parental control.

Marriage for one who has failed to achieve a complete psychological weaning is almost certainly doomed to bring unhappiness to one or more of the parties involved. Mother-in-law troubles are notorious; and many of them are traceable to imperfect psychological weaning. Sometimes a poorly emancipated daughter marries and expects her husband to be like her father and to treat her as a father treats his little daughter. Sometimes the mother-in-law seeks to dominate both daughter and son-in-law because her habits have never been changed. Obviously there may be many possible forms and variations of this pattern of childhood habits carried over into the years when happiness depends upon independence and a new devotion.

While the descriptions just given are of necessity of the more extreme forms of weaning troubles, milder and less conspicuous behavior effects of the experience are doubtless far more frequent. They may be so mild and generally undisturbing as to be passed by with little more attention than the thought that they are but other instances of the vagaries and instabilities of adolescence. Wiser parents anticipate the necessity of guiding their children into independence, and begin the course early. Wiser parents also anticipate the years when their children will be mature and independent, plan for them, and aid by gradually changing their own habits and interests. By so doing they vastly minimize the possibility of their children developing any of the more extreme forms of behavior troubles which might otherwise appear.

Weaning troubles are sometimes traceable to false beliefs concerning parental desires. Not infrequently young people think that they must continue to do as they believe their parents desire because of conscientiousness, a feeling of obligation for what they are aware their parents have done for them, when as a matter of fact they are greatly exaggerating parental desires and attitudes. The writer has often found the more serious-minded young people prone to exaggerate their parents' probable opposition to their making efforts to realize their own desires in life.

What the permanent effects upon the personality may be of these struggles of psychological weaning we little know. Perhaps they may often have no lasting effect. Perhaps they may establish timidity or rebelliousness or some other trait as a permanent feature of the personality. The psychoanalysts would have us believe that many of the great reformers of history, as well as lesser folk who are chronically rebellious, are so because of a life-long struggle against the father or what they like to call the "father imago." Perhaps these struggles of adolescent years serve a valuable educational function. They may prepare the growing boy and girl for the larger battles later on. They may give experience in overcoming social obstacles and encourage through the establishment of self-confidence. Generalizations are of course impossible not only because of the lack of systematic studies but also because the effects of the weaning struggle must vary enormously with the many other factors influencing the growth changes in any particular adolescent.

CHAPTER XIII

ROMANTIC LOVE

LOVE THEORIES, LOVE BEHAVIOR PROBLEMS (CHANGEABLE-
NESS, LOVE OF OLDER PERSONS, CRUSHES, LOVE AT FIRST
SIGHT, PETTING, OBSTRUCTED LOVE), ROMANTIC ATTRAC-
TIVENESS

Youth is traditionally the time for love. Everybody knows it;
everybody expects it; and nearly everybody laughs about it.
Many have been the attempts to regularize and control it. Apparently these have been more numerous by far than the efforts
to understand and interpret. Poets have sung about love and
novelists have described love behavior in its myriad forms, but
researchers in the psychology of adolescence seem to prefer to
study almost any other form of behavior. The last twenty years
have seen the production of much theory about love, but extraordinarily little of a factual nature. Consequently the best that
can be done here is to assemble the theories and to apply them
as best possible to the many behavior problems which the loves
of adolescence have brought to the fore.

That adolescence is a period of restraint intervening between
the achievement of sexual maturity and the years when our civilization makes marriage possible has been so often asserted as
to have become a truism. Nevertheless, all who associate much
with youth realize that adolescence is also in the very best sense
a time of preparation. Most normal youth expect eventually to
marry and are highly sex-conscious. As full maturity approaches,
more and more every young person of the other sex is met with
the awareness that this may be the fateful individual; and in like
manner is there a pervasive tendency to appraise all members of
the other sex in terms of their possibility as a future wife or husband. They are liked or disliked, approved or disapproved, ac-

cording to this standard. And there are all the corollary fears and satisfactions arising out of reports and beliefs concerning the judgments of the self by those of the other sex.

This consciousness of the imminence of love and longing for it brings much day-dreaming. The self is the focus of these fantasied experiences. Love scenes of a most romantic nature in which the dreamer is the one beloved by some gorgeous hero, or heroine as the case may be, and in which there are great achievements for the sake of love, fill these moments. Sometimes they are of the "suffering hero" variety. Then illness and even death is fantasied in a manner that brings tears and regret and deathless devotion from the fantasied lover. Sometimes they are less extravagant and involve the more possible or probable events of love with some one then being courted.

In adolescence one may see every variety and stage of love development. There are the well-known "puppy loves" and the "crushes" and the love-at-first-sight sort of experiences, the negativistic reactions or fighting against love, and all the stages and phases of true courtship. Not every individual passes through all of them and there are large individual differences in the intensity of the experiences when they come. Some seem to be highly passionate, mad for love. While others take it all very casually. Between these extremes there is every possible gradation.

For the interpretation of love behavior one must be supplied with the best of the current theories concerning the nature of love. Of these there are many; but not all are useful. Those which have had the wider circulation will be presented here. If any are to be used at all, they should be accepted tentatively as first approximations and as aids to thinking. To some extent, they overlap each other.

Love Theories. One of the older and simpler conceptions is to the effect that all forms of *love* whatsoever are *evolved from the impulse to possess and reproduce* (1). This has achieved wide currency, probably because of its simplicity and because of the large place which the sex impulse does have in some forms of love. Novelists have not infrequently presented their material with this notion in the background of their thinking. Hall [1]

[1] Hall, G. Stanley, *Adolescence*, chap. 11.

tried to work this genetic concept out into a series of stages which should include all forms of love. From a basic, animal-like, selfish love was derived friendship and romantic love, then from romantic love came marital love, then love of children, and as the love became more inclusive there was evolved love of the community, love of the race, and last and highest of all the love of God.

But this is much more logical than it is psychological. Certainly such a succession of stages is far from being the experience of the people we know; and it is very doubtful if such was the evolutional appearance of love forms in the history of the race. At the same time one form of love does seem to make others more easily developed. Not infrequently instances are observed where a love of the community grows out of a love of children. Perhaps in the background of Hall's scheme there is some basic truth which will later be better understood.

In considering any such notion of derivation it is wise not to forget the physiological correlates of the behavior. A love which is purely animalistic must be very largely a matter of the functioning of the sacral division of the autonomic system. Romantic love and marital love certainly involve the sacral division, but also many sympathetic functions and purely cerebral factors. This is not a transformation by some evolutional process; it is rather a complication and a shift of dominance from one pattern to another. Many loves do not involve the sacral division at all. One cannot find it in the love of a child, nor in a pastor's love for his people, nor in a collector's love of his treasures. It is hard to think of these as evolved forms of a sexual reproductive physiological impulse.

The *Shand-McDougall concept of the nature of love* (2) has had a wide popularity and often proves very useful as an interpretative aid.[1] For those who are accustomed to think in terms of organization or integration of simpler patterns into larger wholes this theory will be easy and welcome. Their whole scheme hangs upon the concept of the nature of a sentiment which is very different from the popular meaning of the term and also different from some technical uses.

---

[1] McDougall, Wm., *Social Psychology*, chaps. 2, 3, 5, and 10.

Their theory of the sentiment assumes first that each individual is born with a certain specific list of instincts and that each of these instincts carries with it an emotion which is qualitatively distinct from each of the other emotions. Hence, each of these response patterns may be designated by its instinct name or by its emotional designation. There is for example the instinct called curiosity which has for its psychic aspect the emotion called wonder. These are assumed also to be second-level functions, which gradually, as the individual develops, come under control of the cortex, as the cerebral cortex develops its own response patterns. Two or more of these instinct-emotions may be simultaneously aroused by any stimulating situation; then a complex emotion is experienced. An example of this is to be found when a person comes into the presence of a great natural chasm or a magnificent waterfall. The situation is such as to arouse at the same time those instinct-emotion patterns called flight-fear, curiosity-wonder and submission-inferiority. The fusion of the three gives us the experience which we commonly designate by the term awe.

But a complex emotion is a temporary experience, one which passes quickly with the passing of the appropriate stimulating situation. A sentiment is something more permanent. It is a pattern in the cortex which controls the arousal of certain groups of the instinct-emotion patterns. It is assumed to be in the cortex because it is thought of as the product of perceptual and conceptual experience. A complex emotion may be easily aroused in very young children. For its arousal it is merely necessary that the stimulating situation should include originally effective stimuli to more than one emotion. A sentiment, however, is to be thought of as being in the nature of a habit pattern which is the residue or development of many repetitions of an experience. It is assumed that there are many of these sentiments. Love is one of them. Hate is another. One's affection for one's alma mater another; and so on.

It is further important to observe that these sentiments may be developed as the consequence of much and varied emotional experience with actual physical objects and situations, and that it is also quite as possible for sentiment patterns to develop as the consequence of repeated emotional experiences with ideas or

concepts. One may then have a sentiment pattern developed as
the consequence of much emotional experience with a dog or a
cat or a house or a book or a human being; and one may also
have a sentiment pattern developed as the consequence of much
emotional experience with one's concept of himself, with one's
concept of the mother who died in his infancy, with the concept
of God, or with some treasured scientific idea.

Each of these sentiments tends to the arousal of its own particular group of emotions; but the attachment of a particular instinct-emotion to one sentiment does not at all preclude the possibility of its being attached to another sentiment, and to many
other sentiments. Tenderness, for example, the emotional aspect
of the parental instinct, may be aroused by the sentiment for
one's wife, one's child, one's dog, and many others. As Mc-
Dougall presents the *love sentiment* it is a pattern tending to
arouse any or all of the following instinct-emotion patterns:
flight-fear, pugnacity-anger, curiosity-wonder, submission-inferiority, assertion-elation, parental-tenderness. Not all of these are
aroused every time the sentiment pattern is activated; but
through that sentiment pattern any one or more are easily
aroused; and, as with a well-developed perception, a small part of
the original experience which gave rise to the sentiment can,
when re-presented, activate the sentiment pattern. Every one
who has been in love knows well how quickly the sentiment is
aroused by the mere sound of the voice or the mention of the
name.

There are, to be sure, many different loves. At any one time
any ordinary human being would have several different love
sentiments well established and in good working order. That
does not mean that he is romantically in love with many people
all at once, although it does mean that he has love sentiments for
several different people at the same time. There is the love sentiment for mother, for father, for a brother, a sister, a home, a
school, a club, and so on. Obviously the difficulty here lies in
our language. We lack good terms for the designation of each
of these and are consequently obliged to overwork the word love.
Sometimes we try such weak substitutes as "liking for" or "affection for," but they are not very satisfactory.

More important is it to observe that, as McDougall presents

the love sentiment, there is apparently no place in it for the reproductive instinct with its emotional correlate which he terms lust. But it is also important to observe that these patterns which we here call love sentiments may differ in the number of instinct-emotion patterns to which they are attached, and also in the degree or ease or frequency or intensity with which each is aroused by the sentiment. There may be love sentiments then which easily and frequently involve the reproductive instinct; others which rarely involve it; and yet others which have no attachment to the sex instinct at all. A romantic passionate form of love sentiment would obviously involve the reproductive-lust instinct-emotion; while the love of a pastor for his people would most emphatically not.

This conception of love as a sentiment stands at the opposite extreme from the evolutional conception of love first presented. Here there is not a suggestion that one form of love evolves out of some other. It is merely a matter of whether or not a given person has had certain emotional experiences with a given object, and frequently enough to have eventuated in the establishment of a love sentiment. As a consequence of childhood experiences, a love sentiment for the mother is established. There may be another for the father, another for the cat, another for the house, another for certain books or playthings, and so on. And each may differ from every other sufficiently so that a different term is desirable for its designation.

From this point of view, adolescence is merely that period in which the experiences of life are such as to bring about the establishment of a romantic love sentiment for one of the other sex outside of the family circle. In the process of the establishment of that sentiment, emotional experiences with a number of persons of the other sex may make their contributions. And the romantic love sentiment established in any one person will include a greater or less tendency toward the activation of the reproductive instinct, according to the ideals and training and daydreaming and emotional experiences of that person. A love sentiment is thus likely to be gross or refined as the individuals involved are gross or refined.

It is necessary only to add that a love sentiment like any other sentiment may change with time. Most of them probably do.

Consequently, in terms of this theory, the change from a romantic love into the partnership or marital type of love sentiment, which comes to most who have been happily married and have been able to maintain that relationship, is a progressive change in the pattern of the love sentiment as the experiences of the years accumulate and change.

The reader will find the *psychoanalytic concept of love* (3) more vague and somewhat more difficult to grasp. This is probably not so much due to its greater complexity as to the fact, readily admitted by the psychoanalysts, that it is still quite incomplete. There are many parts of their theory which are not well worked out because, as they say, their studies of the nature of the functions involved have not yet progressed far enough to justify further development.

The key to the understanding of love psychoanalytically lies in the recognition of its thoroughly dynamic conception of the human psyche. And this centers in their concept of libido. The ordinary definition of the term libido is misleading. For the psychoanalysts it ordinarily means an energy which may flow through many different channels, which may be focalized upon certain functions or concepts, and which again may be detached from them. And it is an energy which may actually pass out from the individual to others or to other objects. The forms of this energy, the channels through which it passes, and the means of its control, must be understood in order to understand the psychoanalytic theory of love. Sometimes this libido is designated by the term affect, and practically always the unhampered flow of libido through some channel is a source of pleasure or satisfaction. The blocking of libido flow is ordinarily unpleasant; although such unpleasantness may be avoided by the diversion of libido into other channels of flow which are not so blocked.

In infancy, pleasure or comfort or satisfaction comes through the simple organic-sensory experiences of the organism. Petting, sucking, relief through the physical processes of elimination, being fed, and being made warm are the ways of being made happy and comfortable. These are then spoken of as libido channels. A very little later there is pleasure in seeing, and this is a visual libido. As these forms are all a matter of the infant's own body they constitute a stage called autoerotism. A little later, as the consciousness of the self develops, there is much satisfaction with self-achievements, with what the self does. Libido now flows to the self and is referred to as a stage of self-love, or narcissism. This is followed by a stage of parental love, that is, of love by the child for a parent; and this is usually more for the parent of the opposite sex. Libido now flows outward to another person and is termed object libido with the parent as the object. These are the pre-pubescent forms of love or of libido expression.

With the development of the sex structures and functions at the dawn of adolescence new and important love developments begin. The libido swings definitely outward but through two different channels. One is toward those of the other sex and one is toward members of the same sex. There are thus two love trends in every adolescent, and every adult for that matter, one of which is heterosexual and the other is homosexual. Because of inhibitions which have been established in the ego, the homosexual trend is ordinarily held well in check. It is usually manifest only in the close friendship of a boy for a boy or between two girls. Sometimes it becomes more apparent and is then popularly termed a crush, a form of adolescent love problem to be discussed in greater detail below.

Probably the homosexual trend of libido in adolescence is influenced by the remaining traces of narcissistic libido, left over from childhood years. This would cause a tendency to love a person most like the self, and that would be one of the same sex. There is also another hang-over influence from childhood years, from the experiences of parental love. When the libido swings outward again in a heterosexual manner the tendency is to fall in love with some one who in some manner, not necessarily perceived, appeals as did the loved parent. Hence the psychoanalysts often say that the adolescent boy tends to fall in love with a substitute for his mother and that the girl loves a substitute for her father.[1]

It is further important to keep in mind, as a part of this theory, that earlier forms of libido expression are never entirely lost. The libido channels of infancy and childhood still remain open

[1] For certain other aspects of this theory see chap. XI, where parental influences upon love development are presented.

to some extent and some libido flows through them. In every adolescent there is some love of the autoerotic form, of the narcissistic, of the parental, and, even after a full development of the heterosexual, there are traces to be seen of the influence of the homosexual libido channel. This progressive shift of libido into expression in ways that are socially more and more acceptable is a displacement which is technically termed sublimation. But it is also possible that circumstances may prevent a proper sublimation of the libido. When this happens, when too much libido continues to flow through some one or other of the older channels, the condition is said to be one of fixation. There are individuals who remain always excessively autoerotic or narcissistic or too much devoted to one parent to achieve a proper and desirable adjustment in life. These are fixated cases, with the many other complications which that involves.

Heterosexual love the psychoanalysts look upon as highly complex. While their theory is not yet complete, it has already gone far beyond the simple notion of libido flowing outward toward one of the other sex. In it they claim to see the lingering influences of the autoerotic period of infancy. In the heterosexual stage libido still flows through the eyes and the lips and the skin. The lover wants to look and to kiss and to touch or pet, and finds satisfaction in so doing. There is also an influence of narcissism, the love of the self, through what is called identification. The lover identifies the beloved with himself (or herself) and so the narcissistic libido is satisfied.

And there are two well-defined phases of heterosexual love. One of these is the manifestation of the sex instincts. It is noteworthy that the term is here used in the plural. There is supposed to be a considerable group of them, although no one has succeeded yet in making a satisfactory listing of them all. Probably sadistic and masochistic [1] trends belong in this group, although that is not yet agreed upon. The libido of the sex instincts is the libido of sensual love. There are also the ego instincts which are even less well known. They appear to be a differentiation which accompanies the development of the ego through childhood and of its precipitate or unconscious portion

---

[1] Sadism means pleasure in being the cause of suffering in the other. Masochism means pleasure in being made to suffer by another.

termed the super-ego which appears to be identical with what has hitherto been called the conscience. There is libido here but operative through very different channels from the sexual libido. Here there is foresight, the long look. Here there is the influence of social ideals and conventions which have been written into the ego, and the super-ego, through childhood years. Obviously there is often conflict between non-sensual love impulses of the ego instincts and the emphatically sensual love impulses of the sex instincts. This appears to be the distinction in other language long made between a purely animal form of love or passion and what has been customarily termed a spiritual love.

The psychoanalysts consider the observation of these two patterns or factors in the heterosexual love as of much importance. It explains for them many individual differences in heterosexual love. In one person the ego instincts, the non-sensual love, might be dominant and only in its proper time and place would the sensual factor find expression. In another person, with a very different development and degree of control by the ego and super-ego, the love would be far more sensual because of the greater freedom of development and expression of the sex instincts. One can easily recognize here the possibility of a wide range of individual differences.

Sometimes there are instances of a divided love life. The ego or non-sensual love is in such cases centered upon one person of the other sex while the sexual or sensual love is centered upon another. That such a divided love is highly undesirable must be obvious. It is usually the unhappy consequence of a training which treats all matters sexual as something indecent and never to be associated with respected persons. The psychoanalysts emphatically condemn all that will lead to the development of a divided love attachment. They recognize its abnormality and the certainty of further trouble to grow out of it.

Finally it is important to observe that when trouble arises there may be what is termed a regression. This libido which has been progressively shifted upward into the socially more approved forms of manifestation may, if blocked, draw back and regress (displacement downward) to the older forms of libido expression. There may under such circumstances be a return to homosexual love, to parental love, to the narcissistic, or even to the autoerotic. Maladjustments may then result in the revival of childish ways of living and loving.[1]

There is also current a less well-formulated conviction that *love* phenomena can be very simply *explained in terms of a few instinctive tendencies and the psychology of learning* (4). It assumes the existence of a few intrinsically determined traits which may subsequently be conditioned and re-conditioned. The advocates of this point of view accept something like an original tendency to be affectionate, to enjoy petting and kissing and the like, something possibly comparable to McDougall's tenderness. In addition there would of course be the reproductive instinct itself and also the assumption, allied to the physiological studies of the autonomic system, that there is an urge or drive toward comfortableness, quiescence, the relief of tension. Accepting these, one has merely to add the psychology of learning in terms of conditioning of responses to now one and now another stimulus. Love would then be a pattern of these responses conditioned to the presence of a certain person. Dislike or indifference for another person might be a negative conditioning. Homosexuality would be the consequence of an environment and life experience which unfortunately conditioned the individual to have the love pattern of responses aroused by one of the same sex rather than by one of another sex.

In terms of this theory, adolescence would be the period when a normal love conditioning should be in process of establishment. Conditioning of some of the patterns would have taken place before puberty. Primitive affection and the urge to comfortableness would have been much conditioned during the experiences of childhood. But the new social contacts and new responsibilities of adolescent years would force, if the individual is to be properly adjusted to life, a very considerable further conditioning of his responses. As the definitized sex urge comes with the

[1] A good introduction to the psychoanalytic literature on love may be found through the following:

Flügel, J. C., "Sexual and Social Sentiments," *Brit. J. Med. Psychol.*, 1927, 7, 139-176.
Freud, Sigmund, *Group Psychology and the Analysis of the Ego* (Internat. Psychoanal. Press), chap. 8.
—— *The Ego and the Id* (Hogarth Press).
—— *Beyond the Pleasure Principle* (Internat. Psychoanal. Press).
Wittels, Franz, *Critique of Love*, New York, 1929.

advent of pubescence, then the conditioning of this would be wholly an adolescent experience. Thus the family relations, the course of education, formal and informal, the social pressures, and those agencies especially which influence the development of ideals would all factor together as determiners of the way in which the love reactions would be conditioned.

With these theories of the nature of love in mind one can obtain the best insight into adolescent love behavior as we now know it by turning to a consideration of some of the special problems that arise. It must never be thought that the phenomena which are presented in the following groups of problems appear in a like manner in all adolescents. Of the course of normal or the commonplace development of love in adolescence, we know far less than we do of those developments which cause questioning and sometimes not a little distress. But it is probable that the fundamental processes involved in these problem cases can be seen in a mild form in the lives of most young people; and so, through examining what is the more unusual, a better knowledge may be obtained of that which is usual.

Problems in Love Behavior. The suddenness and *changeableness* of early adolescent love affairs have often been cause for much comment. Their apparent absurdity and the youthfulness of the parties involved have led to the somewhat disrespectful term of "puppy loves." [1] To those directly involved they may be both happy and distressing experiences. There is love no doubt, but of a very unformed and unstable nature. It is intense for a time, with all the familiar manifestations of desire for constant companionship, letters between times, and disruption of the routine of school work. Then there is a break or the whole thing seems to vanish into the void from whence it apparently came. In a little while the whole episode is repeated with another person.

In terms of the evolutional theory of the development of love forms, one would be obliged to say that these are the first appearances of a new stage in the development of love in the particular individual. Their ephemeral nature and changeableness could be explained in terms of their newness. Nature in its growth

---

[1] If any one does not know what these look like or desires case descriptions for any purpose, they will be found in the following: Smith, T. L., "Types of Adolescent Affection," *Ped. Sem.*, 1904, 11, 178-203.

would be reaching out blindly toward the higher stage of development. In terms of McDougall we should be obliged to think
of these puppy loves as but the experiences which eventuate in
the establishment of the love sentiment. That they are brief and
changeable would indicate that perhaps at first they are little
more than complex emotions, and that the sentiment does not
rapidly come into being. They would indicate also the effect
of the yet inexperienced or undeveloped or imperfect organization of patterns in the cerebral cortex.

For the psychoanalysts the puppy love would be an indication
that the libido is turning outward, but, also, that the channels
for heterosexual love may not yet be well established and that
the coordination between the ego love and the purely sex love
is yet to be developed. As the years pass and the youth settles
down into a more permanent romance then there would be indication of better control by the super-ego and a coordination of
the sensual with the non-sensual.

In terms of the learning or behavioristic theory these puppy
loves would be but the learning repetitions which serve to establish the new conditioning of the love responses.

As has been indicated the "puppy love" mode of response or
stage of development is ordinarily outgrown in a few years. The
youth may have been pained a little by each experience, but ordinarily these trials are quickly outgrown and largely forgotten. If
this sort of love behavior is not outgrown with the passage of
adolescent years, there is obviously something which is retarding
the development. It might be traceable to some basic systemic
defect which prevents a normal nervous organization and control; but it is more likely that false ideas concerning the self, the
nature of love and of the other sex, or of family obligations, have
gone into the formation of the ego and the super-ego and that
these are preventing a normal growth and establishment of romantic love. Such may become genuine abnormalities of function for which special guidance is necessary.

Romantic-like love of older persons is not infrequently a puzzling form of pubescent behavior. So far as we know such episodes are most likely to occur very early in adolescent years, and
some have thought that they constitute the first manifestations
of romantic love. Boys and girls in the very early teens falling

desperately in love with people, often their school-teachers, who
are many years their senior has been the source of much entertainment to adults and of temporary distress to the youngsters
so disturbed.[1] Smith[2] has pointed out in her study of a number
of such cases that there is in these love affairs more idealism than
in ordinary romantic love and that probably there are stronger
altruistic factors.

Hall suggested[3] that some sort of a law might be made out of
the fact that in successive love affairs in any individual one might
frequently observe a progressive approximation of the ages of the
parties involved, or that the aggregate age might remain constant. Whether or not a law of love behavior could ever be
worked out concerning this, something of the sort does often
appear to be true. As the boy grows older he seeks a girl who is
nearer his age; as he grows still older he is likely to seek a girl
who is younger than himself; and there are notable instances of
men of middle age seeking wives who are many years their
junior. Perhaps there is some truth in the aggregate age pro-
posal; but, if true, there are certainly many other powerful influences which push this age factor ordinarily well into the background.

The interpretation of this pubescent tendency to love one
much older in terms of the evolutional theory is not clear. In
terms of the behavioristic theory it would probably be that the
youngster's love reactions are already conditioned to a parent or
older relative and so he easily responds to a somewhat similar
stimulus outside the home. In terms of the sentiment theory
much the same conception must prevail. There has been a love
sentiment established in childhood for the parent or older relative and now the school-teacher or some one outside the home
stirs the same sentiment. But that is not entirely satisfactory.
The suddenness of such affections and the intensity of them are
not thus explained. Perhaps a clue may be had from Smith's
emphasis upon the greater influence of the idealistic in these
forms of romantic love. There may have been a new sentiment

[1] For a very able presentation of this in literary form the reader should
see Thomas B. Aldrich, *Story of a Bad Boy.*

[2] Smith, T. L., "Types of Adolescent Affection," *Ped. Sem.,* 1904, 11, 178-
203.

[3] Hall, G. Stanley, *Adolescence,* Vol. II, p. 106.

in process of establishment for some ideal. Such is not at all uncommon in pubescent years. And now perhaps the intense love for the older person may be a combination of the sentiment for the parent with the sentiment of the ideal, both stimulated by the older person outside of the family.

The psychoanalytic interpretation of this love for an older person is made in terms of what they call the mother imago. By this term they indicate both the remaining influence of the stage of special love for the parent of the opposite sex, that channel through which some libido still flows freely, and also an innately established determining influence toward such a love of the mother. Thus there is a two-fold tendency toward loving one of the other sex of a greater age, the one innate and the other the product of experience which supplements. So when in pubescent years the libido swings outward, the determining tendencies are not only for it to swing toward one of the other sex, but also toward one much older than the self. Later on, it will be recalled, when more normal heterosexual tendencies are established, this mother-imago influence is reduced to the mere responsiveness to a girl whó in some manner appeals as did the mother before.

These curious phases of romantic love are ordinarily of short duration. Why they should appear at all, for they appear to be the exception rather than the rule, is probably due to a combination of circumstances and influences peculiar to each case. What the lasting effects of such experiences may be, if any, we do not know. Perhaps they contribute merely to the establishment of a normal heterosexualization.

The *"crush" form of romantic love* is much more frequently a problem to those who are responsible for the guidance of young people. This is an intense affection for one of the same sex. Although comparative statistical studies are not available there seems to be no question of its being much more frequently manifested in the love life of girls than of boys, although male cases are reported.[1] Ordinarily the affection is more on the part of one girl than the other. The girl who suffers the crush experience is usually the younger of the pair involved. The older is

[1] Smith, T. L., "Types of Adolescent Affection," *Ped. Sem.*, 1904, 11, 178-203.

one who has achieved some distinction at least in the eyes of the younger, and is adored for her wonderfulness by the younger girl. Like any lover, she wants to be constantly with her, desires her exclusive attention and affection, is miserable in her absence. The older of the two may reciprocate to some degree. She may actually have some fondness for the younger girl; she may be flattered by the adoration; or may delight in the power she has over her. Sometimes the affection is not reciprocated but rather tolerated, and then come times when it is a nuisance, even a source of irritation. As in normal heterosexual loves there are jealousies, and quarrels, and tearful reconciliations and the rest. There is also a notable absence of that independence of action which characterizes the friendship type of affection.

While in the preceding description an age difference has been noted, it must be recognized that this is far from essential to the crush form of love. The age relationship may be reversed. The older girl may have a crush on a younger, or their ages may be alike. Apparently as many forms of crush love are possible as in normal romantic love.

Figures on the frequency of these affairs are somewhat unreliable because of the vagueness of definition. Some respondents may have a different notion of what is to be termed a crush than have others, and hence reports vary. Blanchard and Manasses [1] in their returns from 252 girls found 30 percent who admitted having had the crush experience. Davis [2] found nearer fifty percent. Doubtless the frequency varies much with the social situation. It is commonly asserted that they are more frequent where girls are kept in some degree of isolation, as in schools and colleges for girls only.[3]

For explanation of such behavior one is almost forced to turn

---

[1] Blanchard, P., and Manasses, C., *New Girls for Old*, chap. 7.

[2] Davis, K. B., *Factors in the Sex Life of Twenty-two Hundred Women*, chaps. 10, 11.

[3] The following will be found useful as general treatises on the subject in addition to the titles already mentioned:

Blanchard, P., *The Adolescent Girl*, pp. 169-174.
Elliott, Grace L., *Understanding the Adolescent Girl*, New York, 1930.
Hollingworth, L. S., *Psychology of the Adolescent*, pp. 130-136.
Richmond, Winifred, *The Adolescent Girl*, pp. 124-127.
Thom, D. A., *Normal Youth and Its Everyday Problems*, pp. 60-66 and 297-305.

to the psychoanalytic theory or to some modification of it. There is the logical possibility of explaining in terms of conditioning, but it is not very satisfactory. To say that these emotional attachments to one of the same sex are due to the way in which the individual has been conditioned, that the love responses have been positively conditioned only to those of the same sex and negatively to all of the other sex, applies fairly well to some extreme cases, but not so well to the occasional outburst of the crush form of love, nor to the instances of crush loves which seem to be the temporary effect of grief or disappointment.[1]

The crush is commonly looked upon as being to some degree a form of homosexual love, but in thinking of this it is necessary to keep in mind that the psychoanalysts have introduced the practice of looking upon even the finest friendships between members of the same sex as forms of homosexual love. Homosexuality thus does not necessarily mean perversion. Thus the crush, while falling in the homosexual class, would come somewhere between friendship and that extreme form of homosexuality which is classifiable as a sexual perversion. But as crush loves are not all alike they would not all occupy the same place on that scale. Some crushes are quite unconscious of any sexual factor, and the persons involved would be shocked if such were suggested. If there are any physical contacts, they are limited to hugging and kissing. Other crushes, while limiting the physical contacts to hugging and kissing, are conscious of there being a mild sex factor. Such would be a little farther along the scale. Still other crushes do come nearer to being a genuine perversion, although because of their temporary nature there may be some question of the propriety of classifying them as such.

Understanding of any of these forms will be much aided by a little knowledge of contemporary thought concerning the nature of pathological homosexuality. Interpretations of this fall today

---

[1] Gordon has reported a most valuable case history of a homosexual who apparently became such because of the very unusual training received through childhood and adolescence. But even here there was a brother, subjected to exactly the same training, who broke away from it in adolescent years and in spite of parental efforts became normally heterosexual. See Gordon, A., "The History of a Homosexual; His Difficulties and Triumphs," *Med. J. and Rec.*, 1930, 131, 152-156.

into two general classes. There are those which are based upon the assumption of an inborn, intrinsic, defect; and there are others which look upon pathological homosexuality as purely a matter of distorted development.

Those who think of pathological homosexuality as inborn look upon it as a condition determined long before birth and as much a basic characteristic of the individual as is the color of his hair or the pattern of his anatomy. Just as there are sexually complete males and females so there are individuals in whom, anatomically considered, the traits of one sex are not so completely dominant as they are in the person who is thoroughly male or female. That there are anatomical gradations in between is now well known, and these grade all the way down to the hermaphrodite who is neither male nor female but to some extent both. It is assumed also that accompanying these differences in the degree of anatomical dominance of the traits of one sex over the other there is a corresponding development of mental traits. And for this every one can recall some evidence in support. In addition to the men who are thoroughly masculine there are men who are somewhat less so although one would hesitate to call them effeminate; and there are those who are decidedly effeminate. Likewise, in addition to women who are thoroughly feminine there are women who are somewhat less so, and there are those who are commonly classified as decidedly masculine in many of their ways. There have even been attempts to measure these degrees of difference.

According to this conception the homosexual is to be thought of as one who is by nature imperfectly sexed, and who has to a considerable degree the traits of the other sex, and whose sex attractions are far from normal. Such a person may be classified as a male but be sufficiently female to be attracted most by members of his own sex; or the person may be classified as a female but be sufficiently male to be attracted most by members of her own sex classification.

The application of this point of view to the crush is complicated by the many different degrees possible. If a crush case should be but very, very slightly homosexual by nature, then it might be but an episode in the development of the personality, a matter of unevenness of development which would soon disappear as the heterosexuality became established. If the crush occurred in a personality which was much less normal, then it might be the first manifestations of an abnormality which was determined by nature long before birth and which would thus be quite unalterable.

If the writer appraises the trend of thought on this subject correctly the tendency is rather away from this theory than toward it. Although a functional interpretation is growing in favor, even its most earnest advocates seem inclined to admit the possibility of there being occasional individuals who are born freaks and who cannot therefore ever be anything but freaks. However, the application of this intrinsic determination theory to any particular case must be made with the greatest caution because of the convincing demonstration that many, very many, crush cases are re-educable and that many disappear for reasons not discovered. Very few of them can be properly classified as manifesting an inherent defect.

The functional theory for the crush assumes it to be a very mild form of homosexuality and that in turn is interpreted as a predominance or fixation of the homosexual stage or phase of adolescent development. Every normal person is assumed to have the possibility of both homo- and heterosexual expression of the libido energy; but normal folk rapidly develop a dominance or fixation of the heterosexual. In adolescence, before this heterosexual dominance is fully established, homosexual trends are more easily produced, especially if there is anything in the experience which emphasizes the homosexual and at the same time tends to block or inhibit the development of heterosexuality. Advocates of this interpretation offer for proof of their position the instances of rather pronounced homosexuality which they have succeeded in re-educating and the large numbers of crush cases which disappear into a normal heterosexuality.[1]

One then turns naturally to learn *what sort of experiences may*

[1] An introduction to this literature may be found through the following:

Carpenter, Edward, *Love's Coming of Age*, pp. 120-140.
Collins, Joseph, *The Doctor Looks at Love and Life*, chap. 4.
Davis, K. B., *Factors in the Sex Life of Twenty-two Hundred Women*, chaps. 10, 11.
Stekel, Wm., *Bi-Sexual Love*, Boston, 1922.
Wittels, Fritz, *Critique of Love*, New York, 1929.

block the normal development of heterosexuality. Of these a number may be listed. Instances are reported of crush cases that are traceable to the blocking of expressions of tenderness (1) through isolation or death. The girl may have recently lost a loved one and suffer much pent-up emotion; or she may be absent from home and the loved ones upon whom she has been accustomed to lavish affection. As social conventions prevent the expression of that affection upon the young men of her acquaintance, the only alternative is the manifestation of them toward some of her female associates. Hence the lavish love of the crush.

There are also instances (2), loosely allied to the preceding, where the girl has lost her mother in childhood and then in adolescent years acquires a longing for the intimacies and expressed affection of a mother. Every mention of it or sight of the happiness which other girls have stirs fantasy thinking and the longing. Eventually some mature girl of her acquaintance, who has possibly done her some kindness, becomes the center of expression for this emotion. Perhaps this should not properly be termed a crush, but complications are easy, and, if there is any blocking of the heterosexual trend, such an affectionate relation might easily take on all the aspects of a crush.

Far too many girls are still brought up with an actual fear of the other sex. Here parental maladjustment results in false teachings (3) which suppress the heterosexual trend and force the girl into the crush form of love if she is to have any at all. Sometimes there are crushes which may be traced to inferiority disturbances (4), where the victim of the crush sees in the girl she loves the realization of all that she would be and believes herself unable to achieve. This would involve that feature of the psychoanalytic theory of love mentioned earlier in the chapter, wherein there is the identification of the beloved with the ideal of the self and thus a shift of the narcissistic libido to the beloved. Allied to these are the instances of notions of sexual inferiority, coming as the consequence of ignorance and misinformation, which lead to the belief that a normal attainment of married life will be forever impossible. Such ideas block the heterosexual development and make the homosexual or crush form of love the only outlet if there is to be one at all.

Strange as it may seem crush cases are sometimes traceable to an over-idealization of the other sex (5). The girl builds up an image of an ideal man, so perfect and so marvelous that the possibility of her ever meeting such is rare indeed. Actual men, as a consequence, soon become disgusting and vulgar because of their inferiority to her ideal. Again there is the blocking of normal heterosexual affection. This may be in whole or in part a father fixation. The girl's ideal lover is one who is as fine and great and perfect as her own father is believed to be. The father may even be dead. Indeed, where the father is dead, such idealistic notions of what he was are thought to be all the more easily developed.

Some very unhappy instances are to be seen where the crush is caused by a blocking of heterosexuality through disgust of marriage as it has been observed (6). The girl's father and mother may have been very unhappy. The father may have been a brute who abused her mother. And the girl as a consequence had established in her perceptions for all men which stirred repugnant reactions. Any latent homosexual trend would thus be the only means for satisfying desires for love and affection. If there is a normal homosexual trend in every person, then such experiences would be certain to bring it into dominance.

In addition to the above list, it should be observed that any too rigid segregation of the sexes, whatever be the form of institution, be it school or college or reformatory, is quite likely to contribute to the effectiveness of any or all of these causes.

After one has achieved an interpretation of any crush case the question immediately arises of *what to do about it*. The answer is not easy, and must depend more upon the particular case and the immediate circumstances than upon general prescriptions. Some possibilities are obviously indicated by the interpretations just outlined. A better understanding of herself, of what is actually going on, of the causes for her behavior, may sometimes be sufficient to change the course of development.

An appeal to her altruism is reported by some to be effective. When a girl can be convinced that her excessive affection is disturbing and possibly even dangerous to the future development and achievement of the girl she so excessively loves, there may be a reaction which will check the crush. Counselling in such a manner assumes of course the possibility of obtaining some degree of cooperation on the part of the girl herself. Sometimes she is so intensely on the defensive that any such personal approach is impossible; and so the question arises of what will happen if the matter is ignored and allowed to run its course.

If ignored, the crush might develop into a permanent perversion, although but a small percentage of crushes do so eventuate. It might develop into a life-long friendship and companionship. Neither would marry and each would be content in the companionship of the other. Most communities can exhibit such cases. The intimacy might run happily for a few years, although always rather one-sided, and then the one least affected by the crush develop a normal heterosexual affection and marry. The other then reacts with resentment and anger. The friendship is broken and the one left behind is likely to continue more or less indefinitely as a maladjusted personality.

Without doing anything at all for the welfare of a girl suffering a crush, the circumstances of life will often remove the cause and the crush stage disappear. No doubt the vast majority of crushes are so "ironed out" by the ordinary growth changes of life.

A forcible separation of the two girls involved is sometimes satisfactorily effective; but its effectiveness must depend upon the nature of the cause. It should obviously not be used blindly. There should first be some effort to discover the motivation of the behavior. A full understanding of the case might make some other plan appear far more likely to succeed, and all the trouble and expense of a separation unnecessary.

Is there such a thing as *love at first sight?* Perhaps this is not exactly a form of problem behavior in connection with romantic love, but it is certainly often a problem. The discussions of the subject usually center around the more obvious of the alleged instances of such sudden falling in love; and it is doubtless for that reason that the preparation for it is overlooked. Certainly no one who has studied the literature with any thoroughness would deny that there are instances where the individual himself becomes aware of his love suddenly and after a very short acquaintance, perhaps even the first meeting. But this merely proves that the love for this particular person made its appearance suddenly.

When one looks carefully into the history behind such love episodes, one will find evidences of a long preparation. Thinking in terms of McDougall's love-sentiment doctrine, one will be quickly led to observe that prior to this sudden falling in love there had been the development of a number of different love sentiments. Perhaps they were not love sentiments for a girl, but they were love sentiments nevertheless. All that happens then, when a man falls in love with a girl at first sight, is the unexpected meeting with a girl who for some obscure reason arouses in the man a love sentiment already established.

Sometimes one can find in these instances of love at first sight evidence of the individual having long fantasied an ideal girl; and, as a consequence, there was established a love sentiment for this girl of his dreams. Or, maybe he had lost his mother when he was but a child; and through the years he had loved his memory concept of her. By so doing he had established a love sentiment for a beautiful young woman. Then some day, when a girl is met who stimulates this love sentiment, acts as a substitute stimulus, as it were, for the dream girl or the fantasied mother girl, he finds himself unexpectedly in love and says that he fell in love at first sight.

In terms of the psychoanalysts' way of thinking, the explanation would not be so different. Love at first sight comes in the years when the individual is heterosexually inclined, when the libido is well sublimated. And the direction of the heterosexualized libido is supposed to be influenced by the earlier experiences of love for the mother. There are the traces of the Œdipus complex, the childish desire to do away with the father and marry the mother, still left in the content of the ego and the super-ego, which has sometimes been termed the heir of the Œdipus complex. This leads the youth to respond with love to the girl who somehow appeals to him as his mother did. Years may pass and he may meet many girls without being much affected by them. Then comes a day when he meets one who makes an appeal like that of his mother, although not perhaps perceptibly so, and he finds himself in love. Unaware of what has been going on he calls it love at first sight.

Petting is more often presented as an ethical problem; but there are those who seek an understanding of its relationship to love. Petting or caressing is obviously a part of the full love-sex experience. The psychoanalysts have rather happily designated the acts called petting as the fore-pleasures of love. They are to that extent related to the sex relation, although under some circumstances they can be quite thoroughly divorced from it. The formal kiss as it is so often used among some peoples can scarcely be termed a fore-pleasure of love. It has become but a symbol of regard.[1]

The psychoanalytic theorists see in the looking and petting and kissing of lovers the remnants of the autoerotic libido channels of infancy. There is still in the mature adult some eye libido and some skin and some oral libido. These are old and with the maturation of the individual do not entirely disappear but rather become more or less transformed. At the same time they become associated with the sex instincts and so are termed their fore-pleasures.

In the language of any theory, the control of petting, keeping it within the bounds of decency and propriety, depends upon the inhibitions established. The language with which these inhibitions are designated may vary, but the underlying functions are just about the same. The converse of this may be found in the reasons given by young people for their first spooning. G. F. Smith[2] has published a number of returns which indicate the following classification of reasons: Infatuation, 52 per cent; curiosity, 40 percent; others did it, 30 percent; lack of courage to resist, 12 percent; desire to please, 12 percent; fear of unpopularity, 11 percent; and others. In most of these one can read the principle of abandonment, the relaxation of control, giving way to impulse. If inhibition had been strong enough, there would have been no such letting go. In terms of psychoanalytic psychology whether or not a person pets, and how much a person pets, will depend upon the content of the ego and the super-ego, and that content comes out of his experiences with life. In other words, it is a matter of the ideals and standards of the indi-

---

[1] Note for example the European custom so often seen in news moving pictures of the general kissing the soldier when a reward of merit is bestowed.
[2] Smith, G. F., "Certain Aspects of the Sex Life of the Adolescent Girl," *J. Appl. Psychol.*, 1924, 8, 347-350.

vidual, and how well they function as inhibiting mechanisms. And here it must also be recalled, that youth is rarely as thoroughly organized, as well controlled, as an adult; also, that there are some people who never can in all probability develop a high degree of control. In this connection it should also be recalled that alcohol and other depressant drugs reduce the ability to control. And so also does fatigue.

The phenomena of what may be technically termed *obstructed love,* but which is popularly referred to as a case of *broken-heart,* is a pathetically frequent problem in adolescent experience. The emotional distress, the loss of sleep, the inability to eat, and to digest, and the general nervousness of the boy or girl who has loved and lost, may bring a smile to the more experienced adult, especially if it occurs more than once or twice in a year; but it is no laughing matter for the boy or the girl who has it to suffer.

In the writer's thinking, the most satisfactory interpretation of this condition is that which sees it in terms of blocked impulses to action. Whether it be thought of in terms of McDougall or in terms of psychoanalytic theory, it is apparent at least that there are many normal impulses which have now no chance for the sort of expression which brings relief and satisfaction. The boy who has been dismissed by the girl whom he loves, longs to see her, to caress her, to care for her, to protect her, and all the rest. And none of these will she have. She may even refuse to talk to him on the telephone. The inability to give expression to his impulses stirs fantasy thinking. He recalls the days of happiness with her and promptly longs to have them again. He thinks of all that he had planned to do for and with her, and realizes that he can do none of it. Everything is blocked; there are conflicts galore within him. He is, so far, in a condition psychologically comparable to that of the mother whose child is seriously ill. There is nothing she can do because more competent nurses and physicians are doing it all. Hence she walks the floor in agony, tormented by impulses which cannot find expression.

In such cases there is often also, perhaps always, a complication through the disturbance of self-regard and all of the feelings and emotions involved. There is a touch of shame, of inferiority, and perhaps even of fear. He wonders what his associates think of him, and fears their teasing. Notions of uselessness and helplessness arise. He thinks of himself as worthless, a good-for-nothing, a failure. Ideas and impulses of escape appear. There may be thoughts of running away, of skipping out, of quitting everything, and even of death. Sometimes these do find expression in overt acts; but more often they are inhibited by the ideals and ambitions now so well established. The result is the addition of still more conflict to that already suffered. That all this should disturb attention and the continuation of normal application to daily tasks is to be expected as the normal effect of emotional disturbance.

Sometimes the conflict is suddenly and quickly resolved by falling desperately in love with another girl who reciprocates the affection. Such rebound engagements and even hasty marriages are not at all infrequent. Their very haste makes them questionable, for they may not know each other well enough to be certain of a happy partnership. There is also in such a solution of the conflict too much of the escape feature to make the thoughtful observer feel confident of its permanence.

The condition bears all the earmarks of a maladjustment in an early and acute stage. And as such it must be handled. The distracted youth, whether boy or girl,[1] must develop a new orientation. By such only can the confusion of thinking be clarified. The intellectual horizon needs expanding. There must be thinking in terms of social responsibilities and of the years to come rather than in terms entirely of the immediate present. There must be much re-valuation of both events and people. Courage is required, and much of it. Emphasis must be so placed as to re-establish the concept of the self in a more inspiring light, to restore self-confidence, and to eliminate the notions of inferiority. The changed interpretations, and the accompanying elimination of much of the emotional conflict, bring relief and rest and restoration of the normal habits of life. Adjustment is slowly achieved; and the result may in the long run, as poets have so often said, be that of a greater poise of personality and a larger sympathy for others in distress.

It should possibly be observed that such readjustments are

---

[1] The above description was for convenience of style expressed in terms of one sex, but it must be obvious that the description and analysis apply equally well to both.

sometimes not achieved. The result is an enduring maladjustment. In later years marriage may be entered into, but with suppressed recollections and regrets for the real love of youthful days. Others may never marry, and go through life steeled against the world. Within, they may be living a life of devotion to a memory. Such lives may be useful; but most of those who live them would probably testify to a wish that others might find a better adjustment before the years of their youth had passed.

Romantic Attractiveness. Why is one member of the other sex especially attractive to one person and not so attractive to others? In what does such attractiveness consist? Such questions have often been raised and a few efforts, theoretical and experimental both, have been made to answer the question. Hall offers a long list of traits which mediate likes and dislikes between the sexes[1] and Mrs. Hollingworth[2] lists such items and comes wisely to the conclusion that it is futile to seek for certain anatomical features or of clothing items as being more attractive than others. Whatever happens to be the feature or item in vogue at the time is the feature or item most attractive.[3] In considering these items of attractiveness and repulsiveness between the sexes, the complex nature of the reaction patterns involved must be ever kept in mind. Curiosity and other established patterns (whether called instincts or not) which are allied to the sex instinct must be included. And there is no doubt a very large influence by whatever standards of beauty have been established in a particular individual. It is obvious that the experiences of life develop great individual differences in these standards, hence what appeals to one as beautiful does not to another. The reverse is quite as important. Standards of what is ugly and repugnant and repulsive differ quite as much, and in these matters of personal attractiveness or unattractiveness are quite as significant.[4]

[1] Hall, G. Stanley, *Adolescence,* Vol. 2, pp. 113-116.
[2] Hollingworth, L. S., *Psychology of the Adolescent,* pp. 111-115.
[3] Similar conclusions could be drawn from Perrin's study. See Perrin, F. A. C., "Physical Attractiveness and Repulsiveness," *J. Exper. Psychol.,* 1921, 4, 203-217.
[4] Counsellors of adolescents will find on this subject many useful suggestions in Laird, D. A., *Why We Don't Like People,* New York, 1931.

Studies of adolescent ideals concerning love and marriage [1] have led generally to the conclusion that the vast majority hope to marry and have rather conventional homes enlightened by the presence of several children. Unwholesome attitudes appear here and there but they are decidedly a minority and one wonders if even these are not temporary notions motivated largely by some rebelliousness.

[1] Blanchard, P., and Manasses, C., *New Girls for Old*, New York, 1930.

Davenport, F. I., "Adolescent Interests," *Arch. of Psychol.*, 1923, No. 66.

Hance, R. T., "Freshman Matrimonial Ideals," *J. Hered.*, 1923, 14, 159-162.

CHAPTER XIV

RELIGIOUS ADJUSTMENT

SOCIAL SETTING OF RELIGIOUS ADJUSTMENT, NEED OF A
WORLD ADJUSTMENT, TYPES OF RELIGIOUS ADJUSTMENT,
(CRISIS CONVERSION, DECISION, GRADUAL TYPE), THEORIES
OF CONVERSION (INTRINSIC DETERMINATION, SUBSTITUTION,
SOCIALIZATION), INTELLECTUAL RELIGIOUS RECONSTRUC-
TION, IRRELIGIOUSNESS OF YOUTH, YOUNG PEOPLE'S RE-
LIGIOUS SOCIETIES, CONTRIBUTIONS TO PERSONALITY DE-
VELOPMENT

Genetic psychologists have always looked upon adolescence as
a most important period in the religious life of the individual.
The first attempts at an inductive study of religious experience
were made at a time when evangelism was popular and religious
conversion a conspicuous phenomenon. These studies revealed
a greater frequency of conversion in adolescent years. As a consequence the notion grew up that adolescence was the nascent
period of maturation of some sort of religious instinct. Examination of the lives of the saints [1] revealed that their religious
fervor frequently reached a high point in adolescent years.

Others have seen in adolescence a period of religious indifference and doubt and scepticism. The literature on religion
in adolescence is extensive but unfortunately much of it is more
pietistic and hortatory than it is descriptive. Much that attempts
to be scientific is unconvincing because our general psychology
of religion is so poorly developed. Unfortunately very little can
be looked upon as the product of systematic inductive study of
the actual experiences of adolescents. The very bulk of this literature, however, reveals at least that the nature of religious experience in adolescence is of sufficient importance to justify seri-

[1] Hall, G. Stanley, *Adolescence*, Vol. 1, pp. 524-532.

ous consideration and to deserve further and better research investigation.

For the purposes of this presentation, the reader should keep in mind that the author thinks of religion as the product of man's effort to achieve a satisfactory adjustment to his world. Religious exercises are the means which man has developed to maintain or to re-establish that feeling of satisfactory adjustment. This does not affirm nor deny the possibility of human efforts being assisted by divine revelation and supernatural inspiration; but it does assume that such revelation and inspiration contribute also to man's understanding of his world and serve as aids to a more satisfactory life therein.

Man has had to do battle with the powers of nature which even yet he but poorly understands. His capacity to think has vastly expanded his world; but it has also brought into his world problems which the animals apparently are never obliged to confront. Man, because he can think, can ask such questions as whence do I come, whither do I go, and why am I here. Man can raise questions as to the value of living. Man is capable of aspiration and disappointment, of hope and despair. Advancing knowledge has meant a continuously changing world, and differences in the degree of human knowledge have made for different individuals very different worlds, in which they individually seek to live. Religious beliefs and ceremonies reach beyond the few facts of which man can be scientifically certain and supply a scheme of interpretation that aids man in understanding, in living peacefully, in his world of bewildering vastness and complexity. Religious leaders are those who have aided conspicuously in this problem of seeking and finding a world adjustment for the individual.

The author also contends that for the purposes of clarity of thinking it is necessary to think of religion as always involving some sort of concept of god or gods. There have been and still are, as most readers know very well, efforts to interpret the world, to supply working answers to man's most difficult questions in terms of schemes of thinking which omit any sort of god or gods. These the writer contends should be thought of as ethical or philosophical systems but not as religious. That these god-less or non-religious efforts in behalf of man's adjustment in the world have rarely endured for long or served the needs of any considerable number of people may or may not be a reflection upon their adequacy. The current effort in Russia to abolish religion may be watched with interest by all students of genetic psychology. The few studies which have come from there indicate enthusiastic rejection of religious notions by the youth of that land growing up under revolutionary influences.[1] If they succeed in establishing a satisfying non-religious form of world adjustment, they will have done what rarely if ever has been done before on a large scale in the history of mankind.

The following presentation will be in terms of the religious adjustment of youth, using the term religious as above defined; and it will be largely in terms of the Christian religion and European-American youth, because practically all of our available studies have been made within that limited field of behavior.

Social Setting of Religious Adjustment. Adolescence is now recognized as a period of many adjustments. The religious adjustment is but one of the many, and is often brought about or made necessary by the other adjustments which the social pressures upon youth make necessary. Most young people grow up in an environment in which religion and religious institutions are well established. That means that religion constitutes one of the many social pressures to which every growing boy and girl is subjected. Just as they are expected to achieve a vocation and an accepted place in some community, to establish a home, to become moral according to accepted standards, and all the rest, so too are they expected by society to become religious in one way or another. Particular environments produce particular differences in the degree and nature of this religious pressure. From the point of view of the growing boy or girl, it may be said that the years of adolescence ordinarily bring a consciousness that somehow or other every person should become religious and affiliate with religious organizations. Childhood years may have been religious in their way; but as adolescence brings self-consciousness and self-control, there comes this awareness of what is expected of one religiously as well as in other ways.

[1] For summary of these studies see Murphy, G. and L. C., *Experimental Social Psychology*, New York, 1931, pp. 360-361.

This consciousness of a social expectancy of religious profession and affiliation is apparently supported or complemented by the desire of the growing youth to be like adults, to be "grown-up" as rapidly as possible. That same urge or drive (will-to-power, perhaps) which pushes one into vocational selection and preparation, and into conformity with the conventions of established society, apparently pushes likewise into a consciousness that some sort of religious experience and profession is also necessary.

Need of a World Adjustment. The history of mankind forces us to think that this response to social pressure is far from the only reason for the religiousness of youth. Pubic initiation ceremonies have all through the ages been a standing recognition of the need of youth for orientation in a world which transcends that of social relations and social institutions.[1] This in turn is evidence that man believes he has discovered, by natural or supernatural means, that which is of importance to a happy life on earth. When growing boys or girls have reached an age which makes understanding possible and necessary, they are initiated into a knowledge of these mysteries.

This observation deserves thoughtful consideration. In childhood, life is comparatively simple, intelligence has not yet reached maturity of development, and a very simple explanation of the world and its problems suffices. But with advance into adolescence, the rapid approximation to maturity, the world of the individual expands and changes greatly. The simple conceptions of life which once satisfied are no longer adequate. The progress of education brings ever new ideas and interpretations. The world for the youth is thus changing rapidly. He is trying to find himself socially and vocationally and also religiously. He may not call it religious, indeed he may not know what it is that is going on within him; but to the thoughtful and observant adult the groping for a working philosophy of life is readily perceptible. Studies of gangs, good and bad, guided and unguided, have revealed that among other contributions they give to their members a philosophy of life.[2] Gangs would not be doing this,

[1] See discussion of pubic initiation ceremonies and their significance in chap. VIII.
[2] See chap. VIII.

especially unguided gangs, unless there were a need and a seeking for some sort of philosophy, something which would make the ways of life meaningful and supply a principle to live by.

Types of Religious Adjustment. This religious adjustment is achieved in several different ways which may be for convenience grouped into three general classes. One is the crisis type of religious conversion, one is the decision type of religious conversion or adjustment, and another is the gradual type of religious adjustment. All these require special consideration.

The *crisis type of conversion* [1] through much of the eighteenth and nineteenth centuries, especially in this country, was the typical and conspicuous form of religious experience. Many religious communions made it a prerequisite to membership. Although the crisis form of conversion may continue to be looked upon as the psychological prototype of all forms of religious experience, there is no doubt of its rapid decline in frequency of occurrence. Clark [2] in a study of 2,174 cases published in 1929 found only 6.7 percent that could be properly classified as of the crisis type. Consequently many young people today may never have seen and know little about this form of conversion which has figured so prominently in religious history and has been the inspiration for many psychological studies.

Where the crisis type of conversion occurs in adolescence, there will frequently be found a Protestant religious background of childhood experience in an environment that has instilled ideas of a stern theological variety—beliefs in hell, damnation, infant depravity and the like.[3] It means growth in an intellectual atmosphere which assumed the reality of sin and the certainty of a God that was relentless and severe in its punishment. It also means growth in an environment in which there was much talk of conversion and the expectancy of religious crisis in

---

[1] It should be observed that the term conversion is commonly used with any one of four different meanings: (1) a transformation of character by supernatural influence; (2) change by conviction from one religion to another; (3) by Roman Catholic authors, the resumption of the obligations of the practical Catholic after a period of negligence; (4) change from a self-centered and irreligious life to a socially-centered religious life. The use of the term conversion in this book will ordinarily appear in conformity to the last-mentioned definition.

[2] Clark, E. T., *The Psychology of Religious Awakening*, p. 47.

[3] *Ibid.*, chaps. 4, 5.

the lives of all who would be saved. Even in such environments childhood and youth are periods of much impulsive conduct, years in which many acts are committed which are contrary to what is known to be better and right. Such youth arrive at mid-adolescence with a consciousness of much wrong-doing, sinfulness, a belief in a stern and just God. They, too, are subjected to all the social pressures already outlined. Tension and emotional stress are inevitable.

Eventually the time comes when, ordinarily, under the influence of some special preacher or evangelist, they are brought into a vivid consciousness of the difference between their present ways of living and life as it should be. The preacher does not hesitate to throw heavy stress upon this contrast. He builds high the ideals of what should be, and presses heavily upon the hideousness of life as it has been. Hence the contrast between the ideal and the actual is brought out into its full possibility if not actually exaggerated. As inferiority feelings come easily in youth, the consequence is intense emotional depression, termed in religious language the conviction of sin. Then there is stress upon the possibility of divine assistance and of the forgiveness of God. The latter is accepted. The old ways of living are definitely rejected. The tension of the conflict is released and the converted person passes from the crisis into a period of joy and exaltation. This has been frequently described, often in language so extravagant as to indicate clearly the unforgettable nature of the experience.

The concluding phase of this form of conversion is a quiet peace or joy accompanied by a new attitude of helpfulness toward all mankind. Adjustment has been achieved. The person so converted feels for a time at least at ease in his world. He believes that he is right with God. Life takes on a peculiar richness of meaning; and through his faith all problems find a satisfying answer. It is important, also, to observe that one so converted is welcomed by those who have been converted in the past much as the newly initiated member of a tribe or clan is met with rejoicing and approval. The expectations of the adults of the community have for the time being been met by the youth who has passed through the conversion. A social adjustment has thus been achieved as well as the adjustment to a world in which God is believed to be an ever-present reality.[1]

In the early days of psychologizing on religion, many studies were made to discover the average age of conversion. These placed the average at about the middle of adolescence. The median age obtained by consolidating a number of studies is 16 years and 7 months.[2] More recent studies have revealed what was at first thought to be a decline in the average age of conversion; but this has since been found to be a change in the type of religious experience under consideration rather than a change in age. The crisis type of conversion still has its mode in middle adolescence. The apparent change of age in the newer studies is actually due to an increase in the frequency of another type of adolescent religious adjustment, that which is here termed the decision type. The average for the decision type is lower by three, or possibly four, years than is that for the crisis type.[3]

The *decision type of conversion,* or pubescent religious experience, has long been customary, expected and approved in certain religious communions, notably the Roman Catholic, the Anglican, and the Lutheran. As a consequence of changes in theological beliefs, and especially because of changes in methods of religious education, the decision type is rapidly displacing the crisis type in those communions where the crisis type was once considered indispensable. Systematic studies of the experience are unfortunately lacking, but apparently it does not differ much from the crisis type in its general features, although the whole experience is certainly far less intense and disturbing in its emotional aspects.

Religious leaders in the communions mentioned seek to bring to the boys and girls of their church families a consciousness of

[1] Detailed first-hand descriptions of the crisis form of the conversion may be found in the following:

Burr, A. R., *Confessions and Confessants,* chaps. 5, 6, 7.
James, Wm., *Varieties of Religious Experience,* chaps. 9 and 10.
Pratt, J. B., *The Religious Consciousness,* chap. 7.

[2] See the author's *Psychology of Religious Adjustment,* pp. 108-110.

[3] A study of conversion in India made by similar methods has produced a very similar distribution of age frequencies. Such differences as do appear can be satisfactorily explained in terms of differences in the social situation. See Annett, E. A., *Conversion in India,* Madras, Christian Lit. Soc. for India, 1920.

their duty to accept the religious beliefs of their people, and to go through whatever ceremonies are required (baptism, first communion, confirmation, joining the church, or whatever they may be called). That this is making conscious of a social pressure must be obvious. There is also the implication that, if any individual does not make the decision and conform to expectations, there is something peculiar or wrong or even bad about him. Here is enough to suggest the possibility of those inferiority feelings which were so conspicuous in the crisis type. One might safely suspect, also, that the talks before them by adults about the responsibilities of the "step they are about to take," and the like, would also stir no little feeling of inferiority, or at least of inadequacy, which may be much the same thing. Then there is the moment of the decision, followed by the experiences of the ceremony itself; and afterward there is the rejoicing and expression of approval by adults.

This decision type must give for a time at least a new orientation in life, a new consciousness of the self with an attitude of having done the proper thing, a consciousness of adjustment to the social situation and also to the world as it is then understood. That it must be followed by further instruction and perhaps other adjustments, as increasing knowledge and growth bring new problems in life, does not set aside the fact that the decision experience is essentially one of religious adjustment.

The third form is the *gradual type of religious adjustment*. All through the history of psychological studies of religion there has been a belief that there are not a few persons who eventually achieve much the same sort of religious adjustment and orientation in their world without ever having been through any definite religious experience either of the crisis or of the decision type. The thought is that these people go through all of those changes and adjustments in a manner so gradual, so drawn-out or prolonged, that there is no one special time which can be recalled as significant above all others in their religious life. Some modern religious educators are contending that this is far the most desirable form of religious development.[1]

One immediately suspects the possibility here of a basic dif-

[1] Coe, G. A., *A Social Theory of Religious Education*, chap. 23.

ference of personality type or temperament, and this explanation has often been suggested; but unfortunately our psychology of types is far too inadequately developed to justify any conclusion other than that such type relationships may someday be demonstrated. Perhaps those who experience the very gradual religious adjustment constitute one extreme of the introversion-extroversion distribution, and those who experience the crisis type of conversion will be found in the other extreme. Perhaps one may be a pyknic (Kretschmer) and the other an asthenic. But, for the present, such notions are no more than possible inferences, interesting as they may be.[1]

Theories of Conversion. Although the suggestion was made above that religious conversion of whatever special form was an adjustment to the world of the individual motivated largely by growing-up impulses coming into contact with social pressures, that is far from the whole of the psychology of conversion and certainly not the only theoretical construct that has been offered for its interpretation. Aside from the purely religious or theological interpretations, there have been at least three other psychological theories of the nature of conversion. These appear in the following paragraphs.

1. *Intrinsic Determination.* The influence of G. Stanley Hall[2] and the popularity of biological thinking in psychology thirty years ago are responsible for the once widespread use of the notion that the religious experiences of adolescence could best be explained in terms of the maturation of a religious instinct. At the proper time, usually thought of as in the earlier years of adolescence, this instinct was supposed to come into fullness

[1] For an introduction to this literature the reader may well begin with the following:

Jaensch, E., "Psychological and Psycho-Physical Investigations of Types in Their Relation to the Psychology of Religion," chap. 31 of *Feelings and Emotions:* The Wittenberg Symposium edited by M. L. Reymert (Clark University Press), 1928.

Starbuck, E. D., *Psychology of Religion,* chap. 24.

Sward, Keith, "Temperament and Religious Experience," *J. Soc. Psychol.,* 1931, 2, 374-396.

Wells, C. D., "Religious Personality Types," *Sociol. and Soc. Res.,* 1932, 16, 232-241.

[2] Hall, G. Stanley, *Adolescence,* chaps. 13, 14. See also the author's representation of this theory in his *Psychology of Religious Adjustment,* pp. 111-113.

of development and to motivate the special interest in and sensitiveness to all things religious. The conversion phenomena were thought to be an intrinsically determined blossoming or efflorescence of the growing personality into the new experiences and adjustments of religion.

Hall gave much weight to the similarities which he observed between religious behavior and the behavior motivated by romantic love. He noticed that young people in love were prone to consider the building of houses in which they might eventually live; and that religious experience has all through the ages been the motivation for the building of houses in which the god could live, or in which the worship of the god could be properly conducted. He noticed also that lovers are prone to think and talk and write about death, and that religiously minded persons also think much about death. And there was the responsiveness of lovers to nature, which he compared to the large place which nature has had in the religious inspiration of human beings. These similarities of conduct and many others Hall pointed to as proof that religion and love must have at base a similar motivation; and, as Hall firmly believed that love was derived from the sex instinct, he was inclined to the belief that the religious experiences of adolescence, especially conversion, were motivated also by an instinct.

The reason why the apex of the curve of conversion came in middle adolescence could be explained perhaps by the recapitulation theory which was a comfortable means of explaining the distribution of delayed instincts, of why some instincts came into nascency at one time and others at another time. But it is also true that Hall did not rest his case entirely upon intrinsic determination. He also allowed for social influences as will be seen below.

This explanation of conversion in terms of an instinct is not so popular today. Instincts are in ill repute, for very good reasons, as a means of interpretation. Furthermore the interpretation of love as being merely a derived form of the reproductive instinct is open to serious question.[1] And then, too, the mere existence of similarities between the behavior of youth in love and in religious expression does not prove a like motivation. There

[1] See chap. XIII.

are dissimilarities to be considered; and instead of both being motivated by instinct it is equally possible that some of the forms and imagery of religion may be taken for convenience of symbolization and description from the ever-present and universal experiences of love.

2. *The Substitution Theory*. This presents a scheme of interpretation far more closely in harmony with current psychological thinking. Careful studies of the classic descriptions of conversion reveal a rather long series of antecedent but associated events. Prior to the apical moment of the conversion there are to be found many indications that the new way of living, the new belief, had been from time to time met with in one way or another and each time rejected. There had been impulses in the new direction, perhaps even desires. There had been some thought about it. The circumstances of life had persistently brought to mind the advantages of the new and the disadvantages of the old. But all of these pointings toward the new had been regularly rejected. Some prefer to say that they had been repressed. The thought is that they were at no time by themselves strong enough to predominate over the pattern of habits which constituted the established way of living and believing. It was the old which dominated over these more or less isolated tendencies toward the new.

It is further assumed that these rejected or repressed tendencies did not leave impressions which gradually faded out. They were not permitted to fade out because of the many like experiences frequently arising. And it is assumed that these rejected impulses and thought patterns became gradually constellated, as memories are well known to do. Eventually this constellation of possible habit patterns became so large and well organized that it constituted a formidable alternative to the dominant pattern of habits constituting the up-to-then established way of living. Then came the moment of change, when the old ways were definitely rejected and the new, which had long been fought off, was accepted and allowed to come into complete dominance. It is this climactic moment of shifting, with all its attendant emotion, which forms the conversion of the crisis type.

The instances of "back-sliding" would in terms of such thinking be but temporary returns to dominance by the old patterns of living. As the new ways of living change the social setting and provide continuing satisfactions, there is less and less to arouse the old patterns; and so, through disuse, they appear less and less often and may be expected to fade as do old memories.[1]

The range of usefulness of this conception is greater than may at first appear likely. Certainly it is applicable to the variety of religious conversion which appears in the well-known evangelistic campaign meetings. In the interpretation of adult conversions, it appears to fit the known facts remarkably well. And it is almost as readily applicable to adolescent conversions of the crisis type. There are in these the premonitions of the change, the holding back, the denials and refusals and rejections, the conflict between the two modes of living, and the eventual triumph of the newer pattern over the older.

In a lesser degree the same features are probably present in the decision type, although here it is easy to recognize the possibility of many variations. There may be some decisions which come about reluctantly and only after much hesitation or inner conflict. These would of course conform to the theory. At the other extreme there may be decisions which come about so hastily or are so skilfully prepared for by systems of education that, although the decision comes quickly, it is merely a logical next step in growth and is desired rather than hesitated over. If there be such instances, then this substitution theory would scarcely apply, because the decision would be merely an action in harmony with the already established and dominant pattern. One might even question the propriety of associating such behavior with the concept of conversion at all.

The applicability of this substitution theory to the gradual type of conversion might be also questioned. Its greatest champion, Sante De Sanctis, however, contends that the gradual type does manifest behavior which justifies the use of this theory. He claims that the gradual type is really a prolonged succession of conflicts and substitutions. It is a step-by-step process of conversion. From time to time there are small conflicts and rejections and eventual acceptations of the new which, when totalled

---

[1] Conklin, Edmund S., *Psychology of Religious Adjustment*, pp. 116-120.
De Sanctis, S., *Religious Conversion*, chap. 4.
James, Wm., *Varieties of Religious Experience*.

up through the years, amount to the same sort of change as takes place in the crisis type of conversion. Of course, in such instances, there could be no development of a large constellation of repressed tendencies. It would be rather that the new is a gradual development and a gradual encroachment upon the old. Perhaps it might be safely described as a succession of small and partial conversions.

It should also be pointed out that this substitution doctrine of conversion may equally well serve for the explanation of other kinds of changes of general pattern. It well suffices for explaining the story-book type of change from hate to love. The girl who hated the hero and eventually capitulated with a sudden rushing change from hate to love suggests that there was probably the same development of a constellation in the background which was suddenly shifted into dominance, displacing the old hate pattern. Changes of political allegiance can often also be explained in like manner, and they often also manifest the temporary defensive mechanism of militant opposition comparable to the hate just mentioned. Conversion then, strictly speaking, can be thought of only as a substitution of dominant patterns where the substitution involves patterns concerned with the relationship of the individual to his God, sometimes otherwise expressed as adjustment to a world in which God is believed to be a genuine and significant factor.

3. *Socialization Theory.* This interpretation of conversion is associated especially with the name of G. Stanley Hall who made much of it in addition to his use of instinct and the recapitulation theory. He was accustomed to say that every individual was born twice, once as an individual and again as a member of the species. For him the function of religion was to make this change complete and perfect.[1]

By his quaint language concerning the double birth, Hall was referring to that change from self-centeredness to other-centeredness which has already been presented at length as a characteristic of the social developmental changes of adolescent years.[2] The experience of the ordinary child in the approximately normal home is that of centering the habits of thought and emo-

[1] Hall, G. Stanley, *Adolescence,* chap. 14.
[2] See chap. VII, section on the birth of altruism.

tional reaction upon the achievements of the self and upon the ambitions and hopes for the self in the future. The social pressures looking toward the responsibilities of maturity as they are felt in adolescence progressively oppose the continuation of this self-centeredness and force an increasing consideration of the welfare of others. More and more the youth is forced to sacrifice his own personal preferences and ambitions for the sake of the happiness of others. The self-centeredness of childhood must be abandoned for the other-centeredness of maturity. Socialization this is sometimes called.

The circumstances of life may bring about a fore-shortening of this change which forces into prominence all of its features. The death of a parent may force the youth to give up long-cherished ambitions in order to care for the other members of the family. And when such tragedies come, one may observe behavior remarkably like this which has been described above as characteristic of the conversion experience. There is the confusion, the awe, the feelings of inferiority (inexperience and incapacity), the vacillation between two ways of doing (ignoring the welfare of others and the manifest duty versus the personal sacrifice and assumption of the new responsibilities), the decision and abandonment of the old way of living, the peace following a hard decision, and the concluding consciousness of proper adjustment to the world in which he is placed. Ordinarily this socialization process is spread out over the years of adolescence, but even then the thoughtful observer will note these same features appearing again and again with a corresponding lower degree of intensity.

The socialization theory conceives of this change of attitude as the core of conversion; but, as with the substitution theory, it needs to be observed that such socialization may, and often does, take place without any accompaniments which may properly be termed religious. But when this socialization takes place in a religious atmosphere, when it is aided and more or less motivated by religious belief and experience, then it may be properly looked upon as a religious conversion. Socialization may thus be looked upon as a part of the process of world adjustment for every individual. But the world in which most individuals believe themselves to live includes the concept of God and of religious duties. Consequently a complete conversion would be one which provides for an adjustment to a world much larger than that of the social setting of human beings in which he lives.

This last conception of adolescent religious conversion can be applied quite satisfactorily to the crisis type and also to the gradual type, but perhaps not quite so well to the decision type. The decision type comes ordinarily, as the reader will recall, somewhat earlier on the average than does the crisis type. The average for it is practically at the beginning of adolescence, before the socialization process has much more than begun. In our ignorance of the essential nature of this decision type, one may suspect that, while it may have some of the features of social and world adjustment, it may be rather more of the nature of a decision to face the problems of adolescent years in the religious way and in the manner of religiously minded people. It may be essentially of the childish self-centered nature, although not necessarily always so. The socialization process must follow, as the years bring the consciousness of social pressure and the exigencies of life force the change of attitude and way of living. The decision type may thus be frequently followed by the gradual type as a normal course of events. Perhaps it is always so.

The final interpretation of adolescent religious conversion must obviously wait until there have been more studies of the gradual type, and certainly until there has been an intensive study of the decision type and its relationship to the remainder of adolescence. For the crisis type, however, both the substitution theory and the socialization theory are useful. Apparently both are true of the crisis conversion and therefore each but a partial statement. The crisis type of religious adolescent conversion might be better described as a religious socialization by the process of substitution. The gradual type of religious adolescent conversion would be but a spreading-out of the same thing over a more or less prolonged period of time. If there be any factors of an intrinsic or religiously instinctive nature at work, they are certainly not yet demonstrated.

Intellectual Religious Reconstruction. Adolescence seems to be a period in which there is both fixation of religious ideas and reconstruction of religious ideas. Where there are profound emotional experiences of a religious nature, there religious ideas are likely to become fixed, at least for a time and perhaps for a lifetime. There is also much evidence in support of the belief that there is much rethinking of religious beliefs and attitudes during adolescent years.[1] Unfortunately, however, this evidence is peculiarly incomplete and unsystematic.

We do know for certain that the religious ideas of adults and of youths in the later years of adolescence are very different from the religious ideas of children.[2] That means of course that somewhere along the line changes have taken place. Presumably this is largely in the years of adolescence, although systematic studies comparing beliefs year by year from childhood up are yet to be made. Leuba has supplied a study of the ideas about God and immortality of a group of college students which indicates some change from year to year at the college level.[3] In a privately published survey conducted by Parsons, returns appear from over four thousand college students about the effect on their religious thinking of their experiences in high school. Of these approximately 39 percent say that their religious belief was strengthened, 28 percent that it was disturbed, 28 percent that it was re-shaped, and 5 percent that it was destroyed.[4]

In an unpublished thesis study made under the writer's direction, Padilla has compared the statements of belief of high school and college students in sufficient numbers to indicate that there is a progressive change through the years both of high school and college.[5] Whether a study of non-academic adolescents would indicate a comparable change no one knows for certain.

---

[1] This is not confined to religion. See Ruediger, Wm. C., "The Period of Mental Reconstruction," *Amer. J. Psychol.*, 1907, 18, 353-370.

[2] For a study of the religious ideas of children see Barnes, Earl, "Theological Life of a California Child," *Ped. Sem.*, 1892, 2, 442-448. For religious ideas of later adolescence see Leuba mentioned below. Also Bain, R., "Religious Attitudes of College Students," *Amer. J. Soc.*, 1927, 32, 762-770.

[3] Leuba, J. H., *The Belief in God and Immortality*, chaps. 7 and 8.

[4] Parsons, Philip A., *A Report on the Survey of Religious and Character Influences on State University and College Campuses.* Eugene, Oregon, 1933. (Privately printed.)

[5] Padilla, S. G., *A Psychological Study of Religious Belief* (A thesis in the library of the University of Oregon). A few other less useful studies have been published. These can readily be located through the bibliographies in the publications mentioned. See also Dudycha, G. J., "The Religious Beliefs of College Freshmen," *Sch. & Soc.*, 1930, 31, 206-208.

The causes of these changes of religious belief are probably not far to seek. Some at least are readily available. The studies of the rise of intelligence indicate that the ability to think grows up to about the middle of adolescence. And in addition to the ability to think there is an ever-widening range of knowledge, or, to put it otherwise, there is an increasing amount of material to think with. Perhaps the rise of self-consciousness and the trends toward self-reliance and independence may also be contributing factors to this reconstruction of religious ideas. Altogether these are but parts of that changing world of the adolescent which has been so often observed in this text. The social pressures of life as well as the urges from within are forcing a progressive remolding of the personality. The changes of religious ideas are necessitated by these other changes of the world in which the youth is progressively living. It is but an aspect of the course of adjustment to the world as the youth knows it.

Religious reconstruction is thus to be thought of as a normal feature of growth. Without it there would be an unfortunate retention or carry-over into later years of childish concepts which are unsuitable. Such changes are expected in other fields of thought and belief; but, unfortunately, many people, sometimes adolescents themselves, have the notion that religious ideas are too sacred for examination and reconstruction. Such reconstruction is necessary for the elimination of childish crudities. No matter how competent the instruction, children are almost certain to acquire many erroneous notions not only of religion but also of astronomy and anatomy and physiology. Reconstruction of astronomical and anatomical and physiological concepts is taken as a matter of course. It is reconstruction in the direction of the ideas held by adults and the most competent thinkers in those fields of study. So the course of religious reconstruction is normally toward those concepts which adults and religious leaders consider best.

Far too frequently the course of religious reconstruction is attended by more or less disturbing experiences with *religious doubt*. The experience of doubting ideas about the sun and the stars and anatomy, and so on, are not ordinarily dignified with the name of doubt probably because they do not ordinarily cause an emotional disturbance. Ideas about non-religious subjects can ordinarily be changed with little attendant emotion. But, because of the setting which has been given them, the changing of religious ideas may be a serious matter indeed. How frequently religious doubt is a disturbing feature of adolescent years no one knows. Nor does any one know to what extent it is related to the type of religious training, to religious interests, or to the lack of them in the parents. But that it exists cannot be questioned. Authentic reports are available even of instances where the distress over religious doubt has culminated in suicide.

There was a time when students of genetic psychology looked for what was called the nascent period for religious doubt. It was then assumed that doubting of religious beliefs was a normal stage of development the average age of which could be determined, and that when so determined could be looked upon as based upon intrinsic determination. Starbuck considered it an adolescent phenomenon,[1] although his distributions reveal instances of religious doubt coming as early as eleven and twelve years of age. And his distributions present no well-defined mode. Hall, as have others, thought of religious doubt as characteristic of the later years of adolescence;[2] and yet, in places, he spoke of religious doubts appearing in childhood. Apparently then the best one can do at present is to recognize that religious doubt may be an important factor in the development of some personalities through adolescent years and leave the question of average or modal age for later determination. Perhaps there may be no average age that has any significance.

Distress over religious reconstruction appears to be attributable to one or more of a variety of factors. The finger of condemnation is frequently pointed to the influences of the study of the natural sciences, biology especially. Here the implication is that the teaching of evolution is the cause of the distress, when the blame might with equal propriety be placed upon the failure to prepare the child for the experiences of high school and college by supplying a religious education that is not antipathetic toward the newer concepts of the sciences. Again it has been claimed that youth has been too much left to itself to make the readjustments in important concepts without competent guid-

---

[1] Starbuck, E. D., *Psychology of Religion*, p. 239.
[2] Hall, G. Stanley, *Adolescence*, Vol. 2, p. 315 et seq.

ance. Perhaps destructive teaching without provision for newer concepts to take the place of the old that are no longer tenable may also be a cause. Certainly there is some case evidence that individuals are allowed to grow up into adolescent years carrying with them the crude religious concepts acquired in childhood. The emotional effect of religious experiences and associations gives to them a profound valuation. When changes eventually become necessary, the youth mistakenly believes that it means the abandonment of his religion. The making of such changes thus appears to be a far more serious matter than the alteration of ideas about the stars or the moon or of the nature of rocks and trees. Hence the conflict and the doubt. Probably the intensity of the doubt bears some relationship to the length of the delay before making the reconstruction.

That youth needs some sort of working philosophy of life has long been recognized. And by this is of course meant a philosophy which will aid in the explanation of the larger problems of living and in world adjustment. This was long ago recognized in the establishment of the primitive initiatory ceremonies provided for pubescent boys and girls [1] as an essential for the proper achievement of full maturity. It is toward this end that the reconstructions of religious thinking in adolescent years tend. The danger lies in the possibility of an incomplete reconstruction as well as in the emotional distress which sometimes accompanies the change. There is also the possibility that some youths may start the process and then become stalled at some stage, with some utterly inadequate belief. Some simple materialism may be accepted as a temporary device and then the youths stop thinking. The reconstruction may drive some into a scepticism from which they never escape and which may leave them permanently ill-adjusted in their worlds. From these inadequacies later troubles and distortions may arise.

Irreligiousness of Youth. The contention is frequently heard that adolescence presents a period of irreligiousness, scepticism, and even anti-religious attitudes. Whether or not youth is irreligious must of course depend upon the definition of religiousness in the mind of the one making the judgment; and, as is

1 See section on savage pubic initiations, in chap. VIII.

well known, there are vast differences of opinion in the popular as well as the scientific mind as to what should be termed religious and religiousness.

The few systematic studies available, however, do not point to any startling abandonment of beliefs about religious doctrines. A number of samplings of student groups in a number of different places indicate much the same thing. In an elaborate study of Syracuse University students in 1926 it was found that 64 percent of a group of over thirteen hundred students in liberal arts held quite orthodox beliefs concerning the nature of God, and 25 percent of more than fourteen hundred students held a most orthodox belief concerning the miracles.[1] Of 97 entering freshmen at Ripon college, 96 percent believed in the existence of God, 98 percent believed that the ten commandments should be obeyed, and 47 percent believed in the existence of the devil.[2] Even Leuba's much-discussed inquiry does not reveal a startling trend toward unorthodoxy. He obtained answers concerning belief in a personal God from 927 students in nine different colleges and of these 56 percent of the men were believers in a personal God and 82 percent of the women. A much smaller number of students in a single college gave the following percentages of belief in personal immortality: Freshmen 80.3 percent, sophomores 76.2 percent, juniors 60 percent and seniors 70.1 percent.[3] Padilla's study, which is not quite comparable because he used a number of different definitions of God, nevertheless indicates as great if not greater percentages of orthodoxy.[4] Parsons's study of students in twelve different colleges and universities in western states in 1932 included the question, "Do you believe in God?" Of the 5,500 students answering, a very small percentage left the item blank, and of those answering it 91 percent did so affirmatively.[5]

[1] Katz, D., and Allport, F. H., *Students' Attitudes,* chap. 15.
[2] Dudycha, G. J., "The Religious Beliefs of College Freshmen," *Sch. & Soc.,* 1930, 31, 206-208.
[3] Leuba, J. H., *The Belief in God and Immortality,* 1916, pp. 202, 216.
[4] Padilla, S. G., *A Psychological Study of Religious Belief.* (Unpublished thesis in University of Oregon library.)
[5] Parsons, Philip A., *A Report on the Survey of Religious and Character Influences on State University and College Campuses.* Eugene, Oregon, 1933. (Privately printed.)

All such studies are subject to question. The method of obtaining information may not be valid. Students may answer what they think they ought to answer rather than to tell the truth. And the phrasing of the questions used is often open to much difference of interpretation. But, even allowing for all such sources of error, it is evident that there is no overwhelming amount of atheism in the college student groups. Perhaps they present a fair reflection of the status of beliefs on such subjects in the world at large in which they are soon to become members. From a study of sixteen hundred college students, Betts has concluded exactly that. He thinks that the students in religious matters are much like the general population, although unfortunately he had no reliable figures on the general population for comparison.[1] The alleged irreligiousness of youth may be due to the activities and expressions of a small proportion, and it may be due to a total misconception of what is going on in the lives of adolescent boys and girls. Certainly progress in the reconstruction of religious ideas, so that they will better serve the needs of maturity, cannot be termed irreligiousness. If scepticism arises for a time in the course of that progress, it may easily be mistaken for irreligiousness. And it is quite possible that many young people in good health, of high mental ability, and enjoying social advantages may not feel so keenly the stresses of life which prove to so many adults the need for a religious faith.

A promising method for study of this subject which may avoid many of the sources of error mentioned above appears in the Thurstone-Chave measure of attitude toward the church.[2] By this method it is possible to compare one age group with another as well as groups with different kinds of religious background. The following figures taken from the Thurstone-Chave study indicate the average attitude toward the church of college student groups expressed in terms of an eleven-point scale. The smaller the figure the more favorable is the attitude toward the church:

[1] Betts, G. H., "Religious Attitudes of University Students," *Relig. Educ.*, 1928, 23, 917-919.
[2] Thurstone, L. L., and Chave, E. J., *The Measurement of Attitude*, Chicago, 1929.

ATTITUDES TOWARD THE CHURCH OF COLLEGE STUDENTS
(*Thurstone-Chave*) *

	No.	Mean	Standard Deviation
Freshmen	548	4.42	2.07
Sophomores	127	5.04	1.93
Juniors	107	4.57	2.02
Seniors	107	4.78	1.93

* Reproduced by permission of the Univ. of Chicago Press.

These figures indicate that these students differed among themselves considerably in their attitudes toward the church. Some thought it a highly valuable institution, and others quite the reverse. The average of each group is about mid-way between the extremes, with a slight leaning toward the favorable side.[1] This looks very much like what one might expect to find in a chance sampling of the general public. One may suspect of course that from pubescence up through the years of adolescence there would be found considerable shifting of attitude toward the church. Certainly individuals manifest such shifts, whether the averages of large groups show it or not. Doubtless these shifts are to be thought of as but symptomatic of the whole mass of changes through which youth is going in the course of socialization, maturation, and intellectual reconstruction.

Young People's Religious Societies. For many years large numbers of adolescents have participated to a greater or lesser degree in these organizations or movements. The Christian Endeavor Societies, the Epworth Leagues, the Baptist Young People's Unions, the Luther Leagues, and others have apparently had a large place in the development of many people in adolescent years. But of the psychological significance and nature of these societies very little is discoverable. Systematic studies of them are few and for many reasons quite inadequate. Membership in such groups apparently provides some genuine religious instruction, some opportunity for religious contacts. There is reason to suspect, however, that they also involve much that

[1] The author in a similar but unpublished study of four different college student groups found the following means: 3.80, 3.18, 2.80, 3.36. These obviously indicate a somewhat more favorable attitude toward the church than that found in the Thurstone-Chave study.

is superficial and affected, and that there is a poverty often of that which would stimulate really critical thinking or originality of attack upon the problems of life.[1] But no doubt much the same can be said of almost any organization of and for young people. Just what they contribute to the developing personality remains to be discovered.

Contributions of Religious Experience to Personality Development. In the present pathetically undeveloped state of our psychology of religion, it would be most premature to make more than suggestions concerning the possible influences of religious experience upon developing personalities. One thing of which we may be most sure is that religious experience in adolescent years can provide a better subsequent understanding of the feelings and attitudes of others. Religion plays a large part in the lives of most people in one way or another. Those who have never had any of its experiences will have but a poor understanding of their associates who have. And if the religious experience approximates that which is normal and wholesome, it can contribute much to the shift from the self-centered life of childhood to the acceptable other-centeredness of maturity. It might also contribute much to the cultivation of sympathy and tenderness for others.

The consideration of religion in this chapter has been as that of an institution which contributes to the orientation of the individual in the world of his experience. As such, religious experience probably contributes much to the orientation of the individual in his world. That it may sometimes confuse and be prejudicial to mental growth must also be recognized.

Religious sentiments, thought of in terms of McDougall as a cerebral pattern governing the group of emotions aroused, are no doubt to a considerable extent molded and remolded by the religious experiences of adolescent years. Thus the religious differences which are so conspicuous in adult years may be attributable in no small part to the experiences of adolescence. How much of this difference is to be traced to adolescence and how

---

[1] The most thorough study of this subject (including an excellent bibliography) which the author has found is unfortunately unpublished. See Niles, Katherine E., *Young People's Societies in Evangelical Churches: A Survey of Conditions in Eighteen Groups.* (An unpublished thesis in the library of Reed College of Portland, Oregon, 1928.)

much to childhood remains to be determined. Doubtless it in-volves large individual differences also, which in turn means that the religious peculiarities of some people, at least, are determined by the experiences and influences of adolescence.

If, as has so often been contended, religion serves as a moral dynamic, then it is quite possible that religious beliefs and atti-tudes established in early adolescent or even in childhood years may serve as a valuable source of balance and poise and moral determination through all the uncertainties that press in upon most young people when they break away from home and find themselves in a world of conflicting standards and practices.

For some, religion may serve as a means of escape from the troublesome realities of youth. It may serve as a means of avoiding the difficulties of mixing with larger social groups, of learning to live with those of different and conflicting ways and ideas, of avoiding the necessity of doing any constructive think-ing. The timid youth may escape much by limiting his ex-perience to a church group and the ideas of a few in that church. If this be desirable is an open question. Perhaps some young people are not fitted by nature to face the storms of life and thus deserve the sheltered environment which some religious circles afford. For the present, however, this stands as little more than a theoretical possibility; and it must so remain until more thorough studies of the religious features of personality development are made available.[1]

The after effects of the conversion experience upon the per-sonality of the individuals who go through it in one form or another have been little considered. As has already been indi-cated, the decision type may not be properly a conversion type at all; and the gradual type is obviously but a description of the progressive religio-social growth of the personality. It is thus primarily a question of what the crisis type of conversion does to the growing personality. It may establish an orientation and an attitude which are stabilizing and healthful throughout life; and

[1] An arresting gesture in this direction is a study of the degree of intro-version and the amount of inferiority feeling in a group of theological semi-nary students. Here the students were found to be more introverted and much more given to inferiority feelings than a comparable group of college students and business men. See Sward, Keith, "Temperament and Religious Experience," *J. Soc., Psychol.*, 1931, 2, 374-396.

it may subsequently come to be looked upon as a disturbing or even a distorting influence. It must depend very much on the nature of the individual temperament as well as upon the social setting.

In persons who are intrinsically weak and unstable the crisis type of conversion might be merely one of many kinds of emotional explosions to which such persons are susceptible throughout life. And yet it might direct the contacts of such into environments that are not the most hygienic for personalities that do not easily become well integrated and stable. If a person of this kind should, because of the crisis conversion, be directed into frequenting the associations of those who are highly emotional and who practice emotionally disturbing forms of religious exercise, then such might contribute rather to the maintenance of the instability than to its stabilization. On the other hand, the crisis type of conversion coming in the youth of one who grows steadily into a well-organized and integrated personality might eventually be looked upon as merely a rapid socialization and religious orientation of lasting value. With all such interpretations, however, the student as well as the scholar must proceed with much caution until more certain knowledge is available. Even then caution will always be necessary when it comes to the interpretation of effects in any given personality.

CHAPTER XV

FAULTS, MISDEMEANORS AND DELINQUENCY

THEORIES OF DELINQUENCY (TYPE, NATIVE DEFECT, FUNC-
TIONAL THEORY), CONTRIBUTING FACTORS (BROKEN HOMES,
DOMESTIC INADEQUACY, PARENTAL FAILURE, PARENTAL MAL-
ADJUSTMENT, SCHOOL, PLAY, MOVIES, GANGS, ENCEPHALITIS,
EPILEPSY), SEX DIFFERENCES (GANGS, OFFENSES COMMITTED,
MENSTRUATION), NOSTALGIC OFFENSES

An inevitable consequence of the growth changes of adolescence is the appearance of much conduct that is contrary to the
customs of parents, to the conventions of society, to the regulations of institutions, and to the laws of city, state, and nation.
Sometimes these violations of requirements are serious and dam-
aging; often they are petty and incidental. The range of such
conduct is wide and inclusive. At the one extreme one finds such
simple misdemeanors as staying out late at night or going to
shows proscribed by the parents or running away from home;
and at the other are offenses as serious as forgery and arson and
assault and even murder. Sometimes such items of irregular behavior are but relatively insignificant episodes in the course of
growth and social adjustment; sometimes they mark the beginnings of a criminal career. Between these extremes there may
be found many degrees of individual difference.

Many kinds of specialists have long been interested in the
study and interpretation of these refractory forms of adolescent
behavior. Naturally the more serious forms of misdemeanor
have attracted most attention. The consequence of this is that
the published studies are far more concerned with delinquent
adolescents, with those whose offenses have brought them into
courts and correctional institutions. But for psychological purposes, at least, the student of such problems must be constantly
aware that for nearly every youth arrested and brought into court

there are not only others who have committed like offenses without being caught, but there are also many, many more whose impulses have led to conduct not looked upon as socially so serious, to conduct which might never lead to arrest and court records. For any one then to think of the problem behavior of adolescence as limited to those whose traits and ways have come to court records would be naïve indeed and might end in serious misconception. Rather must one think of those who have court records as constituting but a portion of that much larger group of adolescents who manifest behavior that is unsubmissive, asocial, and troublesome.

General Theories of Delinquency. Before one can wisely proceed to the study of special forms and factors involved in these behavior problems it is necessary to have clearly in mind the three rather different points of view for the interpretation of delinquency which are current today. Briefly it may be said that there are those who think of the genuinely delinquent group as including many who are criminals by nature and whose nature is first becoming manifest in adolescent years. Then there are those who have discarded the criminal type theory, but are much influenced by a belief that the more serious forms of misconduct are attributable to some inherent defect of personality. And, thirdly, there is the purely functional point of view according to which all misdemeanors and delinquencies and criminality would be interpreted in terms of environmental influences and maladjustment disturbances. These points of view are so influential they must be examined in greater detail.[1]

1. The *type theory.* For this the great Italian criminologist Cesare Lombroso is responsible. He proposed in 1876 that a criminal was an atavism, that he was a born freak, a reversion to an ancient kind of human being. Just as babies are from time to time born with atavistic anatomical structures which were once characteristic of the species, in remote generations, so Lom-

[1] Before going far with the matter of interpretation the student will find it most helpful to read a number of case descriptions of delinquent or criminal careers. Such may be found in the following:

Case studies published by the Judge Baker Foundation of Boston.
Drucker, S., and Hexter, M. B., *Children Astray*, Cambridge, Mass., 1923.
Shaw, C. R., *The Jack-roller*, Chicago, 1930.
—— *The Natural History of a Delinquent Career*, Chicago, 1931.

broso thought that from time to time there were individuals born who developed not into the typical human being of today, but into that which was typical a very long time ago. They developed a peculiar pattern of physical and mental characteristics by which they could be identified and which differentiated them from the race types of today. Large cheek bones, prominent lower jaw, receding forehead, projecting ears and many other physical traits were described. Psychologically this criminal type was presented as lacking the moral consciousness and conscientiousness of the man of today; much of his sensory apparatus, especially for pain, was crude and dull by comparison. The insensibility to pain was supported by the criminal's alleged greater addiction to tatoo marking on his body. And in mental ability or alertness he was thought to be inferior to the fully developed man of our time.

While all the details of this theory cannot for obvious reasons be rehearsed here, it is important to know that as he worked with it Lombroso was led to make a number of modifications. Among other things he came to realize that somehow degeneration was involved, and this led him to think of the criminal type as somehow a combination of atavism and morbidity. He also recognized that there were differences in the degree of criminality, and that some were criminals by act of sudden passion or by the consequence of temporary circumstances. All criminals were thus not to be thought of as belonging to the criminal type; but this did not apparently shake his belief in the existence of the criminal type as an adequate explanation of the behavior of many criminals.[1]

This notion of a criminal type has achieved a remarkable popularity. One frequently hears it said that so and so is a "born criminal." If there be any truth in it, it is of course of prime importance to the student of adolescent problem behavior, because all studies of criminal careers indicate that a vast propor-

[1] For more complete presentations and critical discussion the reader will do well to start with the following:

Aschaffenburg, G., *Crime and Its Repression*, Boston, 1913.
DeQuiros, C. B., *Modern Theories of Criminality*, Boston, 1912. (Summary of Lombroso pages 10-19.)
Lombroso, Cesare, *Crime: Its Causes and Remedies*, Boston, 1912.

tion were begun in adolescence. Perhaps when a boy or girl manifests repeatedly a tendency to delinquent conduct, it should be looked upon as the first indication of the fact that he or she is destined by nature to develop into the criminal type, that the case is hopeless, that all efforts at reformation will be inevitably futile. But before one jumps to such a conclusion concerning any individual one should look at the criticisms of the type theory.

From the very outset there have been thoughtful students who have rejected this type doctrine. It is said that one criminologist was heard to remark that Lombroso's pictures of the criminal type looked remarkably like his own law-abiding friends. Others have pointed out the difficulty of determining what is the normal for any physical characteristic. Far more would it be difficult then to assert with confidence that any form or degree was the atavistic or criminal type. But by far the most serious obstacle to the acceptation of Lombroso's theory of a type is the extensive study made by Goring[1] on the physical and mental traits of English criminals and non-criminals. In the course of this research a very large number of criminals in English prisons were measured and tested and graded in a variety of ways. The same measures were applied to British soldiers, to the inmates of a general hospital, to the students of three great universities, and to others. The very best of comparisons were thus available.

The upshot of all this study is that Lombroso's criminal type does not exist. The alleged physical characteristics or peculiarities of the criminal type did not appear when Goring's criminals were compared with his non-criminals. Even such items as the tendency to greater use of tatooing by criminals did not prove to be true. But Goring did find that the criminal group was on the average physically inferior, emotionally less well controlled, possessed of more anti-social traits, and was in mental ability below the average of his non-criminal groups. Even this, however, must lead to a vastly different conception of the criminal from that of a hopelessly pre-determined atavistic type. One cannot then on any scientific basis condemn a delinquent youth as a "born criminal," predestined to a criminal career.

[1] Goring, Charles, *The English Convict*, London, H. M. Stationery Office, 1913.

2. The theory of *native defect*. Actually this appears in several forms. Perhaps the most famous in connection with delinquency problems is the notion of an intrinsic defect in the capacity for moral judgment and feeling. The conception is not without some rational basis. Differences in intellectual ability have long been known and regularly recognized in the several grades of amentia. Just as one person may be defective in intellectual ability and normal in other respects, so this theory assumes that another person may be defective in moral ability and normal in all other respects. For this condition the term *moral imbecility* is ordinarily used.

In support of this, cases are described in which the persons involved grow up to maturity apparently without sympathy or kindliness, and with a total failure to develop any sort of consideration for the rights or happiness or welfare of others. They do truly appear to be deficient in all that we commonly designate as the moral life. No amount of training seems to have an appreciable effect upon their behavior. But this mode of interpretation is not supposed to be confined to the few cases of extreme or total moral defect, which might be termed moral imbecility. There are also supposed to be individual differences in the degree of endowment in this faculty or factor of moral capacity. Thus the more troublesome youths would be thought of as in need of much more attention and moral training because of their basic moral weakness. They would not be thought of as lacking moral capacity but rather as being to some degree weak in that function.

The drift of thinking and observation, and also of such experimentation as has been made, is, however, emphatically away from all such interpretation as this. The assumption of a moral faculty comparable to that basic ability measured by intelligence tests is now seriously questioned by many and completely discarded by some. Furthermore, those who are constantly at work with delinquents are failing to find cases which conform to the definition of moral imbecility. Healy, after studying more than a thousand cases of delinquency, said that he had failed to find a single case.[1] Cyril Burt, working in England, found not a

---

[1] See William Healy's complete discussion of this subject in *The Individual Delinquent*, pp. 782-788.

single case of moral imbecility in 2,800 delinquents examined.[1]

The experimental studies are not very satisfactory; but, so far as they go, they support the clinical failure to find evidence for thinking that individuals differ in the degree of their native endowment in moral capacity.[2] For these reasons psychologists are not now in the habit of interpreting the misdemeanors of adolescence as manifesting a defect of moral judgment, considered as intrinsic ability. But it must also be remembered that researchers of recent years have been strongly influenced by the critical reaction to all thinking in terms of instincts and faculties. And our methods for the detection of basic abilities in human beings are in their infancy. It is quite within the range of possibility that tests may some day reveal some elemental function or ability necessary to the development of moral judgment and feeling, in the possession of which individuals may differ as greatly as they do in intelligence and in terms of which adolescent misbehavior can be better understood; but it is quite clear that the definition of such an ability or function, if it ever is discovered, is likely to be quite different from that of the moral faculty assumed to exist by those who have defined moral imbecility.

Another way in which misconduct has been interpreted in terms of native defect is by attributing it to *intellectual deficiency*. This dates back to the early days of the mental testing movement. Soon after the introduction of the Binet-Simon tests in this country, the application of them to delinquent youths and children became a popular form of psychological research. The early studies indicated a very high percentage of feebleminded in the delinquent class. Percentages as high as ninety-three were reported. Even those who looked upon the very high percentages as chance occurrences were quite naturally led to the con-

[1] Tredgold, A. F., and others, "Report of a Symposium on the Definition and Diagnosis of Moral Imbecility," *Brit. J. Med. Psychol.*, 1926, 6, 219-227.
[2] Attempts to measure moral judgment have turned out to be merely measures of the same functions as those measured by intelligence tests (See Bridges, J. W. and K. M. B., "A Psychological Study of Juvenile Delinquency by Group Methods," *Genet. Psychol. Monog.*, 1926, 1, No. 5, especially pp. 481-494). A study of the judgment of degree of badness for a list of different acts made upon a group of delinquent women with a control group of university women revealed the two groups so remarkably alike that the author was forced to the conclusion that delinquency could not be due to any absence of moral insight. (See Weber, C. O., "Moral Judgment in Female Delinquents," *J. Appl. Psychol.*, 1926, 10, 89-91.)

clusion that intelligence defect must be a major factor in the production of misconduct. The apex of this emphasis upon intelligence defect seems to have been reached somewhere about 1915.[1] Since then there has been a progressive change of attitude among students of the subject.

The army intelligence tests applied to Leavenworth prisoners revealed a distribution of scores quite like that of all whites drafted into the army.[2] Since the war studies of the intelligence of men in other prisons have produced quite similar results.[3] But one must not make hasty conclusions from such studies as these. It is true that on the surface they do appear to indicate that intelligence defect is no more frequent among the criminals than among non-criminal groups. But those who were closest to the army testing methods caution the rest of us not to place too much reliance upon the accuracy of the scores there made; and furthermore the army tests themselves on guard-house delinquency cases show a notably different distribution of scores from that produced by the testing of Leavenworth prisoners. The guard-house cases constitute a group of less serious forms of delinquency, of course, and it is significant that they manifest a much lower average of mental ability. Apparently low intelligence was a much more influential factor in the production of these less serious cases.

The percentages of frequency of intelligence defect now reported are, it is true, much smaller than in the earlier studies, and this is commonly attributed to the use of improved tests and better testing procedure; but the percentages reported continue to be much above that for the general population. Reports on the frequency of feeblemindedness among delinquents still vary greatly. They range from about 8 percent to about 30 percent. If we accept 2 percent as the frequency in the population at large, then feeblemindedness is to be found from four to fifteen

---

[1] Pintner lists 42 studies of the percentage of feeblemindedness in delinquency. Of these 23 are from 1911 to 1917 inclusive, and they average 47.2 percent. The remaining 19 are dated 1918 to 1929 inclusive and they average 22.5 percent. This very well shows the change from earlier test studies to the later. Pintner, R., *Intelligence Testing: Methods and Results*, pp. 375-376.

[2] *Memoirs National Academy of Sciences*, 1921, Vol. 15, Part III, chap. 12.

[3] Murchison, C., *Criminal Intelligence*, Worcester, 1926.

times as often among delinquents as among non-delinquents.[1]

The conclusion is inevitable that deficiency of mental ability must be in some manner a contributing factor in the production of delinquency. That it is a contributing and not a direct cause is clear, otherwise there would not be so many dull and feeble-minded youths who are not delinquent. How then does mental defect operate in the production of delinquency? To this question a few reliable answers are available. One has already been indicated by the study of guard-house cases in the army. Those of lesser mental ability are less capable of profiting by experience and respond less well to discipline. This means that training in the ways of society, in the making of judgments of right and wrong, whether it come through the home or school or church or playground or whatever the source, is much more slowly effective where the mental ability is low. For such a greater amount of training and probably better methods are necessary. This is, however, still further complicated by the fact that the young people of lesser mental ability come very largely from homes where the parents are themselves of lesser mental ability. The children who need extra and very special training are thus likely to get less training and of poorer quality, because of the inability of their parents. School life for such children also complicates. School programs are not designed for the child of lesser ability. Failures and repetition of work are inevitable. Inability to compete and the slower responsiveness to the methods of training bring unhappiness and distaste and conflicts. Problem behavior of one sort or another is an all too frequent consequence.

In the interpretation then of specific instances of troublesome

[1] For an introduction to this literature the reader should start with the following:

Ackerson, L., *Children's Behavior Problems*, chap. 13.
Bronner, A. F., *A Comparative Study of the Intelligence of Delinquent Girls*, New York, Teachers College, 1914.
Burt, Cyril, *The Young Delinquent*, chap. 7.
Erickson, M. H., "A Study of the Relationship Between Intelligence and Crime," *J. Crim. Law and Criminol.*, 1929, 19, 592-635.
Healy, Wm., and Bronner, A. F., *Delinquents and Criminals, Their Making and Unmaking*, New York, 1926.
Jones, Vernon, "Children's Morals," chap. 13 in *Handbook of Child Psychology*, edited by Carl Murchison.
Pintner, R., *Intelligence Testing: Methods and Results*, chap. 16.
Slawson, John, *The Delinquent Boy*, chaps. 2, 3.

behavior, one may with all propriety and wisdom seek to discover if the intelligence is normal or defective. But, if it be found defective, one has no right to dismiss the matter by saying that the delinquency has been caused by the intelligence defect and as that defect is known to be incurable the case is hopeless. Rather should the discovery of mental deficiency lead to a search for the other factors in the general pattern, centering around the mental deficiency perhaps, which have produced the undesirable behavior. The effects of these other factors are habits and they may quite well be subject to reformation. Of these other factors more will be found in the later sections of this chapter.

A third concept which has led to the interpretation of much delinquency on an intrinsic basis is that of *constitutional psychopathic inferiority*. The condition designated by this term is without doubt highly influential in the production of all sorts of behavior problems; but unfortunately it is difficult to give it yet a very exact definition. As the terms indicate there is the belief that not a few individuals are by nature inferior in some manner which prevents them from ever achieving a normal neuropsychic development.

With the progress of psychiatry and psychopathology in the identification of abnormal forms of human behavior, it has become increasingly evident that there is a class of cases which manifests a chronic inability to achieve the poise and life-adjustment of the ordinary human being. They may for a time be mistaken for any one of many forms of abnormal condition, but they never develop any of these to a definite degree. They are changeable and suggestible and unreliable. They try the patience of their friends and associates, and of all who attempt to get them settled and adjusted in life. Just when they most need to manifest a little self-control they go off on some tangent which causes yet more trouble. Sometimes ·they appear to be hysterical, again they give the impression of being mildly insane, at times they may appear to have some of the traits of an epileptic personality, and yet with longer observation all of these interpretations have to be abandoned. It may be, as some have thought, that this classification as constitutionally inferior is but a label for a condition we do not yet understand; but, certainly until we do understand its essential nature, it is necessary to accept the fact of its existence.

So far as present knowledge goes those individuals who can wisely be classed as constitutionally inferior are incurable. Their condition may by proper care be somewhat improved but the constitutional defect will remain through life. Obviously they do not all become delinquent or criminal, but in delinquent and criminal groups not a few of this kind of personality are to be discovered. A study of 608 admissions to Sing Sing prison revealed 18.9 percent to be constitutionally inferior.[1]

In attempting to understand the faults and misdemeanors of adolescents who do not come into delinquent and criminal classes the possibility of this kind of basic defect in the personality must ever be kept in mind. No doubt it exists in a variety of degrees. In the problem cases of high school and college life, the chronic trouble-makers, those who never seem to be able to learn to get on with their associates nor to conform with any comfortable degree of consistency to institutional and other regulations, may possibly be suffering some degree of constitutional inferiority. But the concept as a means of interpretation must be used with caution and should never be decided upon finally until after a very long period of observation and with the cooperation of expert psychiatric counsel. There are many other possible causes of chronic maladjustment in school and college life and these should be given full consideration.[2]

Allied to and possibly involved in this concept of constitutional inferiority are the occasional cases of pre-psychotic or very mildly psychotic states. A very few of the problem behavior cases are eventually found to be suffering some one of the more serious forms of mental disease popularly called insanity. A case coming under the writer's observation will illustrate. A young man, a college student, was the cause of much disciplinary consideration. He seemed inoffensive and humble and hard working; but

[1] Glueck, B., "Study of 608 Admissions to Sing Sing Prison," *Ment. Hyg.*, 1918, 2, 85-151.

[2] For a more detailed presentation of constitutional psychopathic inferiority and references to the literature see Chap. XVII, and also Bryant, R. H., "The Constitutional Psychopathic Inferior; a Menace to Society and a Suggestion for the Disposition of Such Individuals," *Amer. J. Psychiat.*, 1927, 6, 671-689.

at the same time he was apparently guilty of many minor infractions of regulations. Then more serious disturbances occurred, frightening of women on the darker streets, and later a series of burglaries which appeared to be curiously purposeless. All of these were eventually traced to this man. Upon apprehension it was found that by that time his condition had become such as to leave no doubt of the true nature of his case. He was suffering a progressive dementia. Hospitalization was necessary and he eventually died in a hospital for the insane.

But there are also conditions bordering on mental disease or insanity which are so mild that their identification is very difficult. And such may never become enough worse to make their identification possible. They may remain through life on the borderline of overt insanity and be chronically difficult. There are a great variety of epileptic or epileptoid conditions known to exist, but not very well understood, which may sometimes be the basis for unruly and troublesome conduct. They may manifest very bad temper and impulsive, erratic, inconsistent actions; but it is necessary to keep clearly in mind that there are other and probably more frequent causes of bad temper and such impulsive conduct. Because of the difficulty of identification of such cases, and their true nature so little known, they are frequently included in the constitutionally inferior group.

The cases which are supposed to be most properly classifiable as constitutional psychopathic inferiors manifest conspicuously a lack of self-control. They may know enough and they may be very intelligent, and they may have had the benefit of the best of home and school training; but all apparently without effect so far as the achievement of normal self-control is concerned. They may chronically wander from place to place. Some authorities believe that people can be feebly-inhibited with regard to certain traits, the impulse to wander for example, and that it is an intrinsic condition transmitted from generation to generation.[1] The result is that such people are never absorbed into the life of any community, unless possibly an itinerant community of their own. They are always wanderers, hoboes, or tramps, leading a socially unassimilated existence. Ordinarily we do not look with

[1] Davenport, C. B., *The Feebly Inhibited: Nomadism, etc.*, Washington, Carnegie Institution, 1915.

alarm upon the youthful longing for elsewhere because in the normal personality this eventually becomes offset and controlled, inhibited, by other desires and habits; but where there is a condition of psychopathic inferiority the wandering may never be brought under control.

So far, attempts to measure this peculiarity of personality are not very satisfactory. Long lists of carefully selected questions have been used and scores made in terms of the number of psychopathically significant answers given; [1] but questionnaires do not reveal the presence or absence of a constitutional defect. They do indeed show that many delinquents are more unstable than comparable groups of non-delinquent subjects, that delinquents apparently do not make the same progress with age in the development of control, that emotional reactions of delinquents are less well controlled, that they are poorly adjusted socially, that they are more suggestible, that they are subject to dominating impulses and that they are tenacious rather than adaptable.

All of these traits or features of growth may be found among adolescents who never see the inside of a juvenile court room and are conditions which may anywhere be the background for troublesome behavior. But these characteristics may not be due in any given instance to a constitutional defect. They may quite as well be due to uneven development, to delayed development, to maladjustments of a variety of kinds. It thus becomes obvious that each individual cause must be very carefully studied and observed over a considerable period of time before any one today can be certain that the cause of the misbehavior is safely attributable to a constitutional inferiority.[2]

---

[1] For discussion and excellent bibliography see Symonds, P. M., *Diagnosing Personality and Conduct,* New York, 1931, chap. V.

[2] The literature on this test work is extensive and cannot all be mentioned here. The following are good examples:

Ackerson, L., *Children's Behavior Problems,* chap. 10.

Bridges, J. W., "A Study of a Group of Delinquent Girls," *Ped. Sem.,* 1927, 34, 187-204.

—— and K. M. B., "A Psychological Study of Juvenile Delinquency by Group Methods," *Genet. Psychol. Monog.,* 1926, 1, 411-506.

Bryant, E. K., "The Will Profile of Delinquent Boys," *J. of Delinquency,* 1921, 6, 294-309.

Courthial, A., "Emotional Differences of Delinquent and Non-Delinquent Girls of Normal Intelligence," *Arch. of Psychol.,* 1931, No. 133.

Slawson, J., *The Delinquent Boy; a Socio-psychological Study,* Boston, 1926, chap. 4.

Weber, C. O., and Guilford, J. P., "Character-Trends Versus Mental Defi-

It must be clear from even this brief survey that many delinquents faced life at the outset with one or more of a number of handicaps which were either genuinely native or so early established that for all practical purposes they must be considered as functioning like a native defect. As possibilities we can now list small stature and physical weakness, tendencies to mental disease, malnutrition, birth injuries, transmitted effects of disease in the parents, mental ability anywhere below the average, and constitutional psychopathic inferiority. In any given case the native handicap was not the direct cause alone of the delinquency but was the initiator of a complicated sequence of events which eventuated in a personality so different, so maladjusted, as to produce the kind of conduct commonly termed delinquent. It is this recognition of a psychogenesis of behavior problems which has led to the current preference for a functional interpretation of delinquency and other conduct troubles.

3. *Functional Theory.* This has grown out of the vast number of case studies which have been made in recent years and the discovery of the inadequacies of the type and defect theories. But it does not discard considerations of native defect. Rather do the advocates of this kind of interpretation consider it highly important to discover in any given case what, if any, defects were present in the native constitution, and to determine if possible something of the degree of such defects.

If one learns that the start was made with the handicap of a rather dull mind, then the troubles of school and social adjustments take on a special meaning and a new light is thrown upon present misbehavior. Likewise, if one learns that the start was made with a serious physical handicap but with an able mind,

ciency in the Problem of Delinquency," *J. Crim. Law and Criminol.*, 1925-26, 16, 610-612.

It should also be observed that some researches with these same methods have failed to reveal such differences. Probably this merely emphasizes the fact that all delinquencies are not to be attributed to such conditions of instability. Examples of such studies are as follows:

Asher, E. J., and Haven, S. E., "The Reactions of State Correctional School and Public School Boys to the Questions of an Emotional Inventory," *J. Juv. Res.*, 1930, 14, 96-106.

Guilford, J. P., "An Attempted Study of Emotional Tendencies in Criminals," *J. Abn. & Soc. Psychol.*, 1926, 21, 241-244.

Tjaden, J. C., "Emotional Reactions of Delinquent Boys of Superior Intelligence Compared to Those of College Students," *J. Abn. & Soc. Psychol.*, 1926, 21, 192-202.

then is the reason clear why there is a different pattern of child-hood troubles, and a correspondingly different approach will be made to the present problems of adolescent years. If again one becomes convinced that present behavior faults are attributable as well as those of childhood to that vague something called constitutional inferiority, then must one be ready with yet another program for counselling and guidance.

In addition, it is necessary to learn of the influence upon the growing personality of life in a broken home, of growing up in a bad social environment, of the effect of running in a gang, of the effects of parental mismanagement, of the special differentiating influences of sex difference, and also of the disturbance brought about in the development of the personality through diseases that are either adventitious or of later manifestation.[1] All of these must be considered in some detail.

Contributing Factors. The lack of training and the growth twists suffered by a child who grows up in a *broken home* are now much and properly stressed by all students of delinquency. Clifford Shaw tells a most thrilling story of the life of a delinquent from infancy up to prison sentence[2] in which the un-speakable home life in childhood occupies a large and dramatic place. But the reader of that book should not fail to observe that the hero (!) of the story had a brother eight years older, just enough older to have had the benefit of a period of fairly good maternal care before the home was too badly broken, and that the brother became a respectable socialized citizen. The absence by death or desertion of the father frequently forces the mother to be much away from home during those very hours of the day when the child's habits are in process of formation. The introduction of a step-parent into a home is all too frequently the beginning of favoritism and quarrelling and jealousy.

The frequency of reports of broken homes in the case histories of delinquents varies considerably. Percentages range from 40 to over 70. But of course there are also broken-home

---

[1] This point of view is well represented by the following:

Healy, Wm. and M. T., *Mental Conflicts and Misconduct*, Boston, 1917.
White House Conference on Child Health and Protection, *The Delinquent Child*, New York, 1932. (Note extensive bibliography.)
[2] Shaw, Clifford R., and Moore, M. E., *The Natural History of a Delinquent Career*, Chicago, 1931.

histories to be found in the lives of non-delinquents as well. Such figures can be of significance only by comparison with the frequency of broken homes in the general population. Here again comparisons vary from a very slight difference to as high as six times the frequency in general population statistics.[1]

It should be further recognized that illegitimacy of birth frequently produces a home situation quite comparable to that of the step-parent, or perhaps even worse. Where the illegitimate child of one or the other of the parents is brought into the home, forced upon the home situation under cloudy circumstances, the prospect for the child is far from bright. One American study revealed that delinquency was about twice as likely to occur among illegitimate as among legitimate children. Burt, in his study of English children, found illegitimacy reported nearly ten times as often among delinquents as among non-delinquents. In Massachusetts, however, the frequency of illegitimacy among delinquents is much lower than in the general population. Healy and Bronner, who make this report, suggest that this may be due to the high degree of efficiency to which child-placing work has been developed in that state.[2]

[1] For such frequency percentages and frequency comparisons see the following:

Bridges, J. W., "A Study of a Group of Delinquent Girls," *Ped Sem.*, 1927, 34, 187-204.
Bridges, J. W. and K. M. B., "A Psychological Study of Juvenile Delinquency by Group Methods," *Genet. Psychol. Monog.*, 1926, 1, 411-506.
Burt, C., *The Young Delinquent*, chap. 3
Bushong, E. M., "Family Estrangement and Juvenile Delinquency," *Social Forces*, 1926-27, 5, 79-83.
Crosby, S. B., "A Study of Alameda County Delinquent Boys with Special Emphasis upon the Group Coming from Broken Homes," *J. Juv. Res.*, 1929, 13, 220-230.
Healy, Wm., and Bronner, A. F., *Delinquents and Criminals; Their Making and Unmaking*, chap. 12.
Roach, L., "Record of Juvenile Delinquency in Benton County, Oregon, 1907-1929," *J. Juv. Res.*, 1930, 14, 34-40.
Shaw, C. R., and McKay, H. D., *Social Factors in Juvenile Delinquency*, Washington, Report of Nat. Comm. on Law Observance and Enforcement, Report No. 13, Gov't. Ptg. Office, 1931.
Slawson, J., *The Delinquent Boy*, chap. 6.
Sullenger, T. A., *Social Determinants in Juvenile Delinquency*, Univ. of Missouri Doctoral Dissertation, 1929.

[2] Burt, C., *The Young Delinquent*, p. 62.
Healy, W., and Bronner, A., *Delinquents and Criminals; Their Making and Unmaking*, p. 122.
Lundberg, E. O., and Lenroot, K. F., *Illegitimacy as a Child-Welfare Problem*, U. S. Children's Bureau, Bulletin No. 75, 1921.

If broken homes are so influential a factor in the production of delinquency, they must also be a factor in the production of traits leading to undesirable behavior in the personalities of many who never become classed as delinquents. One thus naturally becomes eager to know just what are the traits which are developed by life in a broken home. Unfortunately this is a question for which our psychological studies do not yet supply very satisfactory answers. Crosby [1] says that he found lack of self-control more frequently present in the delinquent boys who came from broken homes. Bridges [2] reported on a group of delinquent boys sixty percent of whom had come from broken homes, and listed their office record descriptions of character traits. Presumably much of this could be traced to the broken home influence. Among these traits one reads self-centeredness, exaggerated tendencies to anger, depression, exaggerated acquisitive impulses, and lack of sensitivity to social approval. Here again one perceives a lack of self-control, self-discipline, and a decided absence of socialization or the habits which come from the experiences of learning to live happily with others. Doubtless this is a pretty fair indication of the nature of the broken home effect. To it must be added the effects of poverty and viciousness which so often appear in broken homes, and, where there is illegitimacy, the probable effects of living in a home atmosphere charged with jealousy, a mode of living which we now know to be an active breeder of jealousy in children.

It is necessary also to observe that a home may not be broken, as the term is used, and yet present a pattern of such *domestic inadequacy* as to be a serious menace to the developing traits of any child living therein. Any home may of course be judged inadequate by some possible standard. What is meant here, however, is rather to direct attention to those inadequacies which are known to be causes more or less direct of misdemeanors and delinquent behavior in adolescent years.

Parental failure to understand and to appreciate the nature of the *responsibilities* and position *of the parents* in the home is a prolific source of trouble. This is a condition which appears to occur without any relationship whatever to economic status or

1 References same as those given above on frequency of broken homes.
2 References same as those given above on frequency of broken homes.

degree of education. It may be found in any walk of life. Many
of the misdemeanors of adolescence upon examination appear to
have little if any relationship to the immediate setting in which
they occur. They appear rather to be intrusive impulses, as
though the culprit were blindly plunging suddenly into some
sort of activity, thoughtlessly and heedlessly driven by some force
or drive from within. Instances of stealing are constantly being
reported in student life for which there is no explanation in the
immediate setting. The guilty youth appears to be provided
with all that he (or she) needs and sometimes more. The associates neither approve nor participate in such delinquencies.
The home is reported to be among the most respectable in the
community. But when one pries a little into the circumstances
of the home life one finds that the parental relationship is far
from that of companionship and guidance. One or both of the
parents are insistently and persistently and forcefully dominating
the entire life of the child. By adolescent years, as has been
described in other chapters, there is a normal tendency toward
self-reliance and self-direction. In such homes as these this normal tendency is ignored entirely or deliberately opposed; when
such normal tendencies are repressed, they do not die out but
continue to seek expression until eventually they appear in those
impulsive acts which are contrary to anything or everything that
appears to be of a repressing nature.

Why parents should behave in this manner toward their children is another matter, and one not so easily explained.[1] It may
be sheer ignorance. It may be that the parents sincerely believe
that they know so much better than their child what is best
for him that they persist in domination. Sometimes it may be
traced to a genuine dislike for and impatience with all the problems of child raising.[2] Of this there may be many degrees, but
in any of them one may observe in the background a markedly
self-centered attitude on the part of the parent involved. It is
the selfish satisfactions of the parent that are being sought and
not the welfare of the children in the home. By adolescent years,
life in such a home is certain to stir in an otherwise normal ado-

---

[1] See chaps. XI and XII.
[2] A remarkably effective presentation of this may be found in Samuel
Butler's justly famous novel, *The Way of All Flesh.*

lescent much irritation. Pleasures, especially all that involve the enthusiasms and effervescence of youth, are certain to be sought outside of the home. And, as this must be done clandestinely, misdemeanors and delinquency are a likely consequence. In such a home there must be far less molding of the ideals in the direction desired by the parents than the parents suppose, even in their most conservative moments. Sternness and severity of discipline, untempered by any appearance of understanding or sympathy, are almost certain to fail with adolescents wherever they occur.

In adolescent behavior problems of this sort, one not infrequently finds that one parent errs in one direction and the other parent errs in the other. It may be that the father is the stern unbending over-lord and the mother the indulgent, over-affectionate parent whose ways lead to the establishment of fixations in the children so treated. Or it may be quite the other way around. It may be that the mother is the disciplinarian of the family and that the father is the over-indulgent one. Where such an utter lack of team work by the parents occurs, the child is likely to manifest a very uneven development, to be very childish in some traits and quite mature in others. It is this retained childishness which is to be seen in the troublesome behavior.

The domestic inadequacy may take the form of serious *parental maladjustment*. This may be that the parents are unhappily married, that they have never achieved a genuine partnership in living, that they are not well suited to each other. Again, the maladjustment may be some one of the many possible within the personality of one or other of the parents; or, still worse, it may be that both of them are maladjusted personalities. There may be cynicism as a consequence of disillusionment and disappointment. There may be that very disturbing trait of jealousy. And one or other or both of the parents may be seeking to force upon the child the achievement of their own disappointed hopes and ambitions.

All of these mean that the children grow up in a situation which is not planned and guided first of all for the welfare of the children, but rather that the children grow in a family situation involving much cross-play of conflicting motives. That the adolescent coming from such a psychological confusion should be at times difficult and asocial in his conduct is not to be wondered at. And that he does not himself understand the real reasons for his misbehavior is not surprising when one sees that the parents who are largely responsible for the molding of his personality do not understand themselves, and never had an unprejudiced plan for his upbringing.

Some evidence is forthcoming which points to the possibility that larger families may be a little more likely to produce delinquents. The correlation is small but enough to arrest attention.[1] It may mean that in larger families a condition approaching that of neglect appears. Perhaps beyond a certain number of children every increase means a reduction in the efficiency of home management. The limit of the capacity of the two parents to manage and influence wisely may have been passed. In this connection it will be recalled[2] that children in families of three or four children have been found happier, and that boys were in such families more amenable to discipline than those of larger or smaller families. Probably, also, an excessive difference between the ages of children and their parents is at times a contributing factor. Elderly parents are rarely as sympathetic with the ways of childhood and youth, and their patience is easily tried. The possibility of a helpful companionship sort of relation with such an age barrier is very slight. One study of forty cases of delinquents compared with an equal number of nondelinquents has revealed a greater difference between the ages of the delinquent boys and their fathers than existed in the nondelinquent group.[3] More such studies are needed.

When domestic inadequacy and parental maladjustment are further complicated by poverty and poor housing and insanitary living conditions the situation is still worse. Then viciousness and indecency are more likely to enter in. Growth under such circumstances is almost inevitably in the direction of asocial and anti-social conduct. Misdemeanors with such a background are easily understood. Reformation with such a background is a vastly more difficult matter because there is little in the habits

[1] Slawson, John, *The Delinquent Boy*, pp. 398-418.
[2] See chapter XII.
[3] Reinhardt, J. M., and Harper, F. V., "Comparison of Environmental Factors of Delinquent and Non-Delinquent Boys," *J. Juv. Res.*, 1931, 15, 271-277.

and attitudes and sentiments and ideals and hopes and desires of such a personality that does not need retraining if the individual is ever to be happily fitted into any other form of life than that in which he has grown up. Healy and Bronner found in their study of four thousand delinquents that not more than 10 percent came from what could be safely termed good homes.[1] The difficulties confronted by every effort to salvage such personalities are so great it is not surprising that some should take refuge in the theory of the "born criminal." But that such personalities often are reformed is equally incontestable.[2]

It is pathetic but true that delinquency does appear in adolescents whose home background lacks all of the defects above described. Consequently one must be familiar with the nature of those environmental influences outside of the family which contribute to delinquent conduct. Even *schools* may at times have to be placed in this classification. This is because the formal school program does not always suit the needs of particular individuals, and the school cannot for lack of funds or understanding leadership or other reasons provide for special needs. The children who are below the average in mental ability cannot compete to their own satisfaction with their associates of higher mental endowment. They must then seek satisfaction of their desire to achieve and to be superior in other ways. They may be rebellious and difficult in school contacts and bullies on the playground. Children of superior mental ability are likely to get their assigned lessons quickly and then seek other forms of entertainment in ways that breed trouble for themselves and others.

Our attention is thus drawn to the leisure time, the *play hours,* of adolescent years and of the childhood years which lie behind them. Where and how these are spent is a matter of first importance in the formation of character. Thrasher in his study of gang life in Chicago has brilliantly demonstrated the distressing effects of life in "interstitial areas." These are the sections of a

---

[1] Their Chicago study gave 5 percent and their Boston study 10.3 percent.
[2] Much of Healy and Bronner's volume, *Delinquents and Criminals; Their Making and Unmaking,* is devoted to the problems and possibilities involved in the salvaging of delinquents. See also a brilliant presentation of work done in the re-education and reclamation of delinquent adolescents by Wm. Healy, A. F. Bronner, E. M. H. Baylor, and J. P. Murphy, *Reconstructing Behavior in Youth,* 1929.

city which are in process of transformation or decay. Often they are sections which were once respectable or even superior residential areas, but growth changes have brought degeneration. They are termed interstitial because they usually lie between the large business districts and the better residential areas, sometimes between good residential areas. Often they are crowded and dirty and unsanitary. Leisure time spent in such streets and alleys and back lots, even though the parents are conscientious and do the best they can for their children, is certain to be spent in association with playmates from vicious homes subject to their degrading influence.

Where the leisure time is spent in physical environments far different from these, in better residential areas, that leisure time if undirected or unguided is a breeder of troublesome behavior. Boys, especially, as they approach pubescent years seek thrilling experiences. If opportunity is not provided for such, opportunities will be found in ways which may be distressing to their parents. It is a most significant fact that the studies of delinquency reveal that an extraordinarily small percent of the delinquents were active members of such social groups as Boy Scouts, Y.M.C.A. and the like. And Thrasher has shown how easily a gang given to delinquent activity can be moralized by leadership into other activities. What they are seeking is interesting activity for their spare time. By supplying this, social welfare organizations may prevent youths from falling into vicious ways.[1]

In recent years there has been much discussion of the possibly degrading influence of attendance at *movies*. Bad as many of the picture shows admittedly are, specialists in the study of delinquency are increasingly cautious in their generalizations about the actual effect which they have upon young people. That there are individual instances here and there of delinquency which can be directly traced to the influence of a moving picture show no one doubts. Cyril Burt thinks the proportion of such

[1] Thrasher, F. M., *The Gang*, Chicago, 1927.
  Aschaffenburg, G., *Crime and Its Repression*. P. 79 reveals with effective graphs the greater frequency of certain crimes in Europe during the week-end holidays.
  Haynes, F. E. *Criminology*, pp. 150-155.
  Reinhardt, J. M., and Harper, F. V., "Comparison of Environmental Factors of Delinquent and Non-Delinquent Boys, *J. Juv. Res.*, 1931, 15, 271-277.

to the number of delinquents very small indeed.[1]   Healy and Bronner could not attribute more than one percent of cases to this cause.[2]   Burt thinks that they do have a very pernicious effect through their building in the youth a totally false conception of what the normal life of maturity is.   They thus create desires for gaiety and excitement rather than for the responsibilities and the quiet routine of living.

Extensive investigations of the opinions of delinquents themselves concerning the place which the movies had in producing their own delinquency support the belief that evil suggestions and misleading information are obtained from the pictures. When compared with non-delinquent groups it is found that delinquents have had more movie experience.   In their autobiographies the delinquents indicate that they got their desire to carry a gun, do a "stick up," etc., from movie presentations of such conduct.   Desires for luxury are aroused which can only be satisfied by theft.   Information on the technique of committing various kinds of crimes is acquired from the movies.   And there are many reports of sexual delinquency attributed to the movies in a variety of ways.[3]

While these opinions of the delinquents themselves are important, they must not be over-estimated because they happen to be autobiographic.   The competency of such young people to make self-analyses is decidedly limited.   The discovery of conduct motivations is a difficult task for the expert.   Consequently the statements made by young delinquents must be taken cautiously. But even after exercising due caution there is enough to justify the assumption that in many individual instances movie presentations are a contributing and corrupting influence.[4]

Many think that the influence of the *gang* is the most significant single factor in the production of delinquency.   The psy-

---

[1] Burt, C., *The Young Delinquent*, pp. 137-146.
[2] Healy, Wm., and Bronner, A. F., *Delinquents and Criminals; Their Making and Unmaking*, p. 181.
[3] The best sources for first-hand information will be found in the following:

Blumer, H., and Hauser, P. M., *Movies, Delinquency and Crime*, New York, 1933.
Mitchell, Alice Miller, *Children and Movies*, Chicago, 1929.

[4] For possible explanations of the effects upon those who see the same bad movies and are not corrupted the reader should see chap. V.

chology of the gang has already been presented,[1] from which it will be recalled that gang life develops normally in adolescent years as a social group coming between the emancipation from the child's original family and the achievement of maturity and the formation of a new family group. It trains in loyalty, in leadership, in cooperative activity, in the development of individual talents and skills, and instills a certain kind of philosophy of life. Normally the gang is of temporary duration. It breaks up as vocational and mating interests achieve dominance. But it may become permanent and professionalized. Some gangs are known to have been in existence for at least thirty years, recruiting new members from year to year. Such professionalized gangs, living by some illicit activity, retain their members into maturity.[2]

It will also be recalled that the gang is not necessarily a delinquent influence. But it may easily become such without proper leadership and in a socially bad environment. Gangs flourish in urban interstitial areas. There the environment supplies a wealth of criminal material for their talk and discussion. The easiest way for them to get the thrills youth seeks is through imitating the activities of the criminals about whom they hear. This brings police opposition and conflict. Gang depredations may lead them into sections of the city a little remote in which some other gang pretends to hold sway and there may be conflict with the other gang. Then reprisals against police or the other gang or both are talked about and planned, and eventually carried out. Each clash and act of depredation leads to another, and so habits and attitudes of an anti-social nature are established.

The life and thought of the delinquent gang leads to the idealization of the criminal. Where guided group life of social organizations of youth leads to the establishment of socially desirable character traits, the unguided group life of the delinquent gang leads in quite the opposite direction. The one idealizes the achievements of those who are moral and socially worthy; the

---

[1] See chap. VIII.

[2] Every student should be familiar with that fascinating study of the gang by F. M. Thrasher, *The Gang*, Chicago, 1927. It will also be helpful to read Puffer, J. A., *The Boy and His Gang*, Boston, 1912.

other sets up an attitude of antagonism toward law and order, toward property rights, and makes the life of the criminal the one most worthy of emulation. That the criminal frequently ends in reformatories or penitentiaries or on the gallows is accepted as an inevitable consequence and apparently with a little thrill of anticipation. When apprehension and commitment come, they are met with a stoical indifference born of the crude philosophy of inescapable fate acquired in the gang.

That adolescent delinquency is commonly social is attested by figures on first offenses in juvenile court records. In Chicago in one year, only 25.6 percent of the boys brought before the juvenile court were alone in committing their offense. In stealing cases only 11 percent were alone.[1]

A factor now thought to be of no inconsiderable significance in the production of delinquent conduct is *encephalitis lethargica* (popularly known as sleeping sickness). To what extent it is influential no one can yet say. Figures for a variety of reasons are not available. Very many case studies, however, have been reported showing something of the nature of the damage done by this disease to the personality. Many of those who survive are seriously demented and hence fall outside of this consideration. Others recover sufficiently to return to school or industrial life, but soon manifest inconsistencies and peculiarities of behavior quite contrary to what had been their nature prior to their illness. They are impulsive, erratic, and unreliable. In quiet conversation they show no loss of knowledge of what is right and wrong, their ideals appear to be unchanged in content, but their ideals and their knowledge of right and wrong now apparently fail to have the same influence upon their conduct as formerly. That which has so frequently been designated in this book as the synthesis of personality patterns appears to be badly weakened if not broken up. Their behavior indicates no loss of functional patterns; but, as a consequence of this disease, these functional patterns manifest a bewildering tendency to respond in a largely isolated manner. Such persons sooner or later are certain to break laws or regulations or conventions sufficiently to make

[1] Shaw, C. R., and McKay, H. D., *Social Factors in Juvenile Delinquency*, Nat. Committee on Law Enforcement, Report No. 13, Washington, Gov't. Ptg. Office, 1931.

their conduct a matter for serious consideration by those who are responsible for them.

Still more serious is the now established fact that there is a considerable number of cases of encephalitis where the disease appears in a sub-acute or very mild form. The sleeping or stupor which ordinarily identifies it may be very brief or not even appear at all. The case may not even get into the hands of a physician. It may be passed over as a bad cold. But from these sub-acute cases the same disturbances of personality and conduct may follow. Identification of such instances is not easy, and many times may never be certain. The excellent behavior history prior to the appearance of these delinquencies may lead one to suspect the possibility of an encephalitic cause; and so may also the absurd, silly, irrational and motiveless nature of the misdemeanors. As the behavior is so queer and inexplicable, it may lead to the suspicion of being an early stage or mild form of schizophrenia (dementia præcox). In any case, medical aid should be sought for interpretation and advice where such a condition is suspected.

How frequently such cases appear in any considerable group of adolescents no one at present can say. Nor is it possible to say what percentage of delinquent cases coming before the courts are so caused. Their existence has not been known for a sufficient number of years and their identification is yet too difficult for statistical studies. But it is easy to understand why such changes of personality could readily get any one into serious trouble. Whether or not such cases will ever recover normal control, the integration of personality which they have lost, is another question which cannot yet be answered with certainty. Many cases need first to be followed through many years. But on general principles it is probable that they should be protected for a few years at least from the tensions and conflicting strains of student life or from any sort of work which demands more control than they have capacity to exercise.[1]

Troublesome forms of behavior, especially such as are de-

[1] Burt, Cyril, *The Young Delinquent*, pp. 258-260.
   Rosanoff, A. J., *Manual of Psychiatry*, 6th ed., Pt. II, chap. XX.
   Strecker, E. A., and Ebaugh, F. G., *Practical Clinical Psychiatry*, pp. 147-154.
See also chap. XVII of this book.

scribed by the terms bad temper, fits of uncontrollable anger, outbursts of violence and the like, may be basically due to some one of the very many forms of *epilepsy*. So many are the kinds of conditions now termed epileptic, many specialists prefer to think in the plural and always speak of "the epilepsies" rather than of epilepsy. The epileptic fit, or paroxysm, known doubtless to most readers, is far from always appearing in cases classifiable as epileptic. Sometimes the seizures are so brief as not to be observed for what they are. They may occur at night and be unobserved. Or they may not exist in some cases at all. This great variety of degrees or forms seriously complicates the problem of interpretation.

Where the seizures are conspicuous and temporarily incapacitating it is necessary to consider the effect upon the personality of the self-knowledge of the condition. An adolescent so afflicted, and the disease often makes its first appearance in adolescent years, is confronted by a peculiar and difficult problem of social adjustment. He may find it difficult to obtain employment or to retain a position after his condition has been discovered by the employer. In school contacts he may feel himself neglected or overlooked or excluded because of his disease. Irritability and resentfulness are as a consequence easily developed. He may easily become rebellious and difficult. Troublesome if not genuinely delinquent conduct may be the consequence.

Much has also been made by some authors over the so-called epileptic personality. There is the possibility that the disease itself has a direct effect upon the personality organization. This is supposed to be especially manifest in a chronic self-centeredness of behavior and of recurrent spells of bad temper and other items which need not be mentioned here.[1] The number of such cases as these in any group of adolescents, unselected or delinquent, is quite small and so as a general social problem it may not be especially significant; but for all who work with adolescent problems the possibility of there being an epileptic back-

[1] For more complete descriptions and bibliographies, see chap. XVII of this book and the following:

Conklin, Edmund S., *Principles of Abnormal Psychology*, pp. 101-111.
Rosanoff, A. J., *Manual of Psychiatry*, Part II, chap. II.
Strecker, E. A.; and Ebaugh, F. G., *Practical Clinical Psychiatry*, pp. 124-132.

ground to such troublesome traits of behavior as these should never be lost sight of. Where they occur and the diagnosis of epilepsy is certain, then the youth needs to be guided into an orientation in life appropriate to the kind of life which he is unfortunately obliged to live.

Sex Differences. The effect of individual differences due to sex upon conduct problems has been subjected to considerable study. From these studies come a few items of sufficient importance to justify inclusion here. In connection with the problem of delinquent gangs the question has often been raised if girls go in *gangs* as well as boys. That there are social groups of girls comparable to those of boys has elsewhere been presented and discussed.[1] But it is apparently also true that genuinely delinquent gangs are far more frequently to be found among boys than among girls. Thrasher, in his study of over thirteen hundred Chicago gangs, says that he found possibly five or six of girls. He thinks that even in the poorer sections of a city girls are sufficiently protected to prevent the development among them of delinquent gang life.

Burt has accumulated material for a *comparison between the offenses committed* by one hundred delinquent boys and a like number of delinquent girls. From this table [2] one may learn that in the groups he studied most sexual offenses were much more frequent in the female group and that stealing, burglary, forgery, and truancy were more frequently male offenses.

Probably the most important of the sex differences for practical problems in the handling of adolescent behavior is that attributable to the *influence of menstruation* (functional periodicity). The general nature of menstruation and its psychological effects has been elsewhere presented.[3] Its relationship here to behavior problems should be noted. Burt [4] found that approximately four percent of his female delinquencies could be directly traced to conduct effects of menstruation. The physiological and psychological features of the period bring on a condition of irritability and lassitude, of tension and fretfulness. In such a state vagaries of conduct are likely. Burt thinks that con-

[1] See chap. VIII.
[2] Burt, C., *The Young Delinquent*, pp. 14-15.
[3] See chap. III.
[4] Burt, C., *The Young Delinquent*, pp. 215-217.

duct problems are more likely to occur in the pre-menstrual stage. Then the mood is more frequently one of excitement. Self-control is weakened. Temper outbreaks appear and sometimes even acts of physical violence. Sex delinquency is more frequently reported at such times. Concerning all this it must be ever kept in mind that there are large individual differences. There are individual differences in the sex drive, differences in the general degree of control, differences in the ideals, differences in the habitual attitudes, and differences in social setting.

Nostalgic Offenses. Because the study of nostalgia has been so thoroughly neglected for many years, scarcely anything is known of the place that homesickness may have in the production of misdemeanors in contemporary adolescence. The older literature relates many instances of serious delinquency, even including such criminal acts as arson and murder, that were attributed to the emotional disturbances of nostalgia.

In these older cases, the offensive action itself appears to have been of a compulsive nature. It was like an hysterical intrusion, quite beyond the control or understanding of the one who committed the act. The delinquent person would be as much distressed as any one after it was all over, and would be quite unable to give any acceptable reason for the action. The person involved would not even know that it was due to homesickness. The nature of the offenses committed is said to have taken the form of destroying what might appear to have been the most serious obstacle to the possibility of returning home; or else it was the sort of action which would in all probability bring about a situation necessitating a return to the home.

There is every reason to believe that nostalgia today, as seen in school and college and camp life, is psychologically quite different in a number of features from the nostalgia cases presented in the older literature. But how these differences may affect the possibility of delinquent conduct is even less known than the degree to which nostalgia is today a factor in misconduct.[1]

[1] For a discussion of the psychology of nostalgia and for references to the more significant literature, see chap. IX. For summary of nostalgic criminal conduct see Gross, Hans, *Criminal Psychology*, pp. 77-78.

CHAPTER XVI

SPECIAL DELINQUENCY PROBLEMS

SEX DELINQUENCY AND PROSTITUTION, STEALING, DISHON-
ESTY, LYING AND CHEATING, SUICIDE, TRUANCY AND WAN-
DERING, ALCOHOLIC INTOXICATION, TORTURE AND MURDER,
DISCOVERING DELINQUENT POTENTIALITY

The preceding chapter concerns causes of delinquency in general. Ordinarily these are given first consideration because it is the purpose of all scientific endeavor to discover uniformities. Much of what has already been presented may be applicable in any particular case; but there has been enough attention given to the interpretation of certain special forms of misconduct to make possible many other suggestions both for interpretation and advice. The more significant of these appear in the following paragraphs.

Sex Delinquencies and Prostitution. Rarely if ever will it be found that any instance of sexual delinquency can be traced to a single cause. It is safe always to assume that the causes are many and complicated. In instances of wayward girls, the nature of the home life should be investigated. Very frequently the influences of a broken home will be found in the background.[1] Sometimes one will discover a history of life in some public institution. Broken homes and institutional life do not provide the best of sources for the acquisition of high and effective ideals. They may rather be the sources of very undesirable ideals. But even though there be no report of broken home life, it is very necessary to investigate the ideals in any given instance. Many case studies have revealed a serious weakness here. Where

[1] A. T. Bingham ("Determinants of Sex Delinquency in Adolescent Girls, Based on Intensive Studies of 500 Cases," *J. Crim. Law and Criminol.*, 1922-23, 13, 494-586) found that both parents were dead in 11.4 percent of her 500 cases, that one parent was dead in 59 percent, and that a step-parent was present in 23 percent.

ideals are low and sordid only a corresponding type of conduct can be expected. As has been presented in greater detail elsewhere,[1] the content of the ideals is largely, although not entirely, dependent upon the environment from which they come. If the associates are vicious, the ideals may be no better and serve as no deterrent to sexual delinquency.

The degree of the intelligence must also be considered, although more as a clue to other factors than as a direct cause in itself. Frequently the intelligence in sex cases will be found below the average, although very far from always.[2] Where the intelligence is low one may properly suspect that this has been an obstacle to the development of effectively high ideals. It may also indicate the probability of a somewhat correspondingly low home and social environment. Possibly also, especially if the intelligence is below the average, one may be justified in suspecting association with poorly developed, or natively defective, capacity for inhibition.

Far more important still must be the consideration of unfulfilled desires in the life of the personality under investigation. There may be a seriously significant history of impulsive efforts, unguided drives or urges, of conflicts and maladjustments. Such should be looked for no matter what the home life and native endowment of intelligence may be. W. I. Thomas, from his experience in the study of about three thousand sexually delinquent girls, says that at the outset the sex passion itself does not have a very large or significant place.[3] He reduces the drives of life to four: the desire for new experience, the desire for security, the desire for response, the desire for recognition. The second of these, that for security, does not function directly in sexual delinquency, but all the others do.

Seeking a new experience, a thrill, especially where life is dreary and the routine of living drab, is a well-known trait of

---

[1] See chap. VI.

[2] Some studies of sexually delinquent girls reveal an average intelligence considerably below the average of unselected groups. W. E. McClure found a median I.Q. of 76 for 161 cases of unmarried mothers ("Intelligence of Unmarried Mothers, II," *Psych. Clinic*, 1931, 20, 154-157); while M. Seagrave after reviewing several studies comes to the conclusion that the intelligence of sexually delinquent girls is not sufficiently below the average to be an important contributing factor ("Causes Underlying Sex Delinquency in Young Girls," *J. Soc. Hygiene*, 1926, 12, 523-529).

[3] Thomas, W. I., *The Unadjusted Girl*, p. 109.

adolescent years. That it should then be often a motivating factor in sexual delinquency is both logical and psychological. Seeking responsiveness in others and to enjoy the enhancement of self which recognition by others brings are also prominent in adolescent years (although of course not confined to those years). These, too, Thomas found to be frequently in the background of careless conduct which led to serious consequences. Sexual delinquency in girls must then be looked upon in most cases as probably not attributable to an uncontrolled urge for sexual satisfaction; but as a means resorted to, sometimes rather reluctantly, for the satisfaction of these other desires of life. It must here, as so often elsewhere, be kept constantly in mind that these desires may suffer blocking and conflict and all the familiar complications of behavior which follow.[1]

What Alfred Adler has termed the will-to-power drive can be perceived as a prominent factor in many instances of sexual delinquency. Doubtless this is quite as prominent a feature in the sexual delinquencies of one sex as of the other. That girls give way to delinquent practices in order to be popular with their associates is frequently reported. Male sex offenders are now and then revealed to be in truth sexually inferior. Their offenses are a manifestation of this will-to-power drive, to convince themselves, if not others, of their own normality and potency. In other cases there are falsely based beliefs in sexual inferiority which lead to similar efforts to convince. While this urge to a consciousness of normality or of power will often be found a factor in sex delinquencies, it must be rarely thought of as the only cause of the offenses. Along with this drive will be found a lack of effort at self-control, too much attention to salacious conversation and reading, and a lack of ideals which leads to inhibition.

There is ample reason also for assuming that one may find now and then in cases of sexual delinquency instances of actual hyperexcitability of sex. Burt reports that he found this factor in 16 percent of two hundred cases studied.[2] For the interpretation of an individual case, however, where hyper-excitability may be

[1] Mrs. Wembridge, in a clever presentation of these problems, gives illuminating instances wherein one or another mechanism plays a leading although not exclusive rôle. Wembridge, Eleanor R., *Other People's Daughters*, Boston, 1926.

[2] Burt. C.. *The Young Delinquent*, p. 413.

safely assumed as a factor, it is also necessary to observe this in its setting with other desires, the efforts to control or the lack of them, the ideals of the individual, and any other factors which may be discoverable. This is as true of one sex as of the other.[1]

Occasionally instances appear in adolescent years of the sex perversions known respectively as *exhibitionism and observationism*. Exhibitionism as used here indicates an indecent display of the physical person. The interpretation of the trait, although much discussed, is not yet entirely clear. Some think it attributable to an uneven development in which habits of infancy or early childhood are carried over into adolescent years. Others contend that exhibitionism need not have anything whatever to do with sex and look upon it as a conditioned reaction established in the early years of life such that pleasurable reactions are best aroused by the consciousness of being the focus of the attention of others.[2] But whether or not exhibitionism be a trait basically apart from sex, it is nevertheless true that in some instances of sexual offenses there seems to be evidence for thinking that the exhibitionism has become complicated with sexual behavior patterns.

Observationism, manifest in the behavior of so-called "peepers" or "peeping Toms," is the counterpart of exhibitionism. The explanation of this is even more vague than that for exhibitionism. It may also be a carry-over from infancy. It may be perverted or exaggerated development of a genuinely sex trait. It may be simply curiosity which has become through the circumstances of a peculiar life-experience complicated with the sexual behavior patterns. Both of these are traits which will be found in many different degrees of intensity or development. Fortunately the more acute forms which result in offensive conduct are comparatively rare.

As a form of sexual delinquency one will occasionally meet instances of *homosexuality*. As this condition has already been presented in detail elsewhere [3] it needs only to be mentioned here as a possibility in the list of sexual offenses.

[1] The following reference provides an instructive study of female sexual delinquency problems:

Kammerer, P. G., *The Unmarried Mother*, Boston, 1923.
[2] See chap. VII.
[3] See chap. XIII.

After a satisfactory interpretation has been reached for any given instance of sexual delinquency, the problem of what to do with the case is somewhat simplified. In so far of course as the matter can be attributed to undesirable habits, reeducation is theoretically possible. Unfortunately, however, the possibility of achieving the desired reeducation is frequently very slight indeed because the environmental factors may not be within control. There may be no practical way of getting the one needing the reeducation into the proper environment. This may be because of family obligations and desires; it may be because of economic factors that cannot be overcome; and it may be for the very simple reason that cooperation of the person herself, or himself, cannot be obtained. If there are unsatisfied desires which deserve proper satisfaction, or conflicts which call for some sort of psychotherapeutic care for their resolution, then again success will depend upon the possibility of obtaining the indispensable cooperation. Frequently the whole matter will resolve itself into the ingenuity of the one responsible, into his ability to counsel and control after he has satisfied himself as to the nature and operation of the various factors which have brought the present undesirable behavior traits about.[1]

Stealing. This constitutes one of the most chronically annoying forms of misdemeanor. Figures on its frequency in reported cases of delinquency give little idea of its prevalence. Many instances of theft probably traceable to some adolescent are never solved; and a very great many more are handled quietly without ever becoming a matter of record for further study. It is especially annoying because it seems as likely to break out in the conduct of those who have been brought up in good homes, where there is ample provision for the needs of the individual and presumably the best of training. Fortunately the motivations, at least a number of them, are now fairly clear. And in many instances the correctness of the interpretation has been proved by removal of the fault through treatment in terms of the motivation believed to be the cause.

[1] It should be observed that Healy and Bronner report a most discouragingly small number of successes in their years of work for this type of case. See their *Delinquents and Criminals; Their Making and Unmaking*, New York, 1926.

Many instances of stealing can be traced to the presence of *ideals which do not prevent*. The ideals may actually be such as to make successful theft a laudable act. Or, the ideals may not be sufficiently developed to be desirably effective. There may be a vague notion that property rights should be respected, but the notion is not sufficiently clear and well established to effect much in the way of control.

Allied to this are the cases wherein the individual fails to perceive that the act of stealing is really wrong. Stealing rides on railroad trains or the casual appropriation of hotel towels, may not be perceived as stealing at all. High school and college boy thefts of street signs, quarantine notices, and a vast number of other equally absurd offenses are apparently not perceived as being really thefts. Rather are they looked upon as amusing acts of daring. Here is an example of what has elsewhere been described as a lack of pervasiveness of the ideal, for such acts not infrequently appear in the behavior of persons who possess very fine ideals indeed. Hall made much of this as a delayed development of a consciousness of the rights of property [1] and thought that it was to be interpreted in terms of the recapitulation of racial development. As the rights of property are a comparatively recent achievement in the evolution of the race, so he thought that individuals did not normally reach that stage of property rights until adolescent years, and then but slowly, with some individuals much slower than others.

Baker, Decker and Hill have, however, well shown by a careful study of two groups, one guilty of stealing and the other not, that the home life of the non-stealers was much more normal, with more intelligent and attentive supervision on the part of the parents.[2] From such homes came boys with better ideals, more pervasively effective ideals, and a better social adjustment. There was no evidence for a racially determined lack of consciousness of property rights.

The normal boy, and to a considerable extent the girl as well, loves a *thrilling experience*. Such are *sought for* in one way or another, perhaps because of the consciousness of power which

[1] Hall, G. Stanley, *Adolescence*, Vol. 1, chap. 5.
[2] Baker, H. J., Decker, F. J., and Hill, A. S., "A Study of Juvenile Theft," *J. Educ. Res.*, 1929, 20, 81-87.

they bring, power over the environment, over others, over nature, or whatever it may be. In fact, so persistent is this seeking of a thrill that if there is no provision for thrilling experiences, the lack seems to operate much as the blocking of a drive. The urge for the thrill will break out in some fashion, perhaps an undesirable one. Many instances of stealing are traceable to nothing more and nothing less than this seeking of a thrill. The boy stealing from the store, thefts of fruit from the farmer's orchard, stealing an auto for the fun of it, are the common instances.

Perhaps this might be better conceived as a manifestation of the will-to-power drive. We ordinarily think of inferiority feelings as due to blocking of this drive, and we find many instances where such stealing offenses are traceable to feelings of inferiority. Tjaden[1] has reported a very informing study of delinquencies in a group of boys of superior mental ability. He found that inferiority troubles were a factor in 42 percent of his cases, but that the source of the inferiority was at the organic level. This suggests the importance of seeking actual physical inferiorities, or imagined physical inferiorities, when stealing appears in a youth of superior mental ability. Other studies have revealed that aggressiveness is definitely a factor in such offenses[2] and this can probably be taken as further support for the above statements concerning the place of thrill seeking and inferiority feelings as motivations for stealing.

Case studies have shown that many instances of stealing are motivated in part by a wish for *money with which to satisfy immediate desires*. In specific cases this may be found complicated directly or indirectly with the desire for a thrill; and certainly will it be found associated with a lack of proper ideals or with ideals which for one reason or another are, temporarily at least, ineffective. The desire at times may become so strong that even very good and ordinarily effective ideals are overwhelmed. Thefts so motivated are often found to be made for the sake of obtaining sufficient money to go to a movie, which may bring a little variety or a bit of thrill into an otherwise drab existence.

---

[1] Tjaden, J. C., *The Causes of Delinquency in Boys of Superior Intelligence*, Univ. of Iowa doctoral dissertation, 1923.

[2] Riddle, E. M., "Stealing as a Form of Aggressive Behavior," *J. Abn. & Soc. Psychol.*, 1927, 22, 40-51, 157-169.

There may be complications with envy and jealousy, resulting in stealing in order that the self may be provided with that which will bring the feeling of being as good as, or better than, some one else. Girls stealing in order to be prettily dressed are examples in point.

Thefts motivated by this desire for money with which to satisfy some need are unhappily far from always associated with genuine poverty. The youth may be for the first time away from home and inexperienced in the management of his affairs on an allowance. He may make such a mess of things as to be in debt and ashamed to appeal to his parents. Such instances present a curious confusion of inhibitions and impulses. Gambling debts appear in this type of case, and sometimes also entanglement with immoral women.

Persons in positions of responsibility are often bewildered by the apparent silliness or lack of motivation for a theft. Where such is the case one should look for the possibility of interpretation in terms of *rebellion*. It has elsewhere been pointed out that parents or guardians [1] sometimes make the mistake of over-provision and over-regulation. The consequence in adolescent years is a delayed development of self-management and self-reliance, an uneven development of the personality. A healthy vigorous growing youth ordinarily rebels against such domination. For a time, by extra pressure, parents may continue to maintain control, except for momentary impulsive acts of rebellion.

It is because these acts of stealing are sudden and impulsive breaks through the barrier of submissive habits that they appear to the casual observer as absurd and inconsistent and without adequate motives. An example of this may be found in the property offenses of the college girl whose mother had always bought her everything she needed, paid all her bills and made every decision for her, serene in the conviction that her mature judgment was better than the daughter's could possibly be. It must also be remembered that such rebellions against parental domination may easily take the form of rebellion against anything which symbolizes the parents, against officials or regula-

[1] See chap. XI.

tions or anybody or anything which manifests that same parent-like tendency to dominate and control.

The *revenge* motive will be found from time to time. Especially is this reported in gang activities. The motive then seems to be revenge against some one who may have reported the gang or one of its members to the authorities, or done something which stands as an obstacle to the purposes of the group. But this motive may be found where there is no gang involved. Where there is no apparent need or desire for the article stolen, it is well to keep the possibility of this revenge motive in mind.

Instances of absurdly unreasonable theft may actually be due to some really *abnormal* or even *pathological condition*. There may be a delayed development of personality integration. The various behavior patterns may be present but not well organized with each other. Such a condition is characterized by very inconsistent and impulsive conduct, and it may be due to some intrinsic defect.[1] Such absurdly impulsive conduct is sometimes also found in conditions of personality following an attack of sleeping sickness (encephalitis lethargica). It must also be kept in mind that alcoholic intoxication first weakens control by the newer and so-called higher inhibitions. Conduct inconsistent with what is known of a given personality may be manifestations of the behavior of that personality when partially disturbed by intoxication.

It is necessary finally to mention the rare condition called *kleptomania*. The popular mind thinks of this as an inherent defect, but there is no justification at present for thinking of the condition so designated as representing a specific disease entity. The kind of stealing called kleptomania is to be thought of rather as a symptom of some psychoneurotic condition, possibly at times psychotic, which may be varied and complicated by a vast number of intrinsic and extrinsic disturbing factors. Some prefer to think of it as a form of constitutional psychopathic inferiority.

The *possibility of salvaging* the personality which has already begun to commit offenses against the property rights of others will depend largely upon social as well as psychological condi-

[1] See section in preceding chapter on constitutional psychopathic inferiority and also in chap. XVII.

tions. Theoretically any case attributable to ineffective ideals, unsatisfied desire for thrill, poverty or lack of money for immediate desires, or rebelliousness associated with uneven development, should be considered as well within the range of possible reeducation. But that is often unhappily limited by the impossibility of controlling the environment. The boy or girl who has been convicted of stealing may be placed upon probation under the guidance and supervision of some highly competent social worker; but if, as is so frequently the case, the boy or girl must go back to the same neighborhood from whence they acquired their bad habits and low ideals, the possibility of any social worker, no matter how competent, effecting a satisfactory reeducation is very slight indeed. If the environment can be satisfactorily controlled, the establishment of better ideals can be achieved as other habits can be established. The matter is resolvable in large part into the psychology of learning.

Where there is an unsatisfied desire for a thrill, for the consciousness at times of an over-coming superiority, much troublesome conduct can be dissipated by providing opportunity for the enjoyment of thrills. Gymnasia, athletic sports, and summer camps, when properly guided, have done this for many boys and girls. The provisions for gaiety and entertainment under moral circumstances have done it for others.

Aside from actual poverty, the instances where lack of money is a motivation for theft are really instances of bad self-management and bad habits, associated often with undeveloped or inadequate ideals, all of which are subject to reeducation if circumstances are within control. The rebelliousness against parental domination presents a condition of personality which is not hopeless, as has been proved many times, but one which is often very disheartening because it is so likely to appear late in adolescent years when there is danger of fixation of the condition into a permanent trait. The parents themselves often constitute a serious obstacle. For the achievement of a successful reorganization there is need for much tact, firmness sometimes to the point of severity, coupled with the development in the individual concerned of a full consciousness of the real nature of the trouble and what must be done to establish self-determined socially desirable conduct.

Where one suspects the possibility of an abnormal or pathological condition behind the stealing, it should be obvious that the best of expert assistance is imperatively needed. Even then, while some changes for the better may be achieved, cure may not be entirely possible.

Dishonesty, Lying, Cheating. The problem of honesty and dishonesty is always complicated by the difficulty of drawing a sharp distinction between the two. Some there are who try to think in terms of a graded scale beginning with mere expressions of fancy, ranging through careless misstatement, and ending with intentional acts to deceive for a selfish purpose. But even that is not without difficulties. There are intentional acts to deceive which are for the protection or happiness of others. Whether or not such should be classed as dishonest is a problem. And there are the many social conventions, widely used and generally understood, which are actually intentional misrepresentations for selfish ends, but which are winked at, condoned, or accepted as necessary rather than dishonest. Along with these must also be placed many practices in retail selling which are accepted as a matter of course. Even pre-pubescent children have been found to some extent conscious of these problems.[1]

This vagueness of social standards concerning honesty means that adolescent problems of dishonesty must be thought of in terms of growth in an environment where both practice and standards are imperfect and often conflicting. An act which one adult looks upon as a serious offense may not be so appraised by another. The behavior of adolescents in these matters will then be found to reflect the inconsistencies of their adult associates, as it will also be found to manifest the familiar instability and immaturity of youthful stages of development.

Practically all studies of dishonesty indicate *selfishness as the basic motive.* This will at once arrest the attention of any student of adolescent ways who has thought much about the progressive socialization which takes place through pubescent and adolescent years. One would suspect that adolescent dishonesty might occasionally reflect this shifting center of loyalty, from the self to the group, the gang, the club, loved ones, and the com-

---

[1] Tudor-Hart, B. E., "Are There Cases in Which Lies are Necessary?" *Ped. Sem.,* 1926, 33, 586-641.

munity; and this is often found to be the case. Dishonesty is resorted to not only for self-protection and advancement but also for the protection or welfare of chums, gang members, and club associates. When the youth refuses to squeal on a chum the adult is often bewildered. He condemns the act and the effort to conceal the culprit; but at the same time he is obliged to admire the loyalty to the welfare of another. Sometimes such protective dishonesty actually involves very high self-sacrifice. In such acts the youth is obviously placing loyalty to a friend above his loyalty to the welfare of the community as a whole. It is another manifestation of the immaturity of his socialization. Children will be found at the other extreme. It is personal gain which comes first with them.[1]

A chronic manifestation of immaturity, selfishness, and confusion of standards appears in *academic cheating*. Many have bewailed the inconsistency of youth in this. They have pointed out that very fine young people, sometimes prominent in religious and moral activities of a school or college, who would never be guilty of dishonesty in money matters, will cheat in quizzes and examinations with apparently no disturbance of their conscience whatsoever. The following figures taken from the extensive study made by Katz and Allport [2] bring out the inconsistencies and the extent of such academic dishonesty vividly:

Percent

Of 2,855 answering, 30.1 say they never cribbed.

Of 2,855 answering, 4.6 admit they crib freely.

Of 3,448 answering, 26.1 think cribbing as bad as lying and cheating.

Of 3,448 answering, 9.7 think cribbing shows defect in character, but one which is not so bad as lying or cheating.

Of 3,448 answering, 21.1 say it is unfair but not immoral.

Of 3,448 answering, 0.7 think a student should take all he can get.

[1] J. B. Maller has published a very thought-provoking study of this in which he has revealed by test methods that children cheat more when the score achieved counted for personal gain than they did when the score achieved counted for the welfare of the group. Such methods should be extended for the study of adolescent years. ("The Measurement of Conflict Between Honesty and Group Loyalty," *J. Educ. Psychol.*, 1932, 23, 187-191.)

[2] Katz, D., and Allport, F. H., *Students' Attitudes*, Syracuse, 1931, chap. 13. (Reproduced by permission.)

Classroom activities are regarded as somehow different from the world outside, an attitude which has behind it a very long history. Many parents of cribbing students have been known to tell stories of their own prowess in such tricks, and not a few continue to look upon such acts as far less reprehensible than a comparable amount of dishonesty in the world beyond the school and campus. Again there is the reflection in adolescent behavior of the conflicting standards and practices of adult life. That academic cheating is ethically wrong can be easily demonstrated; but the standard of the ethically high minded is but one of many presented to, even forced upon, the contemporary adolescent as necessary and desirable. Doubtless the best that can be done is to continue the emphasis upon the ethical standard and to make academic dishonesty as fraught with danger as possible. It has been shown that the more dangerous such acts are the less they are resorted to, from the experimental studies of learning, that one is more likely to act according to the habits established. Surrounding the examination with every protection against the possibility of dishonest acts will at least avoid the establishment of habits of overt acts of dishonesty in this field.[1]

Efforts to control academic dishonesty through the establishment of some form of the so-called honor system have met with varying degrees of success. Some places report the scheme as working very well, while others report lamentable failure. Student groups when allowed to discuss the possibility of introducing the plan have sometimes decided that it is good but that their school is "not yet ready for it." All this can best be interpreted in terms of what has just been presented concerning the immaturity of the adolescent personalities involved, the conflicting standards of the adults of their world, and the many different degrees of development of similarly conflicting standards in themselves.

[1] In addition to the references mentioned above the following will prove useful to any one working on this subject:

Chambers, E. V., "A Study of Dishonesty Among the Students of a Parochial Secondary School," *Ped. Sem.*, 1926, 33, 717-728.
Kelly, F. J., *The American Arts College*, pp. 141-149 on the honor system.
Mathews, C. O., "Bibliography on the Honor System and Academic Honesty in American Schools and Colleges," U. S. Dept. of Interior, *Pamphlet No. 16*, 1930.

Emotional instability or lack of control has been found by more than one investigator to be associated with dishonesty. The dishonest tend to be more suggestible, more impulsive.[1] In chronic cases, one may properly suspect a rather weak personality synthesis and wisely look for other evidences of such a condition.

There is also evidence of some association of dishonesty with *degree of intelligence.* Hartshorne and May in their test results found a negative correlation of —.49 between intelligence and deceit.[2] Slaght, however, failed to find any correlation between untruthfulness and intelligence.[3] Hartshorne and May also state that where school grades are high there is less tendency to cheat. Perhaps all this is merely saying that the bright child does not have the same motivation for cheating because he can get the assigned work so easily. The duller child feels the same pressure to make grades, at least to pass, and is obliged to struggle harder. There is thus more fear of failure and hence it is reasonable to suppose that there may as a consequence be more temptation to cheat.

Both of these studies, by Slaght and by Hartshorne and May, reveal the *influence of the home environment.* The poorer and less cultured the home, the more is deceitfulness found in the children. All this is in harmony with previous discussions of home influence, establishment of ideals, of self-control and the like.

Instances of *pathological lying* will rarely be encountered and yet there seem to be such. When met with they should not be difficult to recognize because of their absurdity. The lying seems to lack the selfish motive. There seems to be an intent to deceive, but the lying itself appears to be utterly purposeless; frequently it is to the immediate and obvious disadvantage of the liar.[4] It has a most irrational appearance. Whether or not it actually is so irrational and purposeless as it appears is not yet

---

[1] Hartshorne, H., and May, M. A., *Studies in Deceit,* Book I, New York, 1928, p. 193.
  Slaght, W. E., *Untruthfulness in Children; Its Conditioning Factors and Its Setting in Child Nature,* Univ. of Iowa, Stud. in Character, 1928, 1, No. 4.
[2] Hartshorne, H., and May, M. A., *Studies in Deceit,* Book I, New York, 1928, pp. 181-189.
[3] Slaght, W. E., *Untruthfulness in Children; Its Conditioning Factors and Its Setting in Child Nature,* Univ. of Iowa, Stud. in Character, 1928, 1, No. 4.
[4] Healy, Wm., *Pathological Lying, Accusation and Swindling,* Boston, 1915.

clear. There may be a very complicated background of conflicts and complexes and distortions of development which if fully known to others would give to the lies a greater appearance of rationality. If this should prove to be the correct interpretation, then the instances of pathological lying would have to be classed as indicative of a schizophrenic or at least a schizoidal (of the nature of dementia præcox) tendency.

Some cases of pathological lying may be of an hysterical nature. But there may actually be a special form of abnormality properly classifiable as pathological lying. In this connection one should also keep in mind that lies of fancy, from the confusion with reality of the products of a very active imagination, may occur in adolescent years as well as in childhood where they are so much better known. There are individuals who are slow to achieve a full differentiation between fantasy and reality, and there are possibly also some persons who never achieve that distinction.[1]

Suicide. Age tables of suicide frequencies indicate a rise through adolescent years, but the frequency per hundred thousand is quite small in comparison with the frequencies for the decades immediately following. Perhaps the most significant feature of these age tables is the consistency with which they report a greater relative frequency of female suicides in adolescent years. This is not found at any other age.[2]

Press reports of adolescent suicides must be read with caution. In 1927, for example, there was popularly supposed to be an epidemic of adolescent suicide. Certainly the press did carry reports that were both distressing and alarming. It is now clear, however, that there was no suicide epidemic in that year. Beeley has collected figures for each year from 1909 to 1928 which prove that the epidemic idea was an illusion. Doubtless the attention of editors was attracted by some few conspicuous cases, and that led to more attention to such adolescent suicides as did occur than was given in other years. Judgments may have been influenced also by the cumulative effect of a gradual increase in the

---

[1] See section on day-dreaming and Bovarism, in chap. X.
[2] Cavan, R. S., *Suicide*, Chicago, 1928, p. 313.
  Frenay, A. D., *The Suicide Problem in the United States*, pp. 78 and 185.

frequency of adolescent suicides; but the actuality of this increase is still open to question.[1]

Thanks to a number of careful studies of the subject the *causes of adolescent suicide* are fairly clear.[2] Many have pointed to a release of inhibitions or change of attitude toward the taking of one's own life. Death thoughts and wishes are known to be very common. Cavan obtained 201 returns to a questionnaire on the subject and found that only 18.9 percent of these claimed that they had never entertained thoughts of suicide or death wishes. Even these may have had such thoughts and wishes but could not recall them or did not report them because of repression. The conversations, study, reading, and thinking of adolescent years bring many changes of attitude, belief and opinion. Religious, philosophical, ethical, and social beliefs undergo no little reconstruction. Often this reconstruction leads to a very different attitude toward suicide. Much of the horror and repulsiveness of the idea may disappear; and the notion of self-extinction as a possible way out, if life should ever become intolerable, may be entertained in a very matter-of-fact manner. Where such an attitude of indifference, or even of passive acceptance, becomes established, there would certainly be little to inhibit a suicidal impulse should the individual meet with some serious crisis in life.

All studies agree upon the existence in suicide cases of some disorganization of the personality. There is either the beginning of some form of insanity, involving emotional depression and the distorted thinking which leads to delusional formation, or there is a psychoneurotic condition characterized by emotional disturbance and a reduction of the capacity for self-control. Something has brought about a confusion of impulses and reaction patterns within the personality. The progressive adjustment to life has been disturbed by circumstances which produce so much

1 Beeley, A. L., "Was There a Suicide 'Wave' Among College Students in 1927?" *Sci. Mo.*, 1932, 35, 66-67.
—— "Juvenile Suicide," *Soc. Service Rev.*, 1929, 3, 35-49.
Cavan, R. S., *Suicide*, pp. 262-266.
Wolfe, W. B., "Adolescent Suicide," *Hygeia*, 1928, 6, 125-127.
2 Aswell, E. C., "Student Suicide," *Forum*, 1927, 77, 696-703.
Beeley, A. L., "Juvenile Suicide," *Soc. Service Rev.*, 1929, 3, 35-49.
Cavan, R. S., *Suicide*. (This book contains an excellent bibliography with references to still more extensive bibliographies of the subject.)
Hall, G. Stanley, *Adolescence*, Vol. 1, pp. 374-385 and Vol. 2, pp. 317-318.

emotional tension that the inhibitions have been fatigued or completely overwhelmed. Of circumstances which are capable of producing such emotional disturbance and confusion of judgment there are not a few.[1]

Perhaps the most significant of these are the troubles over love and sex. Frustrated love affairs, whatever be the cause, are powerfully disturbing experiences for many adolescents. Thoughts of death and thoughts of love have for countless generations been associated together, although the reasons for such an association are not entirely clear. Certainly to many a youth the future appears dark and unattractive and life not worth living when a love affair has gone wrong.

More serious still, from the point of view of frequency in suicide cases, are the instances of distress over sexual delinquency. The necessity for facing a critical and unsympathetic world after an experience of seduction and abandonment is more than many girls have courage for. The greater frequency of female over male suicides in adolescent years is ordinarily attributed to the greater amount of distress over sexual delinquencies. Much of the delinquency may be essentially innocent because of ignorance; but it is none the less, perhaps even more, shocking when the horrible facts of an illegitimate pregnancy or a serious disease are finally realized.

Such troubles create a life situation that often seems hopeless, utterly unsolvable except by the road of complete escape through suicide. But the cases studied indicate that there are yet other stimuli for the escape motive. The necessity of facing life in a hopelessly crippled condition has produced many pathetic cases. Incurable disease has produced others. Knowledge of insanity cases in the family has engendered belief in the certainty of its recurrence with tragic consequences.

Any situation in fact which appears to the youth as promising nothing in life but distress and suffering, or even the impossibility of ever being free to achieve a normal existence and a chance to realize the dreams of youth, is known to stimulate suicidal impulses and to have been a factor in the production of actual suicides. Sometimes situations appear trivial to the adult.

---

[1] See Cavan, R. S., "The Wish Never to Have Been Born," *Amer. J. Sociol.*, 1921, 37, 547-559.

They may be in the form of family troubles which time would normally solve; they may be school adjustment problems which should have been worked out; and sometimes they are found to be problems of vocational adjustment. But it is not how these situations appear to the poised and experienced adult that is important; rather is it the way they are perceived by the youth who is so troubled.[1]

There are also, although much less frequently, instances of suicide wherein the confusion and emotional disturbance involved seem properly attributable to what may be termed an intellectual reconstruction. Sometimes from an over-protected or too sheltered raising conceptions of the actualities of life are acquired which are far from the rugged realities that must eventually be faced. The discovery and the disillusionment which follow bring on depression, hopelessness, and desperate efforts to escape.

Sometimes the reconstruction involves religious beliefs. Here and there are individual adolescents who must go through the normal reconstruction of religious ideas which were acquired in childhood, or in the less critical years of pubescence, without skilled guidance. Stumbling for some then seems inevitable. The notion is developed that all of their old religious beliefs are worthless. They think of themselves as obliged to abandon all former religious affiliations and associations. This brings conflict, disappointment, confusion, distress, and struggle. For them the future looks as hopeless and as unattractive as in the other cases mentioned. To the more tough-minded folk all reconstructions of thought and belief may seem insufficient cause for emotional depression and suicide. But it is necessary to recognize the existence of some more tender-minded youth who feel more deeply about such matters.

Attention must also be drawn to the *threats of suicide* which persons in positions of responsibility occasionally hear. There is

[1] For case descriptions and for examples of the notes left by suicide cases see the following:

Beeley, A. L., "Juvenile Suicide," *Soc. Service Rev.*, 1929, 3, 35-49.
Cavan, R. S., *Suicide*, chap. XI.
Stearns, A. W., "Suicide in Massachusetts," *Ment. Hyg.*, 1921, 5, 752-777 (includes seven adolescent cases).
Wolf, H., "Suicide Notes," *Amer. Mercury*, 1931, 24, 264-272.

a rather widespread notion that people who threaten suicide never commit it; but this is not a safe rule to act on because it is not true. Beeley found in his study of one hundred cases that twenty-two were known to have threatened to commit suicide or to have made earlier attempts. How many make suicidal threats and never carry them out no one knows but certainly there must be many such.

Threats of suicide should always be taken seriously, although not always fearfully. They should be seriously considered because suicidal threats alone are sufficient evidence of a confused and maladjusted personality. One may be convinced that there is little danger of a fatal outcome, but there is nevertheless need for intelligent guidance in order to work out for such a person some sort of adequate adjustment to the disturbing situation. Sometimes one will find behind such threats an ill-considered effort to coerce some one else. One is not surprised to find behind such threats an emotionally over-wrought condition.

There are also instances of suicidal attempts which when carefully examined appear to be lacking in sincerity. They are carried out under circumstances that appear to be better designed for the attracting of attention than for self-destruction. Many hysterical cases do bizarre things apparently for the purpose of attracting attention to themselves. Clumsy but dramatic attempts at suicide of this sort should be, like suicidal threats, looked upon as symptoms of a confusion and emotional conflict seriously requiring analysis, attention, and resolution.

From the foregoing summary of causes the means of prevention follow quite logically. Youth needs a constructive working philosophy of life which is adequate for the crises that must be faced. There should be older and wiser friends to whom a youth feels free to go for counsel in times of stress. Religious and secular education should be such as to make unnecessary the disturbing reconstructions and disillusionments. An attitude of repugnance toward suicidal impulses should be established. Attitudes of loyalty to friends and family and community, and to the higher causes presented by philosophy and religion, are known to prevent quite effectively much consideration of escape from the troubles of this life through self-destruction. Wisely planned instruction in sex hygiene and self-control will prevent some of the troubles known to be causal factors. Many more can be cared for by all and every means that contributes to the progressive social adjustment of growing personalities. By such means will psychoneurotic states of disturbed control be largely reduced.

Whether or not such preventive measures as these can prevent the adolescent suicides now attributed to psychotic (insane) states is not so clear. There is much difference of opinion. But certainly such preventive measures are, so far as is known at present, the very best kind of mental hygiene and constitute the best of that which can be done to prevent the development of psychoses in adolescence.

Truancy, Vagrancy, Wandering. Our knowledge of this familiar trait of pubescent and adolescent years is curiously inadequate. Attention seems to have been given far more to its possible causes and to the contribution which it makes to criminal delinquency, than to the effects of wandering upon the growing personality. In the studies of delinquency, truancy records are prominent. In Burt's studies, truancy as an offense, from school or from home, stands second only to stealing.[1] And it is far more frequently a male than a female offense.

In addition, however, to the delinquency cases of truancy which become matters of court record, there are a vast number of young people who do a considerable amount of wandering. It may not be done in a manner to be classifiable as an offense, although it may cause parents and school authorities no little distress. Boys and young men who are beyond the school age law not infrequently respond to the lure of elsewhere and wander off, sometimes without even telling their parents that they are going. They may unexpectedly leave school or college for no very serious reason, and be gone for a considerable period of time. What percentage of later adolescents wander as hoboes, or "ship out" for foreign ports, no one knows; but certainly the number of those who do so is not small enough to be ignored.

The causes of truancy that becomes a behavior problem have been rather carefully studied. As might be expected, broken homes, or homes that are in one way or another so defective as

[1] Burt, C., *The Young Delinquent*, p. 15.

to maintain little control, are a prominent factor. The New York State Crime Commission[1] made a careful study of 201 chronic delinquent cases in New York City and found that 30 percent had lost one or both parents by death; another 15 percent had homes wrecked by desertion or divorce or separation; and, in addition to these, there were troubles from unemployment, or employment of both parents, or immorality, neglect, and so on. Clark found abnormal conditions in 68.6 percent of the homes.[2]

In an extensive study of 660 runaway boys made by Armstrong, stable home conditions were found in only 55 percent of the cases examined. There was also evidence of other family troubles because these runaway cases came from larger families on the average than do employed boys. There was a larger proportion of only children among them than among employed boys, and there was marked tendency for the runaway to be the oldest child in the family. For about one-half of them there were also reports of nervous habits, temper tantrums, and other indications of instability.[3]

But there must be yet other motivations because even these studies support the common observation that youths who wander sometimes have excellent homes, morally and economically. When instincts were more used for explanatory purposes than they are today, it was the practice to say that such wandering was motivated by a migratory instinct; and this was supported by dissertations on the wandering habits of the race.[4] Perhaps there is such an instinct, but it could also be demonstrated that much of adolescent wandering is also motivated by a curiosity factor, a desire to see and to know more of the world and its ways.

Then, too, there is the youthful seeking of thrill and adven-

---

[1] *A Study of 201 Truants in the New York City Schools*, pp. 285-302 of report submitted in 1927.

[2] Clark, W. W., "A Statistical Study of 102 Truants," *J. of Delinquency*, 1918, 3, 213-235. In this connection see also the comprehensive study by Edith Abbott and S. P. Breckinridge, although concerned rather more with pre-adolescent cases (*Truancy and Non-attendance in the Chicago Schools*, Chicago, 1917).

[3] Armstrong, C. P., *660 Runaway Boys*, Boston, 1932.

[4] For this type of theorizing see the following:

Hall, G. Stanley, *Adolescence*, Vol. 1, pp. 348-349.
Kline, L. W., "Trunacy as Related to the Migratory Instinct," *Ped. Sem.*, 1898, 5, 381-420.

ture. Home and school seem excessively protected and humdrum and monotonous. Just what this seeking a thrill is psychologically we do not know very well. Perhaps it may be in part a
manifestation of that which is termed the will-to-power drive.
The thrilling experience may bring a consciousness of power
which the routine of home or work or school does not produce.
Again there is the probability that not a little of the wandering
of adolescence is motivated by that frequently noted tendency
of youth to rebel against parental domination, and whatever
stands as surrogate for parental control. Elsewhere lures because
of the prospect of complete freedom and self-reliance. There
may be other factors, but something of these is likely to be found
in any given case.

The effects of truancy and wandering are usually presented
from the point of view of the studies of criminality; and the
people who make these studies are profoundly impressed by the
numbers of criminals whose careers seem to have begun in truancy. No doubt that is true; and it is proper to say that truancy
may easily lead into ways that are criminally delinquent. When
away from home, even though the home be poor and lax, the individual feels a release from restraint. Offenses may be committed without regard for public opinion, and without much regard
for the local authorities because in a life of wandering the individual wanderer is usually too far away by the time local authorities begin to act. It is notorious that even moral, law-abiding
folk feel a little less socially responsible when away from their
home community. Such wandering far too often throws the
wanderer into very bad companionships. Life in hobo camps
and jungles is not a place for training in socially desirable ideals.
It is more likely to provide a training in ways of delinquency.

There is always the possibility that habits of wandering may
become established as permanent traits of the personality. This
is no doubt true of the chronic tramps and hoboes of the world.
If there really is a migratory or nomadic instinct, then such habits can be thought of as growing out of the instinct and reinforced by it.

Another effect is obviously the retardation of the educational
process, so far as formal education is concerned. In Clark's study
it was found that only twenty percent of his truancy cases were

at or above the normal school grade for their age.[1] The wan-
derings of older adolescents inevitably take time out of school,
sometimes a year or more at once. Whether such losses are desirable or not must depend largely upon the habits and information acquired during the periods of wandering. Sometimes there
can be no question of their great value.

There are instances where a period of wandering has satisfied
the desire for self-management. There is risk of course when a
youth goes off wandering in such a fashion; but risks are frequently necessary in life. Just because there is the possibility
of delinquency and the acquisition of bad habits one cannot
therefore condemn all wandering. The risk may be exaggerated
by adults, and the chance of great progress in self-reliance and
self-management may far exceed the dangers that are faced.

Some degree of prophylaxis or immunization against wandering may be achieved through provision for adventure and thrills
and travel under partially controlled conditions. No doubt this
is effective in a very large number of cases. If it were not we
should probably have far more truancy and vagrancy than now
exists. But there are likely always to be not only the thoroughly
bad homes which exert no control and even stimulate to truancy,
but also the good homes where there is a surplus of domination
and no proper effort to provide the youth with thrills and opportunities for the development of self-reliance.

Alcoholic Intoxication. It is necessary to consider alcoholic
effects in this section on special problems because of the double
standard existing in present-day society concerning the use of
alcohol as a beverage. There are large numbers of people who
consider any use of alcohol by adolescents as a misdemeanor, and
who would classify any chronic use of it as a serious delinquency.
On the other hand, there are many who look upon a moderate
use of alcohol in about the same way that they look upon the
use of tea or coffee. They have it regularly in their homes, and
themselves introduce their children to its use. Within these
circles the occasional use of alcohol by adolescents would be
taken as a matter of course. They would consider as misde-

[1] Clark, W. W., "A Statistical Study of 102 Truants," *J. of Delinquency,*
1918, 3, 312-335.

meanors only the excessive use of it, and the use of it at improper times and in improper places.

All who are in positions of responsibility for the guidance of youth find themselves confronted by the consequences of this double standard. Some parents insist upon the treatment of any use of alcohol as a serious misconduct, while others consider such treatment extreme and radical and unjustifiably severe. There is also evident in any considerable number of adolescents the consequences of these differences in training. Their standards are frequently confused on the matter and often in consequence rather ineffective. Intolerance is easily established. It is therefore exceedingly difficult to determine upon regulations for youth which will be satisfactory to the parents and public involved; and having determined upon some plan the enforcement of it is certain to appear an imposition to some youth and an unpardonable laxity to others. The world of youth here very well reflects the confusion which exists over similar problems in society at large.

That the use of alcohol does contribute to the performance of misdemeanors must be admitted by every one. It is now well established that alcohol is a depressant to the central nervous system; and it is also well established that the newer and higher functions are the first to be affected. This means that inhibitions are early weakened by the alcohol, that self-control is reduced. Consequently impulses to action are not judged and ordered by the best that is within the individual. His impulses are allowed a progressively freer expression. The emotions are far less controlled. Anger is easily aroused, and when aroused the associated impulses are more likely to find expression. Thus criminal actions of any degree of seriousness are far more likely to be committed under the effects of alcohol.[1]

A number of answers are now available to the question often raised of why adolescents use alcohol at all. Obviously many use it for the same reason that they use tea and coffee, because they grew up in homes where it was so used. Others no doubt follow in their wake because its use appears to give pleasure, adds

[1] For a general consideration of the literature on alcoholic effects see the author's *Principles of Abnormal Psychology*, pp. 365-372. See also Emerson, H., *Alcohol and Man*, New York, 1932.

to the gaiety of life; and, also, because it is so often presented as
the daring, thrilling thing to do. In many adults, drinking can
be traced to an escape motive. There is the impulse to find relief from the troubles of the present through the depressant effects of alcohol. Occasionally that motive may be observed in
adolescent drinking. Hall believed that youth was predominantly seeking whatever gave to the self a feeling of exaltation,
and that the use of alcohol presented an aberrant means of
achieving such feelings.[1] Patrick advocates the explanation of
adult drinking as an artificial means for the achievement of relaxation.[2] He thinks of life today as demanding a high degree
of tension from which the depressant effect of alcohol brings
release, and there do seem to be instances of adolescent drinking
where that theory appears to be the most satisfactory.

It should also be observed that the habit of escaping from the
problems of life by the easy route through drugs of any sort is
one that becomes easier with each repetition; and that after the
escape a return to the disagreeable reality is eventually necessary. During the interval the conditions of life do not change,
and upon his return the one who has sought escape rather than
a straightforward facing of reality is no better equipped for the
struggle. The temptation to escape comes again and is more
easily accepted.

The depressant effect of the habitual use of alcohol cannot be
without its effect upon the progressive establishment of control
through synthesis, which is the normal course of development
of personality in adolescent years. From the point of view of
education and hygiene, every effort must be applied in adolescent
years toward the establishment of organization, adjustment and
control. This means integration and the establishment of inhibitory or controlling functional patterns. The habitual or
even frequent use of a depressant drug would appear to be a
practice the effect of which is directly opposite to the normal, or
the healthiest, course of development. Permitting emotional
and spasmodic impulses uncontrolled expression cannot be an
aid to the development of personality organization; it must open
the way to the commitment of acts which, much as they may be

[1] Hall, G. Stanley, *Adolescence*, Vol. 1, pp. 367-370.
[2] Patrick, G. T. W., *The Psychology of Relaxation*, chap. V.

regretted in sober moments, are likely to stand as a serious handicap to the progress and professional achievement so much desired in youth.

The solution of the problem in individual cases, as well as in the mass, must come through education, through a dissemination of knowledge of the effects of the drugs and the habits involved, and through a clarification of ideals and opinions related to the use of alcohol.

Torture and Murder. Cases of this form of delinquency are fortunately rare, although the amount of publicity which they receive when they do appear is such as possibly to make readers of the daily papers think otherwise. Torturers apparently find an intense pleasure or satisfaction of some sort through the perception of suffering in others brought about by their own efforts. The stories of such cases are as hideous as those told of the treatment of captives by savages. Unfortunately they are not well understood. There is the possibility, attractive to many perhaps because it is easy, to think of such cases as intrinsically or congenitally determined perverts. Ordinarily this assumes that there is a native tendency in all human beings to find pleasure to some extent in the suffering or discomfiture of others. Teasing is a common manifestation of this. In the torture cases this tendency has been, by some cause unknown, developed to an excessive and exaggerated degree. Some have looked upon this as an atavistic form of development.[1]

But there is also the possibility of interpreting such cases in terms of a will-to-power drive which, through some curious pattern of circumstances, has been directed into this method of finding satisfaction. The psychoanalysts look upon such cases as having a highly complicated motivation related to sexual maladjustments. Certainly the normal development of ideals and attitudes toward others and of the control of impulses is lacking. Whether or not there is a possibility of torturer cases being successfully reeducated, reorganized, is not yet clear.

Adolescent murderers are sometimes quite as difficult of interpretation. Ordinarily they are found to be suffering some form of insanity, dementia præcox (schizophrenia), epilepsy, or ex-

[1] Hall, G. Stanley, *Adolescence,* Vol. 1, pp. 358-360.

haustion psychosis. It is necessary of course to distinguish between impulsive homicide and premeditated killing. The impulsive forms may be traceable to psychoneurotic conditions of poor control, to the temporary loss of control through alcoholic intoxication, or to a condition of developing psychosis (insanity).

In instances of premeditated murder, alcoholic and psychoneurotic states can be ruled out as major factors; but there may be an influential psychotic (insane) condition of the personality. Where this condition is such that the ordinary observer can recognize its presence, no serious questions arise, unless perhaps that of why the patient was not cared for and society protected before the tragedy occurred. But there are other instances where the morbidity is not so obvious. Then questions do arise. This has been true of many of the cases of youthful murderers which have attracted so much attention in recent years. Unfortunately most of these have not been thoroughly studied and consequently scientists, as well as the general public, can learn little about them.[1]

Infanticide is occasionally committed by later adolescent women. Here the case studies report uniformly a condition of insanity as the cause.[2] The depleting strains of childbirth and lactation, supplemented perhaps by much anxiety and emotional conflict, will bring on a condition usually called puerperal insanity that may take any one of several forms. There is also the possibility that such strains and conflicts may be the irritating factor which brings out a latent insanity of some other form. Where the puerperal disturbance develops melancholia and delu-

---

[1] For brief notes on a number of these see Milton Mackaye, "Youthful Killers," *Outlook*, 1929, 151, 2-6 and 33-35. The Loeb and Leopold cases were quite thoroughly studied. The details concerning them may be obtained through the following:

Glueck, S. S., "Some of the Implications of the Leopold-Loeb Hearing in Mitigation," *Ment. Hyg.*, 1925, 9, 449-468.
McKernan, M., *The Amazing Crime and Trial of Leopold and Loeb*, Chicago, 1924.
Smith, H., and Fairweather, A., "The Case of Richard Loeb and Nathan Leopold," *J. Ment. Sci.*, 1925, 71, 80-92.
Urstein, M., *Leopold and Loeb*, Chicago, 1924.
(Anon.) "The Crime and Trial of Loeb and Leopold," *J. Abn. & Soc. Psychol.*, 1924, 19, 223-230.
(Various) "The Loeb-Leopold Case," *J. Crim. Law and Criminol.*, 1924, 15, 347-405.
[2] Hopwood, J. S., "Child Murder and Insanity," *J. Ment. Sci.*, 1927, 73, 95-108.

sions of unworthiness, there is danger of both suicidal and homicidal tendencies.   It is probable that by far the larger number of infanticide cases by young mothers occur in this condition.

Discovering Delinquent Potentiality.   Not a little thought has been given in recent years to the problem of discovering delinquent potentiality.   Prevention has been much talked about. A number of tests have been developed, some of them very good as tests, for this purpose.[1]   It must, however, now be clear that the causes of misdemeanors and delinquencies in adolescence are too many and too complicated for a single battery of tests to reveal.   Any youth who is intoxicated may commit a misdemeanor.   Hysterical conditions may develop rapidly in a personality ordinarily quite stable, if suddenly subjected to excessive fatigue and emotional overstrain.   Others of the many causative factors listed may not be discoverable by test methods because they can appear as unanticipated and unanticipatable changes in the circumstances of living.   Nevertheless, much can be done to discover the potentially delinquent, to know in advance who are most likely to be problem cases in any given group.

All that indicates the tendencies to psychoneurotic or psychotic conditions, personal case histories that reveal evidences of chronic bad temper or of encephalitis or of trouble with family discipline or of broken homes or other known significant social factors, tests for honesty, tests for attitudes toward law and order, toward parents, toward suicide, toward ethical standards, and so on,—all such test scores and personal case history studies should reveal much to student and employee supervisors that could be valuably used in the preparation of programs for counsel and guidance looking toward the stabilization and socialization of the personalities involved.   While such methods are now largely in their formative stages, enough has been done to indicate the possibility of achieving much more.   The prospect is really promising.

[1] For an introduction to this extensive literature see the following:

Cady, V. S., *The Estimation of Juvenile Incorrigibility*, J. of Delinquency Monog. No. 2, 1923.

Hartshorne, H., and May, M. A., *Studies in Deceit*, New York, 1928.

Jones, Vernon, "Children's Morals," being chapter 13 of *Handbook of Child Psychology*, edited by Carl Murchison, Worcester, 1931.

Raubenheimer, A. S., *An Experimental Study of Some Behavior Traits of the Potentially Delinquent Boy*, Psychol. Monog., 1925, 34, No. 159.

CHAPTER XVII

ABNORMALITIES OF PERSONALITY ORGANIZATION AND ADJUSTMENT

FATIGUE, ALCOHOL, TOBACCO, CAFFEIN, MORPHINE AND CO-
CAINE, CONSTITUTIONAL PSYCHOPATHIC INFERIORITY, EPI-
LEPSY, PSYCHONEUROSIS, SCHIZOPHRENIA, MANIC-DEPRES-
SIVE PSYCHOSIS, ENCEPHALITIS LETHARGICA, SEXUAL ABNOR-
MALITIES

The best approach to an understanding of the abnormalities of adolescence can be made by way of the concepts of instability and maladjustment. Both of these terms have at times been sadly overworked and sometimes abused. They are nevertheless useful because they designate very real forms of abnormality which are the sources of the more serious disturbances of adolescent development. Both are indicative of conditions prevailing within the personality pattern.

All through the pages of this book adolescence has been considered as a growth period in the molding of personality. The course of personality integration has been outlined and many different factors of influence, extrinsic and intrinsic, have been presented, with their various effects. The same point of view should be held for the consideration of the mental abnormalities of adolescence. As stability, poise, control, are achieved through the development and integration of patterns in the cerebral cortex, so any condition or influence which delays that development, or reduces the effect of such organization as has been achieved, may be expected to produce a condition of relative instability. If the stresses of adolescent years, the struggles to meet social demands and the like, result in accidents or modes of adjustment which are inadequate and inefficient, the inevitable consequence is the building within the personality of patterns which are in serious conflict with other patterns. Whenever these disturbers are activated there is consciousness of inadequacy, conflict, and struggle to get along somehow. Unless some corrective appears, such undesirable patterns may be the cause of an accumulation of maladjustments which distort the personality into abnormal forms. Diseases of inherent or acquired origin, or traceable to combinations of both inherent and acquired effects, may produce genuine abnormalities of personality, both through the disruption or depression of cerebro-cortical control, and through the production of maladjustments and their cumulative effects. Normal growth is to be thought of as change in the direction of stability and adjustment; while the abnormalities of adolescence are to be thought of as disturbances of stability and of adjustment.

The conditions which delay or disturb such growth are many, far too many for any but the specialist in psychopathology to fully comprehend. Even the specialist is obliged to recognize that many of them are still beyond his understanding. But the general nature of many of these disturbing factors can be understood by almost any intelligent person and if the knowledge be cautiously used, it may be of much service.

Prolonged or frequent illness may be a seriously retarding or distorting factor. And it should be ever kept in mind that the effect of such illnesses may be both direct· and indirect. The weakened physical condition may actually delay the development within the cerebral cortex; and it may also bring about delays of development through its provocation of over-protection and coddling by parents and other elders associated. Loss of sleep and fatigue are common adolescent causes of instability and inadequacy. The ingestion of drugs of a number of kinds may in not a few cases be significant factors. Sometimes there seem to be native defects which prevent the full development of normal control. The mild or borderline forms of mental disturbance commonly designated as hysterical and psychasthenic behavior need to be included. And, while fortunately less frequent, it must be recognized that in adolescent abnormalities there will here and there be found instances of insanity. There are psychoses, as the more serious forms of mental disease are technically termed, which often make their first appearance in adolescent years. Sometimes the troublesome behavior of adolescents turns out to be but the early stages of some one of these psychoses. It is of these retarding and distorting conditions and influences that the remainder of this chapter treats.

Fatigue. This is a far more frequent and insidious cause of adolescent abnormality than most adults who are associated with young people are likely to assume. Fatigue states are easily mistaken by the amateur psychologist for something far more serious. The emotional depression which fatigue often brings on may be mistaken for melancholia. The inattention, mind wandering, and erratic behavior may be mistaken for early stages of schizophrenia. What appears to be hysterical or hysteroid behavior may clear up promptly and completely when a rested condition of mind and body is reestablished. Fatigue states appear so frequently in adolescent years that it is a wise rule for the inexperienced, and not a bad rule for the experienced, to think first of fatigue as a possible cause when the behavior of a youth is such as to provoke interpretations in terms of abnormality.

A boy or girl in the teens easily overlooks or ignores the possibilities of fatigue. Some think that being tired is somehow something of which one should be ashamed, as if perhaps it were some relic of childhood which should have been outgrown. Youth is eager and animated. There is a delight in living. Thrills are sought and easily found. Hence life is so interesting that sleep and rest may be neglected. A series of social affairs which appear as honors to the individual, or a number of appointments to committees and offices of various kinds which also appear as honors to be welcomed, in addition to the regular work may actually be far more than a given adolescent is capable of handling without excessive fatigue. But the youth is so thrilled by the honors and the opportunities that a little (sic) thing like fatigue does not enter his thoughts, at least not for long. Caffein or other drugs may be resorted to as aids to keep going. And then when the reaction comes, when fatigue does finally become manifest, there may be distress.

The effects of fatigue upon attitudes and feelings and conduct are now pretty well known. Ordinarily the newer or higher functional patterns are most easily affected. Attention is easily disturbed. Complaints of inability to keep one's mind upon one's work are familiar to the student of fatigue. Recollection is poor—the student complains of being unable to recall material which he had known quite well. There is a growing disinclination to work. All work may be done with an effort. And what work is done is slow and far less efficient. Errors creep in. Errors of judgment appear because of the poverty of recall. Hasty and impulsive actions take the place of a normally good self-control, indicating reduction of cortical control and disturbance of cortical organization. There is much irritability, languor, feelings of inadequacy and even of genuine depression. There may be emotional outbreaks quite inconsistent with the person's reputation for poise. The general pattern of fatigue effects must be expected to vary not a little from individual to individual as the differences in personal background, degree of development, and so on, enter into the picture; but these are the common indications of fatigue. Some of these items may of course be produced by other causes than fatigue. Caution in interpretation of the troubles of any youth must be exercised here as always.

In any consideration of fatigue, the capacity of the human being to compensate for a time by special effort should always be kept in mind. This capacity for temporary compensation not infrequently produces quite remarkable results, and may be correspondingly misleading. Not a few experimental studies of fatigue effects have failed completely because the subjects were able for the period of the test to apply themselves and with effort make as good scores on the tests used as they had done in a rested condition. A youth who has manifested many of the above-mentioned indications of fatigue may startle the adult by appearing soon after in a condition of animation and apparent effectiveness. This does not mean that the fatigue has been eliminated, nor that the fatigue interpretation was mistaken. It is merely an example of the possibility of youth to throw off temporarily the effects of fatigue. The next day the fatigue effects may return in an aggravated degree.

The ordinary causes of fatigue are commonly known. Loss of sleep, sleep of poor quality, and overwork (either physical or mental or both) are the usual causes. But those who have much to do with young people will discover that emotion is also a frequent cause of fatigued states. There may be worry over money matters, or there may be a love affair which is not going well, or there may be family troubles. Anything, in fact, which troubles the youth, and there is much to trouble young people, may be a large contributing factor to a fatigued state. A vicious circle is often set up. The emotional upset disturbs sleep; or the worried youth tries to get along with too little sleep. The loss of sleep adds to the fatigue, and in a fatigued condition the youth is far less able to think effectively. Conscious of his inability to solve his problems a feeling of helplessness creeps upon him. Then the blues or emotional depression comes. He worries about all this and his sleep is still more disturbed. So the circle continues until something happens to break it. Not infrequently it is necessary for friends to step in and help him straighten out his world in order to get him sufficiently rested so that he can do things for himself again. Much emotion is probably also directly fatiguing, as the effort to control it most certainly is.[1]

Alcohol. It is quite necessary that every one who would understand the ways of youth should understand the effects of alcohol upon behavior. Whether one likes to admit it or not, it is a fact that many adolescents use alcoholic beverages to a greater or less degree. One study at least has indicated that the habit of using alcohol was begun by more than a third of the cases investigated prior to the age of twenty.[2] Many are brought up in homes where it is regularly used, and youth not so brought up will sooner or later be thrown into association with those who were. There is strong social prejudice for and against its use. Consequently it constitutes one of the problems which every youth must face and to which some adjustment must be made.

The mental and physical effects of alcohol are fortunately very well established.[3] It is now quite certain that the chief effect of alcohol is upon the central nervous system and that the effect is that of a depressant. With all such drugs the effects are first

---

[1] For more technical material on fatigue see the following:

Offner, Max, *Mental Fatigue*, Baltimore, 1911. (Has an excellent bibliography.)

Renshaw, S., Miller, V. L., and Marquis, D. P., *Children's Sleep*, New York, 1933. (Includes an excellent bibliography.)

[2] Emerson, H., (Ed.), *Alcohol and Man*, New York, 1932.

[3] For an excellent and authoritative summary of these see Emerson, H. (Ed.), *Alcohol and Man.*

upon the higher or more recently acquired functions. Hence control and inhibition first manifest this depressant effect. There have been some studies which seemed to indicate that there is at first a slight stimulation. Others have contested it. But whether or not there be any initial stimulation all agree that the further and larger effects are those of depression.

All of the specific effects of alcohol are but symptoms of this central depressant effect. Inhibitions are released and the person talks too much, and often does things which in more sober moments are regretted. There is a feeling of freedom from restraint. Self-criticism is deadened. There is therefore a dangerous abandon, although at the time it is enjoyed. Conflicts between ideals and lower impulses disappear.[1] Judgment is less acute. If work of any sort is attempted, there is a reduction of efficiency both in the quantity and the quality of the work done. This depressing of the higher functions, associated as it is with certain physiological effects producing sensations of bodily warmth, combines to produce a spurious euphoria or feeling of general well-being. For this reason it is often attractive, especially if there be disagreeable life situations which can by this means be easily escaped for a time. And it must also be evident that the alcohol-user's own judgment of its effects is unreliable, because he will recall the well-being and pleasant freedom and may thus be easily led to think that he can work better when under the effects of small amounts of alcohol. Obviously this has contributed to the popular belief that alcohol is a stimulant, although the systematic studies everywhere reveal that the apparent stimulation is actually due to the removal of control or inhibition.

That there are large individual differences in the matter of alcoholic effects has been well demonstrated. Much of this must depend upon the personality organization involved. Two people may be superficially trained into daily routines that are much alike, but their personal backgrounds and histories may be very different. Then when their ideals and inhibitions are depressed

---

[1] There is thus in alcoholic intoxication much that is similar to the release and freedom of play. This led Professor Patrick to treat the subject as a phase of relaxation. See Patrick, G. T. W., *Psychology of Relaxation*, chap. 5.

by alcohol the differences of background become apparent. The old patterns released in one may be quite different from the old patterns set free in the other. Age differences are also significant. Well-integrated adults are more resistive to intoxication than are children. Adolescents obviously come in between. And, furthermore, it will be recalled that adolescents manifest large individual differences in the degree of organization and integration achieved. For their chronological age some are developmentally much older or younger than others. Hence it must be expected that some adolescents will be much more easily affected by alcohol than others.

It is also noteworthy that emotional excitement and fatigue both may increase or supplement the effects of alcohol. And it will be recalled at once that adolescence is a period of much emotional excitement as well as much fatigue. These are also well-known disturbers of inhibition and control. This explains those instances of apparent intoxication which most observers of youth have noted, where interpretation in terms of alcoholic effect was difficult because of the comparatively small amount of alcohol consumed. But in the light of the knowledge that alcohol and fatigue and emotion all work in the same direction, of reducing control by the higher cerebral organizations, such cases become more intelligible.

For an answer to the question so often raised of why young people should use alcohol at all there are unfortunately no systematic studies to which one may turn with confidence. There is a wealth of speculation and no little acute observation, and it is from such that one must draw answers at present. If these are to be relied upon, there are many motivations for the use of alcohol, any one or more of which may be functioning in any given instance. Some drink for social approval. There is that ever-present desire of youth to feel that others, especially those a little older, welcome their presence and approve their conduct. It might perhaps be better to say that youth fears to be looked upon by those with whom they associate as queer or childish or timid or in any wise unacceptably different. Some apparently drink as a manifestation of rebellion against parental domination or overly strict home discipline.

It has been thought that young people sought through alcohol to achieve a thrill, an enhancement of personal feeling of vigor, and this may be true in some instances. Obviously this interpretation is allied to the escape motive which no doubt prevails in many instances of youthful intoxication. Through the depressant effects of alcohol the youth who is worried about his work or social affairs or what not can easily find relief. He forgets that the relief is but temporary, and that there is an inevitable morning after with realization that life is just as complicated and difficult as before.

No doubt alcohol is often resorted to as a quick means for the breaking down of restraint, and the establishment of freedom in social relations. With the finer inhibitions and judgments deadened, speech flows more easily and the simpler feelings and emotions are more easily stirred.

Even this brief presentation has probably brought to the minds of many readers the fact that the effects of alcohol in youth are in the opposite direction to that of normal growth in adolescence. As has been so often pointed out, adolescence is a period of primary stress upon the future. There is much consciousness of the need to grow up, to be mature, to be adult as soon as possible, of much fear of doing the socially wrong thing, of appearing ridiculous and so on. The goal of adolescent years is the achievement of the control and integration and social adjustment of full maturity. The effects of alcohol are in the opposite direction. The depressant effect of alcohol is first of all upon those sought-for inhibitions, with the consequent release of older patterns which are permitted to find expression in unguided ways. To what extent, if any, the habitual use of alcohol in adolescence retards the development of integration and control little is known, but one may wisely suspect that it might be a seriously retarding factor in the lives of some individual adolescents at least.[1]

Tobacco. Of other drugs there is less to be said. Either they are not so much used in adolescent years or their effects are of

---

[1] For more detailed presentations of alcoholic effects and theories about its use the reader should see in addition to the references mentioned above the following:

Conklin, Edmund S., *Principles of Abnormal Psychology,* pp. 365-372.
Rosanoff, A. J., *Manual of Psychiatry,* chaps. 9 and 10.

less significance. Tobacco, if used to excess in the earlier years of adolescence and especially if the smoke is inhaled, may have seriously retarding effects upon physical development. Throughout adolescence and in normal maturity the use of tobacco increases the pulse rate and makes the heart more susceptible to excitement. The finer coordinated reactions are made less accurate and reliable. A manual tremor often appears. But of mental effects which are directly traceable to the use of tobacco there is little evidence. The best of experimental studies here show but very slight difference between the mental achievements under tobacco and those of a control group without the tobacco effect.[1]

There is a persisting belief that the use of tobacco in adolescence is the cause of both poor scholarship and many forms of delinquency. A number of studies have been reported in which there can be no question that smokers showed a poorer school grade average than the non-smokers.[2] But there is also a high probability that the two are associated because both are traceable to the same cause, rather than that the one is the cause of the other. The boy who has the means and the time and the inclination to loaf is the boy who smokes and neglects his studies. The same may be said of the alleged relationship between tobacco and delinquency. It is more than likely that they are associated rather than that the use of tobacco is the cause of the delinquency.

The student of adolescent behavior problems will do well to recognize also that young people, as well as adults, easily become habituated to certain patterns of stimuli. This is why many find that they can do their best work only while smoking. The presence of the cigarette or pipe or cigar is not a direct cause but merely one of the familiar items in the situation to which their working reactions have become conditioned. Without the cigarette or pipe or cigar, they find it difficult to "settle down" to work, to keep their attention upon the task in hand. They are irritable. Sometimes young people in a fit of extra seriousness,

---

[1] Hull, C. L., *The Influence of Tobacco Smoking on Mental Efficiency,* Psychol. Monog., 1924, 33, No. 3. (Includes an excellent bibliography.) See also the author's *Principles of Abnormal Psychology,* pp. 373-378, and 385-386.
[2] In addition to the references given above, see also Earp, J. R., "Tobacco and Scholarship," *Sci. Mo.,* 1928, 26, 335-337.

very likely just before examination time, will try to abandon the habit of smoking by suddenly stopping altogether. Obviously such is a bad time to "swear off," because the absence of the familiar item makes study more difficult rather than less; and that at a time when everything is needed to improve the mental work done. Perhaps the youth should stop smoking, or reduce the amount; but certainly the change should be made at some period when the irritation incidental to the change will be less disturbing both to himself and his associates.

The current vogue for smoking among adolescent girls has given rise to much comment and not a little wild rumor. If there are sex differences in the effects of the use of tobacco, they are not yet known; and the indications of available evidence are against there being any great sex difference. Probably all that has been said above will apply as well to the girl as to the boy. In the matter of motivation there may be more difference. Perhaps there is a greater influence of rebellion against authority in the girl's smoking than in the boy's, but even that is uncertain. It is a matter of common talk (a very unreliable source of information) that girls who smoke often smoke to excess more frequently than boys. If this is true, it would indicate that the pleasure of the experience is but a small part of the motive; or, what is less likely, that the girl on the average has poorer control than does the boy. Research on sex differences here might prove to be more than usually illuminating.

Caffein is far less a cause of difficulties in adolescent life partly because the use of caffein, either as coffee or in certain popular soda fountain drinks, is not associated with as much social disapproval. There are instances of young people who make excessive use of caffein and become serious behavior problems; but even then the problem is but incidentally one of drug effects. The motivation of the excessive use is by far the more important feature.

Experimental studies of caffein effects are quite inconclusive. The most certain indication from them is the existence of large individual differences in caffein reactions. In small doses, about that to be found in a full cup of coffee, it appears to be slightly stimulating to mental functions; in larger doses it is more clearly a depressant.[1] Mistakes are sometimes made, especially by students facing examinations, for a lack of knowledge of this. Caffein may also produce a misleading feeling of freshness. Probably this is due to a depressant effect upon those processes underlying the feeling of fatigue. Consequently it is easy for young people, or others, by the use of caffein to overwork themselves, or dissipate their store of energy.

When such behavior is found, investigation should promptly be made into the motivation for the excessive use of the caffein. A tangled state of affairs is usually revealed. There may be an ill-advised effort to make up for lost time, to compensate for loss of work through worry or other emotional disturbance. Correction of the difficulty then lies not primarily in advising less use of caffein but in removing the cause.

Morphine and Cocaine. Addiction to the use of the more serious drugs, such as morphine and cocaine, is fortunately far less of a problem than it was twenty-five years ago. But unfortunately it may yet be met from time to time. Careful studies reveal that a very large proportion of drug addicts acquire the habit during adolescent years [2] and of course the question immediately arises of why it should be so.

The effects of drug addiction are complicated and belong properly in a study of pathology, but analysis of cases has revealed that the beginning usually lies either in that characteristic effort of adolescents to be like somebody else, to find approval, to take a dare and get a thrill, or in an effort to escape from a situation which appears to be intolerable. Perhaps a genuinely psychopathic condition of some sort with its weakening of self-control has been developed upon either an hereditary or acquired base or both. Then the impulsive escape through the drug route

[1] Hollingworth, H. L., "The Influence of Caffein on Mental and Motor Efficiency," *Arch. of Psychol.*, 1912, No. 22, 166.
—— "The Influence of Caffein Alkaloid on the Quality and Amount of Sleep," *Amer. J. of Psychol.*, 1912, 23, 89-100.
Lashley, K. S., "The Effects of Strychnine and Caffein upon the Rate of Learning," *Psychobiol.*, 1917, 1, 141-169.
Renshaw, S., Miller, V. L., and Marquis, D. P., *Children's Sleep,* New York, 1933, chap. VIII.
[2] Kolk, L., "Drug Addiction: a Study of Some Medical Cases," *Arch. Neur. & Psychiat.*, 1928, 20, 171-183.
Rosanoff, A. J., *Manual of Psychiatry*, pp. 235 et seq.
Treadway, W. L., "Drug Addiction and Measures for Its Prevention in the United States," *J. Amer. Med. Assoc.*, 1932, 99, 372-379.

is all the easier. The use of alcohol sometimes precedes the use of the more dangerous drugs. Here the course is simple. The alcohol is used because, by its depressant effect, there is temporary release from some trouble or complication of troubles. The alcohol reduces control and in some time of special stress the use of morphine or cocaine or something else is begun as a further means of escape.

The handling of a case of drug addiction even in its early stages will ordinarily require the association of medical skill with the interpretation and guidance which the psychologist can contribute.

Constitutional Psychopathic Inferiority. This is a concept of personality defect or disturbance which seems destined to occupy a much larger place in the thinking of students of adolescent personality problems than it has in the past. The definition is not yet agreed upon, and the cause is unknown; yet there is so much experience with a baffling type of abnormality which does not fit into any of the older categories, students of abnormal behavior problems are being forced into the recognition of a form which is now most frequently designated by this admittedly crude term "constitutional psychopathic inferiority." [1]

The behavior of these cases is characterized especially by its inconsistency and lack of educability. There seems to be a notable lack of balance, a defect of control, and a conspicuous failure to evaluate past conduct with anything like an approximation to the ways of healthier associates. The consequences of acts seem to be recognized but not appreciated. Inconsistencies of conduct appear in annoying ways. There may be disgusting manifestations of meanness associated with most kindly and generous conduct; there may be, and often is, a marked selfishness broken by impulsive acts of a highly altruistic nature. Stealing is frequently reported. Such cases sometimes have the reputation of being kleptomaniacs. Sexual delinquencies of a like impulsive and inconsistent nature also appear in the reports. But there is strangely no correlation of all this with intelligence defect so far as is known. In fact, some are rather inclined to think

---

[1] Not a few other terms will be met: constitutional immorality, psychopathic personality, moral insanity, constitutional psychopathy, socio-path, and even psycho-satipath.

that it is more often associated with high intelligence. Certainly associates are often misled by knowledge of their ability and also by the elaborate and plausible rationalizations which such people so easily and freely develop when confronted by the facts of their misconduct. For rationalization they seem to have an almost characteristic facility. Punishment and discipline have no discoverable effect.

As one reads the descriptions of their conduct one is inclined to think that they are merely cases of delayed development, because so many of their ways are childish. This has frequently attracted attention, and there are those who contend that such is the nature of these cases. They think that some yet undiscovered defect, or complex, or what not, has caused a delay in the development of integration, hence the childishness, and inconsistency of behavior. But, if such were the true nature, time and effort at reeducation should bring improvement. This, however, seems not to be the case. Time and educational efforts have been expended upon them in large measure with only the most disheartening results. They do not respond. Consequently there must be something more involved than merely a delayed development.[1]

The greatest possible caution should be used in the application of this classification. Much harm could be done by any person in authority who should too hastily think that cases of delinquency or chronic trouble-making among their charges were cases of constitutional psychopathic inferiority. Specialists in behavior abnormalities use this classification only when every effort to treat as something less hopeless has failed. It is the current belief, however, of many psychopathologists that many cases of delinquency and drug addiction and of chronic trouble-making are personalities suffering this kind of a defect. Unfortunately there is no method available at present, except this one of slow elimination, by which the presence of this defect can be certainly determined.

The significance of all this to those who are placed in positions of responsibility with adolescents is obvious. While the abnormality may make its appearance in childhood, it is ordinarily

[1] For important relationships of this condition to delinquency problems see discussion in chap. XV.

not recognized until sometime in adolescent years, or even later. Apparently it is one of those defects which becomes manifest as adolescence progresses. If anything can be done to prevent the condition becoming permanent, it must be done before the condition is too well established, which means doing something while adolescence is still in progress. The early reference of such cases to competent psychiatric care is therefore indicated. Even that will often be found difficult, because the persons so affected will not cooperate. The outlook for them at present is not bright; but the subject is attracting more and more attention. Consequently it is safe to hope that a better understanding may come at almost any time.[1]

The Epilepsies. These constitute a group of little understood but nevertheless very important disturbances of personality development in adolescent years. It is estimated that probably not much less than seventy-five percent of the epilepsies make their appearance before the sufferer has reached the age of twenty years. Many of these appear in childhood, but by far the larger number become apparent in adolescence.

The traditional epileptic seizure in which the patient loses consciousness, falls with a fairly widespread rigidity of the skeletal muscles, which soon changes to an irregular contraction and relaxation of these muscles, slowly recovers consciousness, experiences a period of somewhat clouded consciousness and is greatly fatigued, and then gradually regains the normal state, is one which doubtless most students of psychology have seen occasionally. It has been known from very ancient times. But it is now

[1] A good introduction to the literature on this subject may be had through the following:

Bryant, R. H., "The Constitutional Psychopathic Inferior a Menace to Society and a Suggestion for the Disposition of Such Individuals," *Amer. J. Psychiat.*, 1927, 6, 671-689.

Huddleson, J. H., "Connotation of Constitutional Psychopathic Inferiority Without Psychosis," *J. Amer. Med. Assoc.*, 1926, 86, 1960-1964.

Kahn, E., *Psychopathic Personalities*, New Haven, 1931.

Karpman, B., "Psychopathic Individual: a Symposium," *Ment. Hyg.*, 1924, 8, 174-201.

May, J. V., *Mental Diseases*, chap. XVII.

Orbison, T. J., "Constitutional Psychopathic Inferior Personality," *J. Delinq.*, 1926, 10, 428-433.

Strecker, E. A., and Ebaugh, F. G., *Practical Clinical Psychiatry*, chap. XI.

Visher, J. W., "A Study in Constitutional Psychopathic Inferiority," *Ment. Hyg.*, 1922, 6, 729-745.

known that there are a very great many forms of epileptic seizure. In extreme contrast to the above are those which manifest merely a lapse of consciousness. Between these extremes there is every possible gradation and variation of emphasis. And then there are also what is known as epileptic equivalents. Running amok, fits of uncontrollable anger, and ecstatic states are some of the conditions which psychopathologists believe at times properly classifiable as forms of epileptic disturbance.

Some epileptic seizures have many features which may make the distinction from hysteria difficult. Ordinarily, however, the competent physician or psychiatrist can make the distinction. And this differentiation is important. A case of hysteria in school or place of employment must be treated quite otherwise than that which is a clear case of epilepsy. The one may be of no danger to self or associates while the other may be a menace to all.

Whatever the cause and the essential nature of the epilepsies may be, it is quite certain that no one yet knows what they are. There are at least two very diverse modes of thinking about them. Some pathologists look upon epilepsy as at base an organic disturbance, while others think of the seizure as incidental to a distortion of personality of psychogenic origin. Into this controversy, fascinating as it soon becomes, it is impossible to enter here. The heredity problem is almost equally uncertain. Some think that there is a basic defect of personality, others of biochemical processes, which may be inherited and transmitted to future generations. But any careful survey of the studies of epileptic heredity are quite unconvincing for any conclusion other than that the matter is unsettled. One serious confusion for the heredity studies lies in the uncertainty about the nature of epilepsy and of what to classify as such.

The personalities of those disturbed by epileptic seizures usually present certain traits which sometimes have been thought to be characteristic and diagnostic. The epileptic personality is said to be egotistic, sensitive, conceited, emotionally unstable, unadaptable, cruel, lazy, manifesting a very bad temper, and impulsive. Not all of these terms will be found applicable to each case but not a few will be. All of them indicate distortion of mental development which may easily result in problem behavior.

Not much reflection is necessary for any one to realize why many of the traits of the epileptic just mentioned should appear. The youth who must face all the adjustments and social pressures and conflicts of adolescent years with the recurrent experience of the epileptic seizure, and the knowledge that he is epileptic and incurable, faces a life situation far more complicated even than that of the ordinary youth. The problem of finding employment and earning a living is aggravated by the fact of the epilepsy; the normal desires for marriage and a home are blocked by it; the youthful ambitions for social recognition and approval often find in the epilepsy a serious obstacle. That the youth so afflicted should appear at times to be more self-centered than ordinary, that he should rebel at times in a manner to appear bad tempered or cantankerous, could be explained in terms of the conflict between the normal drives or urges and the complicated life situation. There is, however, the additional possibility that the cause of the seizures, whatever it be, may also prevent or delay the normal course of personality integration. Perhaps the seizures themselves may have the effect of weakening the organization. But of the fact that the epileptic youth faces a life situation more complicated and difficult than that of the average youth is the fact for those interested in adolescent welfare to have first in mind. Even a partial solution of that would contribute something to the normalization of the personality development.

For this it is necessary to know that the handicap of the epileptic is not wholly insuperable. Proper medical care can do much to reduce the frequency and the severity of the seizures. For the remaining problems help in the direction of the development of a working philosophy of life will aid much. Assistance in working out the vocational problem will also bring relief, as it brings at least the promise of adjustment. Assisting the afflicted youth to a full understanding of his own condition and of the attitudes of others toward himself is ordinarily recommended. And the knowledge that many have lived, even to distinguished achievement, long and useful lives in spite of their epilepsy might be somewhat consoling if not genuinely inspiring.[1] Per-

[1] The list of the great who have been, or are by some thought to have been, epileptic includes Napoleon, Molière, Julius Cæsar, Peter the Great, Mohammed, Swift, Dostoyevsky, and St. Paul.

haps a little more protection than is wise for the average healthy youth may here be necessary. All are seeking security, but the epileptic youth may often discover the prospect of finding security distressingly difficult. Consequently it is not surprising to find psychiatrists saying that epileptics often get on best in life situations which are well routinized, where conditions are standardized. There is then not quite so much responsibility thrown upon the afflicted youth himself.[1]

Psychoneurosis. By this term is designated a large group of allied abnormalities of behavior which appear frequently in adolescent years. They are in general caused by disturbances of organization or control on the one hand, and an over-excitation of some or many emotions on the other. Adolescence, with its many emotional tensions and its immaturity of control development, is thus a time of life when psychoneurotic disturbances can easily appear. They are to be thought of as purely functional in nature and quite without any organic defect. They may be produced in the healthiest of youths, but they are more likely to appear in the less healthy and more nervous. There is a possibility that some persons are predisposed to them by an intrinsically determined weakness, but of this psychopathologists are none too sure.

Ordinarily the psychoneuroses are divided for convenience of thinking into two groups—the hysterias and the psychasthenias. And in each of these there are many forms. All, however, have certain basic similarities which may not appear to the casual observer but which upon careful study do become evident. The lack of organic defect is one similarity; imperfection of control is another; emotionally driven intrusions into consciousness constitute another. Others can be noted but must be left to more technical presentations.[2]

---

[1] For general presentations of the epilepsy problems see:

Conklin, Edmund S., *Principles of Abnormal Psychology*, pp. 101-111.
Lennox, W. G., and Cobb, S., *Epilepsy*, Baltimore, 1928.
May, J. V., *Mental Diseases*, chap. 15.
Rosanoff, A. J., *Manual of Psychiatry*, pp. 90 et seq.
[2] Bagby, English, *Psychology of Personality*.
    Conklin, Edmund S., *Principles of Abnormal Psychology*, chaps. 6, 7.
    Fox, C. D., *Psychopathology of Hysteria*.
    Janet, P., *Major Symptoms of Hysteria*.
    Strecker, E. A., and Ebaugh, F. G., *Practical Clinical Psychiatry*, chap. 10.

The best-known form of hysteria is "hysterics," and it presents a good example of the general nature of all forms. When carefully examined it will be seen to be the uncontrolled expression of a more or less complicated mass of emotional excitement. The person so disturbed has been excited until control has been overcome. Often the control has first been worn down by the fatigue. Because this does not always take the form of uncontrolled laughing and crying as in "hysterics," it is better to think of the "hysterics" as but one form of an hysterical emotional convulsive seizure. Such cases, as most people have discovered, can as a rule be readily handled by startling them into some degree of cortical domination and then providing both rest and freedom from the emotionally exciting situation.

The other forms of hysteria will be met from time to time, although far less frequently. Sometimes there is an hysterical paralysis of a limb or some group of muscles which identifies itself by the patient's lack of distress over it and by the discovery that the functioning of the limb is still intact in sleep. To find a paralyzed limb perfectly used when the possessor is asleep or half asleep is both startling and convincing. Then there are the hysterical anesthesias, areas of the body which are apparently insensitive to pain stimulation, or to any sensory stimulation. These will be found variable in location and extent and not to conform to the distribution of the sensory nerves. Sometimes the hysterical disturbance takes the form of a muscular tic, in which some small group of muscles contracts quite regularly. It may be a twitching of the arm or hand or side of the face or almost any mobile portion of the body. This takes place apart from the subject's personal consciousness and will disappear when attention is called to it, only to reappear when attention moves to other matters. Again the hysteria may take the form of a continuous contraction of some group of muscles, pulling the head to one side or twisting the body, for example.

There are some other forms of hysteria with which the student of adolescence should be familiar, although they will not be seen as often as those just described. Instances are reported of the hysteria taking the form of a fugue. In such the subject is apparently dominated by an uncontrolled urge to escape. The subject of the fugue will disappear suddenly and wander off, perhaps even for several days, acting rather strangely, and then come to himself with a memory only for those events prior to the advent of the fugue.[1] Perhaps the least frequent of all the hysterias is the hysterical somnambulism. This must not be confused with the nocturnal somnambulism, although nocturnal somnambulism (sleepwalking) is usually an indication of weakened control or of excessive emotional excitement. It is an intrusion of what looks quite like sleepwalking into the affairs of waking life. The business of the day is suddenly interrupted by the acting out of some episode, after the conclusion of which the subject either repeats it or forgets all about it, and promptly thereafter takes up the affairs of the day where they were left off as though nothing had happened.

Psychasthenic phenomena indicate the loss of control, although in these the subject is fully aware of his inability and is distressed by it. In this group are the obsessions, in which annoying and disturbing ideas persist in consciousness. It also includes the phobias, morbid uncontrollable fears of open places or of closed places, of bridges, of railroads, or almost anything, in fact. Sometimes this uncontrollable process takes the form of an impulse to some admittedly absurd and unnecessary action, a compulsive act as it is technically termed. The subject experiences the uncontrollable impulse to touch something, wash the hands, to enter a door always with the same foot first, or something equally annoying and absurd. There are also psychasthenic tics which appear only when the subject thinks of them and fears that they will appear. Distraction of attention away from them causes them to subside and even to disappear for the time being.

Neurasthenia may be of a psychasthenic nature. Neurasthenia may be produced by overwork and is a condition of greatly reduced functional capacity. The subject can do little work, is too easily fatigued, is often depressed, is hyperesthetic (responding too easily to any and every sensory stimulation), is irritable, presenting in fact the general picture of both weakened control and reduced ability to function. But this condition may also be of a

[1] All cases of wandering with loss of memory must not be thought of as hysterias. They may be epileptic or they may be a form of disturbance known as Korsakoff's syndrome, which is usually of alcoholic origin.

psychasthenic nature. The subject may suffer an obsession of inability to work rather than an actual exhaustion, and the other symptoms be but incidental to the general state of psychasthenia.

The interpretation of the psychoneuroses is far less simple than has been indicated above. There is to be sure the weakening of control, and there are the functional patterns activated beyond or outside of the control of the personality integration; but this is far from being the whole story. The particular form and symptoms must be accounted for and this calls for an elaborate and skilled study of the personal history. In general it is found that these cases present complications of development by the effects of unhappy memories, conflicts between sexual impulses and ideals, misunderstandings of the nature of sexuality, or conflicts between other impulses and ideals which cause the person chronic fear that the undesirable may break loose in some fashion. The individual psychoneurotic symptoms in the light of the personal history become but evidences of an inadequate effort to meet the situations of life in spite of internal conflicts. The repressed or dissociated material intrudes and disturbs every effort to achieve a normal adjustment to life. They are thus essentially growth disturbances or distortions.

One may think of these cases as probably curable by skilled reeducation. Often this requires the knowledge and training of a skilled neuropsychiatrist; but there are instances which clear up readily as a consequence of guidance and counsel on the part of some older person in whom the afflicted youth has full confidence. Sometimes the cause can be readily discovered, and the trouble straightened out by assisting the youth to a complete understanding of the cause and of its relation to his present troubles. It may be the lingering influence of an old family trouble of which he is ashamed; there may be some past delinquency which is being fearfully concealed; there may be some sexual shock behind it all; there may be inferiority complexes which need facing and reeducation. These are but suggestions of the sort of disturbance which may be at the root of psychoneurotic troubles. Any given case may easily have in the background something quite other than these mentioned, but it will be something which is causing a serious conflict within the personality organization.

In studying any instance of such psychoneurotic distortion of personality development, the observer should keep in mind the possibility of being misled in any one of a number of ways. The life story may be badly distorted through the inclusion of what has actually been the content of fantasy thinking rather than actual social experience, and this quite without any intent to deceive. There may appear what is known as defense mechanisms. These may be of many forms, but always lead the investigator away from the truth. Sometimes the defense mechanism appears in the form of a very pleasurable explanation offered by the subject, but which, although plausible, leaves the investigator quite helpless. This is known as a rationalization. Another is the projection. In this defense the concealed impulses of the subject are projected upon other persons, other persons are accused of various acts or intentions of a dishonorable nature, when as a matter of fact they are but the repressed desires of the subject of the psychoneurosis. Highly trained experts are not infrequently led astray by these falsifications and defense mechanisms. They are characteristic of the psychoneurotic.

Schizophrenia (dementia præcox). Under the earlier name, dementia præcox, this condition was long known as the insanity of youth. While this is one of the most common forms of mental disease and does appear in a large proportion of cases in adolescent years, it is no longer thought of as peculiarly an adolescent disease. About one-half of the cases studied have had their onset after the achievement of adulthood, and in the last few years some instances of what appears to be the same condition have been reported as appearing even in the earlier years of childhood (dementia præcossisima). For these reasons, many now prefer to use the term schizophrenia for its designation; but the student should be equally familiar with both the older and the newer designations, because both appear so frequently in the literature of the subject.

Any brief description of this disease form is certain to be inadequate, and possibly misleading; nevertheless there are certain features or symptoms which do appear with a fair degree of regularity. These can be safely mentioned, if the student will keep in mind that any one of a vast number of variations and combinations may be met with in actual contacts with the disease.

The lack of normal emotional and feeling reactions to the situations of everyday life is usually evident. There is an indifference amounting often to apathy. Sometimes the observer will note emotional reactions but of a highly incongruous nature. That which should amuse appears to cause sorrow, and the like. Delusions are usually discoverable. These may be of persecutory, greatness, or other form. Hallucinations also are ordinarily present. The behavior may be silly and incomprehensible. The patient may be willing to sit about doing nothing, or perhaps content with a world of day-dreams. To the normal mind the behavior of the schizophrene is peculiarly incomprehensible and irrational. Frequently there is resistiveness and negativism. Some psychiatrists like to designate such persons as having a "shut-in" personality, and that term does very well characterize some of them.

The onset may be slow or rapid. In the former case, the associates gradually become aware that the afflicted youth is not normal, is characterized as queer, as indifferent, uncooperative, preferring to be alone, and perhaps the possessor of strange beliefs. The indifference may first appear in a loss of interest or care for the personal appearance. Sometimes the onset is rapid, and, when so, the changes are promptly observed by associates because of the contrast with what the person has formerly been. Eccentricity of behavior marks them immediately.

It is customary among students of psychopathology to think of these cases as falling into four groups, although there are many which are to be so classified only with much hesitation. If delusional formations are the dominant and outstanding feature they are termed paranoid schizophrenia; if the impulsive, eccentric, silly behavior is the dominant feature, they are termed hebephrenic schizophrenia; if the resistiveness, the negativism, the shut-in features are most prominent, then they are termed catatonic schizophrenia. Sometimes the apathy and inactivity are about all that is discoverable. If there be delusions and hallucinations, they cannot be discovered because of the lack of response to the examiner. In such instances it is customary to term them simple schizophrenias, or simple dementias.

The essential nature of the disease is not known. The behavior leads the casual observer to think at once that there must be some progressive change taking place in the brain tissue. There are psychopathologists who believe this to be true. But so far post-mortem examinations have failed to demonstrate organic changes which can be positively accepted as causes of the mental condition. There are other psychopathologists who contend that the disease is wholly psychogenic in origin and that whatever physical changes are discovered are but the consequence of the altered functional processes. It is thus evident that the student of genetic psychology must take the controversy as it stands and suspend his judgment until more reliable interpretations are available.

The older textbooks of psychiatry state that except for periods of remission of symptoms during the early months of the disease it is a condition without hope for recovery. Today the attitude of psychiatrists toward the prognosis is undergoing a change. Many cases do seem to be cured, especially if they are caught and subjected to re-training early in the course of the disturbance. Many are, however, neglected until it is too late; and there are not yet many psychiatrists sufficiently skilled to do the type of re-training necessary. To what extent heredity hinders recovery, as well as to what extent it may be causative, remains an unsolved problem.

Those who are in positions of responsibility need to use their knowledge of these abnormalities with caution. It is easy to make mistakes and mistakes are often freighted with very serious consequences. While it is wise that schizophrenias be early recognized and provided with proper care, it is also well to know that there are near-schizophrenic conditions which are easily confused with the genuine. There is what is known as the schizophrenic episodes, a period of comparatively short duration in which the youth so disturbed manifests what certainly looks like the onset of a true schizophrenia, but which clears and disappears without recurrence. The lack of proper nutrition is known to have produced behavior mistaken for dementia. Instances are reported of students striving to get an education without adequate funds, who have so starved themselves as to bring on this misleading condition of mental disturbance. Fatigue to the point of exhaustion may also be a complication in such instances. Rest and proper feeding will soon clear away the trouble, if fatigue and hunger be the only cause.

Then, too, there are the little understood conditions known as schizothymia and the schizoid personalities. There are personalities so organized that they are asocial, suspicious, apparently unresponsive and negative. Such persons make one suspect at first the possibility of their becoming eventually genuine cases of schizophrenia, but they never do. When they are chronically close to the borderline of a pathological condition they are classed as schizoidal personalities; when they are not so much like the pathological cases, merely standing out in their social setting as more than ordinarily characterized by these traits they are often classed as schizothymic personalities.[1] It is frequently assumed among students of personality that such persons as these will, if they should become mentally diseased, be more likely to develop schizophrenia than any other form of psychosis. While this appears to be logical, there is yet no systematic study by which the generalization can be safely supported.[2]

Manic-depressive Psychosis. Observers of adolescence will occasionally see disturbances of personality organization such as to present the appearance of a manic-depressive psychosis, rather more often perhaps in the depressed phase than in the manic. Such a diagnosis should, however, be made only after careful observation, and at best with the guidance of one trained in psychiatry, because depressed states in adolescence may be but a melancholy mood, a fatigued state, or a psychasthenic condition. Genuine cases of manic-depressive psychosis, however, do appear in adolescent years.

This is essentially a disturbance of emotional behavior, and whatever distortions of thinking appear are but incidental to the emotions and do not indicate any intellectual deterioration. In the depressed phase, especially, there is often a recurrent fear that there may be a permanent impairment of the intelligence and of

[1] For a full presentation of this scheme of personality type classification, the reader should see Kretschmer, E., *Physique and Character.*
[2] An introduction to the literature of schizophrenia may be found through the following:

Conklin, Edmund S., *Principles of Abnormal Psychology*, pp. 80-90.
May, J. V., *Mental Diseases*, chap. 13.
Rosanoff, A. J., *Manual of Psychiatry*, Part II, chap. 3.
Strecker, E. A., and Ebaugh, F. G., *Practical Clinical Psychiatry*, chap. 8.

the cognitive processes, but for this fear there is no justification. When the emotional disturbance has passed the mental functions are found to be uninjured. As the name implies, the psychosis may appear in either the exalted phase or the depressed. To the novice these appear strikingly different; but to the trained observer there are many psychological similarities. There is in both a limitation of the range of thinking; in both there is a certain chronicity or persistence of certain ideas; and in both the more extreme degrees manifest a distinct loss of self-control. Frequently the same patient will be at one time depressed and at another time elated. Sometimes these follow each other in a regular cycle; sometimes both phases appear with no regularity of alternation; sometimes only one phase will appear and that at a fairly regular rate of recurrence. In the excited or elated phase there is marked euphoria, a self-exaltation, a rapidity of thinking and action, and usually an anger response pattern that is too easily aroused and badly controlled. The depressed phase presents the familiar appearance of melancholia, sometimes to an extreme degree, although far from always so. The patient is very unhappy, cries easily, moves slowly and believes the condition hopeless, and whatever is thought about is interpreted in a lugubrious manner. The suffering which those in even a mild degree of depression experience is easily under-estimated by a healthy youth or adult.

The nature of this disease is unfortunately also not well known. Post-mortem examinations do not reveal any explanatory changes of brain tissue. The known close relationship between emotional reactions and endocrine functioning makes students of physiology and psychology both think that the explanation must be found in some disturbance of the endocrine pattern; but the nature of that disturbance, if it exists, has not yet been established.

McDougall believes that the condition is basically due to a disturbance of or defective development of the self-regarding sentiment, which for him is the master sentiment of the personality. And, as that sentiment is supposed to involve primarily the positive and negative self feelings (elation and inferiority), a disturbance or defect might permit one or the other to react excessively. Others have worked out psychogenetic interpretations in terms of psychoanalytic thinking. But explanations are still in the realm of speculation.

When a suspected manic-depressive condition does appear in adolescent years, the best obtainable medical and psychiatric counsel should be sought. The prognosis is always good for a recovery from the depressed or elated condition present at the time; but if it be a true manic-depressive psychosis there is always the possibility of its recurrence. Everything possible should be done to prevent the establishment of the condition as a permanent feature of the personality. As depressed states sometimes result in suicide such a possibility must be kept in mind and proper precautions taken.

While all mention of psychological types must be made today with the greatest of caution, because of our ignorance concerning them, nevertheless the student of adolescent behavior should know that there are personalities which in many features so resemble the manic-depressive psychosis as to have led to their characterization in terms of that disease. They are known as the cyclothymic and the cycloid personalities.[1] Persons so classified live on a wider emotional scale than do most people. When they are happy they are much happier, and when they are blue they are bluer than the rest. They seem to run to emotional extremes. If this condition does not differ too much from that of the more placid person, they are termed cyclothymic, but if the condition seriously approximates the abnormal then they are termed cycloid. The notion is current that should either of these forms ever suffer a genuine mental disease, it would be most likely that of the manic-depressive psychosis; but the notion is yet without adequate verification. The importance of all this typological thinking to the student of adolescent behavior problems lies in the possibility that adolescent development brings out into full establishment type peculiarities which have been of very early or perhaps intrinsic determination.[2]

[1] For full presentation see Kretschmer, E., *Physique and Character*.

[2] An introduction to the technical literature on the manic-depressive psychosis may be had through the following:

Conklin, Edmund S., *Principles of Abnormal Psychology*, pp. 93-101.
May, J. V., *Mental Diseases*, Part II, chap. XI.
Rosanoff, A. J., *Manual of Psychiatry*, Part II, chap. IV.
Strecker, E. A., and Ebaugh, F. G., *Practical Clinical Psychiatry*, chap. VI.

Encephalitis lethargica. This disease is also termed epidemic encephalitis and is popularly called sleeping sickness.[1] The disease itself cannot be described here. It is a purely medical problem. But the after-effects of the disease frequently become a troublesome psychological problem. Of those who recover sufficiently to return to the ordinary routine of living not a few manifest serious disturbances of personality. There appears to be no loss of intelligence but a marked deterioration of personality organization. They quickly become behavior problems. They are impulsive and erratic, cantankerous and antisocial, frequently delinquency cases, often appearing like children with the powers of later adolescent or adult degrees of development. It often seems as though through the ravages of the disease these persons had lost the effects of home and school disciplinary training of many years.

Whether or not such cases can be re-trained entirely is still an open question, but certainly re-training is what they obviously need. They must be taught again to live according to the ways of the society in which they are placed. They have to be looked upon as children in organization and patiently but firmly subjected to constant supervision and systematic discipline.

It should also be known that without doubt there are many cases of encephalitis lethargica of a mild or subacute form which do not manifest sleep states or phases, but which do unfortunately have the same disintegrating effects upon the personality organization. So, in instances of persistent erratic and troublesome behavior in adolescent years, one should look for the possibility of an encephalitic disturbance as a cause—not forgetting of course the possibility also of the case being a constitutional psychopath.[2]

Sexual abnormalities. These always constitute a troublesome phase of adolescence. The interpretation of sexual misbehavior in adolescent years necessitates having at one's command a familiarity with practically all phases of adolescent psychology and

[1] Not to be confused with the African sleeping sickness.
[2] The literature on encephalitis lethargica is now incredibly vast, although not yet well precipitated into book form. A useful introduction will be found through the following:

Rosanoff, A. J., *Manual of Psychiatry*, Part II, chap. XX.
Strecker, E. A., and Ebaugh, F. G., *Practical Clinical Psychiatry*, pp. 147-154.

of its psychopathology. A single instance of sexual abnormality which on the surface appears quite like another instance may be very differently motivated. Consequently general statements are impossible, unless perhaps they are so general as to be of little value.

Much sexual misbehavior is a matter of immaturity and poor ideals, rebellion, and poor judgment.[1] But there are instances of sexual misconduct which reveal a condition approximating the abnormal if not genuinely pathological. The control of proscribed modes of expression may have been weakened by alcohol or other drugs, or even by fatigue. Control may be weak because personality development has taken the form of a constitutional psychopathic inferior; or the ability to control may have been lost or broken up by an attack of encephalitis. The misconduct may have been a part of some form of epileptic disturbance. It may have been due to a psychoneurotic condition. And it may also be incidental to the distortions of an early stage of schizophrenia. All these conditions and every possible phase of them must be kept in mind while working on the interpretation of any given instance of serious sexual misconduct.

The sexual abnormalities known as exhibitionism, investigationism, nymphomania, satyriasis, fetichism, sadism, masochism, homosexuality, autoerotism and the rest are to be thought of when they are met in adolescent years as attributable to some disturbance of normal development or social adjustment. They are to be taken as individual instances and their causation traced out in terms of growth changes and the influences which disturb and distort. They may be related to over-protection, to fixations (hence an unevenness of development), to psychoneurotic conditions of some sort, possibly to schizophrenia or to the after-effects of encephalitis, or perhaps to the emergence of a psychopathic personality. They may be highly complicated and resistive to reeducational procedures; and they may prove to be very simple and quite responsive to training.

Finally it must be noted that the abnormalities of development here presented may easily occur in combinations. That this still further entangles the way for those who would understand adolescent behavior is unfortunate but nevertheless true. Hysteri-

[1] See chapters on delinquency.

cal phenomena may appear with epilepsy, in a constitutional psychopathic personality, in combination actually with any other abnormalities mentioned. Schizophrenic abnormalities may manifest some of the features of a manic-depressive psychosis and vice versa. Fatigue and drug effects may be combined, and both may appear with psychoneurotic or some form of psychotic disturbance. When the possibilities of distortion and disturbance of normal growth changes are fully canvassed, they are always found to be distressingly many and intricate. Fortunately, however, those which are the most frequent are not so difficult nor so complicated. And it should never be forgotten that a huge proportion of the misconducts and apparent abnormalities of development are ironed out by the forces of growth and the accidents of living. The "give and take" of life, the "rough and tumble" of living, frequently serve as cures for the disturbances of development as well as a cause.

INDEX

Abbott, Edith, 390
Ability, and vocational choice, 112
Abnormalities, Chap. XVII
Academic cheating, 381
Acceleration, periods of, in growth, 19, 20
Achilles, P. S., 32
Ackerson, Luton, 223, 349, 353
Active sympathy, in family relationship, 249
Activity, periods of special, 8
Adaptability, and homesickness, 210
Additon, H., 98
Adler, Alfred, 196, 372
Adolescence, definition of, 1
Adults, ideals in, 122; social pressures, 233
Adventure, seeking, 82
Aikins, H. A., 50, 204
Alberty, H. B., 111
Alcohol, age differences in effects of, 404; depressant effect of, 393, 394, 403; effects of, in general, 402; escape motive, 394; seeking thrill, 405; self-control, effect on, 313; stimulating effect of, 403; weakening of restraint, 405; why used, 393, 404
Alcoholic intoxication, 392
Aldrich, T. B., 302
Allen, C. M., 198
Allen, C. N., 41
Allport, F. H., 17, 52, 151, 207, 208, 263, 336, 381
Almack, J. C., 188
Altruism, 9; appearance of, 152; decline of, 157; effects of, on personality, 157-159
Amusement, nature of, 69
Amusements, 90
Anderson, T. H., 88
Anderson, W. A., 107
Angell, R. C., 187, 277

Anhedonia, 246
Annett, E. A., 323
Anxiety over growth changes, 31
Appetite changes, 36
Appleton, L. M., 72
Aristotle, 8
Arlitt, A. H., 79
Armstrong, C. P., 390
Arnold, C., 108
Aschaffenburg, G., 344, 362
Asher, E. J., 354
Aswell, E. C., 385
Athletics, 74; effect on personality, 78; preference for watching, 76
Attitudes, adolescent, 52; changed by social pressure, 154; definition of, 147; influenced by other constellations, 149; influences in changing, 156; loyalty, 125; measurement of, 150; movie effects upon, 94; relation to emotions, 148; relation to instincts, 151; social, 51
Austin, F. M., 107
Autoerotism, 31, 260, 296

Bagby, English, 414
Bain, R., 332
Baker, H. J., 375
Baldwin, B. T., 20, 24
Barker, R. H., 281
Barnes, Earl, 115, 118, 332
Baylor, E. M. H., 361
Bedale, E. M., 54
Beebe, Wm., 14
Beeley, A. L., 385, 387
Bender, I. E., 276
Berry, Elmer, 78
Betts, G. H., 337
Bingham, W. V., 106
Biological theories of development, 13
Blanchard, P., 29, 304, 316
Blanton, S. and M. G., 275

427

7